Colonial Granville County *and* Its People

By:
Worth S. Ray

Southern Historical Press, Inc.
Greenville, South Carolina

This volume was reproduced from
A personal copy located in the
Publisher's private Library

Please direct all correspondence and orders to:

www.southernhistoricalpress.com
or
SOUTHERN HISTORICAL PRESS, Inc.
PO Box 1267
375 West Broad Street
Greenville, SC 29601
southernhistoricalpress@gmail.com

Originally published: Austin, TX. 1945
As: The Lost Tribes of North Carolina, Part II
ISBN #0-89308-900-1

Printed in the United States of America

SPECIAL NOTICE

This work was reproduced by the photo-offset process from the original mimeographed edition. A characteristic of mimeographed copy - from which the offset printer must work - is that the copy is often very light and uneven, while at the same time over-inking may be present, such as, for example, when individual letters appear as a smear. Every effort has been made by the printer to produce as fine a reprint of the orginial mimeographed edition as possible.

Southern Historical Press, Inc.

BY THE AUTHOR

This book is about Colonial Granville County and its earliest residents. Where did they come from? Where did they go?

It is just a few loose leaves from a larger volume containing several hundred pages, in course of preparation and which it will take some time to complete, entitled "The Lost Tribes of North Carolina".

An impatient public shows some evidence of "being in a hurry" to see the notes and these pages have been set apart for separate binding and made available to the impatient ones, who may not even want the more ambitious project when it is completed. These may, or may not be, a fair sample of the more elaborate compilation.

We have discarded the old fiction of dividing the work into so-called "Chapters" and have arranged the notes according to convenience. Where some appear out of place and out of bounds, reference to the index will enable the reader to place them where they belong. Many afterthoughts occur and it takes too much time to revamp the whole manuscript in order to get them in where they should have been in the first place.

The family histories and charts are not to be classed as "genealogies", but as mere deductive studies, the aim being to answer the pertinent points of the author's theme: "Where did they come from? Where did they go?". If they were "genealogies" as that term has been customarily applied they would necessarily be bristling with "Sir John So and Sos", "Lord This and Thats" and a brilliant array of family "crests", "mottoes" and "coats of arms" designed to tickle the fancy and pride of thousands of descendants.

The studies are based on such information as is available at the time they are written, always subject to later correction and amendment, should new evidence turn up, even before the book is completed.

We make no pretense of being hide-bound as to positive proof. Every lawyer and student of evidence knows that a fact may be established by circumstances as well as by direct testimony. If we are reasonably certain as to where the subjects "came from" we try to state the reasons and the facts as they appear. The same yardstick is used in determining where these North Carolina tribes "went", when they settled elsewhere. We leave it to the clever and enterprising genealogists to furnish them with the stereotyped "background of royal descent" and the pretty $10.00 "Coats of Arms".

On page 304 Mr. Francis B. Hays, of Oxford, North Carolina, has furnished us with a pretty complete list of the old "First Families" of Colonial Granville, which is especially valuable as a guide to the correct spelling of the names. When in doubt we suggest his list be turned to and consulted.

Box 1111 WORTH S. RAY

Austin, Texas.

TABLE OF CONTENTS

Early Marriage Bonds and Records:

Family Charts:

Studies:

BUNCOMBE COUNTY. GENEALOGY of the COUNTY. It was formed in 1791, from BURKE and RUTHERFORD, BURKE being formed from ROWAN and ROWAN came out of ANSON. RUTHERFORD came out of TRYON, a short-lived County, which also came out of ANSON COUNTY, so that before the days of ROWAN, all of the present BUNCOMBE, and the counties SOUTH and WEST of it (1753) (though overrun with the Indians, then) were in ANSON COUNTY.

Deeds and other instruments between 1791 and 1808, dated in BUNCOMBE COUNTY, may have applied to HAYWOOD, which was formed from BUNCOMBE the latter year, so that the early history of BUNCOMBE, covering the first 17 years, is also a history of HAYWOOD.

The writer is indebted to MR. W. C. ALLEN'S "The Annals of Haywood County" for much of the material on BUNCOMBE which appears below.

COL. ROBERT LOVE, a revolutionary soldier and his brother GEN. THOMAS LOVE were early residents of BUNCOMBE COUNTY, they having settled in that part of the county which was taken from BURKE in 1791 to form BUNCOMBE. Both were sons of SAMUEL LOVE and his wife DORCAS BELL and were born near TINKLING SPRINGS MEETING HOUSE in Augusta County, Virginia, ROBERT in 1760 and GEN. THOMAS in 1765. SAMUEL LOVE was the son of one EPHRAIM LOVE, and DORCAS BELL was the daughter of JAMES BELL. Both ROBERT and THOMAS LOVE, who came to BUNCOMBE COUNTY, lived for a time in the WATAUGA settlements in what is now EAST TENNESSEE. THOMAS LOVE was one of the first Representatives from BUNCOMBE and afterwards served also from HAYWOOD when that county was organized in 1808. When serving BUNCOMBE in the Legislature he passed the bill organizing HAYWOOD COUNTY, where he made his home. In his later years, THOMAS LOVE moved to MAURY COUNTY, TENNESSEE, & served that District in a Legislative capacity until the time of his death. A Great Grandson of THOMAS LOVE, of BUNCOMBE and HAYWOOD, in 1907 was Speaker of the Texas Legislature, and afterwards an Assistant Secretary of the Treasury under Woodrow Wilson. His name was also THOMAS B. LOVE, and at this writing (1945) he is living, hale and hearty, and a prominent lawyer in the City of DALLAS, TEXAS.

REVOLUTIONARY SOLDIERS. The following Revolutionary soldiers, who came to BUNCOMBE COUNTY, are buried in HAYWOOD COUNTY:

Col. Robert Love
Captain John Henry
William Allen
Thomas Abel
George Hall
Edward Hyatt
Christian Messer
John Messer
Hugh Rogers
Jacob Shook.

JAMES ROBERT LOVE, son of COL. ROBERT LOVE and his wife MARY ANN DILLARD was born in BUNCOMBE COUNTY, N. C. in November, 1798.

The first Justices of HAYWOOD COUNTY (all of whom, of course, up to that time had been residents of BUNCOMBE) in 1809, were THOMAS LOVE, JOHN FERGUS, JOHN DOBSON, ROBERT PHILLIPS, ABRAHAM EATON, HUGH DAVIDSON, HOLLIMAN BATTLE, JOHN McFARLAND, PHILLIP T. BURFOOT, WILLIAM DEAVER, ARCHIBALD McHENRY and BENJAMIN ODELL.

JOHN DAVIDSON and JAMES CHAMBERS were granted lands in BUNCOMBE COUNTY on PIGEON RIVER shortly after the revolution.

DAVID ALLISON bought land on PIGEON RIVER in BUNCOMBE COUNTY in 1796.

ROBERT MARTIN bought land on PIGEON RIVER in BUNCOMBE COUNTY in 1798.

JOHN PENLAND, JACOB SHOOK, SPENCER RICE, and DAVID MEHAFFEY came from BURKE COUNTY to BUNCOMBE. JOHN PENLAND'S farm was on what is or was known as "CRYSTAL" Creek.

What was known in the old days as TWELVE MILE CREEK, was later called FINE'S CREEK, & among the early settlers along this course when it was in BUNCOMBE COUNTY was DAVID RUSSELL, HUGHEY ROGERS and JOHN RAY.

WILLIAM CATHEY was one of the earliest settlers in the PIGEON VALLEY and his son COL. JOSEPH CATHEY was born in BUNCOMBE COUNTY on MARCH 12, 1803.

THOMAS ISAAC LENOIR was the son of COL. THOMAS LENOIR, who came from WILKES COUNTY to BUNCOMBE in 1799. He bought lands in the County, but after a residence of some thirty years moved back to WILKES COUNTY, the old home of the LENOIR FAMILY, where he died in 1850. He was the son of WILLIAM LENOIR who married one of the BALLARDS and some of whose descendants settled in what is now ROANE COUNTY, Tennessee, where they built the town of LENOIR on the Tennessee River, some thirty miles South of KNOXVILLE.

In 1828 HODGE RAYBURN settled in BUNCOMBE. He was from BURKE COUNTY, where he had served as State Senator. In 1838 he was also Senator from BUNCOMBE COUNTY. He was born in Rowan County in 1759, the son of WILLIAM RAYBURN, from Virginia. He is said to have been a descendant of POCAHONTIS and a first cousin of a Georgia Governor of the name of RAYBURN. A SAMUEL RAYBURN served in the State Senate of Alabama, and both, this writer believes, were relatives of HON. SAM RAYBURN, of TEXAS, now (1945) Speaker of the National House of Representatives.

JONATHAN CREEK (now in HAYWOOD COUNTY) was named for JONATHAN McPETERS who was one of the first white settlers to come to BUNCOMBE COUNTY.

COUNTIES TAKEN FROM BUNCOMBE were HAYWOOD, MACON, CHEROKEE, JACKSON, SWAIN, CLAY & GRAHAM. All of these, of course were originally in the territory of ANSON COUNTY, from which BUNCOMBE came through TRYON, RUTHERFORD, ROWAN and BURKE.

HUGH ROGERS married NANCY THORNTON, who was the daughter of JOHN THORNTON, who lived at the foot of KING'S MOUNTAIN, where the famous revolutionary battle was fought, where he manufactured powder that was used by the patriots in that fight. Hugh and Nancy were married in 1781. The ROGERS family to which HUGH belonged lived before the American Revolution in Mecklenburg County, N. C. JOHN ROGERS a son of HUGH and his wife NANCY THORNTON, married POLLY McCRACKEN in 1824. John died in HAYWOOD COUNTY in 1852.

LAWYERS OF BUNCOMBE. Among the first of the lawyers to practice in BUNCOMBE COUNTY were WALLACE ALEXANDER, JOSEPH McDOWELL, JOSEPH SPENCER, BENNETT SMITH and ROBERT WILLIAMSON. These all attended court from other parts of the country, as same met in BUNCOMBE. The first lawyer who actually lived in BUNCOMBE COUNTY was ROBERT HENRY, who was admitted to practice at the JULY Term of Court in 1802. He was a native of LINCOLN COUNTY and had a most interesting history.

MORE LAWYERS. The lawyers who were admitted and licensed to practice in the Courts of BUNCOMBE after ROBERT HENRY and between the year 1804 and up to 1812 were THOMAS BARRON, ISRAEL PICKENS, who afterwards was Governor of ALABAMA, Joseph Wilson, Joseph Carson, ROBERT BURTON, who was a Judge on the Bench, HENRY HARRISON, Sanders Donoho, John C. Elliott, HENRY Y. WEBB, Tench Cox, JR., A. R. Ruffin, and JOHN PAXTON, a Judge of some distinction.

JOHN BURTON received a grant of land JULY 7, 1794, which he divided into town lots, thus giving the first start to what is now the CITY of ASHVILLE.

SAMUEL LUSK in 1795 bought Lot No. 13.

COL. WILLIAM DAVIDSON bought Lot No. 21.

JAMES DAVIDSON bought Lot No. 26.

HUGH TATE bought half of Lot No. 13, from the original purchaser, SAMUEL LUSK.

JOHN PATTON bought Lot. No. 16.

PATTON & ERWIN bought Lot. No. 4.

This list, of course, constitutes an incomplete list of the original purchasers of lots in what is now the City of Ashville.

PATTON & ERWIN afterwards acquired an interest in the BURTON property and sold off large numbers of the lots as the town gradually began to expand and grow.

A FEW EARLY DEEDS IN BUNCOMBE

REASON DAVIS sells 5[illegible] acres of land on TURKEY CREEK to JOSEPH HARRISON, January 25, 1811. Book D p 127.

CLEMENT DAVIS sold JOSEPH HARRISON 100 acres of land on TURKEY CREEK Sept. 29, 1810. Book D. page 97.

STATE OF N. C. to JOHN HARRISON, grant to land No. 706, December 6, 1799; land located on French Broad River.

THOMAS HARRISON sold JOSEPH HARRISON 100 acres on North Turkey Creek, November 27, 1804. Book B 222.

JACOB KELLER sold THOMAS HARRISON, 100 acres of land on TURKEY CREEK, March 22, 1802. Book E, p. 347.

JOSEPH HARRISON sold to WILLIAM HARRISON 200 acres of land on SANDY MUSH CREEK in BUNCOMBE COUNTY, July 8, 1806. Book 8 page 8 of Buncombe County Records.

JAMES MURPHY sold to THOMAS HARRISON 125 acres of land in BUNCOMBE COUNTY located on Turkey Creek, October 22, 1805. Recorded Book 10, page 152.

NATHANIEL HARRISON received a land grant from the State of North Carolina, No. 2926 to 100 acres of land on TURKEY CREEK January 3, 1831. Book 19 p. 347.

WILLIAM CASSADY sold NATHANIEL HARRISON and others 100 acres on TURKEY CREEK in BUNCOMBE County, October 29, 1835. Book 21 page 496 of the Deed Records of BUNCOMBE COUNTY.

WILLIAM KING bought 100 acres of land on SANDY MUSH CREEK from NATHANIEL HARRISON on April 2, 1811, in BUNCOMBE COUNTY. Book C. page 291 of BUNCOMBE COUNTY.

JEREMIAH DAVIS bought 100 acres of land on SANDY MUSH CREEK from NATHANIEL HARRISON March 10, 1819. Book 11, page 540.

PATTON & ERWIN, on May 5, 1807, bought 10 acres of land on a branch of CANEY RIVER from JESSE HARRISON. Book A p 304 Deed Records of BUNCOMBE COUNTY.

ASHBURN BALL bought 50 acres of land on [illegible] BRANCH in BUNCOMBE COUNTY, from THOMAS HARRISON November 31, 1806. Book E page 58, Deed Records of BUNCOMBE COUNTY.

JOHN PLEMONS, bought 100 acres of land from THOMAS HARRISON in BUNCOMBE COUNTY, December 1, 1806.

RICHARD STOCKTON'S WILL, written January 14, 1826, was recorded in BUNCOMBE COUNTY in Will Book 1 p. 74, in the month of FEBRUARY in 1840, in which he mentions "my daughter, MARY HARRISON.

M. H. GARRISON on March 7, 1838 sold 24 acres of land on CAMP BRANCH in BUNCOMBE COUNTY, to NATHANIEL HARRISON. Book 21, page 170.

JAMES BLACK on August 12, 1826, sold LUKE HARRISON 87 acres of land on BEAVER'S BRANCH in BUNCOMBE COUNTY. Book 21, page 497. NATHANIEL HARRISON, Clerk of the Court.

REV. JOSEPH HARRISON, ancestor of the HARRISONS who figure in most of the above recorded deeds in BUNCOMBE COUNTY at about the time or a little after its formation, was a revolutionary soldier, and a contemporary of RICHARD GENTRY, AARON JOHNSON, WILLIAM BALDWIN, RICHARD JACKS and DAVID SMITH. Rev. Harrison was the minister of the historic old "THREE FORKS BAPTIST CHURCH" of Western North Carolina.

A revolutionary soldier's marker has been placed at his grave in the old TURKEY CREEK burying ground near LEICESTER, a short distance from ASHVILLE, where he lived at the time of his death, on which the date of his birth is given as 1733 and his death as 1811.

The account of the marking of his grave declares that his wife was MARGARET HILL, who was the daughter of a N. C. revolutionary soldier. His descendants do not agree on a list of his children. We think they were probably:

(1) NATHANIEL HARRISON, High Sheriff and Clerk of BUNCOMBE.
(2) WILLIAM HARRISON (See Deeds above).
(3) JOHN HARRISON of TURKEY CREEK DEEDS.
(4) THOMAS HARRISON.
(5) JEREMIAH HARRISON
(6) LUKE HARRISON
(7) RACHEL HARRISON m. SNELSON.
(8) ELIZABETH HARRISON m. a man named BOYD.
(9) JANE HARRISON m. CASSADY.
(10) LIZZIE HARRISON married a GARRETT.
(11) MOURNING HARRISON.

SOME NOTES FROM THE RECORDS OF ANSON COUNTY

ANSON COUNTY. It's ancestor is NEW HANOVER COUNTY, which was formed in 1728, from which BLADEN COUNTY was taken in 1734, and thereafter in 1749 ANSON was established out of a part of BLADEN, so that, genealogically speaking, NEW HANOVER was the grandfather of ANSON. For a period of FOUR years ANSON COUNTY comprehended all of the Western Part of the State, and except for claims of the Indians extended through Tennessee to the Mississippi River. Deeds or grants of land located in ANSON COUNTY between 1749 and 1753, otherwise not identified, may have been anywhere WEST of Wadesboro, the county seat in this day. ROWAN COUNTY was carved out of this huge area in 1753 & embraced approximately the Northern half of ANSON including SURRY, WILKES, IREDELL and all that tier of counties; deeds, grants and other such instruments for the following NINE YEARS (1753 to 1762) labelled ANSON belonged somewhere in the area now covered from WADESBORO, West to the Tennessee line including Union, Mecklenburg, Cabarrus, Lincoln, Gaston, Rutherford and other counties farther on West. In 1762 both Mecklenburg and Tryon were established, but after SEVEN YEARS, Tryon was abolished and LINCOLN and RUTHERFORD in (1779) came into existence. Rutherford was the BIG COUNTY and extended to Tennessee, while LINCOLN included only its present area and the new county of GASTON. All this to enable the reader to more clearly "place" records here cited from ANSON COUNTY, by a comparison of these dates. (Authority: Wheeler.).

The following items are taken from the records of ANSON COUNTY, N. C. on file at WADESBORO, the county seat:

JAMES ARMSTRONG, will; dated May 11, 1760; he names his sons WILLIAM, JOHN, MARTIN, JAMES, JOSEPH, BENJAMIN and MATTHEW (the last two his youngest sons) and daughter MARY ARMSTRONG. Children JAMES ARMSTRONG and daughter MARY his executors. CHARLES MOORE, JOHN BETTY (BEATTY) and JAMES PRICE, witnesses (Vol. 1, p.8). (It is likely these were the ARMSTRONGS who lived on the South Fork of the CATAWBA RIVER in what was then ANSON, but is now in either LINCOLN or GASTON).

JOSEPH MARTIN, will. Dated February 13, 1787. Names wife CATHERINE and children JESSE, NANCY and JOHN HAIL MARTIN (Book 1 p. 56.)

JOHN HICKS, will. Dated April 24, 1760. Wife OBEDIENCE HICKS; sons WILLIAM and JOHN HICKS, and daughters FRANCES and MARY HICKS; grand-daughter SARAH HICKS. Signed JOHN HICKS. Witnesses were ALEXANDER GORDON and WILLIAM HICKS (Book 1 p. 12)

HENRY ADCOCK, will. October 1802. Names his wife SUSANNAH, and children HENRY, JAMES, ELENDER, NANCY and JOHN ADCOCK. (Book 2 p 2).

THOMAS ADCOCK. April 8, 1823. Will names wife SARAH and children NOSMETY, MARY, DELILAH, FRANCES, MOURNING, BARSHEBA, MATILDA and B. B. ADCOCK (Book A. p 84).

WILLIAM LOVE, will. Dated May 7, 1753. Leaves all of his property to his father. Done in presence of ROBERT x LOVE and BENJAMIN x LOVE. Signed WILLIAM LOVE.

ANDREW BERRY (BARRY?) Inventory of his goods, chattels, rights and credits, by RICHARD BARRY, administrator. No date, but about the year 1765.

WILLIAM RATLIFF, will. Dated February 10, 1777. Names wife SUSANNAH and children WILLIAM, ZACHARIAH, THOMAS, JAMES, JOHN, ROBERT CLOVEN RATLIFF and ELIZABETH CURTIS (Probably the wife of SAMUEL CURTIS); WILLIAM THOMAS and PHILEMON THOMAS executors, and THOMAS DICKSON, G. JEFFERSON and SAMUEL CURTIS witnesses (Book 1, p. 26).

STEPHEN VAUGHAN, will. Dated March 5, 1785. Names wife MARY and children WILLIAM, HARMON and SARAH VAUGHAN; Witnesses were JEREMIAH LEWIS and THOMAS LEWIS (Book 1).

JOHN McCLENDEN WILL. Dated April 9, 1784. Children ANN, DENNIS, SAMUEL, REBECCA and SIMON McCLENDEN (Book 1).

SAMPSON LANIER, will. Dated June 8, 1789. Mentions his son JAMES LANIER, and appoints BURWELL LANIER, WILLIAM LANIER and COL. JOHN STOKES his executors. Witnesses were JOHN JENNINGS, BENJAMIN FELKY and JAMES B. PORTER (Bk 1 p. 70).

ROBERT McCORKALL. An inventory of his estate, July 23, 1757. Wife MARGARET is mentioned Inventory taken by JAMES McCORKALL, MARGARET M. McCORKALL and JAMES LINN, witnessed by JOHN CROCKETT. (Book 1, p. 123).

ROBERT JARMON. Inventory of his estate in 1782, but not other name mentioned. (Bk 1.)

JOHN DAVIDSON. Inventory of his estate in December 1, 1749. Taken by JAMES McILWEANE and HILL MORRISON (Book 1).

JAMES LOWRY. Inventory of his estate taken by ELIZABETH LOWRY (No date) (Bk 1 p.139)

ANN BAKER, deceased. Inventory of her estate April 1, 1782, taken by D. JAMESON (Bk 1).

JAMES ROPER. Inventory of his estate in 1782. MARY ROPER mentioned (Bk 1 p 145).

JOHN HICKS. Inventory of his estate taken by JOHN HUSBANS and FRANCES x HUSBANDS, in October, 1772.

MATTHEW PATTON. Inventory of estate taken about 1780, with ELIZABETH PATTON and JAMES PATTON mentioned. (Book 1 p 151).

RICHARD TOUCHSTONE and SARAH TOUCHSTONE. Inventory of estate about 1765 (no date given) with HENRY TOUCHSTONE and FREDERICK TOUCHSTONE mentioned. (Book 1 p 132).

MOORMAN, BENJAMIN. Will dated March 26, 1798, mentions sons WILLIAM MOORMAN and MICHAEL MOORMAN, with CHARLES HISON and ARMSHE CREW as witnesses. (Book 2).

SMITH FIELDS. Will. Dated March 15, 1792. Names children JAMES, JOHN, MISAJAH, CELIA and ELIZABETH FIELDS. Signed SMITH x FIELDS. Witnesses were JOHN AUID, JOHN CASON, JAMES LEGGETT. (Vol 2 p. 37).

SARAH JACKSON. Will in 1813. The witnesses were JAMES COLEMAN, SR. and JAMES COLEMAN JR.

TOD ROBINSON, Clerk of ANSON in 1814.

RICHARD ODOM will. Dated Sept. 4, 1797. Names wife HONOUR ODOM and children WILLIAM, NANCY, JAMES, ELIZABETH (FRANKLIN), DAVID, RICHARD and ISAAC ODOM and daughters LUCY FAIR and CHARITY RUTHERFORD. Friends STEPHEN HYDE and JAMES MARSHALL executors; witnessed by ROBERT LEE J. WATE, Mc DAVIDSON and JOHN SCOTT (Book 2, p. 118

JONATHAN YARBOROUGH will. Dated March 6, 1811. Names one son WILLIAM YARBOROUGH and a son in law JOHN CULPEPPER; witnesses AMY MARSHALL and TEMPY COB (COBB); recorded at the October session 1812. TOD ROBINSON, CLERK.

SAMUEL MOORE and SARAH his wife convey to PETER CLUB, 250 acres on the South side of the CATAWBA RIVER, on both sides of KILLIAN'S CREEK, between the lines of KILLIAN and ROBERT LEEPER, October 19, 1753. Recorded in ANSON COUNTY Deed Book B-1 p. 370. (NOTE: The land described in this deed was in what is now LINCOLN or GASTON COUNTY, through which KILLIAN'S CREEK runs; but at the date of the execution of the deed (1753) it was a part of ANSON COUNTY.)

DANIEL HILL left will in ANSON COUNTY in 1826. His wife was MARTHA HICKMAN, and the children named are SARAH, MARY, NANCY, WILLIAM HICKMAN HILL, GREEN HILL, MILDRED HILL, ELIZABETH, LUCINDA and SUSANNA SMITHERS HILL. (NOTE: WILLIAM HICKMAN HILL died in TEXAS in 1867, where he left numerous descendants, and ELIZABETH HILL married HENRY CLAYTON EWING of Nashville, Tenn.).

MATTHEW MOORE, of ANSON COUNTY died before 1794 and left HENRY MOORE his heir, who employed JOSIAH DOBBS that year to recover a slave from JOHN BELK. (Book D-E p. 71).

SOME RECORDS FROM CASWELL COUNTY

CASWELL COUNTY - GENEALOGY. According to WHEELER Caswell County is a descendant of two of the old original precincts, CRAVEN and BLADEN. In 1751, ORANGE, its immediate parent was formed from GRANVILLE, JOHNSTON and BLADEN. Edgecombe and Johnston both came from CRAVEN, and GRANVILLE was taken also from Craven. From 1746 until 1751, FIVE YEARS, Caswell territory was a part of GRANVILLE, and after that until 1777, for 26 years it was a part of ORANGE until the Legislative Act that established it as CASWELL. All instruments between 1751 and 1777 in the territory that is now CASWELL bore the name of ORANGE, and for five years prior to that period GRANVILLE. The leading men of CASWELL in its earliest years was JAMES WILLIAMSON, COL. JOHN WILLIAMS (brother of JAMES WILLIAMS, the gallant officer killed at King's Mountain during the revolution,) the GRAVES, BURTONS, SHELTONS, LEAS, (Luke Lea family of Tennessee) Marmaduke WILLIAMS ROMULUS SAUNDERS, BARTLETT YANCEY, the McADENS, BROWNS and KERRS, according to WHEELER'S records. Dolly Payne Madison is said to have been born in CASWELL COUNTY. In our visits to YANCEYVILLE we collected the following records:

ROBERT RAY left will in 1786 in which he mentions his wife ANNIE and his children, without naming them. (W. B. B p. 138).

JOHN COBB left will in 1838, in which he names wife JANE and children MATINDA, SAMUEL, LOUISA (m. ABRAHAM WOMACK 1838), JOHN, HENRY, HUGH, MARTHA GARDNER (also MARTHA MADDEN) and DEBORAH GRANT. (W. B. N, p. 202.

WADDY TATE, died leaving will in (1789) in which he mentions his wife ANN TATE and his children, without naming them. His wife ANN and friend TYRE HARRIS Executors (W. B. B. p. 275).

JOHN LEWIS, SR. and JOHN LEWIS JR. indenture with SARAH TAYLOR the wife of PHILLIP TAYLOR. Witnessed by N. CUNNINGHAM. (Book A) 1790.

JAMES SANDERS and WILLIAM HUTSON execute an instrument in the form of an indenture on March 3, 1783, relating to the adoption of NATHAN WINGFIELD, an orphan . (From Book A. p. 233.

MATTHEW DUTY died and left will in 1782 in which the name of his wife is not mentioned, or wther living. He named the following children: JOHN, LITTLETON, THOMAS, MARY, ANN, WILLIAM, SOLOMON and RICHARD DUTY (Will Book A, p. 215.)

HUMPHREY DONALDSON died leaving will in 1781 in which he mentions his wife MARY, and his children WILLIAM, ANDREW, ROBERT, EBENEZER and HUMPHREY DONALDSON. (Will Book A. p. 144.)

JAMES WILLIAMS (This was evidently COL. JAMES WILLIAMS who fought and was killed in the battle of KING'S MOUNTAIN) left will dated in 1780 in which he named his wife MARY and his children DANIEL, JOSEPH, JOHN, ELIZABETH, MARY, SARAH, JAMES and WASHINGTON WILLIAMS (From W. Book A p. 113.)

HENRY WILLIAMS died and left will in 1786 in which he mentions the following children: DANIEL (m. ANN RICE in 1786), JOSEPH, NATHAN, HENRY, ELIZABETH, MARY SLADE, NANCY RICE, ELIZABETH, SUSANNAH, WESLEY DUKE PEOPLES, SALLY BROOKS and JANE WILLIAMS. (From W. B. B p.92).

SAMUEL FARMER left will in CASWELL in 1779 (two years after the county had been organized) in which he names his wife CASSANDRA, and children DANIEL, WILLIAM, STEPHEN, NATHAN, RACHEL WILSON, MARY WILSON, SUSANNA FARMER and ELLINER McMAHON. Witnesses were RICHARD HOLMAN, WILLIAM DENNIS and SAMUEL HOLMAN. (From Will Book A. p. 234.)

JOHN WILLIAMS died and left will in 1805, in which he mentions his wife BETSY and his children DUKE WILLIAMS (Hon. Marmaduke Williams, M. C. at that time) BETSY GRAVES, and HENRIETTA SIMPSON and her children. (From Will Book E p. 168.

NATHANIEL WILLIAMS, JR. died and left will in 1816 in which he mentions several children. (Will Book g p. 133).

NOAH COBB, died leaving a will in CASWELL COUNTY in 1808, in which he mentions his wife ELIZABETH and children EBENEZER, ELLINER, LEVI, NATHAN, NOAH and NANCY PAGE (Will Book F p 3).

HUGH WALKER, left will in CASWELL COUNTY in 1845, and mentioned his wife FRANCES and children JEFFERSON, JOHN, JAMES, NANCY ENOCH, MARY BROWN and FRANCES McCAULEY (Will Book P p. 188).

RICHARD WILLIAMS died leaving will in 1819 and named wife ELIZABETH and his children RICHARD WILLIAMS and ELIZABETH WILLIAMS; JOHN CHISHUM to be Executor. The witnesses were R. POWELL and GEORGE COKER (Book H p. 205).

DANIEL WEBB left will dated AUG. 23, 1827, and mentions DANIEL WEBB, grandson THOMAS JEFFERSON, grand-daughter ELIZA WEBB, DANIEL DAVIS, my half-sister's son; JOSEPH WEBB and my grandchildren ALEXANDER M. WEBB, DANIEL JEFFERSON WEBB and MARY A. ELIZABETH WEBB. Sons DANIEL WEBB and JOSEPH WEBB, Executors, and the witnesses were RICHARD W. BARBER and WILLIAM H. TRENT (Book H. p. 409).

WILLIAM STEELE left will in CASWELL COUNTY dated September 9, 1774; names wife ELIZABETH & children JOHN STEELE, MARGARET GILLESPIE and ROBERT STEELE; witnesses were JAMES KERR and D. OSBORNE (Book A. p 168).

THOMAS SWANN left will in CASWELL COUNTY dated November 21, 1795, and names his wife CATHERINE and children WILLIAM, ELIZABETH, THOMAS, ISAAC, ANN (wife of ABRAHAM LAWRENCE), MARTHA, MARY, MATTHEW and JAMES SWANN; wife CATHERINE & ABRAHAM LAWRENCE, Executors. (Book D p. 27).

ANDREW HARRISON left will in ORANGE COUNTY, N. C. (In that part which in 1777 became CASWELL COUNTY) named wife JANE (DILLARD) and children WILLIAM, THOMAS, ANN (m. JOHN WARE) NINIAN (son) ELIZABETH, MILDRED (m. WILLIAM MOORE) MOLLIE, NANCY, JANE and ANDREW HARRISON.

JAMES WILLIAMS left will in 1787 in CASWELL COUNTY and named wife ELIZABETH and children BENJAMIN, NEAL, MARY, LUCY, MARTHA and ELIZABETH MOORE, a married daughter.

JOHN WALKER left will in CASWELL 1790 named wife RACHEL, and children THOMAS, BETSY, BENJAMIN, WILLIAM, POLLY and BARBARA WALKER.

SAMUEL WALKER left will CASWELL in 1798 and named wife ELENER and children JAMES, JANE LONG and ELIZABETH LONG, daughters.

WILLIAM WILLIAMS died leaving will in CASWELL COUNTY in 1786, naming TOBIAS, MARY, AGNES and OBEDIENCE WILLIAMS.

JOHN DOUGLAS, ESQ. and MARTIN COOPER, contract dated January 20, 1791 in CASWELL COUNTY in which SOLOMON MANGUM, an orphan now four years old is indentured to MARTIN COOPER to live after the manner of an apprentice. Witnessed by A. E. MURPHY. H. HARALDSON, Clerk of the Court for CASWELL COUNTY.

SOME MARRIAGE BONDS IN CASWELL COUNTY.

Azariah Denny to Elizabeth McKinney, September 26, 1823.
Shadrack Dye to Eleaner Westley, Nov. 26, 1802.
Alexander A. Daniel to Isabella Brandon, Nov. 6, 1866; Fleming Daniel security.
James K. Dameron married BARSHEBA Bateman, Nov. 28, 1829.
James B. Dameron to Elizabeth Connolly Dec. 12, 1829.
John Dameron to Nancy Love, January 22, 1828.
William I. Dameron to Alsy S. Travis, Sept. 28, 1841.
Solomon Debow to Nancy Murphy March 22, 1804.
Ashley Davis to Anny Kennon, Sept. 8, 1814; Azariah Graves, security.
John Daniel to Jane Murphy, July 25, 1805.
Thomas Daniel to Nancy Hardridge in 1815; with Martin Daniel, security.
Simon Denny to Polly Bartán, April 26, 1796; Lewis Barton, security.
John Daniel to Rebecca Huston, October 21, 1822.
Robert Daniel to Miss Jiles A. Norfleet, August 27, 1812.
John W. Dick to Martha Graves, May 31, 1822.
John M. Daniel to Cornelia A. Carter, July 6, 1836.
Richard Duty to Tars McNeill, July 21, 1791; Thomas McNeill, security.
Benjamin Walling to Sarah Sargent, June 5, 1782.
John Webster to Mary Whitlow, Nov. 6, 1817.
Solomon Whitlow to Nancy McDaniel, Nov. 13, 1822
Thomas Winston to Patsy Coleman, Dec. 29, 1796; Noel Coleman, security.
John Wood to Polly Anderson, March 11, 1797.
William H. Walters to Sally Ingram, Dec. 26, 1816; Geo. W. Jeffrey and Jas. Daniel, sec.
James Wallace to Polly Robinson, Sept. 21, 1796.
Josiah H. Whitlow to Lucy Ann Bradley, April 25, 1836.
Watson Winters to Nancy Womack, Feb. 5, 1815.
Thos. W. Wilks to Mariah L. Graves, Oct. 31, 1837; Tom C. Connolly, security.
Silas T. Ware to Sarah Cannon, Sept. 4, 1837; Stephen T. Ware, security.
Theodore L. Williamson to Mary Sneed, April 2, 1828.
John White to Elizabeth Williamson, Oct. 26, 1796; William Dickens, security.
Thomas White to Sally Mitchell, Jan. 12, 1802; John Mitchell, security.
David White to Sally Pond, Nov. 19, 1800.
Thomas Wray to Rebecca Fowler, Nov. 15, 1790; Thomas RAY, Sr. security.
Major Wallace to Susannah Burton, April, 1802; Drury Burton, security.
Azariah Walker to Jane Walker, Dec. 8, 1837; John M. Walker, security.
Phillip Walker to Frances Martin, Dec. 27, 1833; William Walker, security.
Benjamin Walker to Susan Rice, March 1, 1833.
Samuel Walker to Barbara Walker, May 29, 1834.
Jethro I. Walker to Anne Graves(?) Dec. 26, 1829.
Alex I. Walker to Mary Ann Dill, December, 1832.
Abraham Walker to Elizabeth Smith 1833.
Henry Willis, Jr. to Betsy Evans, Jan. 20, 1830.
John White to Elizabeth Ingram, Jan. 10, 1834.
Alexander Wiley to Polly Kerr, Dec. 28, 1807.
John Westley to Nancy Randall, Jan. 22, 1806; James Randall, security.
Epaproditus White to Lydia Walker in 1806.
Hampton Wade to Ann Durham, Nov. 12, 1796.
John Williams to Fanny Dunnavant, Nov. 13, 1822
Duke Williams to Edy Harris, October 19, 1790; Robert Williams, security. (This was the celebrated Col. Robert Williams of Va. and N. C., and his signature on this marriage bond is a positive model).
Daniel Williams to Ann Rice, Jan. 5, 1786; with Anthony Thompson, security.
Joseph Walker to Priscilla Zachary, March 17, 1800; John Garr, security.
Jeremiah Walker to Batha Cross, May _ 1805; Joshua Pike, security.
Thomas Walker to Peggy Swann, Oct. 28, 1811.
Davis Womack to Delilah Graves March 24, 1800.
Abraham Womack to Louisa M. Cobb, Nov. 29, 1838

Thomas White to Mary Carroll, Jan. 8, 1781.
Benjamin Williamson to Miss Eliza A. Hinton, Nov. 15, 1848.
David Walker to Luffy Carver, Dec. 24, 1825.
Hardy Wells to Elizabeth Parker, Oct. 20, 1784.
David Walker to Patsy Dalton, January 30, 1806.
James Walker to Elizabeth Elliott, Nov. 21, 1791.
James White to Nancy Ware, August 30, 1813.
Thomas Nesbit Williams to Mary Fuller, Nov. 7, 1789.
Hall Williamson to Nancy Smith, October ___1791.
Nathaniel Williams to Mrs. Stone, Jan. 17, 1832.
Henry Williams to Polly Gooch, Dec. 3, 1799; Alexander Murphy, security.
Alfred Williams to Mary Terry, Dec. 12, 1836.
Warner Williams to Elizabeth M. Lewis, March 16, 1813; Thomas Baldwin, security.
John Wiley to Jennie Mitchell, Sept. 5, 1815.
Robert Williams to Nancy Elam, Feb. 16, 1835.
James Williams to Elizabeth Sawyers, June 18, 1806; William Sawyers, security.
Paul Williams to Lucy Donohoo, Oct. 8, 1791; Thomas Donohoo, security.
Crafton Williams to Betsy Yates, March 3, 1798.
John Williams to Susannah Dixon, Jan. 10, 1800; Duke Williams and John Williams, security.
William Williams to Jemimah Page, Dec. 3, 1788.
Nathaniel Williams, Jr. to Elizabeth Dixon, June 25, 1792; Robert Harris security.
*Marmaduke Williams to Agness (Payne) Harris, October 26, 1798; Alexander Murphy, security.
Robert Westley to Delilah Dye, March 22, 1799; William Dye, security.
Jefferson H. Walker to Mary Cooper, Oct. 20 '54.

COL. JAMES WILLIAMS, whose last will and testament was probated in CASWELL COUNTY at the December Court in 1780, an abstract of which is contained in the foregoing items, was the son of Daniel Williams and his wife URSULA HENDERSON. He is said to have been born in 1740 in Hanover County Virginia. His mother was a sister of Samuel Henderson and an aunt of Judge Richard Henderson, of Transylvania (Ky.) fame. Col. James Williams was also the brother of Col. John Williams, of Caswell County, and a first cousin of Judge John Williams, of Granville County, N. C. He was also a brother of Henry Williams, an abstract of whose will in CASWELL COUNTY, N. C. in 1786 is given in the foregoing notes. In fact, the will of Daniel Williams in Granville County in 1759, abstract of which will be hereafter given under that county's records, shows that he had five sons, Henry, James, John, Joseph and Daniel. A more complete abstract of the Col. James Williams will is given herewith, to more assuredly identify him:

"Will of Col. James Williams, of 96 District, South Carolina, but now in the State of North Carolina, as a refugee. Wife Mary Williams certain lands in 96 District, South Carolina, along the line of the land I bought of John Caldwell. Son, Daniel Williams, 250 acres and other lands, and a child's part of all my estate when he becomes 21. Sons Joseph Williams, lands, etc; John Williams the same. Daughters Elizabeth Williams and Mary Williams, certain lands and each a child's part of the estate; daughter Sary Williams, cash to buy land, etc. Son James Williams, land, etc. Son Washington Williams, the land which was left to his mother for her life-time. All the lands, stallions, still, wagons and horses and horse creatures to be sold at public sale and the store, books and bonds and notes and other due collateral, to be divided among my eight children. Executors are son Daniel Williams, brother Henry Williams and Joseph Hays. Signed June 12, 1780. Probated at December Court 1780. Witnesses, William Rice, James Goodman and James Cook."

Daniel and Joseph Williams, sons of Col. James Williams, were respectively 17 and 13 years of age when at King's Mountain; and a year later were slaughtered by "Bloody Bill" Cunningham at Hoyes' Station. John Williams, a younger brother, went towards the close of the war to Virginia, to keep the negroes from the Tories; and while there, took suddenly ill and died - supposed that he was poisoned for money, but he had none. But the negroes were saved to the family. (Logan MSS, Vol. 3 Joseph Habersham Chap. D. A. R. Records pp 109, 110).

* MARMADUKE WILLIAMS, who married Agnes (Payne) Harris, Oct. 26, 1798, as shown in the marriage bond records above, was born in CASWELL COUNTY, N. C. April 6, 1772, and became a lawyer & a member of the State Senate in 1802; thereafter he was a member of the 8th, 9th and 10th United States Congresses from N. C. (1803-1809). He moved to Huntsville, Madison County, Alabama, in 1810, and to Tuscaloosa, Alabama in 1818, where he was a member of the Constitutional Convention of Alabama in 1819, and the same year a candidate for Governor, although defeated. Thereafter he served 11 terms in the Alabama Legislature and was Judge of the Tuscaloosa County Court for 10 years (1832-1842). He died in Tuscaloosa, Alabama in 1850.

Other marriage bonds copied from the CASWELL COUNTY records were as follows:

Israel Dickson to Frances Ware (?) March 4, 1812; Nathaniel Graves, security.
Andrew Donaldson to Mary Motheral, July 18, 1791; James Richmond, security.
John P. Daniel to Jane C. Higginson, April 30, 1857; Thomas W. Graves, then Clerk.
John Denton to Miss J. Payne, July 8, 1812.
Jesse Dickson to Frances Moore, Nov. 7, 1791; Herndon Harralson, security.
Samuel Dunnaway to Kesiah Barksdale, Feb. 20th 1792.
Walker Dowell to Nancy Thomspon, Dec. 29, 1806; William Swann, security.
James Davis to Susanna Parker, April 7, 1822.
Solomon Draper to Joyce Taylor, July 4, 1790; a William Draper, security.
Michael Delks to Elizabeth Starkey, Jan. 29, 1782; Jonathan Starkey, security.
Isaiah Durst to Rebecca Barnett, De 6, 1788.
iam M. Daniel to Adaline H. Williamson; 1839.
William Donaldson to Margaret Motheral, Sept. 5, 1793; Jos. Richmond, security.
John Daniel to Lucy Walters, March 29, 1841.
Elias J. Daniel to Susan R. Turpin, April 5, 1843.
Samuel Driskill to Irby Dudley April 20, 1820.
John Daniel to Martha Mangum Feb. 5, 1860; David Walker security.
John Dennis to Rachel Grant Feb. 3, 1796.
Jonathan Davis to Mary Austin April 17, 1781.
Daniel Darby to Elizabeth Gibson Feb. 9, 1791.
Joseph Duty to Polly Fitch July 23, 1826.
William Duty to Rachel Warren, Feb. 13, 1783.
Robert Donaldson to Elizabeth Richmond, Jan. 6, 1799.
Thomas Dyer to Betsy Matlock, Aug. 18, 1796.
Richard Dillard to Sarah Holt, Dec. 12, 1796.
John Darby to Elizabeth McDaniel Sept. 15, 1794.
Nathan Duncan to Jane Rainey, Nov. 8, 1792.

GENEALOGY OF CHATHAM COUNTY. Chatham County territory originally, as near as may be estimated, prior to 1733, was a part of CRAVEN COUNTY or PRECINCT. Edgecombe came out of Craven, Granville out of Edgecombe, Orange out of Granville, and Chatham County out of ORANGE in 1770. Mr. WHEELER tells us it was born mainly out of the "regulator troubles" of about that period. It was named for WILLIAM PITT, Earl of CHATHAM, and the county seat was called PITTSBORO in further compliment to the great English statesman. Deeds to land in what is now CHATHAM dated prior to 1770 would appearin ORANGE back to 1751, from there back to 1746 in Granville, then Edgecombe, and back of 1733 in CRAVEN, assuming that our hypothesis is correct. As a matter of fact the early precincts like CRAVEN had no well defined Western boundaries, and even the others were somewhat hazy. But there were few deeds in this territory at that period and even the boundaries of many of the large grants were in grave doubt. The material shown below was gathered on several different visits to PITTSBORO by the writer and his wife.

WILLIAM RAY, will, dated in May, 1792. To beloved wife PATTIE RAY, a negro boy, Kios, etc., and the land I live on during her natural life. Children, NANCY, ANNIE, WINNIE, MILLY and JOHN. To son JOHN the residue of the land I live on. He mentions two grandsons HENRY and JACOB RAY. His friend JAMES LANGSTON and wife PATTIE executors. Witnesses JAMES LANGSTON and LEWIS BRINKLEY. (Bk. B. pp. 41-42).

THOMAS RAY, will, dated April 19, 1854, mentions wife KATHERINE and sons WILLIAM F. RAY and THOMAS M. RAY. CARY BYRUM and JOHN T. DAVIS executors.

KATHERINE RAY, her will, dated August 28, 1865. (Evidently the widow of THOMAS RAY who died in 1854) mentions children, MARGARET RAY who married a DISMUKES, CATHERINE RAY married a CLARK, DAVID RAY, NANCY RAY, married JOHNSON and son JOHN RAY.

WILLIAM DUTY died leaving will in CHATHAM COUNTY in November 1815; mentions his wife CATHERINE and children THOMAS, WILLIAM, RUSSELL and MATTHEW DUTY, REUBEN CLAYTON (relationship not given), NANCY (son SOLOMON), SARAH HACKNEY and SUSANNA who married WILLIAM DORSETT; To THOMAS DUTY, son of WILLIAM, 1 share, and to SARAH HACKNEY COLLINGS' three oldest daughters, 1share. Signed, WILLIAM DUTY. Witnesses were WILLIAM DORSETT and DUTY DORSETT.

HENRY CRUTCHFIELD, will, dated August 28, in 1787, names his wife MILLY CRUTCHFIELD and the following children: JAMES CRUTCHFIELD (not yet 21), JOHN CRUTCHFIELD, (at 21, my negro boy Daniel), HENRY, ELIZABETH, WILLIAM, THOMAS, BENJAMIN, EDWARD, ANDERSON and STAPLETON CRUTCHFIELD. Witnesses GEORGE DISMUKES and TURNER CRUTCHFIELD. (Book B p. 28).

THOMAS CRUTCHFIELD left will in CHATHAM COUNTY in May, 1844, and named the following children: WILLIAM H. CRUTCHFIELD, ELIZABETH who married a WHITEHEAD (John), MARTHA CRUTCHFIELD who married a JOHNSON and NANCY CRUTCHFIELD who married JAMES CLARK.

JAMES W. RAY, died leaving a will in CHATHAM COUNTY, dated January 1, 1912. Did not copy as it was too recent.

BENJAMIN RUSH left will in CHATHAM, dated April 29, 1801, in which he named his wife ELIZABETH and the following children: WILLIAM RUSH, ANN who married PEYTON, ALICE who married DEVINNEY, ELIZABETH married TERRILL, the children of SUSANNAH BROOKS, FRANCES RUSH who married a WADDLE, AMY RUSH who married STRINGFELLOW, MARY RUSH married a WILLIAMS, and BENJAMIN RUSH; my three daughters RUTH, JUDIE and ELIZABETH; his wife, son WILLIAM and THOMAS STOKES, friend, executors. The witnesses were THOMAS STOKES, HARDY WHILLERS and ALLEN RAINES.

MARGARET MARKS, left will in CHATHAM dated February, 1848, and named the following children: Sons RICHARD, WILLIAM, NICHOLAS & JAMES, and daughters SUSAN married GEORGE HEIGHT, MARGARET, NANCY married RICHARD SLOAN, SARAH married a FERREL, and to LLOYD MARKS, the residue, including two negroes, stock, etc. My worthy son WILLIAM MARKS, Executor. Signed, MARGARET MARKS, in the presence of W. BUCHANAN and R. S. MARKS. Proven. W. A. STEDMAN, County Court Clerk at February session 1848.

JOHN MOORE, left will in CHATHAM dated SEPT. 19, 1843, in which he named his wife PHENEBY, and "my grandson JAMES MOORE, son of COUNCIL MOORE"; MARY P. HILL, ROMETHA MOORE and RACHEL MOORE, heirs of my son HENRY MOORE, deceased; deceased daughter MARY HERNDON; son ALFRED MOORE, of Alabama; daughter SARAH MOORE who married a WARREN; son COUNCIL MOORE, daughter, ELIZABETH HUCKLEY and my son WORTEN (WOOTEN?) MOORE, of Alabama. Witnessed by THOMAS BELL, ALLEN ELLIS and THOMAS WHITEHEAD.

GEORGE WILLIAMS, SR. left will in CHATHAM COUNTY, dated February 20, 1833, in which he mentioned wife DELPHA and children JOHN, MARMADUKE, WILLIAM, RICHARD, ELIZABETH MOORE, PATSY STONE, HENRY WILLIAMS, and the lawful heirs of GEORGE WILLIAMS, JR., viz: DAVID P. WILLIAMS, JOHN D. WILLIAMS and POLLY E. WILLIAMS. Signed GEORGE WILLIAMS. Witnesses to the will were R. C. COTTON and WILLIAM FORSHEE.

JOHN WILLIAMS left will in CHATHAM dated November, 1816, in which he mentioned his beloved wife PHILADELPHIA, and his children SOPHIA LOUISA WILLIAMS, CHARLES JUDSON WILLIAMS and BENJAMIN WILLIAMS; son in law JOSEPH HENRY WALTERS, and makes his wife, JOSEPH BAKER and JAMES BAKER his executors. Signed by JOHN WILLIAMS. Witnessed by CHARLES MANLY and BASIL MANLY. (Book a p 282).

ANN LACY left will in CHATHAM COUNTY dated in 1811, in which, stating that she was old & infirm, left her property to the following children: ANN LACY, wife of STEPHEN JUSTICE; PHILEMON LACY, LUCY LACY married MONTREY, MARY LACY married LLOYD, MARTHA LACY married BROWN, ELIZABETH LACY married an ADCOCK, and SALLY LACY married WEST. Son, PHILEMON LACY and son in law STEPHEN JUSTICE, Executors. Signed by ANN x LACY, May 30, 1810. The witnesses are THOMAS SNIPES and ROBERT GATES (Book A p. 189).

PHILLIP (PHILEMON) LACY, PHILLIP LACY SR. and JOHN LACY were all on the U. S. Census for the year 1800 in CHATHAM COUNTY, North Carolina; also WILLIAM DUTY, GEORGE DISMUKES, JAMES BAKER and JAMES, JOHN, JOSEPH and WILLIAM MARKS, also GEORGE MARKS.

CHATHAM COUNTY, N. C. was erected out of ORANGE COUNTY in 1770, and among the old deeds to land showing on the records are the following:

JAMES RAY and wife WINNIFRED sold land to BENJAMIN WATTS by deed dated February, 1772 in Book A at page 62; in 1773 they deeded lands in CHATHAM to ROBERT RUTHERFORD, Book A p. 142; in 1778 they sold land to WILLIAM PETTY, JR. which is recorded in Book d p. 515.

THOMAS RAY, in 1789 sold land by deed to one GEORGE LUCAS, Book D p. 556; his wife was CHARLTY (TEAGUE) and they sold land to JAMES BRIDGES in 1795, as shown by Book G pp 380-381; and they also sold land to ISAAC TEAGUE in November 1796, as shown by Book H p. 291.

JOHN RAY deeded land to JAMES LASSITER in the year 1804 (Book N p. 424).

DAVID RAY, deed to JOSEPH J. BALDWIN in 1835 Book A-D 259.

ABRAHAM HINTON executed a deed in 1786, Book D. p. 134. He also sold land to GEORGE BROWN in 1798, Book J. p 260.

WILLIAM HINTON deeded land to LARD SELLERS in 1798 (Book L p 60).

MATTHEW JONES sold land to AARON HARLAND (or HOLLAND) in November, 1772; Book A p. 132.

JOHN H. JONES deed to JAMES BUCKNER in May, 1774. Book A p 243.

MATTHEW JONES also sold land to GEORGE HARLAND in August, 1794. Book A p 319.

AQUILLA JONES sold land to HUGH DANIEL about the same time. Book D p 182.

NATHAN JONES (NATHANIEL, of course) deeded land to TIGNALL JONES, SR. and TIGNALL JONES JR., and they all sold same to JACOB FLOWERS. (Book J. pp. 37-38-39.

NATHANIEL JONES sold land to E. CAIN (ELIJAH) in 1797. (Book J. 37-38-39).

JOSEPH BURTON, of "Deep River" in CHATHAM CO. deed to WILLIAM DANIEL, sold tract of land on North Side of DEEP RIVER, beginning at the mouth of INDIAN CREEK, south along WILLIAM POWELL'S line, and East along THOMAS SMITH'S line, 270 acres. Signed JOSEPH BURTON and MARY ELIZA BURTON. (It may have been BENTON, but appears to be BURTON in another deed). Witnessed by EDWARD GRIFFIN, CONNER DOWD and JOHN PHILLIPS. (Book A pp.370-372.

RICHARD DANIEL sold land by deed to SAMUEL WARD in 1778; Book B p 123.

HUGH DANIEL received a grant of land from the State of North Carolina in 1779. Book B p 206.

MARMADUKE DANIEL received a grant of land in CHATHAM COUNTY from the State of North Carolina in 1780. (Book C p. 32).

ISHAM DANIEL received a grant of land from the State of North Carolina in 1780. Book C, p. 516.

GEORGE DANIEL received a grant of land from North Carolina in 1782. Book B, p. 428.

JESSE DANIEL received a grant of land from the State of North Carolina in 1795. (Book L, p. 358.

ROBERT T. DANIEL deeded lands in 1799 (Book L, p. 2) and also in 1802 (Book M, p. 94).

GILLIAM DANIEL deeded lands to RICHARD DANIEL in 1780. (Book B, p. 365).

WILLIAM DANIEL sold lands to JACOB VARDEMAN in 1783 (Book C, p. 10).

WILLIAM DANIEL sold lands by deed to the estate of GEORGE DANIEL in 1784 (Book 6, p. 280).

JESSE DANIEL sold lands to ISHAM DANIEL in the year 1787. (Book D, p. 386).

JOHN DANIEL, JR. sold land by deed to JACOB FLOWERS, JR. in 1794. (Book G p 293).

GILLIAM DANIEL sold land to MARMADUKE DANIEL in 1803; Book N p 136; and GILLIAM also received a grant of land from the STATE of North Carolina (Book N p. 475).

BENJAMIN DANIEL and NANCY B. DANIEL deeded land to JOHN BRANTLEY'S ESTATE in 1806; Book S p 261.

LITTLETON DANIEL sold land to ISAHAM DANIEL in 1815. (Book T p 346).

ROBERT T. DANIEL deeded lands to WILLIAM BARB in 1818. (Book V p. 18 and Book X pp 32 and 229.

DEEP RIVER CHURCH IN CHATHAM COUNTY, N. CAROLINA

REV. PHILLIP MULKEY, a Baptist Minister of the "Separatist" persuasion, early established a Church and Congregation on DEEP RIVER in what is now CHATHAM but was then a part of ORANGE COUNTY (1759). Mulkey was born in HALIFAX COUNTY, North Carolina. Those who established the DEEP RIVER Church were PHILLIP MULKEY and wife, STEPHEN HOWARD and wife, JOSEPH BREED and wife, OBEDIAH HOWARD and wife, BENJAMIN GIST and wife, CHARLES THOMPSON, THOMAS THOMPSON & RACHEL COLLINS. (Paschal's History of the Baptist Church in North Carolina. The persons named, headed by the minister PHILLIP MULKEY emigrated from DEEP RIVER to Fair Forest in S. C. before 1760, but many of the members did not accompany the contingent who moved South, and among those remaining in CHATHAM COUNTY in 1764 were NATHANIEL POWELL, CONRAD DOWD and his wife, ISAAC BROOKS and wife, MARY BROOKS, MR. HODGE, JAMES STEWARD, SIMON POE, ROBERT CALLEH and SAMUEL MARSH, also NEHEMIAH HOWARD (Journal of Morgan Edwards). Long after the establishment of the DEEP RIVER CHURCH, the names of its old members - many of them - appear on the records of the State of GEORGIA, including PHILLIP MULKEY and NEHEMIAH HOWARD (Who left will in GEORGIA) and the descendants of ROBERT RUTHERFORD and the MARSH FAMILY, who drifted to S. C. and other parts.

SOME MARRIAGE BONDS IN CHATHAM

John Culberson to Peggy Webster, January 22, 1811.
Joseph Culberson to Anne Henson, September 26, 1814.
John Crutchfield to Sally Williams, March 20, 1827.

JOHN CRUTCHFIELD to Ruth Stout, February 3, 1819.
James Crutchfield to Dinah Crutchfield, Sept. 3, 1831.
Tapley Bolling to Sallie Ellington, January 16, 1838.
Tapley Bolling to Drucilla White, February 10, 1817.
William Moore to Martha Cummings, September 25, 1833.
Alexander H. Moore to Elliner F. Prince, March 25, 1834.
James O'Daniel to Polly Marsh, January 31, 1815.
Joel O'Daniel to Lucy Bright, November 11, 1830.
Pinckney Ray to Margaret Burns, December 5, 1851.
Rittenhouse Ray to Susan Patterson, Feb. 11, 1841.
David Walker to Ferreby Johnston, Oct. 17, 1814.
Coleman Walker to Peggy Thrift, November 15, 1813.
Thomas Williams to Ann Horton, August 25, 1833.
Andrew Wright to Nancy Crutchfield, April 22, 1833.
Arthur Whitehead to Elizabeth Crutchfield, Nov. 9, 1833.
William Straughan to Sarah Moore, Sept. 29, 1831.
George Rives to Mary Crutchfield, March 10, 1842.
Jesse Rogers to Mahala Crutchfield, March 27, 1832.
John Moore to Elizabeth Crutchfield, January 13, 1818.
Jonathan Moore to Hannah Lynch, Dec. 26, 1820.
Matthew Patterson to Leah P. Daniel, March 2, 1828.
William Duty to Jemimah Edwards, January 7, 1811.
William Cooper to Jane Ray (no date).

HERE ARE SOME UNITED STATES CENSUS RECORDS OF CHATHAM COUNTY FOR YEAR 1850:

JOHN CRUTCHFIELD, 43, born in N. C., wife SALLIE CRUTCHFIELD, 41; children William 21, and Franklin 18, Ruth 15, Mary 12 and Elizabeth 7.

WILLIAM F. RAY, 23, born in NORTH CAROLINA, and wife ANN J. RAY 21; one child JAMES M. RAY, two months old.

DANIEL BAKER aged 44, born in North Carolina and wife FLORA BAKER 34, the same. Children are Mary E 14, William J. 12, Flora Ann 10, John C. 8, Henry Clay 6, Daniel M. 3 and Margaret J. 1 year old.

NATHAN B. BRAY aged 42, born in N. C. and his wife MARY W. BRAY 36, the same. Ancelet M. 14, Ruth M. 13, Eliza W. 11, William S. 9, Jasper N. 6, Anne 3 and Mary C. 2 years old.

JOHN CHEEK, SR. 50 years of age in 1850, born in North Carolina; wife JANE CHEEK 42 also born in N. C. Children Elizabeth 13, Randall 10, Nancy J. 9, Lydia C. 6 and Noah R. Cheek 2 years old. (Must have been related to the pioneer NOAH CHEEK who came to Texas long before 1850).

JOHN D. CHEEK, 24 years old, born in N. Carolina, wife MARTHA 22, the same, and one son JOHN H. CHEEK 2 years old.

WILLIAM MARKS 43 years old in 1850, born in North Carolina; wife SARAH MARKS aged 39 also b. N. C., with children: Abner 18, Louisa 16, Letitia 13, Thadeus 11, James 9, Julia 7, Mary 3, and William Marks 1 year old.

CHRISTOPHER BARBER aged 59 years, born in N. Carolina, with wife JANE BARBER 57 also born in N. C. Children George 25, Martha 22, Simpson 21, Elizabeth 19, and Matthew Barber 17 years old.

OBEDIAH HENDERSON 50, born in N. C. and wife MARY, 45, born in N. C., and the following children: Isaac 18, James 15, Mary 13, Frances 11, Martha 8, Hezekiah 5 and James G. Henderson 2 months old.

BUCKNER FAMILIES. The records at Washington show many families on the census in CHATHAM COUNTY for 1850 named BUCKNER.

JOSHUA LINDLEY age 72, born in N. C., wife MARY 73, born N. C. and children as follows: Thomas P. 37, Sarah 33, Elijah 25, George Fox 22 and EZEKIEL HORNADY 15 also born in North Carolina.

JAMES LINDLEY and family. He was 76 years old in 1750.

WILLIAM L. LINDLEY and his family. He was 38 and his wife 36.

JAMES RAY 54 born in N. C. and his wife MARY 57; Henry M. 20, Mary C 18, and BRICE RAY 9. Rachel Gibson lived with the family at that time and was 80 years old.

JOHN RAE age 66 born in N. C., wife MARY T. aged 58; Margaret L. 26 and Emily C. 22 years old; George W. Dismukes 24, Ann Sophia Dismukes 24 and Daniel Hickman 8, all appear to have been members of this family.

COMELING WOMBLE age 57, born in N. C. and wife NANCY aged 45. Children Eliza 24, John J. 23, Samuel T. 22, William J. 19, Ruth C. 15, Mary E. 12, Comeling H. 8 and Lydia J. 6 years of age.

DIXON FAMILIES. Many families are shown on the 1850 census for CHATHAM by name of DIXON.

DAVID ALLRED aged 31 years, born in North Carolina, wife EDITH 35 and children Arply 9, Emeline 5, Boaz 2 and Jane 1 month.

THOMAS FLOWERS aged 30 born in North Carolina and his wife ELIZABETH, the same, aged 21 years. Three children Everett 23 (perhaps brother of Thomas), James E. 6 and William 1 year old.

WILLIAM DANIEL 60 years old, born in North Carolina.

RICHARD MARKS 45 years old, born in N. Carolina had children Jane Marks 20 and William L. Marks 1 year old. MARGARET BUCHANAN aged 30 apparently a member of the family.

JOSEPH STALLINGS aged 65 years born in NORTH CAROLINA. Children Martha 26, Sally 24, Mary 22, Esther 20 and Matilda 18. DAVID WOMBLE listed with the family aged 23.

THOMAS RAY aged 52 years, born in NORTH CAROLINA; wife CATHERINE RAY 49 born also in N. C. with children Louisa M. 25, William F 24, Eliza 22, Sarah J. 20, Thomas M. 1[illegible], Margaret 17, James W. 15, Catherine 12, John H. 10, Nancy E. 8 and David A. [illegible] 3 years.

PINCKNEY DANIEL aged 38 years, bo[illegible] N. C. wife CATHERINE and Susan 14, Nan[illegible] [illegible]1, and Martha 9, Mary 6 and James M. 3 years old.

MARKS, ZACHARY, 26 b. in N. C. wife EMILINE 29, William H. 6 and Lucian H. 5 years old.

A FEW NOTES FROM CLEVELAND COUNTY

CLEAVELAND COUNTY. Genealogically this County was for 62 years prior to its formation a part of Lincoln and Rutherford Counties (1779 to 1841), which two counties had been taken out of Anson and called TRYON in 1762. As ANSON came from BLADEN, Cleaveland was originally therefore a part of BLADEN. The County was named for the old King's Mountain hero Colonel BENJAMIN CLEAVELAND, who died long before his name was thus honored. King's Mountain lies partly within this County. At Shelby, the County seat, we copied the following from the county court records:

JAMES WRAY, will dated September 22, 1849 (eight years after the county was established) he names his children JANE RAY married a DICKSON, PEGGY RAY married a STALLINGS, WILLIAM WRAY, RUTH WRAY married a BAILEY, ESTHER WRAY married SHUFORD; grandchildren MARY ELIZA GRAHAM, JAMES P. GRAHAM and WILLIAM W. GRAHAM; their mother was ELIZABETH WRAY who married GRAHAM; NARCISSA WRAY married a LEWIS and had NANCY LEWIS, SARAH JANE LEWIS and JAMES LEWIS; F. A. L. WRAY another son mentioned. Signed JAMES WRAY. Names his son WILLIAM WRAY, Executor. The witnesses were JOHN R. LOGAN, E. McCARTHER and CHARLIE BLANTON.

SAMUEL LATTIMORE in a will (about 1848) names his wife LUCINDA LATTIMORE and makes her his Executrix. The names of no children are mentioned. The witnesses to the instrument are A. S. Elam and J. T. Miller.

COLEMAN DOGGETT left will in CLEAVELAND COUNTY dated December 20, 1852, in which he names his wife MARY DOGGETT. The will is witnessed by W. J. T. MILLER and one H. HAMRICK of Cleaveland County.

FRANCIS LATTIMORE left will in CLEAVELAND COUNTY dated February 14th, 1857, and names his wife SOPHIA and children SALLY, CHARLOTTE and DANIEL LATTIMORE, SAMUEL LATTIMORE, SUSAN LATTIMORE. DAVID CLINE made Executor. Witnessed by J. G. Williamson and W. B. McCall.

HOWARD - MULKEY FAMILIES. On page 7 of the MORGAN EDWARDS note book (appropos of CHATHAM COUNTY, N. C.) appears the following: "The following persons came from Opekon, in Virginia, and settled in the neighborhood of SANDY CREEK (later in CHATHAM COUNTY, but then in Orange) viz: REV. SHUBAL STEARNS and wife, DANIEL MARSHALL and wife, JOSEPH BREED and wife, SHUBAL STEARNS, SENR, and his wife, EBENEZER STEARNS and wife, ENOS STINSON and wife." This was in 1756. At first they had no ordained ministers but exhorters, met TIDENCE LANE and JAMES BILLINGSLEY. Then, from pp 385-386 of Paschall's History of the N. C. Baptists: "The first body of Separatists to go from North Carolina was a large portion of the DEEP RIVER Church (in CHATHAM COUNTY) which as a traveling church went first to the Broad River section (S. C.) and there in August, 1759, established organized worship with PHILLIP MULKEY as minister. Those who formed this church were PHILLIP MULKEY and wife, STEPHEN HOWARD and wife, JOSEPH BREED and wife, OBEDIAH HOWARD and wife, BENJAMIN GIST and wife, a CHARLES THOMPSON and THOMAS THOMPSON and RACHEL COLLINS. Here they remained for two years in which time their church had increased to 104 members, then the THIRTEEN who had come from the DEEP RIVER Church, left this young Church and went to FAIR FOREST farther South". OBEDIAH HOWARD and PHILLIP MULKEY of the above notes were the founders and ancestors of a numerous inter-mixed family of both names, in Tennessee and Kentucky.

The wife of JOSEPH BREED was PRISCILLA AVERY, and they had a daughter PRISCILLA BREED who married OBEDIAH HOWARD, the two families having met on DEEP CREEK at the old Baptist Church sometime after the STEARNS and BREEDS arrived there from OPEKON in 1756. PHILLIP MULKEY was, I am quite sure, a grandson of the PHILLIP MULKEY who died leaving a will in EDGECOMBE COUNTY, N. C. in 1736 (See p 112 of this volume) and probably the son of JONATHAN MULKEY, who witnessed the will. The REV. PHILLIP MULKEY had a son JONATHAN, who also became a noted minister in East Tennessee, who, in turn married in 1772 NANCY HOWARD, a daughter of OBEDIAH HOWARD and his wife PRISCILLA BREED. Rev. Phillip Mulkey (Of Deep Creek, later of Broad River, S. C. and GEORGIA) died in Georgia, as has been mentioned heretofore, and among his sons were REV. JONATHAN MULKEY who married NANCY HOWARD. The name of Rev. Jonathan Mulkey is mentioned often in the annals of Tennessee. He established the first Baptist Church West of the Blue Ridge, said to be the ancestor of the one now located at Jonesboro or Johnson City, Tennessee; also the first Church at Dandridge, Jefferson County, Tenn., in 1787, a list of the members of which is given in GOODSPEED'S TENNESSEE HISTORY. Rev. Jonathan Mulkey died and left a will in Washington County Tennessee, which is dated August 3, 1826 in which he names the following children: ISAAC, REBECCA (m. a SLAUGHTER), ELIZABETH, JOHN, PHILLIP, JONATHAN, MARY (m. a MANN), NANNY (m. a son of JAMES BILLINGSLEY mentioned above - or a grandson), SARAH (m. MENEZ). He mentions his sons in laws WILLIAM SLAUGHTER and JOHN MURRAY and his friend NATHAN SHIPLEY. (W. B. 1 p. 180).

OBEDIAH HOWARD (From DEEP CREEK, CHATHAM COUNTY, N. C. to S. C.) who married PRISCILLA BREED was a Revolutionary soldier, as attested by a receipt signed by his agent JOHN McCOOL on August 28, 1786 "for militia duty pay with BRANDON'S REGIMENT before the fall of Charlestown" and certified to also by A. S. Salley, Jr. in 1928, Secretary of the Historical Commission of South Carolina. OBEDIAH HOWARD, in his old age, moved to BARRON COUNTY, Kentucky, with his children and also with REV. PHILLIP MULKEY (son of JONATHAN and grandson of the PHILLIP of DEEP CREEK) where he died leaving a will in 1804. His children were STEPHEN HOWARD, WILLIAM HOWARD, NANCY HOWARD (wife of REV. JONATHAN MULKEY of Tennessee), ELEANOR HOWARD who married JAMES THOMAS, HANNAH HOWARD who married AARON HAYS, ANNE HOWARD, and perhaps others who may have died before their father. In BARRON COUNTY, KENTUCKY (that part of same, which later was erected into MONROE COUNTY) these HOWARDS were numerous, and included the names CHRISTOPHER (or KIT), JESSE, JOHN B., LOT HOWARD and many others. The descendants of "BENJAMIN GIST and wife" of DEEP CREEK, were also settlers there. They married into the CHISHOLM, DUNCAN and JOHN RAY family. Rev. PHILIP MULKEY III left there and settled at MULKEYTOWN, ILLINOIS. The descendants of these families are all over the SOUTHERN STATES.

SOME RECORDS FROM DUPLIN COUNTY

DUPLIN COUNTY. Genealogy. Wheeler tells us it was formed as early as 1749 from the upper part of NEW HANOVER COUNTY. Thus it is about the same age as GRANVILLE, ANSON and several of the other early counties taken from the original North Carolina Precincts. It is surrounded by the counties of WAYNE, SAMPSON, LENOIR, JONES, ONSLOW and NEW HANOVER. Among many others the following wills appear on its records:

THOMAS HICKS died in DUPLIN County 1776, and left a will. Wife mentioned but her name not given. Had daughter REBECCA the wife of a JAMES MILLS, and the following grandchildren: HICKS MILLS, LEONARD MILLS, BEULAH MILLS, THANKFUL MILLS, REBECCA MILLS, ANNE MILLS, SERENA MILLS, BETTY MILLS and SARAH MILLS. Wife and ROBERT SOUTHERLIN, JR. Eexecutors (Book A p 186).

JOHN MOULTON died in DUPLIN COUNTY in 1790 and names his father ABRAHAM MOULTON, his wife and daughters MARY, SARAH, ELIZABETH and CATHERINE MOULTON all minors. His brother MICHAEL MOULTON is made an executor, with JOSEPH DICKSON and THOMAS JAMES. Witneses were KADER BRYAN, JANE DICKSON and ANN BRYAN (Will Book A p 287).

THANKFUL HICKS died leaving will in DUPLIN COUNTY, N. C. in 1785, and names her daughter REBECCA MILLS, and the following grand-children: THANKFUL MILLS, ANN TILLIS, HICKS, MARY, JAMES, SHADRACK and FREDERICK MILLS. (Will Book 1 p 185).

GEORGE KORNEGAY, SR. of DUPLIN COUNTY N.C. died in 1808 and in his will names GEORGE KORNEGAY, son DANIEL, DAVID, BASIL and JACOB KORNEGAY. His wife was MOURNING. Also mentions a daughter SEVILL and her children, the wife of a JOHN KORNEGAY. (Will Book A p 266).

MARY KORNEGAY died in DUPLIN and left will in 1826, in which she mentions sons BRYAN and HENRY KORNEGAY, daughter PENELOPE GARNER, daughter MARY CARRAWAY and the following grand-children: MARY NORRIS, NANCY JONES, ZACHARIAH KORNEGAY, WARD KORNEGAY, MARTHA KORNEGAY and LOVY BLALOCK. Sons BRYAN and HENRY KORNEGAY, Executors of her will. (Will Book A p. 265).

WILLIAM THOMAS, SR. died in DUPLIN COUNTY N. C. in 1782. Will proved in JANUARY that year. Daughters ELIZABETH HOLLINGSWORTH and RACHEL RHODES are mentioned, and sons WILLIAM THOMAS & BAILEY (or WILLEY) THOMAS, and JAMES HOLLINGSWORTH (who married his daughter ELIZABETH); also grandsons ISAAC, WILLIAM and ARCHIBALD THOMAS all minors. Son WILLIAM THOMAS and BENJAMIN RHODES (who married his daughter RACHEL THOMAS) named as Executors. Will witnessed by WILLIAM HOUSTON, BENJAMIN SMITH and JOHN HUMPHREY. (Will Book A, p. 477.

BENJAMIN RHODES (who married RACHEL THOMAS, daughter of William THOMAS SR.) died & left will in DUPLIN COUNTY, N. C. in 1804, probated 1805; mentions his wife RACHEL and sons JACOB, JOHN F. and JOSEPH T. RHODES, and two daughters RACHEL NEWKIRK and NANCY POWELL, and MASSEY BRICE, and several grandchildren; son JOSEPH THOMAS RHODES Executor. JAMES T. RHODES (maybe a brother) and NATHAN WALLER were the witnesses. (Will Book A p 415).

JAMES GILLESPIE, died in DUPLIN COUNTY, N. C. and left will dated in 1804. Among his legatees, after his wife, whose name is not given, are sons DAVID GILLESPIE and JOSEPH GILLESPIE; grandson JAMES GILLESPIE, daughters LUCY GILLESPIE, ELIZABETH MORGAN, JANE GILLESPIE and MILDRED ANNE GILLESPIE. CHARLOTTE and JOSEPH MUMFORD (whom the testator raised, and considered members of the family) are mentioned in a Codicil to this will; daughter ELIZABETH was the wife of AARON MORGAN; also mentions JAMES WASHINGTON MORGAN, a grandson, and JAMES GILLESPIE also a grandson. The executors named were sons DAVID and JOSEPH GILLESPIE, and COL. WILLIAM DICKSON and EDWARD PEARSALL were mentioned as Trustees.

WILLIAM HALL left will in DUPLIN COUNTY, N. C. in 1826. Wife ELIZABETH and sons JAMES and NICHOLAS HALL, WILLIAM HALL (deceased), LEWIS HALL, EDWARD P. HALL, THOMAS P. HALL and ISAAC N. HALL (Will Book A p 192).

JOHN SHUFFELL, died in DUPLIN COUNTY, N. C. leaving will in 1791, wife ELIZABETH and children WILLIAM, WRIGHT, ISHAM, EPHRAIM, WEST and ARTHUR and BRYAN SHUFFELL. His wife's son WILLIAM GRADDY, and his daughters NANCY SCREWS, LEVISA SHUFFELL, POLLY SHUFFELL, CATHERINE and TABITHA SHUFFELL (or SHEFFEL). The Executors named were LEVIN WATKINS and FRANCIS OLIVER. (Will Book A p. 427).

ROBERT SLOAN died in DUPLIN and left a will in 1840 in which he names son DAVID SLOAN, daughter MARY wife of JAMES HOWARD and SUSANNEH NIXON wife of WILLIAM NIXON, also daughter MARGARET DICKSON, deceased, and her children ROBERT SLOAN DICKSON, BARBARA ANN CHAPMAN, WILLIAM DAVID DICKSON, MARTHA DICKSON and EDWARD DICKSON; mentions his son in law WILLIAM DICKSON, who with his son DAVID SLOAN is made an executor of the will.

JOHN SLOAN died in DUPLIN COUNTY leaving will proved in 1827, in which he mentions his daughter MARY BRYANT (BRYAN) wife of JACOB BRYANT. His son WILLIAM SLOAN. JACOB BRYAN, his son in law is made Executor. Witnesses were JOHN McCANN and JOHN POWELL. (Will Book A. p. 444).

WILLIAM THOMPSON left a nuncupative will in DUPLIN COUNTY in 1785, in the proven memorandom of which he mentions sons JOHN and BENJAMIN THOMPSON and grandsons EZEKIEL CARTER and LAWRENCE THOMPSON. (Will Book A p. 256).

ABRAHAM KORNEGAY died leaving a will in DUPLIN COUNTY, N. C. in 1825, in which he names his wife ANNE, three eldest daughters and his youngest daughter and three sons without calling them by name. His "friend" HENRY KORNEGAY made Executor. Witnesses were JOHN B. WHITFIELD and J. BROWN.

LUKE KORNEGAY died in DUPLIN COUNTY, N. C. in 1819-20., in which he mentions a brother JAMES and JAMES' wife MARY CARROWAY, his brother HENRY KORNEGAY, NATHAN GARNER and his own wife PENELOPE; also a brother ABRAHAM KORNEGAY; his mother MARY KORNEGAY and another brother BRYAN KORNEGAY. The witnesses to his will are ROBERT WILLIAMS and MATILDA PRICE. (Will Bk. A pp. 251-3).

JAMES DICKSON died leaving will in DUPLIN COUNTY 1812. Wife SUSANNAH. Names 7 youngest children and six oldest children, and land in Tennessee. (Will Book A. p. 119).

JOHN CARROLL died leaving a will in DUPLIN COUNTY, N. C., dated Jan. 12, 1761, and recorded in March of the same year, in which he named his wife MARY CARROLL, sons JOHN CARROLL and JOSEPH CARROLL and daughters DORCAS and RACHEL CARROLL. Named his wife MARY and son JOHN as Executors, & the will was witnessed by DEMPSEY BENTON, HENRY HOLLINGSWORTH and JOHN BACHUS. (Book C p 100).

ALEXANDER GRADY, JR. of DUPLIN COUNTY, N. C. left will dated 1846 but not recorded until 1854 in which he mentions four sisters, and the "lands of Alexander Grady Sr." Also A. O. Grady, Fred Grady and ABNER GRADY, and "oldest brother" OUTLAW GRADY, and lands purchased of ISLER KORNEGAY and KEENAN GRADY, son of JAMES GRADY, SR. The will is witnessed by J. W. OUTLAW and S. H. SIMMONS.

THOMAS KENAN (Or KENNAN) of DUPLIN CO. N. C. died leaving will dated 1762, but proved in 1765. Names his wife ELIZABETH; sons THOMAS and MICHAEL KENAN under age, and daughters ARABELLA, ELIZABETH PENELOPE and JANE KENAN. Two oldest sons mentioned but not by name. His Executors his wife and DAVID THOMPSON. The witnesses were EDWARD MATCHET, JOHN MATCHET and EDWARD GANNONE. He mentioned in codicil a son in law RICHARD CLINTON. Witnesses were WILLIAM HOUSTON and ISAAC HUNTER. (NOTE: The name KENAN was simply a veriation of KENNAN, KANNON and even CANNON, as notice the spelling of EDWARD "CANNONE" in the will as a witness. These variants are common in the same families all over the Virginia and Carolina counties even among KNOWN members of the same family.)

ELIZABETH KENAN (wife of THOMAS KENAN of the preceding note) died leaving will in DUPLIN COUNTY, N. C. in 1790. She mentions three granddaughters SUSANNAH LOVE, ELIZABETH MORRICEY and NANCY TORRENCE; sons JAMES and MICHAEL KENAN; her daughters JANE MORRICEY, ELIZABETH TORRENCE and PENELOPE CLINTON (wife of RICHARD CLINTON); her daughter in law NELLIE KENAN. Her Executors were RICHARD CLINTON and GEORGE MORRICEY. The witnesses were DANIEL HICKS, SERENA HICKS and JAMES THOMPSON (Will Book A p 259).

JAMES KENAN, of DUPLIN COUNTY, N. C. died leaving will in 1810. His wife was SARAH and he mentions his son DANIEL LOVE and THOMAS KENAN, & land sold to BENJAMIN JOHNSTON and JAMES TORRENCE (spelled TORRENS); daughters JANE and SARAH KENAN, SUSANNAH GREEN, ELIZABETH PRICE and their children. Executors appointed were THOMAS KENAN and DANIEL LOVE KENAN. (Book A p. 257).

JOSEPH GREEN left will in DUPLIN COUNTY in N. C. in 1829, in which he mentions children JOHN A. GREEN, THOMAS K. GREEN, CATHERINE E., SUSAN E., HALION J., JOSEPH W., DANIEL K. and ROBERT F. GREEN. (Deed Book 2 p. 239).

SARAH KENAN died in DUPLIN COUNTY, NORTH CAROLINA in 1819, leaving will in which she names sons THOMAS KENAN and DANIEL L. KENAN (Daniel Love) and daughters ELIZABETH PRICE and children; SUSANNAH GREEN and children; SARAH MORRICEY and JANE HALL; grandson THOMAS D. KENAN son of THOMAS KENAN; grand-daughters CATHERINE E. PRICE and SARAH HOLMES. Her Executors were to be THOMAS and DANIEL L. KENAN; and the witnesses were JAMES LAWSON and ANN STANFORD. (Book A p 255).

BRYAN GLISSON, died leaving will in DUPLIN COUNTY, N. C. in 1824. (Book A p 182).

WILLIAM BARNES died in DUPLIN COUNTY, N. C. in 1769, leaving will in which he mentions only two children, LEWIS BARNES and a MARY BARNES. The Executors of this will are given as WILLIAM GOODIN, GEORGE SMITH and a FELIX KENAN.

SAMUEL DAVIS, died leaving a will in DUPLIN COUNTY, N. C. in 1838 in which he names his wife CATHERINE and children ELIZABETH PIPKIN CALVIN DAVIS, JAMES P. DAVIS, HEPSIBAH ADELIA JERMAN, SETH DAVIS and IRA DAVIS, when he becomes 21 years of age; JOHN EDWARD T. DAVIS, NANCY DAVIS, WINNIFRED DAVIS, EMMA DAVIS, MARIA C. DAVIS and SAPHRONIA E. DAVIS. Son JAMES P. DAVIS and JAMES H. JERMAN Executors.

WILLIAM H. HURST left will in DUPLIN COUNTY, N. C. in 1837, in which he mentions his brother JOHN J. HURST, Uncle HOGAN HUNTER, and sister SARAH A. HILL; children of sister CATHERINE COLVIN; sister NARCISSA HURST, brothers ANDREW J. and JAMES R. HURST, and his mother (name not given). Appoints his brother JOHN J. HURST his Executor, with CHARLES WINDERS and HENRY WINDERS, witnesses.

SARAH HALL died leaving will in DUPLIN COUNTY, N. C. in 1789 in which she mentions her grandson JAMES T. RHODES, and grand-daughters MARY HALL and MARTHA WILLIAMS; daughters MARTHA WILLIAMS and PATIENCE WILLIAMS, and son DRURY HALL. JOSEPH T. RHODES and JOHN HUMPHREY named her Executors, with CHRISTIAN WILLIAMS, SUSANNAH SMITH, JOHN HUMPHREY and J. T. RHODES the witnesses (Will Book A p 193).

BENJAMIN HERRING executed a division of lands in DUPLIN COUNTY, N. C. in 1815, with HENRY GRADY the Surveyor, in which is mentiored THOMAS GRADY, THOMAS PARRISH, LUKE HERRING, WILLIAM CREECH, BENJAMIN HERRING, DANIEL HERRING and EDWARD CREECH. (Deed Book 5 p 376).

STEPHEN B. HERRING, bill of sale in 1814, mentions wife ELEANOR and children BRIGHT M., MARY N., CATHERINE, ROBERT N., SARAH ANN and ELIZA. D. MIDDLETON and ROBERT MIDDLETON the witnesses (Book 5 p 253).

JAMES HERRING, SR. executed a deed in DUPLIN COUNTY, N. C. in 1789, in which he mentions his daughter ANN, sons BRYAN, JAMES, JR., and LEWIS WILLIAMS HERRING. Witnessed by OWEN O'DANIEL. (Book E p. 362).

(OWEN O'DANIEL was the son of CHARITY WHIT-FIELD and FREDERICK O'DANIEL; and after the death of his father, his mother married DANIEL HERRING, her sisteŕs widower. CHARITY WHITFIELD was the daughter of WILLIAM WHITFIELD and Elizabeth Goodman, who had a son WILLIAM who married RACHEL, the daughter of NEEDHAM BRYAN.) See (1-568).

JAMES PEARSALL, died in DUPLIN COUNTY, N. C. and left a will in 1813, in which he names his wife ANN (She his third wife, it is said); sons EDWARD, JAMES, JEREMIAH, JOSEPH DICKSON, HUGH and WILLIAM PEARSALL. Daughters MARY McGOWAN and son in law JAMES McGOWAN, and ELIZABETH PEARSALL. Exrs. sons EDWARD and JAMES PEARSALL.

RICHARD BARFIELD died leaving will in DUPLIN COUNTY in 1754, sons HENRY, JESSE and SOLOMON BARFIELD. His Executors were sons SOLOMON and JESSE BARFIELD. (See p. 6).

ALEXANDER GRADY, SR. left will in DUPLIN COUNTY, N. C. proved in 1825, in which he names his wife ANNA and mentions children but does'nt give their names. (Book A p. 178.)

WILLIAM BIZZELL died in DUPLIN COUNTY N. C., with will, in which he mentions his wife HANNAH and several children, including HARDY, whose wife was MARGARET DENMARK, ISAAC, ARTHUR and JAMES and daughters NANCY and RACHEL WOODARD, and grand-daughters MARY WORRELL, PATTY WORRELL, SARAH CHERRY, ELIZABETH GOODMAN and a NANCY ROGERS.

JAMES BIZZELL died in DUPLIN COUNTY in 1822 and by his will he appears to have had daughters CATY SAUNDERS, BETSY, MOLLY, ALSEY, NANCY GULLY and SALLIE SWINSON, and sons SAMUEL, ELIJAH and JAMES and WILLIAM BIZZELL.

ALEXANDER O'DANIEL died in DUPLIN COUNTY, N. C. in 1816, and in his will gives his wife's name as ANN. He also mentions son WILLIAM, who was then under 21. His executors were JAMES PEARSALL and OWEN O'DANIEL. The witnesses were OWEN O'DANIEL, CHARITY HERRING. (CHARITY HERRING, who signs by mark, had been CHARITY WHITFIELD, daughter of WILLIAM WHITFIELD and his wife ELIZABETH GOODMAN and was an aunt of the testator and his brother OWEN O'DANIEL). (Will in Book A p 370).

DAVID SLOAN died in DUPLIN COUNTY, N. C. in 1785 and gives the name of his wife as MARGARET; sons JOHN, DAVID and GIBSON, daughters MARGARET, SUSANNAH and POLLY BROCK. The Executors were MARGARET SLOAN, LEWIS BROCK (who had married POLLY SLOAN) and DAVID SLOAN. (Will Book A p 447).

JOSEPH SCOTT died in DUPLIN COUNTY, N. C. leaving will proved in 1781. Name of his wife not given. Sons JOSEPH, JONATHAN and NEHEMIAH SCOTT and daughters JEAN CHESTNUT, JERUSHA, PEGGY, ADER (ADAIR), ASHEA and MARY SCOTT. The Executors were MARTHA and JOSHUA CHESTNUT. (Bk. A p 445).

JAMES OUTLAW died leaving will in DUPLIN COUNTY, N. C. in 1827 in which he gives the name of his wife as ELIZABETH, mentions his son in law JACOB WILLIAMS who first married his daughter MARY OUTLAW; and after her death his daughter PATIENCE OUTLAW; also his son JOHN and his children PATIENCE, MARY, OLIVE, LEWIS, ALEXANDER, LOTTIE and ELIZABETH OUTLAW; also his own sons JOHN, EDWARD, ALEXANDER, WILLIAM and LEWIS OUTLAW. Testator also mentions HENRY GRADY, ALEXANDER GRADY and WILLIAM WHITFIELD. The Executors were his sons WILLIAM and EDWARD OUTLAW.

JAMES OUTLAW left will in DUPLIN COUNTY, N. C. in 1806, the will being dated JULY 31, of that year. In it he mentions his daughters MARY WILLIAMS, PATIENCE GRADY, ELIZABETH GRADY, CHARITY GRADY and NANCY OUTLAW, and sons EDWARD, JAMES, JOHN, ALEXANDER, WILLIAM and LEWIS OUTLAW. Executors, sons EDWARD and JOHN OUTLAW. This will was witnessed by JONATHAN KEATHLEY, EDWARD OUTLAW, POLLY PEACOCK and WILLIAM OUTLAW. (Alexander, the son of this testator, removed to JEFFERSON COUNTY, TENNESSEE (then a part of N. C.) where he became a distinguished lawyer, Speaker of the State Senate of the THIRD LEGISLATURE and a compatriot of General JOHN SEVIER, GEORGE DOROTY, and other distinguished men, associates of ANDREW JACKSON and the founders of the State of Tennessee.)

SAMUEL HERRING died in DUPLIN COUNTY, N. C. sometime in 1909, when his will was proven. In his will he names his wife RACHEL, and his sons WILLIAM and FREDERICK HERRING and DRURY HERRING and daughters POLLY and ALLY (ALICE). JOHN ELLIOT was Executor, and the witnesses were SOLOMON and LEWIS ROUSE. (Book A p 208).

ALEXANDER HERRING, of DUPLIN COUNTY died in 1819, with wife REBECCA. In his will he names his son LEWIS STEPHEN HERRING and makes his friends DAVID WRIGHT and DAVID HOOKS his Executors. (Book A p 202).

BENJAMIN HODGES died in DUPLIN COUNTY, N. C. and his will was proved in 1824. Daughters NANCY BOURDEN and MARY HERRING, ELIZABETH, SUSAN and FRANCES HODGES and sons HOLLOWELL, WILSON and WILLIAM HODGES. Sons WILSON and WILLIAM HODGES, Executors, and JAMES and WILLIAM RHODES, and DAVID D. HUNTING the witnesses. (Book A p 197).

WILLIAM DICKSON died leaving a will in DUPLIN COUNTY with a Codicil, both of which were recorded in 1820. In the will it is shown that the children of the testator were all grown and settled for themselves and some are deceased at the time the codicil was written and executed. The will is very interesting and throws much light on the DICKSON FAMILY HISTORY, items from which follow:

Grand-daughter CORNELIA ANN DICKSON (a daughter of son WILLIAM DICKSON, late of the State of Tennessee) unmarried and under 21 years of age.

Son JAMES DICKSON, deceased, had wife ELENER and three children, MARIA, ELIZA and PATSY DICKSON, who are provided for in this will.

Son LEWIS DICKSON, also deceased, with two minor daughters PATSY and ELIZA who are mentioned in the will. Lands of DAVID WRIGHT, JOSEPH DICKSON, ELISHA HERRING, ELIAS FAISON, LEWIS DICKSON and DAVID HOOCKS are mentioned in this devise.

Son JOSEPH DICKSON. His wife was LUCY and they had a son WILLIAM DICKSON mentioned by his grandfather.

Daughter ELIZABETH DICKSON became the wife of EDWARD WARD of ONSLOW COUNTY and died without issue.

Daughter SUSANNA DICKSON married JOSEPH GILLESPIE and they had son WILLIAM GILLESPIE, mentioned in the will of his grandfather.

Daughter ANN DICKSON married WILLIAM LANIER and had daughter FRANCES ANN who married a man named GRAHB.

Daughter MARY DICKSON married ISAAC LANIER and had a daughter MARY LANIER.

In another paragraph the testator mentions his four daughters ANN LANIER, FRANCES PICKETT (wife of WILLIAM R. PICKETT) MARY LANIER and SUSANNA GILLESPIE. His daughter ELIZABETH WARD was then deceased without any heirs. Executors named in the will were JOSEPH DICKSON, DAVID WRIGHT and DAVID HOOKS; witnesses were JOHN DICKSON, D. L. KENAN and ANN DICKSON.

The Codicil repeats a lot of the above same infomation. (Book A p 115).

ROBERT DICKSON left will in DUPLIN COUNTY, N. C., which was proved in 1815 and it is presumed he died that year. He mentions in it his mother BARBARA WILKINSON and his brother WILLIAM DICKSON, and nephew ROBERT DICKSON HOOKS, son of DAVID HOOKS his brother in law. (Book A p 100).

WILLIAM BIZZELL left will in DUPLIN COUNTY in 1800 and mentions his wife HANNAH, sons ISAAC, HARDY, ARTHUR, daughters NANCY BIZZELL, RACHEL WOODWARD, and others. HARDY and ISAAC BIZZELL were the Executors.

THOMAS ROUTLEDGE, SR. died in DUPLIN COUNTY in 1801, and states that he was in his 73rd year. Leaves land to his son THOMAS ROUTLEDGE on DUCK RIVER in TENNESSEE, one third of which belonges to JOHN DICKSON, of Cumberland County, N. C. for locating and surveying the same. DR. WILLIAM DICKSON is empowered to sell said land. Mentions a grandson THOMAS ROUTLEDGE, son of THOMAS, and grand-daughter CATHERINE ROUTLEDGE; daughter SARAH LEDDON. Executors sons THOMAS and STEPHONS JAMES and EDWARD FEARSALL. (Book A p 411).

GEORGE HOLMES died leaving will in DUPLIN COUNTY, N. C. in 1791, in which he mentions his wife HEAD and ten children, five of whom were HARDY, FREDERICK, WILLIAM, GEORGE and JOHN HOLMES (Book A p 223).

JACOB BONEY died leaving a will in DUPLIN COUNTY, N. C. in 1761. Mentions his wife but does not call her name. Mentions "my children" including son JACOB and youngest child JOHN BONEY. Executors were JOHN BROCK and DAVID JONES; witnesses JOHN COOK and WILLIAM McCANN (Spelled McCANNE). (Book A p 61).

EDWARD HOLMES died in DUPLIN COUNTY N. C. in 1761. In it he mentions only his brother GABRIEL, daughters MARY and DOROTHY HOLMES and his son JOHN HOLMES. (Book A p 466).

PHILLIP ROUSE died in DUPLIN COUNTY, N. C. in 1784, in which he names his son MARTIN and a daughter ELIZABETH ROUSE. PRISCILLA MURPHY and BARBARA SHEPARD have their names written on the back of the will, but no relationship is mentioned or connection given with the testator. The witnesses were ADONIJAH GARRISON and EPHRAIM GARRISON. (Book A p 415).

DAVID SLOAN died leaving a muncupative will in DUPLIN COUNTY, N. C. It was reduced to writing a few minutes before he died but when he attempted to sign it he passed away. He mentioned his two children DICKSON and CASANDRA SLOAN to whom he devised lands in Tennessee patented by JAMES MIDDLETON and DANIEL WILLIAMS. Will was dated in 1801. JAMES MATHIS and ANDREW THALLY are named as Executors. (Book A).

PATRICK POWELL died in DUPLIN COUNTY, N. C. leaving a will dated July 22, 1769. His wife was MARY MAGDALENE. His oldest son was GEORGE POWELL. He mentions "my four children" and another on the way. Wife MARY MAGDILENE and ALEXANDER HOLDEN are named Executors. ROBERT DICKSON made the overseer and guardian of his children. The witnesses were JOHN DICKSON, CHARLES WARD and RICHARD MILLER. Witnessed by A. ROUTLEDGE.

GEORGE ROUSE died in DUPLIN COUNTY, N. C. in 1810. His wife was RHODA. Mentions a son NATHAN and a grandson DAVID, son of NATHAN. Three other sons GEORGE, REUBEN and DAVID ROUSE. The Executors named were JOHN CARR and JOHN GILMAN, and the witnesses were JAMES ALLEN and JAMES HARRELL. (Book A p 418).

ROBERT DICKSON left will in DUPLIN in 1790. Son JOHN DICKSON, and daughter ANNE BRYAN. WILLIAM DICKSON and JOSEPH DICKSON the Executors. (Book A p 98.)

ROBERT DICKSON (another one, who died at nearly the same time) left will in DUPLIN in 1790. One is recorded in Book A at page 98 & the other in the same volume at page 101. But they are not the same. This one had wife BARBARA, who had been a widow SHUFFIELD, and who had children by her first marriage. This ROBERT DICKSON had sons EDWARD, ROBERT and JOHN DICKSON. His son JOHN DICKSON and brothers WILLIAM and JOSEPH DICKSON were made Executors of the will. Witnessed by JAMES DICKSON, DOROTHY DICKSON (relationship not known) and JANE DICKSON. (Book A p 101).

BENEDICT DICKSON left will in DUPLIN COUNTY, N. C. proved in 1838, in which he mantions children JOSEPH, SUSANNAH, ANNIE, BRYANT (BRYAN, WILLIAM, ALFRED, JAMES and ELIZABETH JANE DICKSON. Executors were BRYANT MALLARD and a DAVID SOUTHERLAND. Witnesses were HUGH MAXWELL, JESSE BOYETTE and JAMES MANER (Book A p97).

LEWIS DICKSON died leaving a will in DUPLIN COUNTY, N. C. in 1815. His wife was CATHERINE and he had PATSY and ELIZA DICKSON who were both minors and unmarried. His wife was named Executrix and his friends DAVID HOOKS & ELIAS FAISON Executors. Witnesses were LEVI BORDON (Another place this name is spelled BOURDEN) and DICKSON HOOKS. (Book A p 130).

STEPHEN HERRING died in DUPLIN COUNTY N. C. in 1797. His children were STEPHEN BRIGHT HERRING, ALEXANDER HERRING, ALATHEA HERRING & SAMUEL HERRING, CATEY CROOM (Dau), SALLY GLISSON (Dau) wife of DANIEL GLISSON, also a daughter PEARSIS GLISSON, and another daughter NANCY NEW. Sons STEPHEN BRIGHT HERRING and ALEXANDER HERRING were made the executors, and the will was witnessed by WILLIAM DICKSON, a JAMES STUART, WILLIS HERRING and SARAH CROOM. (Book A pp 209-213).

SUSEY MORRIS DICKSON died leaving will in DUPLIN COUNTY in 1803. In it she mentions her son in law GEORGE DREW who married her daughter LUCY, whose first husband had been WILLIAM JONES, also children SARAH DICKSON, HANNAH PHILLIPS, JOHN DICKSON and JOHN'S son SAMUEL DICKSON. Daughter FANNY WARD is menmentioned, and her son BENEDICT DICKSON; the last named being nominated as her Executor. The witnesses were JOHN and GEORGE SOUTHERLAND and JAMES REARDON. (Book A p 120).

HENRY KING died leaving a will in DUPLIN COUNTY, N. C. in 1762, in which he mentions his wife ANN KING, and sons HENRY, STEPHEN & CHARLES KING, and daughter MARY KING. His Executors were wife ANN and MICHAEL KING and ABRAHAM HERRING. Witnesses JOHN and JAMES YARBOROUGH and JOHN KING. (Will Book A. p. 260).

ALEXANDER DICKSON died in DUPLIN COUNTY N. C. leaving a will dated 1813, in which he mentions his brother ROBERT DICKSON of Blocke's Ferry in CUMBERLAND COUNTY, a nephew JOSEPH McGOWAN and another JONES DICKSON, nephew JOHN son of his brother ROBERT. Witnesses were STEPHEN GRAHAM and WILLIAM MALLARD. (Book A 95)

JOSEPH WHITFIELD died in DUPLIN COUNTY in 1765. In it he names his wife MARY WHITFIELD and children JOHN, JOSEPH, WILLIAM, BRYAN, HENRY and TIMOTHY WHITFIELD, daughters ELIZABETH OUTLAW, HESTER GRADY, SALLY WHITFIELD, CHARITY LOFTEN (a married daughter) & RACHEL WHITFIELD. (Will Book 1 p 64).

NOTES FROM FRANKLIN COUNTY

FRANKLIN COUNTY. GENEALOGY. FRANKLIN County was formed from BUTE in 1779. BUTE came from GRANVILLE in 1764, and GRANVILLE came from EDGECOMBE in 1746, and EDGECOMBE was cut off of CRAVEN in 1733. FRANKLIN and WARREN COUNTIES were political twins, born the same year, from the extinct county of BUTE, an in a genealogical sense they were great great grandchildren of old CRAVEN, as shown.

The territory embraced in FRANKLIN therefore was

CRAVEN up to 1733.
EDGECOMBE from 1733 to 1746.
GRANVILLE from 1746 to 1764.
BUTE from 1764 to 1779.
FRANKLIN from 1779 to date.

SOME DEEDS TO LAND

GABRIEL RAY and his wife MILLY, of FRANKLIN COUNTY, N. C. sell lands to SYLVANUS PUMPHERY, of NASH COUNTY, N. C., a tract beginning at the line of JACOB BASS on the lower side of BARLOW'S BRANCH, by line to ROOT BRANCH. Dated December 2, 1786. Signed by GABRIEL RAY and MILLY RAY (both by their mark).

GABRIEL RAY and wife MILLY to FRANCIS WILLS, 140 acres on the PETER HILL branch, witnessed by WILLIAM GARNER and GRAY ANDREWS, March 10, 1789. JOHN WILLS witnessed.

THOMAS RAY, of FRANKLIN COUNTY, N. CAROLINA, to THOMAS GAY, a tract of land beginning on the corner of PHILLIP PIERCE, running South to ISAAC STRICKLAND'S corner and to THOMAS GAY corner, October 3, 1795. Signed by THOMAS RAY his mark. Witnesses were MOSES UPCHURCH, RICHARD UPCHURCH and JOHN CARPENTER.

THOMAS GAY sells land to THOMAS RAY, on both sides of MOCCASON SWAMP, 73 acres more or less, on STRICKLAND and PIERCE line. December Court 1787. Date of deed October 4, 1787. Signed THOMAS GAY. Witnesses were MOSES UPCHURCH, JAMES PRICE (his mark) and CHARLES UPCHURCH.

DEMPSEY GATTIN sells land by deed, on February 19, 1781, located on the North side of RANSOM'S ROAD, being part of a tract of land which ISAAC SAUNDERS bought of SIMON MURPHY on PETER HILL'S branch, 140 acres more or less. Signed DEMPSEY GATTIN; witnesses JOHN HOFF and ELISHA HUNTER.

ELISHA STRICKLAND of WAKE COUNTY sold to THOMAS RAY, of FRANKLIN COUNTY, N. C. 42 acres on the line of JAMES PIERCE, and his corner, to the line of THOMAS GAY. November 18, 1794. Signed by ELISHA STRICKLAND. Witnesses were PHILLIP PIERCE and ISAAC STRICKLAND.

WILLIAMSON RICHARDS, of FRANKLIN COUNTY, N. C. on November 1, 1800, sold land to DANIEL RAY near the FRANKLIN COUNTY line, containing 118 acres more or less. Signed WILLIAMSON RICHARDS. Deed was witnessed by JEREMIAH BELL.

DANIEL RAY executed a deed to JAMES RAY in FRANKLIN COUNTY, N. C., same being part of the said DANIEL RAY'S tract where he now lives (Jan. 10, 1825) beginning at SANDEFORD'S line, then with WILLIAMSON RICHARD'S line, fifty acres more or less. Signed DANIEL RAY (by his mark); witnessed by I. PATE and EPHRAIM PERRY.

DANIEL RAY married PATSY JONES, Dec. 3, 1822, in FRANKLIN CO. WILLIAMSON RICHARDS, Sec.

RESIDENTS OF FRANKLIN COUNTY, NORTH CAROLINA IN 1800.

From the records of the UNITED STATES CENSUS in 1800, the following persons, among others were living in FRANKLIN COUNTY that year:

Green Hill
Jordan Hill
Thomas Hill
Robert Hill
Richard Hill
Henry Hill.
Aaron Bledsoe
Thomas Gunby
William Harrison
John Wooten
Parks Beman
Arch. Wiggins
Sampson Wiggins
Richard Browning
Harwood Pope
William Rae
John White
James Dew
James Perry
Joshua Perry
Solomon Perry
Anthony Winston
George Cunningham
James Upchurch
Seth Collier
William Penny
John Allen
Anthony Winston, Jr.
George Winston
Robert High
John Penny
Obediah Green

Phillip Daniel
Green Walker
William Wood
Joshua Gordon
Jonathan Thomas
Elisha Williams
Nicholas Long
John Cooly
Edward Cooley
Thomas Gay
John Wadkins
William Collins
Peter Collins
Jesse Denton
Lavisa Gay
Joseph Freeman
William Harrison
John Wills
Joel Terrell
John Alford
William Cooper
John Elliott
William Coppage
Charles Coppage
Jesse Coppage
John Pease
John Myrick
John Cooper
Robert Gill
Benjamin Rush
Sterling Cooper
Eason Alley

SOME MARRIAGE BONDS FROM THE RECORDS OF FRANKLIN COUNTY, N. C.

William Richards to Dolly Freeman, February 22, 1809.
Archibald Richards to Sarah Grumby, Jan. 15, 1829.
Howell Reams to Elizabeth Elliott, Oct. 23, 1812.
Jesse Reed to Mrs. Polly Perry, Jan. 16, 1828.
Burrell Reed to Frances Perry, June 25, 1807; Simon Jeffreys, security.
Ezekiel Reed to Margaret Edwards, Nov. 21, 1829
Albert Ray to Jacky Bryant, Oct. 29, 1853; John Wiggs, security.
Richard Russell to Ann Hawkins, March 21, 1824.
Green Ross to Susan Harris, Oct. 2, 1822.
Willie Roland to Obedience Bridges, Dec. 1, 1879.
John Rayley to Polly Mabry, Feb. 7, 1796.
Christopher D. Robertson to Lucy T. Fisher, Jan. 24, 1827.
William Robertson to Keziah Mitchell, Nov. 5, 1816.
Michael Riley to Lucy Upchurch, Dec. 20, 1815.
Micajah Rayley to Elizabeth Stallings, Dec. 16, 1812.
William H. Ray to Mollie L. King, Oct. 19, 1864.
John Richards to Elizabeth Perry, August 17, 1832.
Erastus H. Ray to Christian D. Gill, Eaton Davis, security. (About 1830).
Bennett Richards to Nancy Freeman, Dec. 27, 1831.
Ransom Rae to Anny Woodley, October 20, 1818.
George Richards to Lyddy Vinson, October 24, 1789.

Charles Ransom to Mary Dew, April 5, 1842.
James D. Ridley to Elizabeth J. Alston, Nov. 27, 1815.
Solomon Rogers to Gillie Hogwood, Dec. 5, 1826.
John Tayler to Tabitha Ramon, Dec. 15, 1801.
Isaac Winston to Polly Barron, May 9, 1821.
Joseph Winston to Betsy Dorsey, Oct. 25, 1821.
Jordon Winston to Delaney Walker, Dec. 12, 1832.
C. Winston to Martha J. Hester, Oct. 6, 1834.
Young A. Winston to Agnes Upchurch, Dec. 20,1844.
Newton Winston to Frances H. Young May 31, 1832
John Winston to Sarah Winston, Jan. 14, 1828.
William Winston to Frances Mayfield, July 1, 1814.
John Winston to Mary Thomas, Oct. 17, 1815.
John Wyatt to Alley Rains, Dec. 2, 1802.

Benjamin Winston to Miss Cook, Dec. 12, 1805. John A. Cook, security.
Anthony Winston to Mildred Yarbrough, Oct. 11, 1825; Claiborn H. Cook, security.
Marsallis C. Winston to Carmichael Dent, Sept. 7, 1837.
Richard Winston to Mary A Winston, May 17, 1825.
Robert Walker to Martha Winston, Jan. 15, 1833
Thomas Walker to Patsy Vream Sept. 15, 1812.
Thomas White to Sarah Johnson, April 4, 1821.
Joseph John Williams to Betsy Norfleet, Jan. 13, 1797.
Wyatt Wills to Nancy Garner, August 14, 1802.
Marmaduke Williams to Betsy Alford, Aug 19 1824

GREEN HILL. The marriage bond of Wyatt Wills to Nancy Garner, dated August 4, 1802, was witnessed by GREEN HILL, Clerk of Franklin County, who was a son of the GREEN HILL, born, as Boddie says on page 312 of his "Seventeenth Century Isle of Wight" Nov. 14, 1741 in BUTE COUNTY, N. C. and died in Williamson County, Tennessee in 1826. This is error because the text of the account shows that the 1741 date would apply to EDGECOMBE COUNTY, as even then, GRANVILLE COUNTY had not been set aside and organized. So, this shows, that the GREEN HILL who lived South of Louisburg across the Tar River, where Bishop Coke held the First North Carolina Methodist Conference at his home in 1785, which Bishop Asbury attended, was in Williamson County, Tennessee, in 1812, and it was his son GREEN HILL, who was Clerk of Franklin in 1812. (Green Hill, father of the 1741 Green, married GRACE BENNETT, daughter of WILLIAM BENNETT and was father also of many children, including GREEN and JORDAN HILL, whose name appears on the 1800 census list given in this sketch.) The Green Hill who was Clerk of Franklin in 1812 married Mary Long, who was obviously a daughter of GABRIEL LONG and his wife SUSAN RICHARDSON, of Halifax County. Gabriel Long was the son of COL. NICHOLAS LONG, of Halifax. Nicholas Long, son of Nicholas and brother of Gabriel, appears on the 1800 census in Franklin also, though the Georgia Records show that he was and had become a leading citizen of WILKES COUNTY, GEORGIA, a little after or about this time. The GREEN HILL who was Clerk of Franklin County in 1812, and who married the grand-daughter of COL. NICHOLAS LONG, of Halifax County, probably did not remove to WILLIAMSON COUNTY, Tennessee, with his father, since the father was living in Tennessee in 1808, according to Bishop Asbury (p. 312 Boddie's 17th Century) while his son was still in Franklin County even four years later, holding a county office. However, GREEN HILL the younger afterwards moved to ALABAMA and settled in GREENE County, where his family also went, including a son GABRIEL HILL, born in 1811, evidently in Franklin County, N. C., who married ELIZABETH EPPS MURPHY. The son GABRIEL HILL and his wife ELIZABETH had WILLIAM, RICHARD, GRACE, GABRIEL and ANNE LIZA HILL, the latter becoming the wife of NICHOLAS TURNER SORSBY (b. N. C. 1817), son of ALEXANDER SORSBY, who died in NASH COUNTY, N. C. in 1818, believed to have been the son of SAMUEL SORSBY who died in Nash County in 1791. Nicholas Turner Sorsby and his wife ANNE LIZA HILL were the parents of EUGENIA REBECCA SORSBY (b. 1859) who married ROBERT JEMISON or JAMISON, who was in some way related to the SEARCY FAMILY, of GRANVILLE County, who settled in TUSCALOOSA, ALABAMA.

JOHN ALLEN, of FRANKLIN COUNTY. The old JOHN ALLEN home is about two and a half miles from the town of Louisburg, in FRANKLIN COUNTY. The one on the 1800 census was either the father or grandfather of the famous "Spelling John" Allen, who is credited with having possessed a most phenominal memory and aptitude for the spelling of words. It is said that he could spell a word and tell where it stood by page and line in the Old Webster Blue Back Spelling Book. He won a prize as the best speller in the State of North Carolina and used to proudly exhibit a letter of congratulation on this subject which he had received from General Robert E. Lee, testifying to his abilities along that line displayed while a student in Washington & Lee. The John Allen of spelling fame was a half brother of Orran Randolph Smith, who is credited with having designed one among the first flags of the Confederacy. A drinking fountain on the courthouse lawn at Louisburg commemorates this act of Smith's.

THOMAS RAY (whose name appears on the several deeds in Franklin County) it is said, by one of the family genealogists, was the only soldier of the revolution by that name from North Carolina (the only THOMAS Ray, is meant). The account says that he enlisted from Wake County in 1779, and that his service ended in 1781. He was in the battle of EUTAW SPRINGS. In Franklin County, N. C. in 1782-3 he married ELIZABETH PEARCE (perhaps PIERCE) who died November 13, 1844 in SHELBY COUNTY, Indiana, where he, himself died November 16, 1829. According to this same account THOMAS RAY and ELIZABETH PEARCE (PIERCE) had children: HUDSON RAY, REV. JAMES RAY (a Methodist minister) GILLY RAY (m. a BYERLY), SUSANNAH RAY (m. BASS), MARTHA RAY, married a man by the name of HAIL and CHANEY RAY, who married HUGH CAMPBELL.

The writer, whose relationship to the RAYS of FRANKLIN COUNTY, N. C., is undoubted, is not in agreement with all of the statements in this account, and merely reproduces it because it may be credited by others who claim to know, and will interest them. My grandfather was MASSENBURG PEARSON RAY, and the MASSENBURG FAMILY, from Virginia, (Sussex and Williamsburg) were at one time numerous in Franklin County.

PHILLIP PIERCE, of these same deeds in FRANKLIN COUNTY, was the grandfather of Rev. BISHOP GEORGE PIERCE, of the Methodist Church, and the father of the noted minister of the same Church, Rev. Lovick Piece. The mother of LOVICK PIERCE and the wife of PHILLIP PIERCE of these records was LYDDIA CULPEPPER, whose identity has not been fully identified at this writing. She was perhaps a daughter of another minister of some note in North Carolina, the REV. JOHN CULPEPPER.

RECORDS AND GENEALOGICAL NOTES PERTAINING TO GRANVILLE COUNTY, N. C.

GRANVILLE COUNTY. GENEALOGY. The noted WHEELER says: "GRANVILLE COUNTY was formed in 1746, from EDGECOMBE COUNTY, and was so called in honor of the owner of the soil". As EDGECOMBE came out of CRAVEN about 1733, GRANVILLE is therefore a grandson of CRAVEN. When it was first established in 1746 GRANVILLE embraced for a period of FIVE YEARS, until 1751, not only WARREN, FRANKLIN and VANCE, but most of ORANGE, including the present PERSON, CASWELL, ORANGE & WAKE, CHATHAM, DURHAM, ALAMANCE, a part of GUILFORD and perhaps all of ROCKINGHAM, a vast territory, of which one WILLIAM PERSON was the first Sheriff. After 1751 ORANGE COUNTY and GRANVILLE dominated this wide Virginia line area until WAKE and CHATHAM were formed around 1770, for the evident purpose of forestalling the restless and embryonic "regulator" element, who were becoming enraged over the aggravating fees and burdens levied by the prosperous "office holders" of the two large domains. In 1764 a county called BUTE was established out of the territory now embraced in Warren and Franklin Counties, and thus GRANVILLE'S size was again appreciably trimmed down. From 1764 until 1851 - a period of eighty-seven years GRANVILLE COUNTY included its present area, plus the territory now in VANCE COUNTY.

FIRST MEETING OF COURT EVER HELD IN GRANVILLE COUNTY

From a tattered fragment of an old record in the Department of Archives and History at RALEIGH, N. C., this writer obtained a very brief account of what was the first County Court ever held in GRANVILLE COUNTY. It set forth the substance of:

Act of the North Carolina Assembly for erecting the upper part of EDGECOMBE COUNTY into a new County by the name of GRANVILLE.

The minutes of this first court recite:

That the courthouse be erected at ROCKY CREEK, as near as may be to the BOILING SPRINGS.

That WILLIAM PERSON and WEST HARRIS be appointed commissioners to confer with the Court of EDGECOMBE COUNTY.

WILLIAM PERSON was appointed Sheriff.

Members of the Court who were present at this first meeting were WILLIAM EATON, JOHN MARTIN, JAMES PAYNE, EDWARD JONES, JOHN WALKER and GIDEON MACON.

It was ordered that the Court adjourn to meet at the home of MR. EDWARD JONES.

(The above meeting was held, apparently at the home of EDWARD JONES on SEPTEMBER 3, 1746.)

Court met a second time at the home of MR. EDWARD JONES on December 2, 1746, at which meeting the following members of the Court were registered as being present: JAMES PAYNE, JOHN WADE, JOHN MARTIN, WEST HARRIS and JONATHAN WHITE.

(Here ended the record).

NOTES FROM AN OLD MINUTE BOOK OF THE COURT OF GRANVILLE COUNTY

June 1755 (p 18) In an action of trespass on the case between WILLIAM WILLIAMS, SOLOMON WILLIAMS, PHILLIP ALSTON and BENJAMIN WYNNS, the Executors of SAMUEL WILLIAMS, deceased, Plaintiffs, and WILLIAM BLAKE, defendant, the jury finds for the Plaintiff 55 shillings and 8 pence. It is considered by the Court that the plaintiff recover, with his costs, etc.

June 20, 1758 (p. 51). In an action of trespass upon the case, etc. JAMES DANIEL, Plaintiff and JAMES KNOTT, Defendant. Considered, and the defendant shall pay, etc.

June, 1758 (pp. 47-48). In an action of trespass on the case between THOMAS WILLIAMS, Plaintiff, and SAMUEL HENDERSON, the Defendant; the jury finds that the defendant did assume to pay, etc., and that there was a non-performance of said obligation; that Plaintiff recover the sum of five pounds, ten shillings, which is assessed against him.

In 1760. In the action of trespass on the case between FRANCIS RAY, Plaintiff, an JOHN ELLIS, Defendant, a jury being elected, tried, and sworn the truth to speak upon the issues joined, upon their oaths do say that the Defendant did assume, in manner and form, as the Plaintiff against him has declared; and they do also assess the Plaintiff damages by occasion of the non-performance thereof, to three pounds, eleven shillings, eight pence. Wherefore it is considered that the Pliantiff recover against the Defendant the damages assessed aforesaid, in form aforesaid; and assessed with costs.

February 5, 1765 (p. 126). CHRISTMAS RAY, Plaintiff, and DRURY GLOVER, a jury being selected, tried, and sworn the truth to speak upon the issues joined, upon their oaths do say that they find for the Plaintiff, fourteen pounds, four shillings and four pence, proc'd money. Wherefore it is considered by the Court that the Plaintiff recover against the Defendant and WILLIAM HESTER, the Garnishee, the damages aforesaid, in form aforesaid; assessed with costs.

At an Inferior Court of Pleas and Quarter Sessions held for Granville County, the 18th Day of May, A. D. 1764. Present, His Majesty's Justices, the following causes came on to be heard, viz:

JAMES BOYD v. JOHN WALKER.
WILLIAM TABB v. WILLIAM BIRD.
WILLIAM TABB v. JOHN PRITCHARD.
NATHANIEL BULLOCK v. JOHN GLOVER.
CHARLES JOHNSON v. THOMAS REID.
DAVID MITCHELL v. ROBERT DUKE.
BLAKE BAKER v. ROBERT LOVELL
JOHN SHEPHARD v. NICHOLAS COOK

NOTES FROM THE COURT RECORDS OF GRANVILLE COUNTY OF A LATER DATE

Tuesday, August 7, 1787. At a meeting of the Granville County Court, JOSIAH DANIEL was fined for his non-attendance as a juror.

HENRY POTTER asks for a Bill of Sale from JOHN MINOR.

LEWIS POTTER proved the execution of a deed from WILLIAM HURT (or HUNT).

LEWIS POTTER proved a Bill of Sale from JOHN POTTER.

STERLING YANCEY proved a Bill of Sale from PHILLIP YANCEY to THORNTON YANCEY.

RICHARD TURNER ALLEN was the orphan of DAVID ALLEN, aged 11 years.

Court for GRANVILLE COUNTY met on Wednesday, August 8, 1787. Present were the following Justices of the Court:

THORNTON YANCEY.
THOMAS SATTERWHITE
JOHN DICKERSON
JOHN MANIER.

It was ordered that ISAAC KITTRELL, JOHN DICKERSON, JR. (Sr.?) and HENRY SMITH be searchers in the Fishing Creek Section of GRANVILLE COUNTY.

Other "searchers" (whatever their functions may have been) appointed by the GRANVILLE COURT at this meeting on the date given (which thus discloses the "District" of their residence, apparently) were:

ISLAND CREEK DISTRICT. Samuel Williams and Knight.

ALRA PLAIN DISTRICT. William Byars and one THORNTON YANCEY.

COUNTY LINE DISTRICT. MEMUCAN HUNT.

GOSHEN DISTRICT. DR. WILLIAM BENNETT.

HENDERSON DISTRICT. WILLIAM ELEY.

RAGLAND DISTRICT. CASH and MITCHELL.

TAR RIVER DISTRICT. PETER BENNETT.

NAP O' READ DISTRICT. JOHN TAYLOR.

EPPING FORREST DISTRICT. McDONALD.

FISHING CREEK DISTRICT. JOSHUA BELL, AMBROSE BARBER and P. WOOD.

FORT CREEK DISTRICT. BULLOCK.

BEAVERDAM DISTRICT. BULLOCK.

DUTCH DISTRICT. BULLOCK.

Other proceedings on this date (AUG.8,1787):

The last will and testament of JOHN MORGAN was proved by the oath of GRANT ALLEN.

WILLIAM HUNT proved a deed to land he had sold to JAMES BRAZLEY.

Meeting of the GRANVILLE COUNTY COURT on the first Monday in May, 1786:

The Commissioners who were appointed to run the line between the County of WARREN and GRANVILLE, rendered them providing into court. They were, JOHN MASON, JOHN WILLIAMS DANIEL, PLEASANT HENDERSON, who were appointed for that purpose.

The case of PAINE, ESQ. v. WILLIAM KENNON came on to be tried. The jury, consisting of SAMUEL HUNT, WILLIAM ROBERTS, JOSEPH DANIEL, JOHN ROGERS, SAMUEL JOHNSTON, MICHAEL SHEARMAN, JOHN SHEARMAN, PETER CASH, WILLIAM YANCEY, JOHN WASHINGTON, ANDERSON SMITH and VINKLER JONES found for the plaintiff.

The case of ISAAC HICKS v. DANIEL NOLAND came on to be heard, and the jury, which was as follows: SAMUEL HUNT, WILLIAM ROBERTS, JOSEPH DANIEL, JOHN ROGERS, SAMUEL JOHNSTON, MICHAEL SHEARMAN, JOHN SHEARMAN, PETER CASH, JOHN PARHAM, BOLLING ADCOCK, DAVID HICKS and VINKLER JONES found for the plaintiff.

AARON PINSON was exempt from taxes because he was blind.

HOWELL LEWIS executed and signed the bond of WYATT HAWKINS.

STEPHEN BRAZLEY was appointed overseer of a road from BEARSKIN CREEK to GIDEON CRENSHAW'S.

Meeting of the GRANVILLE COUNTY COURT on Thursday, August 9, 1787.

JAMES W. DANIEL returns a list of the insolvents for the FISHING CREEK DISTRICT, for the year 1786. (He must have been the Sheriff). Among those listed were HARRIS MAULDIN, THOMAS W. DANIEL, GEORGE BRISTOW and JUSTICE PARISH.

Administration of the estate of FRANCIS OLIVER, deceased, granted to JOHN OLIVER, who entered into bond with HOWELL LEWIS, ESQ. and PETER BENNETT his sureties, etc.

Meeting of the GRANVILLE COUNTY COURT on August 10, 1787.

The following jurors were appointed to attend the HILLSBORO SUPREME COURT: SAMUEL HARRIS, RICHARD WILKINS, WILLIAM BENNETT, SAMUEL SNEED, JOHN WASHINGTON, WILLIAM GILL, ESQ., RALPH GRAVES, JAMES DOWNEY, JR., and JONATHAN KNIGHT.

Partial list of jurors selected to attend the County Court: WILLIAM KNIGHT, PHILLIP YANCEY ALLEN HOWARD, THOMAS HICKS, JOHN HUNT, ROWLAND GOOCH, SAMUEL CLEMENT, REUBEN RAGLAND, MARK WHITE, JAMES W. DANIEL, JOHN PARHAM, SR., and WILLIAM REEVES, or REAVES.

The case of PETER EPPS v. JOHN DUNCAN came on for trial and the following were among those selected on the jury: SAMUEL HARRIS, MICHAEL SPEARMAN, WILLIAM SANTHORN, JOHN MORRIS, JOHN RUSSELL, JAMES JENKINS, THOMAS HICKS and JOHN DICKERSON, CHARLES MOORE, JOHN PEACE and JOHN OLIVER.

MICAJAH BULLOCK presented his resignation as County Surveyor.

Meeting of the GRANVILLE COUNTY COURT on the first Monday in November, 1787.

Some members of the Grand Jury were:

SAMUEL CLEMENT
WILLIAM KNIGHT
GEORGE MELTON
THOMAS HICKS

Meeting held again on November 8, 1787.

JAMES DOWNEY was appointed guardian of THOMAS POTTER, ROBERT POTTER, POLLY POTTER and SALLY POTTER, the orphans of ABRAHAM POTTER, deceased.

JOHN POTTER renders into court his account as guardian of the estate of ABRAHAM POTTER.

Again the Court met on November 9, 1787.

Present as justices were JOHN POPE, THOMAS SATTERWHITE and ZACHARIAH HIGGS.

A jury was appointed to view the road from OXFORD to COL. JOHN DICKERSON'S.

JOSHUA BELL was allowed five days pay for attending court.

Meeting of the GRANVILLE COUNTY COURT on the first Monday in February 1788.

Justices present were:

CHARLES R. EATON
MICAJAH BULLOCK
ROBERT BURTON
ROBERT REID
HOWELL LEWIS.

Meeting of the GRANVILLE COUNTY COURT on the first Monday in May 1788.

Justices present were:

MEMUCAN HUNT
WILLIAM HUNT
EDMUND TAYLOR.

Members of the Grand Jury selected for Granville County Court, and recorded, were: WILLIAM GROVES, JOHN KENNON, SAMUEL CLEMENTS, DAVID KNOTT, GIDEON GOOCH, JOSEPH GOOCH, JOHN DICKERSON, WILLIAM DICKERSON, CHARLES MOORE, SOLOMON THORNTON and others.

Meeting of the GRANVILLE COUNTY COURT on May 7, 1788. List of the JUSTICES who were present and the name of the DISTRICT from which they came, is as follows:

COUNTY LINE DISTRICT. Memucan Hunt and Joseph Hart.

ABRAHAM PLAINS DISTRICT. Samuel Smith, Sr. and JOHN RAVENS.

GOSHEN DISTRICT. Thomas Owen and James Chandler.

TAR RIVER DISTRICT. William Gill and GROVES HOWARD.

NAP O' REED DISTRICT. Barnett Pulliam & OBEDIAH CLEMENT.

EPPING FORREST DISTRICT. Charles R. Eaton and James McDaniel.

FISHING CREEK DISTRICT. JOHN DICKERSON and William Dickerson.

BEAVERDAM DISTRICT. John Pope and JOHN PEWETT (or Prewett).

DUTCH DISTRICT. WILLIAM HUNT and a JOHN C. PEEK.

(From the above list it is easy to note the names of the leading residents and most prominent men in each of the named districts)

At this meeting (May 7, 1788) an order was passed exempting JAMES HUNT from the payment of tax levies, he being sixty (60) years of age.

The following jurors were selected and appointed for the next court:

ISHAM HARRISON
SAMUEL WILLIAMS
JAMES JOHNSTON
ABRAHAM DAVIS
LEWIS AMIS
JONATHAN KNIGHT
WILLIAM MALLORY and others.

The case of HOWELL LEWIS v. RANSOM SUTHERLAND came on to be tried and among the jurors selected to serve were HENRY MELTON, SAMUEL PARKER, RALPH WILLIAMS and STEPHEN CLEMENT.

ARCHIBALD HENDERSON was Clerk of the Court of GRANVILLE COUNTY in 1788, and most of the material shown in these abstracts was copied in his fine handwriting.

Meeting of the GRANVILLE COUNTY COURT on the first Monday in February, 1789.

The following persons appeared and qualified as Grand Jurors for this term:

JOSIAH DANIEL
GIDEON GOOCH
JOHN HART
REUBEN RAGLAND
JOHN HOWARD
SAMUEL CLEMENTS
WILLIAM GRAVES.

GROVES HOWARD was permitted to resign his office of Constable for the TAR RIVER DISTRICT.

Present as members of the court at this meeting were HOWELL LEWIS, JOHN BRODIE and MEMUCAN HUNT.

HOWELL LEWIS acknowledged a deed of sale to CHARLES LEWIS for 720 acres of land.

Agreeable to an order of the last Court the following commissioners WILLIAM BIASS, JAMES LEWIS, JOHN TAYLOR, LEONARD SIMS and ROBERT BURTON, ESQ. in re estate of JESSE HARPER, deceased.

ARCHIBALD HENDERSON is allowed $15 for drawing the list of taxable property for the year 1788, alphabetically, which is ordered paid.

FIRST COURT OF GRANVILLE COUNTY. This writer is convinced that the first court ever held in GRANVILLE COUNTY was at the home of EDWARD JONES in the lower edge of what is now WARREN COUNTY at the "BOILING SPRINGS", later called SHOCCO and JONES' SPRING, and not at the home of COL. WILLIAM EATON as some writer has stated. Both Colonel Eaton and Edward Jones, who appear to have been the moving spirits at this birth of COLONIAL GRANVILLE COUNTY were present. On page 43 of this work, the writer thinks he is in error in stating that JONES lived in the Northern part of FRANKLIN, but now believes that his home was over the line in WARREN. These statements are based on the record discovered in the old minute book of the court detailing briefly the account of the first two meetings held, and upon data found among the notes of Col. Ashe relating to the JONES and MACON FAMILIES which disclose that the JONES and MACONS (descendants of GIDEON) lived in that vicinity. Some of the facts relative to this meeting and relative also to COL. EATON will be found on page 43 hereof, to which reference is made.

GIDEON MACON who met with the first court of GRANVILLE COUNTY at the home of EDWARD JONES on September 3, 1746, was a son in law of EDWARD JONES, having married his daughter PRISCILLA, by whom he had ANN HART MACON (m. CAPT. JOHN ALSTON), SARAH MACON (m. CAPT. JOHN HAWKINS), MARTHA MACON (m. JOSEPH SEAWELL), JOHN MACON (m. JOANNA TABB), HARRISON MACON (m. HANNAH GLENN), NATHANIEL MACON (m. HANNAH PLUMMER), and GIDEON HUNT MACON, who m. (1) MARY GREEN, (2) MARY HARTWELL. GIDEON MACON was deceased before 1763, and his widow PRISCILLA (JONES) MACON married JAMES RANSOM on February 9th of that year. MARTHA, the sister of GIDEON MACON married ORLANDO JONES, son of the REV. ROWLAND JONES, of Bruton Parish, in YORK COUNTY, VIRGINIA, and her daughter FRANCES JONES, who married COL. DANDRIDGE was the mother of MARTHA WASHINGTON. For the names of the children of EDward JONES see page 43 (this book).

JAMES PAYNE another one of the persons present at the first meeting of the first Court of GRANVILLE COUNTY on September 3, 1746, was a brother in law of EDWARD JONES, he having married ALICIA JONES, a sister of EDWARD, long before coming to North Carolina, as shown by the will of EDWARD JONES, SR. in Farnham Parish, in Virginia, recorded in 1715.

WEST HARRIS, another member of this little band of GRANVILLE COUNTY pioneers was also related to EDWARD JONES. WEST was the son of EDWARD HARRIS who died leaving a will in ISLE OF WIGHT COUNTY, Virginia in 1734, whose ~~sister~~ JOHN HARRIS married a JONES. The wife of WEST HARRIS is said to have been MARY TURNER. This West Harris, of GRANVILLE was the ancestor of HON. ISHAM HARRIS, the beloved Governor of Tennessee. While the HARRIS genealogists have failed to furnish us with a list of his children, it is more than likely that WEST HARRIS was the father of ROBERT HARRIS who, in the days of GOVERNOR DOBBS appears to have been a kind of "political Boss" of GRANVILLE COUNTY. As a member of the Assembly ROBERT HARRIS must have said some uncomplimentary things about Dobbs, for which he was hailed before the Governor and penalized by having his name left off the lists of Justices for Granville County, whereupon his more fortunate fellow-citizens who had been reappointed, refused to serve.

ROBERT POTTER, the orphan who is mentioned with his brother THOMAS and sisters POLLY and SALLY, and for whom JAMES DOWNEY at a meeting of the GRANVILLE COUNTY COURT on November 8, 1787, was a son of ABRAHAM POTTER, and his subsequent history, while not very creditable, as same is related by the Historian Wheeler, yet his meteoric rise in GRANVILLE COUNTY and NORTH CAROLINA politics to a seat in Congress, his fall back into the position as a member of the State Legislature, his trial for indignities against the peace and dignity of the State of North Carolina, and his final departure from the Old North State, headed for Texas, provides a historical " thriller " for people who like such narratives. On his arrival in Texas he became almost immediately a confidant of the leading men of what was then the REPUBLIC OF TEXAS, and was elected to serve as a member of the CONGRESS of that budding commonwealth, but only served for a brief period, because, the hot blooded Texans, who did not like his "style" ended his career in the midst of tragic circumstances. He "died with his boots on".

Meeting of GRANVILLE COUNTY COURT the first Monday in May, 1786:

GROVES HOWARD asked to record a deed of sale to ALLEN HOWARD. Granted.

THOMAS HENRY proved a deed of gift from WILLIAM ALLEN.

Will of DAVID BAIL (BAILEY?) proved by JOHN JOHNSTON and ABSALOM JOHNSTON.

Members of the Grand Jury empannelled & sworn were as follows:

Robert Coleman	Absalom Davis
David Knott	John Taylor
Samuel Pointer	William Williams
John Webb	G. Smith.
Josiah Daniel	Joseph Taylor
Henry Graves	P. Davis
Samuel Sneed	Ransome Sutherland
Henry Melton	Samuel J. Kittrell
John Rust	Benjamin Beardon.

An inventory of the estate of JAMES DANIEL, deceased, was rendered into Court, under oath, which was approved.

JAMES HUNT GREER, ESQ., produced into Court a license to practice as an attorney in GRANVILLE COUNTY COURT, which was admitted. He took the oath of the said office.

The will of JAMES DANIEL referred to in the above minutes is recorded in Will Book No. 1, p. 452. It was dated October 10, 1785.

Mentions his wife Sarah Daniel. To his son JOHN DANIEL he leaves 210 acres of land & some negroes and cattle; to his son REUBEN he leaves 210 acres of land; to his son WILLIAM he leaves 210 acres of land near the head of DEEP SPRING BRANCH"; to his son RICHARD DANIEL he leaves two hundred and ten acres "after my wife dies"; to son JOSEPH DANIEL he leaves land and his interest in a still. Mentions his daughter MARY DANIEL, the wife of DAVID ROYSTER, and her children, LUCY, POLLY and BECKY ROYSTER; his daughter ANN DANIEL, and refers to his son in law EDMUND SMITH.

The following abstract of the will of JOHN DANIEL, father of the JAMES DANIEL who executed the above will, is made from a certified copy in the hands of the writer, as furnished by CHARLOTTE EASTON, Assistant Clerk of the Superior Court of Granville County, where said will is on file, being Numbered 88. Said will was executed June 19, 1762, and proved by the oath of JOHN WALKER the same year, DANIEL WELDON so certifying as Clerk. The will was witnessed by JOSEPH LINSEY, JOHN WALKER and a JOHN DUNKIN. The devising clause of the will is copied in full below:

"Item. I lend to my beloved wife ANNE all my estate both real and personal during her life and after her decease all my estate, both real and personal to be equally divided between my FIVE CHILDREN, vizt: JAMES DANIEL, JOHN WILLIAMS DANIEL, SARAH HARRISON, MARTHA BARBEY(it should be BARBER) & Elizabeth DUDLEY, to them their heirs and assigns forver.

"AND as I am informed that I did some years past make a deed of gift to my daughter ELIZABETH DUDLEY, wife to CHRISTOPHER DUDLEY, my negro wench HANNAH, together with her increase, I do hereby declare the said gift to be void and entirely contrary to my will, I not being in my proper senses at the execution of the said Deed of Gift; and do by this present writing appoint JAMES DANIEL and JOHN WILLIAMS DANIEL my executors to this my last will and testament.

JOHN DANIEL (Seal).

The will of SIMON CLEMENT, dated April 3, 1800 is recorded on the records of GRANVILLE COUNTY, in which he mentions his wife MARY FREDDEN CLEMENT; other legatees being as follows: OBEDIAH CLEMENT, ZEPHANIAH CLEMENT, STEPHEN CLEMENT, SIMON CLEMENT, JOHN CLEMENT, son in law CHARLES JONES, daughter ANNE CLEMENT (who married TERRY), SAMUEL CLEMENT, WILLIAM CLEMENT, ISABEL CLEMENT and MARY CLEMENT. (Book and page not copied).

Following is an abstract of the will of AARON PINSON, found on the records of GRANVILLE (Dated before 1800) in which he mentions his wife DELILAH, evidently a widow CUNNINGHAM, when he married her as his second or third wife. The legatees mentioned are WILLIAM CUNNINGHAM, JAMES CUNNINGHAM, SALLY CUNNINGHAM, who shall have their mother's part of the estate; THOMAS PINSON, ELIZABETH CAMPBELL, DORCAS AUSTIN, SARAH HEAD and ANNIE CUNNINGHAM, WILLIAM PINSON, AARON PINSON, MARY EVANS, ZACHARIAH PINSON and ISAAC PINSON; (the last list evidently being the children of the testator, one of whom, ANNIE, had married a CUNNINGHAM). The witnesses were JOHN GRAVES, RALPH GRAVES and JOHN STOVALL.

(A large contingent of these PINSONS & CUNNINGHAMS, of Upper Granville County, moved down into Laurens County, S. C. where numerous wills, deeds, etc., identify them, on the records there. Old AARON PINSON is mentioned in the "JOURNEY TO THE LAND OF EDEN " by COL. WILLIAM BIRD in 1733, who at that time lived up on the Roanoke, probably above Clarksville. The CUNNINGHAMS were of that set, from Virginia, originally, who owned the CUNNINGHAM STORE near the Virginia line on HYCO CREEK.)

The MORROW FAMILY lived in the ISLAND CREEK section of GRANVILLE COUNTY, probably in Vance County now, and in the vicinity of the MORROW CHAPPEL shown on BUCK'S MAP. Following is an abstract of the will of DANIEL MORROW:

Will of DANIEL MORROW, dated February 8, 1817. My beloved wife ELIZABETH, and my children DRURY MORROW, ALEXANDER MORROW, THOMAS MORROW; my daughters NANCY MORROW, ELIZABETH MORROW, EASTER MORROW (married one of the STOVALLS), and the children of WILLIAM MORROW, deceased, and DANIEL MORROW, deceased. To the three sons first named "the tract of land I now live on, on the South side of ISLAND CREEK, to be equally divided between them"; three slaves to my trusty friend JAMES WORTHAM, and my son DRURY MORROW for the benefit of my daughter EASTER STOVALL. James Wortham, wife and DRURY MORROW, executors, and A. BURWELL, Alexander F. Morrow and THOMAS MORROW, witnesses.

Will of ELIZABETH MORROW (widow of DANIEL MORROW) dated June 16, 1836. To my daughters NANCY LEWIS, EASTER LEMAY and ELIZABETH MORROW, and my sons THOMAS F. MORROW, DRURY MORROW and ALEXANDER MORROW, the two trunks which formerly belonged to WILLIAM and DIANA MORROW; witnesses JAMES LEWIS, HOWELL L. HERD and JOHN A. RAMELL

For DANIEL MORROW'S will see Will Book H. page 43; EASTER MORROW married first, one of the STOVALLS and second a LEMAY.

The name of DANIEL MORROW appears on a tythe list of PRINCE EDWARD COUNTY, Virginia, in 1748-49; and in the census of MECKLENBURG COUNTY, Virginia in 1790.

Last will and testament of JOSIAH DANIEL, of GRANVILLE COUNTY, N. C., dated APRIL 3, 1811, and recorded in GRANVILLE COUNTY. In his will he mentions his wife ELIZABETH and fourteen children, as follows: James K., Thomas, Leonard, NANCY GRAVES, MARTHA BROWN, William, MARTIN, Chesley, Henry, Josiah, Joshua, Walter, Samuel and Elizabeth Daniel. The wife of WOODSON DANIEL and JOSIAH DANIEL were named executors, and the witnesses were CHESLEY DANIEL and DAVID KNOTT, JR.

Will of JOSEPH DANIEL, dated FEB. 18, 1819, in GRANVILLE COUNTY, N. C. (Vol. 8 p. 224). He mentions his wife MILLY DANIEL & children SALLEY KEY (m. DANIEL KEY, Nov. 26 1796), ELEANOR KEY (m. MARTIN KEY, Nov. 28, 1796), POLLY SMITH, ELIZA DANIEL, LUCY WIGGINS, JOHN DANIEL (to whom he left a tract of land in WARREN COUNTY adjoining lands of JOHN DANIEL, SR.), SEPHAS DANIEL, and "my two grandchildren, WILLIAM DANIEL and CHESLEY DANIEL, sons of CHESLEY DANIEL. The witnesses were I. WIGGINS, THOMAS DANIEL and JOHN DANIEL, SR. & they were the executors also.

Will of JOHN DANIEL of GRANVILLE COUNTY, dated DEC. 15, 1778 (Book 1 p. 235) his wife named CELIA DANIEL; to son MARTIN DANIEL, when of age, and appoints his brother WILLIAM DANIEL, Executor, who qualified at the Court in MAY, 1779. Witnesses were LEWIS AMIS, LUKE SANDERS and JOHN DILLON.

Last will and Testament of one WILLIAM GRAVES, of GRANVILLE COUNTY, N. C., dated APR. 24, 1786, in which he mentions his wife MARY, and the following legatees: To MARY HESTER - land in VIRGINIA; ELIZABETH MONTAGUE, NANCY GRAVES, HENRY GRAVES (land bought of JAMES WALKER), WILLIAM GRAVES, LYDIA GRAVES, NATHANIEL GRAVES, ANNA GRAVES and MARTHA GRAVES. His wife and sons WILLIAM and NATHANIEL were made Executors, and the witnesses were HENRY GRAVES, RACHEL GRAVES and JOHN WILLIAMS GRAVES.

Will of JOHN WILLIAMS GRAVES (omitted to set down the date, but about 1786-7) mentions his wife MARY GRAVES and sons JOHN GRAVES, RALPH GRAVES and WILLIAM GRAVES. The witnesses were MEMUGAN HUNT, JOHN HART and JOSEPH HART.

Last will and testament of AGNES WILLIAMS (widow of JUDGE JOHN WILLIAMS) dated March 29, 1802, and recorded in GRANVILLE COUNTY, North Carolina. The following legatees are mentioned:

Daughter FRANCES RIDLEY.
Grand-daughter SARAH RIDLEY.
Great Grand-daughter FRANCES KEELING BURTON.
Grandson JAMES RIDLEY.
Grand-daughter FRANCES RIDLEY.
Grand-daughter POLLY RIDLEY.
Grandson ROBERT RIDLEY.
Grand-daughter PEGGY SATTERWHITE.
Grand-daughter NANCY SATTERWHITE.
Grandson EDWIN SATTERWHITE.
Grandson HORACE SATTERWHITE.
Grandson JOHN HENDERSON.
Grand-daughter ELIZABETH ALEXANDER.
Grandson JAMES RIDLEY.
Grandson LEONARD HENDERSON.
Great Grand-daughter FANNIE HENDERSON.
Daughter AGATHA BURTON.
Grandson FRANK H. W. BURTON.

The last named is referred to as the Executor of my deceased husband.

—

Last will and testament of WILLIAM WILLIAMS, of GRANVILLE COUNTY, N. C. Dated Dec. 5, 1775. Legatees sons JOHN WILLIAMS and SAMUEL FARRAR WILLIAMS. Wife (not named) and COL. RICHARD HENDERSON, Executors.

Last will and testament of DAVID RAY, in which no children are mentioned, and who left all of his property to his wife ISABELLA, including land and land claims. He (testator) is referred to as "late of N. C." in the will. The witnesses were WILLIAM MERRIMAN and CHAS. MERRIMAN. (W. B. 1 p. 308).

ISAAC WHITE makes bond to JOHN WILLIAMS GRAVES, for Five Hundred Pounds Continental money, February 4, 1779. Signed ISAAC WHITE The witnesses were JAMES WILLIAMS and MATTHEW HARRIS.

DEED OF GIFT from WILLIAM WASHINGTON to his son EPHRAIM, "land where I live". Wit. by JOHN WASHINGTON and JAMES LANGSTON, Feb.1779.

THE DANIEL FAMILIES OF GRANVILLE COUNTY. There were two different DANIEL FAMILIES in GRANVILLE COUNTY. They were not related, and to this good day the descendants of both families are confused as to the different identities and relationships. Mr. Hayden, in his "Virginia Genealogies" got them mixed, also. The confusion is due mainly to the fact that back in Virginia there were two JAMES DANIELS who belonged to different sets, one being a Sheriff of GOOCHLAND COUNTY, and the other being Sheriff of ALBEMARLE COUNTY almost, if not quite contemporaneously. James Daniel, Sheriff of Albemarle (1751-2) had a list of nine children whom he mentioned in his will in 1761. They were CHESLEY, ABRAHAM, JOSIAH, JAMES, JOHN, MARY, NANCY and SUSANNA, and a son LEONARD. His wife was JANE HICKS. The other JAMES DANIEL, Sheriff of GOOCHLAND COUNTY, married ELIZABETH WOODSON, the daughter of BENJAMIN WOODSON. The first JAMES was the grandson of WILLIAM DANIEL, of MIDDLESEX COUNTY, Virginia, and belongs to what is known as the "MIDDLESEX DANIELS". The second JAMES was the Grandson of JOHN DANIEL, of YORK COUNTY, Virginia, who died in 1689. The first JAMES was born in MIDDLESEX and the second JAMES in YORK COUNTY, Virginia. So far as the actual records show the names of the children of the first JAMES DANIEL are all known, whereas there is no positive factual proof of the names of any of the children of the second JAMES DANIEL and his wife ELIZABETH WOODSON. A certain BENJAMIN WOODSON DANIEL of WAKE COUNTY, who lived to be over 100 years of age and moved to TENNESSEE, and served in the revolution, is almost sure to have been one of several sons, but deductive evidence must be depended upon altogether to identify any of their other children. The JOSIAH DANIEL who died in GRANVILLE COUNTY, whose will was recorded in 1811, married ELIZABETH KEY, and was a son of JAMES DANIEL of ALBEMARLE and his wife JANE HICKS. CHESLEY DANIEL, father of HON. BEVERLY DANIEL, one time ATTORNEY GENERAL, of RALEIGH, was another son of JAMES DANIEL and JANE HICKS, CHESLEY DANIEL lived ten miles Northwest of the present town of OXFORD, GRANVILLE COUNTY. The JOHN DANIEL, whose will, dated June 19, 1782, in GRANVILLE COUNTY, which is abstracted on the preceding page, was a BROTHER of JAMES DANIEL, who married ELIZABETH WOODSON. These latter DANIEL resided on NUTBUSH, in what is now VANCE COUNTY.

Last will and testament of JOSEPH WILLIAMS, dated NOV. 5, 1775, in GRANVILLE COUNTY, N. C. and recorded in Will Book 1 page 38. He names his wife SARAH, and leaves to her his lands on the West side of NICO ROAD, beginning at COL. HENDERSON'S BRIDGE on GREAT ANTHONY CREEK; "which I bought from my brother JOHN WILLIAMS" certain lands left to his daughter MARY WILLIAMS. To my brother JAMES WILLIAMS leaves lands, including those and the plantation whereon SAMUEL HENDERSON, JR. formerly lived. He makes his wife, RICHARD GARRISON & JOSEPH WILLIAMS, his Executors.

July 25, 1782. Indenture by DANIEL WILLIAMS, SR. (from Book 1 p. 308). He for a certain sum paid by JOHN WILLIAMS, son of DANIEL WILLIAMS, and JOHN WILLIAMS, JR. (Of 96 District in S. C.), sells twenty-seven negroe slaves. Signed DANIEL WILLIAMS. Witnesses are HOWELL MOSS and DANIEL WILLIAMS, JR.

Last will of CHESLEY DANIEL dated 1814. (W. B. 7 p. 475) names his wife JUDITH and (among others) JAMES, WOODSON and BEVERLY DANIEL.

Last will and testament of another CHESLEY DANIEL, dated in 1838. Names his wife NANCY and their children.

Will of THOMAS DANIEL (W. B. 12, p. 182) dated 1831. Legatees were MERIMAN DANIEL, THOMAS HARRIS, NANCY HARRIS and the children of SUSANNAH WILKINSON.

Last will and testament of THOMAS GARDWELL in 1800. (W. B. 5 p. 48). Those named in his will were his children THOMAS, LEONARD, WILLIAM, JOHN, PATTY NANCE and MRS. THOMAS GARDWELL.

SOLOMON WALKER left will in GRANVILLE CO. N. C. dated August 16, 1790, in which he mentions his wife MARTHA WALKER, and gives her the use of the TAR RIVER land he had bought from W. LEWIS POTTER; and he names his son JOHN WALKER. Nominates his friends ELIJAH MITCHELL and WILLIAM HUNT, Executors. Witnesses were JOSEPH TAYLOR, JOS. P. DAVIS and WILLIAM MARSHALL. (W. B. 1 p. 214). SOLOMON WALKER was the son of JOHN WALKER (W. B. 1 p. 37.)

Last will and testament of JOHN STOVALL of GRANVILLE COUNTY, recorded in W. B. 1 p. 213, and dated July 29, 1781. His legatees named in the will were BARTHOLOMEW STOVALL, JOSIAH STOVALL, WILLIAM STOVALL, DRURY STOVALL, BENJAMIN STOVALL, JOHN STOVALL and GEORGE STOVALL. Mentions also his son in law O. GRIFFIN, grandson JOHN STOVALL, son of THOMAS STOVALL (deceased?), and son in law AARON PINSON.

Last will and testament of THOMAS HOWELL of GRANVILLE COUNTY, N. C., executed in July, 1790, but proved in 1791. Wife was REBECCA & he had sons THOMAS, JOHN and ROBERT and daughters CHEXIA, FORTUNE, MARY and ELIZABETH HOWELL. His wife and JEREMIAH FRAZER and JOHN IOCK are named his executors.

JOHN MANGUM left will in GRANVILLE COUNTY dated August 26, 1842, but not probated until the year 1846 (Book 16 p. 536). His wife was SARAH and he had sons JAMES M. MANGUM, SAMUEL MANGUM, WYATT MANGUM and WILIE MANGUM.

The last will and testament of HENRY HUNT proved in GRANVILLE in 1780. Wife AGNES; children JAMES, HENRY, WILLIAM, JAMES, JOHN & ELIZA.

Last will of BENJAMIN COOPER proved in GRANVILLE COUNTY, N. C. in 1761, in which he names sons [illegible], JAMES, WILLIAM, JOHN and GEORGE COOPER, and daughters SARAH and GRACE COOPER and MARY [illegible], and [illegible]. Wife ELIZABETH. JOHN [illegible] and [illegible] witnesses.

Will of DENNIS LINDSEY, dated sometime in 1762, was probated the same year in GRANVILLE COUNTY, N. C. He mentions his sons WILLIAM and BENJAMIN, and daughters MARY, WINIFRED, ELIZABETH, CATRON and MARGARET LINDSEY; mentions also a son in law ROBERT PHILLIPS and another EPHRAIM CLANTON and one ROGER THORNTON, and a grandson.

Will of ROBERT COCHRAN was recorded in GRANVILLE COUNTY, N. C., dated in 1794. Wife SARAH and sons WILLIAM, JOHN HINES, HENRY & DAVID [illegible] COCHRAN. Also his son in law SAMUEL JONES.

Last will and testament of PHILLIP WALSTON (said to be the oldest recorded will in GRANVILLE COUNTY, N. C. - at least MRS. HIGGS so informed the writer); it is dated November 27, 1749 and was recorded the same year. Testator mentions his wife but does not give her name. He had sons PHILLIP and JOSEPH and a daughter named MARY. The witnesses were THOMAS CHRISTIAN, MARY DAY and JAMES KNOTT. (This PHILLIP WALSTON came from BERTIE CO. N. C. See page 174 of this book for the WALSTON FAMILY notes.)

Last will and testament of WILLIAM BECKHAM on record in GRANVILLE COUNTY N. C. dated in the year 1776, but proved in 1777. He mentions his wife PHILLIS and their children WILLIAM, THOMAS, SIMON, PHILLIS and MARY. (These Beckhams were related to the HENDERSON family, and like they, came from Hanover County, Virginia.)

Last will and testament of SHEM COOK, of GRANVILLE COUNTY, N. C. dated in 1792 & probated in 1796, in which he mentions his wife ANN COOK, daughters ELIZABETH TURPIN, and sons WILLIAM and JOHN COOK, deceased; DELPHIA ROBERTS, and sons SHEM, CLAIBORNE, ROWLAND, JOHN, JAMES and MACK ROBERTS.

The will of WILLIAM BELL was proved in GRANVILLE COUNTY, N. C. in 1772, but was dated a year earlier. He mentions his brother NATHANIEL and JOHN DAVIS BELL, a MARY MERRYMAN and sisters BETTY and SARAH BELL, and his mother SARAH BELL, who was still living in 1771; brother JOSHUA BELL and his father GEORGE BELL. In the will he mentions property he owns in ANN ARUNDEL COUNTY, MD.

(This WILLIAM BELL, we are quite sure, must have been the son of DAVID BELL or his brother GEORGE —the latter, of course - of NEW KENT COUNTY. See Bell's OLD FREE STATE II pp 122-3).

The will of WILLIAM REEVES was proved in GRANVILLE COUNTY, N. C. in 1782, same being dated that same year. Wife was MARGARET and they had sons WILLIAM, JAMES, BENJAMIN and BURGESS REEVES, and daughters ANNIE, ELIZABETH, MARY CARPENTER, SARAH HICKS and an ZELIVE or OLIVE REEVES.

(In the family genealogy of the REEVES, it is claimed that the name is properly spelled RIVES)

Will of GIDEON MACON, of GRANVILLE COUNTY, N. C. dated 1761 and proved in 1763, gives the name of his wife PRISCILLA, and sons HARRISON, JOHN, NATHANIEL and GIDEON; daughters ANN ALLSTON, PATTY, MARTHA, MARY MACON, and son in law JOHN ALSTON.

Last will and testament of SOLOMON ALSTON recorded in GRANVILLE COUNTY in 1771, the year it was executed. Mentions wife SARAH, daughter CHARITY ALSTON (under 21), son LEMUEL, son HENRY, and ROBERT LEWIS (called BIRD ROBERT LEWIS) Executors were JOHN WILLIAMS and WILLIAM ALSTON

Last will of WILLIAM BULLOCK, of GRANVILLE COUNTY, N. C. dated 1794 and proved in 1796; in it he names his wife ELIZABETH, and children ELIZABETH MARTIN, WILLIAM BULLOCK, and FRANCIS BOYD. Grandson JAMES BULLOCK and son in law JAMES LEWIS.

Last will and testament of RICHARD BULLOCK of GRANVILLE COUNTY, N. C. proved and recorded in 1766, in which he mentions the following children: SARAH SIMS, AGNES WILLIAMS, WILLIAM, ZACHARIAH, NATHANIEL, JOHN and LEONARD HENLEY BULLOCK.

RICHARD BENNETT died leaving a will in GRANVILLE COUNTY, N. C., which was dated in the year 1783 and probated in 1786. In this will he mentions his wife ANNE, and sons THOMAS, MICAJAH, WILLIAM, PETER, BARTLETT and LEWIS BENNETT; daughters SARAH ASTES (ESTESS), ANNA DUKE. The witnesses were CHESLEY DANIEL and NANCY BLACKWELL.

Last will and testament of BENJAMIN HARRISON, dated January 17, 1773 and proved in MAY, 1774. Mentions his wife ELLEN; mentions his daughters SUSANNAH WHEELER, AILSEY HARRISON, & sons SAMUEL, BENJAMIN and VINSON HARRISON. The witnesses were CHESLEY DANIEL, JAMES DANIEL & JOSEPH ROBERTS.

(For the identity of the above BENJAMIN HARRISON see Vol. 6 Tyler's Mag. pp. 206 et seq.)

Last will and testament of SAMUEL BENTON, executed and probated in GRANVILLE COUNTY, N. C. in 1770. In it he mentions his wife as being FRANCES, and sons SAMUEL and JESSE BENTON; daughters BETTY BRUCE, PENNY, PATTY and son AUGUSTINE BENTON. Executors were JESSE BENTON and CHARLES BRUCE; the witnesses were BROMFIELD RIDLEY, SAMUEL HENDERSON and THOMAS HENDERSON.

(From 1764 until 1770, SAMUEL BENTON served both as REGISTER OF DEEDS and CLERK OF THE COURT for GRANVILLE COUNTY. REUBEN SEARCY, a son in law of SAMUEL HENDERSON, followed Mr. BENTON as Clerk of the Court & JESSE BENTON, his son, succeeded his father as REGISTER of DEEDS.)

SOME EARLY MARRIAGE RECORDS IN GRANVILLE COUNTY, NORTH CAROLINA

Hannah Daniel to JEREMIAH WALKER, Feb. 11,1775.
Mary Daniel to David Royster Jan. 11, 1775.
Elizabeth Daniel to William Clements March 15, 1775.
Elizabeth Daniel to Samuel Hopkins December 1, 1779.
Rowland Harris to Sarah Daniel, August 21,1783
Robert Hester to Dely Daniel, April 29, 1785.
George Daniel to Martha Daniel, March 30, 1786.
David Hughes to Judith Daniel, Jan. 21, 1786.
John Denton to Sarah Stark, 1797.
Samuel Hogg to Sarah Williams May 14, 1792.
James Daniel to Nancy Macklin in 1809, with Samuel Hogg, security.
Walter Daniel to Milly Overby in 1809.
Josiah Brown to Patsy Daniel June 6, 1794.
Thomas Daniel to Elizabeth Satterwhite, Jan. 29, 1793; Thomas Daniel security.
Leonard Daniel to Mary Ann Graves Dec. 21, 1789. (Both living and on the 1750 U. S. Census in Rutherford County, N. C.)
John Daniel to Elizabeth Jenkins, Sept. 22, 1791; Elias Jenkins security.
Ransom Cunningham to Sarah Peace Feb. 28, 1821.
Daniel Key to Sallie Daniel, Nov. 28, 1796.
John Watkins to Susanna Daniel, Oct. 26, 1786.
William Gard to Polly Daniel, Dec. 11, 1799.
Martin Key to Eleanor Daniel, August 7, 1804.
John Knott to Charlotte Daniel Oct. 20, 1810.
Zadock Daniel to Elizabeth Lewis, July 24, 1792.
Lewis Daniel to Martha D. Lanier, Jan. 21, 1812.
John Cobbs to Mildred Lewis, Sept. 6, 1769.
Charles Kennon to Mary Lewis, April 19, 1770.
John Bullock to Catherine Lewis, March 11, 1771.
Thomas Harp to Elizabeth Lewis, Nov. 3, 1778.
John Harp to Mary Lewis, June 3, 1778.
William Ridley to Elizabeth Lewis, Feb. 7, 1780.
James M. Daniel to Nancy Rogers, May 22, 1790.
James Daniel to Sarah Cocke August 6, 1771.
Reuben Daniel to Elizabeth Harrison, Dec. 12, 1781.
David Daniel to Margaret Lynch, Feb. 13,1781.
John Daniel to Elizabeth Incore, May 1, 1781.
Chesley Daniel to Agnes Williams Nov. 2,1807; Willis Williams, security.
Willie Daniel to Sarah Wilkinson 1811.
Thomas Daniel to Eliza Daniel 1813.
John Daniel to Martha Harris 1815.
Cephas Daniel to Clarrissa Harris in 1821.
Chesley Daniel to Lucy Noblin in 1826.
Zachariah Daniel to Martha Crutchen 1860.
Henry M. Daniel to Sarah L. Blount 1828.
Elijah Daniel to Lucy Cavendish 1829.
Willis Daniel to Elizabeth Ellis 1832.
Woodson Daniel to Mary Mealor 1832.
William Daniel to Martha Jones 1832.
Jesse Daniel to Eliza Summerhill 1832.
Beverly Daniel to Eliza Jane Daniel 1840.
George W. Daniel to Caroline Blackwell 1846.
Rufus Daniel to Susan J. Overby 1847.
R. V. Daniel to Mary G. Venable 1847.
Stith G. Daniel to Sarah F. Wilkinson 1848.
Samuel Daniel to Lucy A. Wilkinson 1852.
Richard A. Daniel to Louise Land 1852.
William H. Daniel to Martha Currier 1852.
Morris S. Daniel to Emily Watkins 1853.
Robert M. Daniel to Ellen Daniel 1855.
Jesse Daniel to Nancy Boswell 1855.
Thomas B. Daniel to Martha J. Puckett 1858.
William Lewis to Elizabeth Howard Oct. 21, 1773.
Willis Lewis to Mary Ann Taylor Oct. 10, 1790.
Nathaniel Lewis to Sallie Harris Nov. 29,1790.
Charles Lewis to Nancy Smith, April 15, 1793.
Joseph Lewis to Elizabeth Walker, 1800.
David Key to Sally Daniel, Nov. 28, 1796.
James Key to Mary Daniel Jan. 3, 1792.
John Ray to Elizabeth Mize, Sept. 2, 1783.
George Boswell to Martha Ray, 1832.
Job Rogers to Sarah Rust, Sept. 7, 1790.
Stephen Rogers to Permelia Wood, Aug. 12, 1782.
James Rogers to Nellie Bailey in 1794.
Peleg Rogers to Elizabeth Bailey in 1794.

John Rogers to Ellener Preddy in 1802.
John Jenkins to Matty Thomas, Dec. 19, 1789; John and Jesse Jenkins securities.
Elias Jenkins to Sally Taylor, Dec. 19, 1789.
Elias Jenkins to Patsy Morse, Sept. 22, 1800; W. Jenkins, security.
Anrita Jenkins to William Upchurch in 1803.
Moore Lanier to Jennie Jenkins in 1806.
Henry Jones to Winney Jenkins in 1809.
Samuel Hunt to Sarah Howard, May 20, 1780.
Robert Jones, of Northampton County, N. C. to Mary Jordan, Feb. 2, 1756; John Jones, security.
James Jones to Charity Alston; Solomon Alston, Jr., security (no date given).
Richard Henderson to Elizabeth Keeling, John Williams, security.
Isaac Hunter to Martha Alston, April 18, 1760; Joseph Johnson, security.
Nathaniel Henderson to Sarah Jones, Oct. 31, 1763.
Charles Harris to Sarah Allen, August 12, 1760.
Daniel Williams to Ann Henderson, July 30,1755.
James Thornton to Elizabeth Jones, March 2, 1762.
James Ransom to Priscilla Macon (widow) Feb. 9, 1763; Daniel Weldon, security.
Daniel Weldon to Miss Betty Eaton, Jan. 17,1763 Blake Baker and Samuel Swann JR. security
Leonard Henley Bullock to Fannie Hawkins, daughter of Philemon Hawkins, Nov. 17, 1760.
Nathaniel Bullock to Mary Hawkins, daughter of John Hawkins (date?)
John Bullock to Mary Mitchell, daughter of JAMES Mitchell, Nov. 12, 1759.
John Alston, Jr. to Ann Hunt Macon, March 17, 1760, daughter of Gideon Macon; with Solomon Alston, security.
Charles Kennan to Mary Lewis, April 19, 1770; Joseph Taylor and Thomas Person, sec.
William Kennon to Bettie Bullock, March 1, 1771; William Bullock, security, and John Bullock, witness.
John Bullock to Catherine Lewis, March 11,1771; William Bullock, security.
Leonard Henley Bullock to Susannah Goodloe, Aug. 16, 1766; John Hamilton and Robert Goodloe, Jr. security.
Thomas Satterwhite to Ann Keeling, Oct. 15, 1772.
Ellis Drury to Amy Rose, Aug. 6, 1771; with Joseph Rose and Jesse Benton sec.
John Henderson to Sarah Alston (wd. of Solomon Alston, June 4, 1772; Samuel Henderson and Reuben Searcy, security.
Robert Crowley to Mary Taylor, July 15,1767; Joseph Davenport and Charles Gilliam.
Joseph Williams, Jr. and Rebecca Lanier, on Sept. 11, 1772; John Henderson, sec.
William Lewis to Elizabeth Howard, Oct. 21, 1773. Groves Howard, security, and Rebecca Searcy, witness.

Last will and testament of SUGAR JONES; proved in GRANVILLE COUNTY, N. C. July 15, 1761. Names children EDWARD, DRURY, SAMUEL, JAMES, NANCY and MOLLIE JONES, with wife, GIDEON MASON and ADKINS McLEMORE Exrs. Witnesses SOLOMON ALSTON JR., JAMES and EDWARD JONES.

Last will of EDWARD JONES, proved in 1750 in GRANVILLE COUNTY. His wife was ABIGAIL. Children named: SUGAR, JAMES, EDWARD, DANIEL, SARAH, OBEDIENCE, RABON and PRISCILLA MASON.

EDMUND TAYLOR, Granville Co. N. C. will proved 1808. Names children LOUIS, RICHARD, HOWELL, JOHN, EDMUND, JAMES, MARY BRODIE, ELIZABETH BUCKS and FRANCES MOORE; wife and sons LOUIS and RICHARD, Exrs.

JOHN TAYLOR (Son of JAMES TAYLOR of CAROLINE CO. VA.) will March 6, 1780, in GRANVILLE CO. N. C. (W. B. 1, p. 275) His wife was CATHERINE PENDLETON. He names his children: EDMUND TAYLOR (m. ANNE LEWIS) JOHN TAYLOR (m. Kyrn), JAMES TAYLOR (m. Pollard); PHILLIP TAYLOR (m. MARY WALKER); WILLIAM TAYLOR (m. ANDERSON); MARY TAYLOR (m. PENN); JOSEPH TAYLOR (m. FRANCES ANDERSON); CATHERINE TAYLOR (m. MOSES PENN) ISABELLA; ELIZABETH (m. (1) JAMES LEWIS (2) WILLIAM BULLOCK.

EDWARD JONES. The first Court ever held in GRANVILLE COUNTY was at his home in the lower part of what is now WARREN COUNTY, as has been mentioned before in some of these notes (see pp 43 and 209). His will was proved in 1750 and that of his son SUGAR JONES in 1761. At the time these wills were filed neither the extinct county of BUTE, nor what is now WARREN COUNTY had been established, so they were necessarily recorded in GRANVILLE COUNTY. Had they died after 1764 the records would appear among the records of BUTE later filed in WARREN COUNTY. The wife of EDWARD JONES was ABIGAIL SUGHE, a member of a HUGUENOT family, from MANIKINTOWN, from which CAPT. SUGAR JONES obtained his Christian name. EDWARD JONES was the son of another EDWARD JONES whose will was proved in RICHMOND COUNTY, VIRGINIA, September 2, 1715, in which he named four sons and one daughter, SANFORD, JOHN, EDWARD, CHARLES and ALICIA JONES the wife of a PAYNE (either the JAMES PAYNE who was present at the first court of Granville County in 1746, or a son of that PAYNE who married ALICIA JONES, sister of EDWARD). SANFORD PAYNE, the elder brother of EDWARD of GRANVILLE, died in RICHMOND COUNTY, Virginia, in 1717, and in his will names his "cousin" ANNE PAYNE. EDWARD JONES (son of EDWARD of GRANVILLE County) married MARY HILL, a sister of GREEN HILL (b. 1714, the son of HENRY APPLEWHITE HILL) who married GRACE BENNETT (daughter of WILLIAM BENNETT of Northampton County, N. C. and Virginia), and WILLIAM HILL (son of GREEN HILL) married MARY JONES, daughter of EDWARD JONES and MARY HILL. SAMUEL JONES, sister of MARY JONES and son of the younger EDWARD, married ELIZABETH SHORT GOODLOW and had a daughter SARAH APPLEWHITE JONES who married a nephew of GEN. JAMES ROBERTSON of Nashville, Tenn., (JAMES COCKRILL). Hon. Jo. SEAWELL JONES (of SHOCCO, in WARREN COUNTY - the old EDWARD JONES estate, was a grandson of JOSEPH SEAWELL (whose namesake he was also) and his mother was a MRS. GORDON (she having married a second time) a sister of JUDGE HENRY SEAWELL, her mother being a sister of Hon. Nathaniel Macon, son of GIDEON MASON and his wife PRISCILLA JONES (who married second JAMES RANSOM - see marriages). In 1824 JOSEPH SEAWELL JONES was a student at the University of North Carolina, later of HARVARD, and was affectionately known as "SHOCCO JONES". He was an eccentric, but served in the United States Congress for a long term of years and was one of the founders of the North Carolina HISTORICAL SOCIETY.

REUBEN SEARCY. This man and his family played an important role in the history of Colonial Granville County. He was a brother in law of JUDGE RICHARD HENDERSON, of Transylvania, Kentucky and North Carolina fame, having married a daughter of the original SAMUEL HENDERSON - one SUSAN HENDERSON - as his first wife, by whom the family historian (Hon. W. H. H. Searcy, of Griffin, Georgia) says, he had ten children. This family historian adds that after the death of his wife SUSAN HENDERSON, REUBEN married again, and had eight more children. REUBEN SEARCY left GRANVILLE COUNTY and moved to MADISON COUNTY, KENTUCKY, where he lived for a time, where doubtless his second set of children were born, after which he settled in Tennessee. (Mr. Searcy says in TURNER County, but as there is no TURNER County, the writer is quite sure it was in RUTHERFORD County). Eight of the children of REUBEN SEARCY and his wife SUSAN HENDERSON are given in the one and only account available, as THOMAS, who married ANN MARTIN, ASA SEARCY, BENNETT SEARCY, ROBERT SEARCY, WILLIAM SEARCY, HENRIETTA, POLLY and ELIZABETH SEARCY WHITE; (apparently the wife of HENRY L. WHITE, SR., a revolutionary soldier, who was born July 1, 1755, in North Carolina, & died in Rutherford County, Tennessee, Oct. 6, 1830 - See Acklen's Tenn. Bible Records, p. 33). REUBEN SEARCY'S will has not been located, and if a record of it exists, it is probably in RUTHERFORD COUNTY, Tennessee, where I am sure he must have died. He was Sheriff of old GRANVILLE COUNTY during the period of 1764, succeeding JAMES YANCEY in that office, who was the ancestor of HON. WILLIAM L. YANCEY, the famous Southern orator of South Carolina and Alabama. Prior to Yancey, Searcy, Phillip Pryor, LEONARD HENLEY BULLOCK and ROBERT HARRIS, the office of SHERIFF had been held by SAMUEL HENDERSON, Searcy's father in law, and JOHN MARTIN, who was a member with Col. William Eaton and Edward Jones, of the first Court of GRANVILLE COUNTY in 1746 (See page 43), and whose daughter, ANN MARTIN married THOMAS SEARCY, son of REUBEN. It appears to have been this JOHN MARTIN who emigrated to KENTUCKY and established what was known as MARTIN'S STATION, where BARTLETT SEARCY (brother of REUBEN) and his brother REUBEN obtained lands after the revolution. and not far from where BARTLETT is said to have been killed by the Indians (a fact that I have been unable to verify). After serving GRANVILLE COUNTY as Sheriff, and being later charged, along with James Yancey, Phillip Pryor, Leonard Henley Bullock and Robert Harris with a shortage of his accounts (for which, it seems, he had failed to give bond) REUBEN continued active in politics and in 1770 , after the death of SAMUEL BENTON, he succeeded the latter as Clerk of the Court. Before continuing farther, I shall break off here and say someting of

THE ANCESTRY OF THE SEARCY FAMILY. Hon. W. H. H. SEARCY (long since deceased) of GRIFFIN, GEORGIA, was the son of DANIEL BARTLETT SEARCY, who was the son of a WILLIAM SEARCY, who settled in GEORGIA in a very early day, who was the son, in turn, of a DANIEL SEARCY, of JOHNSTON COUNTY, N. C., who was the son of a JOHN SEARCY, JR., a brother of REUBEN SEARCY, the early Sheriff and Clerk of GRANVILLE COUNTY. He claims, in his account, that the SEARCY FAMILY in N. C. were ALL the descendants of a JOHN SEARCY (who died leaving a will in GRANVILLE COUNTY, N. C. in 1787 - which I have not located) in which he gave the names of his children as JOHN, BARTLETT, REUBEN, WILLIAM, RICHARD, ELIZABETH, MARY, SUSANNAH and SARAH SEARCY. The wife of JOHN SEARCY, the ancestor was PHOEBE, and he and his wife settled on a farm in GRANVILLE COUNTY, N. C. in 1727 or 1728. Of course, this could NOT be true, because GRANVILLE COUNTY was unheard of at that period. Even Edgecombe County, from which it was taken, had no existence, and the County of CRAVEN, so far as the territory of GRANVILLE is concerned, was non-existent (according to WHEELER) who says it was formed in 1712, but was known as CRAVEN PRECINCT; it was some years later before there was a CRAVEN COUNTY (Olds.).

JOHN SEARCY, according to Mr. Searcy, had only two brothers, ROBERT and RICHARD SEARCY, neither of whom left children. He believes they came from NOTTINGHAM, ENGLAND, where the names of SEARCYS are found on old tombstones from 1733 to 1785. He says ROBERT SEARCY died at HALIFAX Courthouse, in Virginia, in 1733. He does not dispose of RICHARD at all, except to say that he left no children. This is all simply a case of "traditional family genealogy", the truth being that the SEARCYS were numerous in VIRGINIA, and particularly in HANOVER COUNTY, VIRGINIA. ROBERT SEARCY did not die in HALIFAX C. H., Virginia, in 1733, because no such County existed in the Colony of Virginia until 1752, nine years later. On the contrary the ROBERT SEARCY, who died in Virginia in 1733, lived in HANOVER COUNTY, and his will was proved in 1733, and is shown on the records of that county. He had children, but only one daughter, SUSAN, is mentioned. The proof that JOHN SEARCY was NOT in N. C. in 1727-8, as claimed, is refuted by the following item from the record: "June 6, 1734, RICHARD PHILLIPS, of ST. GEORGE'S PARISH, in Spottsylvania County, Virginia, (which joins HANOVER) deeds to JOHN SEARCY, of St. Martin's Parish, in HANOVER COUNTY, VIRGINIA, 400 acres of woodland, adjoining the lands of CAPT. CARR, MARTIN DAVENPORT and JOHN WILSON." Incidentally, the SHERIFF of HANNOVER COUNTY, Virginia, at the time this deed was executed was none other than SAMUEL HENDERSON, father of SUE HENDERSON, who married REUBEN SEARCY. The will of ROBERT SEARCY, of Hanover, mentions his wife SUSAN and his daughter SUSAN, and was witnessed by EDWARD BULLOCK, JR., THOMAS HAWKINS and ANN BULLOCK. (Sounds like the old NUTBUSH DISTRICT, in GRANVILLE COUNTY, N. C.). It is possible that ROBERT SEARCY, who died in HANOVER COUNTY, Virgina in 1733 married SUSAN BULLOCK, but this fact has not been established by positive proof. In addition to ROBERT and JOHN SEARCY, of HANOVER COUNTY, Virginia, there was a WILLIAM SEARCY who was granted 400 acres of land on SANDY RIVER or CREEK in what is now PRINCE EDWARD COUNTY, Virginia, in 1746. At that time the land was in AMELIA COUNTY, that part of which in 1754 became PRINCE EDWARD COUNTY. He could hardly have been the son of JOHN SEARCY of HANOVER, as he is bound to have been of full age when the land was granted in 1746. It is probable that he left children and other descendants, as, for instande, ROBERT SEARCY of HENRY COUNTY, Virginia, who took the oath in 1777. Also, on the tythe lists of LUNENBURG COUNTY, Virginia, in 1764, will be found the name of an ABRAHAM SEARCY. Who was he? Last, but by no means least, the name of a REUBEN SEARCY appears on the tythe (tax) lists of MECKLENBURG COUNTY, Virginia, in 1750, 1751 and 1752, and this could not have been the obstreperous REUBEN, of GRANVILLE, North Carolina, who was elected Sheriff in 1763-4, and had been tax collector before that time and was charged with being short in his accounts. (18 N. C. Hist. Rev. p. 359). Or could it have been?

Anyway, the foregoing evidence should be enough to show that the SEARCY FAMILY of GRANVILLE COUNTY, North Carolina (supposed descendants of JOHN SEARCY and his wife PHOEBE) came to that part of the Colony of North Carolina at or about the time GRANVILLE COUNTY was orginized in 1746, and NOT in 1727 as claimed by the genealogists. One has but to review the roster of the older and most prominent of the settlers of the County to ascertain that a great many of the others who appeared there at the same time had a common back-ground. SAMUEL HENDERSON and his family, the BULLOCKS, SIMS, the WILLIAMS, DANIEL and other families arrived at about this same period, and also came from HANOVER COUNTY, VIRGINIA. REUBEN SEARCY, in all probability, married SUE HENDERSON in HANOVER COUNTY, Virginia, and it is even possible, and not improbable, that some of his children were born there. JUDGE JOHN WILLIAMS, of WILLIAMSBORO settlement on NUTBUSH CREEK, was a nephew of SAMUEL HENDERSON'S wife, who was a WILLIAMS, and was a native of HANOVER COUNTY & a first cousin of JUDGE RICHARD HENDERSON and of SUSAN, his sister, the wife of REUBEN SEARCY. A study of the early marriage records of GRANVILLE COUNTY, shown herein, will disclose a relationship between nearly all of these families, indicating very strongly that there were close ties between them, which are bound to have been contracted back in HANOVER COUNTY, Virginia.

BARTLETT SEARCY. The records are confusing in regard to BARTLETT SEARCY. There were TWO Searcys named BARTLETT who were almost contemporaneous. One of them went to KENTUCKY, and "was killed by the Indians" according to the family genealogist. He left a will in "FIAT" (intended for FAYETTE) County, Kentucky, which was proved in 1790, tho' written in 1789, so it is to be presumed he died in Kentucky, and was probably the one who was "killed by the Indians". The other BARTLETT SEARCY evidently died in GRANVILLE COUNTY, N. C., where his will was proved in 1784, though it was later probated also in MADISON COUNTY, KENTUCKY in 1795, eleven years, apparently, after his death. REUBEN SEARCY (the old Sheriff of GRANVILLE) had a brother BARTLETT, and REUBEN'S brother JOHN SEARCY, JR. had a son BARTLETT. Which one was the brother, and which one was the KENTUCKY INDIAN FIGHTER? Below is given the abstracts of the two wills copied from ARDRY'S "Kentucky Court Records" (pp. 66 and 99):

SEARCY, BARTLETT, "Of GRANVILLE County, N. C." Wife LUCY; when youngest child is fifteen years of age property to be sold and divided. Exrs. wife, son SAMUEL, JOHN WILLIAMS, ESQ., REUBEN SEARCY. Written July 28, 1780. Wits.: THOMAS SEARCY, REUBEN SEARCY, ELIZABETH SEARCY, LEONARD HAYS. Proved GRANVILLE COUNTY, N. C. Nov. 1784, when LUCY SEARCY, REUBEN SEARCY and SAMUEL SEARCY qualified as the Executors. Probated MADISON (Ky.) 1795.

SEARCY, BARTLETT, "Of Fiat Co. Va., " (Fayette? Co. Ky.) To wife ANN; son, JOHN MORGAN SEARCY; daughter ELIZABETH SEARCY, land held in partnership with COL. MARSHALL to be held for schooling of son and dau. JOHN and ELIZABETH. Exrs.: wife, COL. DANIEL BOONE, & W. FLANDERS CALLOWAY. Written Sept. 17, 1784. Wits.: ANDREW PAULL, SQUIRE BOONE, and JESSE BRYAN. Codicil: Two children, JOHN and ELIZABETH. Atty: JOHN BROWN to bring suits, to have charge of land assigned by JOHN BROWN of Bedford Co., to himself and JOHN FOWLER. Dated Jan. 8, 1789. Wits: WILLIAM PHILLIPS. Probated Sept. 1790.

It is interesting to note that the witness to the will of BARTLETT SEARCY of "FIAT" County, Kentucky, was one WILLIAM PHILLIPS and to then turn back to 1733, in HANOVER COUNTY, VIRGINIA and see where JOHN SEARCY (whose wife was PHOEBE) bought 400 acres of woodland from RICHARD PHILLIPS "Of Spottsylvania County, Va." Just another link in the proof that the SEARCYS came from HANOVER COUNTY, Virginia; also that both of the above BARTLETT SEARCYS had children who were minors. I am inclined to the belief that the BARTLETT of "Fayette County" was the INDIAN FIGHTER, who had his "brush" with the Indians in 1787 and was recommended to the Governor as a proper person to be appointed a militia officer of WOODFORD COUNTY Kentucky as late as JUNE, 1789. (Vol. 4, Va. State Papers, p. 285). He may have died from wounds received in the fight sometime prior to September, of that year, when the will and codicil was proven. The family genealogist says that the INDIAN FIGHTER (Of Ky.) was the son of JOHN SEARCY, JR. (brother of REUBEN, the SHERIFF) who had a son BARTLETT, as well as a RICHARD. Assuming this last to be true, the following item from the Woodford County (Ky.) records, tends to clear up the mystery: "March Court (Woodford County) 1793. JOSEPH REARDON and wife, ANN, and Exrs. of the will of BARTLETT SEARCY, deceased, appoint RICHARD SEARCY, of Madison County, Ky., atty, to recover land in CLARK COUNTY, on HOWARDS CREEK, entered by said BARTLETT SEARCY in his life time, given by law to RICHARD SEARCY, and deeds issued to ROBERT BURTON, of GRANVILLE COUNTY, N. C., and conveyed to said BARTLETT, deceased, and now claimed by JAMES SPEED, of Mercer County, Kentucky". (Ardry's Records p. 163-4). But it does NOT clear it up entirely, because REUBEN and his brother BARTLETT had a brother named RICHARD also. But it will be noted that the will of the other BARTLETT in GRANVILLE mentions REUBEN and JOHN WILLIAMS, ESQ., which is a strong indication that the one who died in GRANVILLE COUNTY, N. C. was the brother of REUBEN (the old Sheriff) and the other BARTLETT may have been his NEPHEW.

WILLIAM W. SEARCY, one of the sons of REUBEN SEARCY (the old Sheriff of Granville County, North Carolina) moved to the general vicinity of MURPHREESBORO, TENN. He was born, according to the family Bible on January 1, 1769, and was married three times, (1) to ELIZABETH HARRIS, of WARREN COUNTY, N. C., a relative in some degree to HON. ISHAM G. HARRIS, beloved Governor of the State of Tennessee, on whose head old "Parson" Brownlow (Governor) placed a "price", following the War Between the States. They were married Jan. 22, 1797. Among their children was HON. ISHAM G. SEARCY, a brilliant lawyer, who came to TEXAS and practiced law at old WASHINGTON on the BRAZOS; (2) to SARAH MORTON, of RUTHERFORD COUNTY, Tennessee, by whom he had a son ANDERSON SEARCY who d. April 3, 1847 in the 36th year of his age; who married BETSY SEARCY WHITE (his cousin) and had ANDERSON SEARCY, Colonel in the Confederate Army, who was born in 1832, and died May 11, 1910. William W. SEARCY, son of WILLIAM W. SEARCY and ELIZABETH HARRIS, died in 1880 in the 80th year of his age, and was the father of HON. WILLIAM W. SEARCY, for forty or fifty years one of the leading members of the Bar of Texas, who died at BRENHAM, TEXAS, where he had spent the greater part of his life in the practice of his profession, about 1939. His son W. W. Searcy is at this writing a practicing attorney of many years standing, located at CORPUS CHRISTI, Texas. There are many descendants of WILLIAM W. SEARCY and his first wife ELIZABETH HARRIS living in Texas; (3) his third wife was SARAH CAMPBELL, whom he married May 6, 1838. Probably no issue.

ROBERT SEARCY, (son of REUBEN, the SHERIFF) was the second Grand Master of the Masonic Lodge in the State of Tennessee, he being elevated to that position in the year 1815, as the successor of THOMAS CLAIBORNE, who was the first; then in 1820 no less a person than ANDREW JACKSON, afterwards President of the United States, occupied this high office. ROBERT SEARCY located in Tennessee, therefore, prior to 1815, possibly many years before that time. According to W. H. H. Searcy, a portrait of this son of the old Sheriff of GRANVILLE COUNTY, N. C. hangs in the State Masonic Hall at Nashville, Tennessee.

RICHARD SEARCY (according to W. H. H. Searcy, of GEORGIA) was another son of REUBEN, of GRANVILLE COUNTY, and evidently settled in the State of Arkansas, since the town of SEARCY, Arkansas, is named for him.

BENNETT SEARCY, another son, was a lawyer of ability, and practiced his profession at Memphis, Tennessee, where he may have died.

BETSY SEARCY, one of the daughters of REUBEN, the Sheriff of GRANVILLE, married a WHITE. This information is taken from an account of the family given in a well known book about the HENDERSON family, written by LUCY HENDERSON HORTON, of Maury County, Tennessee, many years ago in which she gives the names of EIGHT of the children of REUBEN SEARCY and his wife SUSAN HENDERSON. The writer was a relative of REUBEN SEARCY'S wife, but fails to give the name of BETSY SEARCY'S husband, other than to say that his name was WHITE, so that we are relegated to other sources for information on that subject. In ACKLEN'S TENNESSEE TOMBSTONE RECORDS (pp 34 to 40) will be found many BIBLE RECORDS taken from the WHITE FAMILY BIBLE, of a family living in RUTHERFORD COUNTY, TENNESSEE, at the same time and contemporaneous with the SEARCYS, who came there from GRANVILLE COUNTY, N. C. A study of these entries will disclose some startling facts that reveal, the writer thinks, the identity of BETSY SEARCY'S husband, her children and their descendants. In these records, the ancestor was HENRY WHITE, SR., a revolutionary soldier, who was born in [illegible]; the record says he married [illegible] [illegible], a widow, but one of his sons was named ASA WHITE (probably for ASA SEARCY, son of REUBEN) as a HENRY WHITE, JR. married MRS. LUCY SEARCY Dec. 8, [illegible]; another entry says that HENRY S. WHITE, born Nov. 15, 1814, married ANDERSON SEARCY, and the last couple were the parents of COL. ANDERSON SEARCY, C. S. A., grandson of WILLIAM W. SEARCY, the son of WILLIAM (son of REUBEN, the Sheriff). No doubt but what WILLIAM W. SEARCY (son of REUBEN) was named for the revolutionary hero COL. WILLIAM WASHINGTON, who lived in the TAR RIVER district below OXFORD, in Granville County. On the Muster Roll in 1754, of COL. WILLIAM EATON'S GRANVILLE COUNTY regiment was a company of sixty men under the command of CAPT. ANDREW HAMPTON, and one of these men was VALENTINE WHITE (Vol 22 N. C. Records p. 379). In 1750, THOMAS, VALENTINE and MARK WHITE were residents of the "FISHING CREEK DIST" of GRANVILLE County. Captain SUGAR JONES commanded another Company in Col. Eaton's regiment in 1754. These facts all considered, the writer believes that BETSY SEARCY married into this same WHITE FAMILY, and moved with her brothers, ROBERT, WILLIAM W. and her father (REUBEN) to RUTHERFORD COUNTY, Tennessee, and there lived and died, and that the WHITE BIBLE RECORDS mentioned deal with her descendants and White family relatives.

THOMAS SEARCY (son of REUBEN, the Sheriff) married ANN MARTIN and they lived and died in GRANVILLE COUNTY, N. C. That ANN was a daughter of JOHN MARTIN, who met with the first court of GRANVILLE COUNTY, for the reason that about 1780 JOHN MARTIN was the agent of REUBEN SEARCY to locate lands known as "MARTIN'S CABINS" (Station) in KENTUCKY, as shown on page 105 of ARDERY'S Kentucky Court Records. Beginning with the children of THOMAS SEARCY and ANN MARTIN, the family records, still preserved in the hands of the descendants of this couple, in TUSCALOOSA, ALABAMA, makes the writing of this record easier. They were the ancestors of the TUSCALOOSA SEARCYS.

THE TUSCALOOSA (ALA.) SEARCY FAMILY. Thomas Searcy and Ann Martin had NINE children: RUTH (b. 1794), SUSAN (b. 1796), JULIA (b. 1799), [illegible] (b. 1801), WILLIAM (b. 1803), REUBEN (b. 1805), SALLIE (b. 1808), ALEXANDER (b. 1810), THOMAS (b. 1815).

DR. REUBEN SEARCY, a pioneer Alabama Physician (b. 1805, d. 1887) was the son of THOMAS SEARCY and his wife ANN MARTIN, and the grandson of REUBEN SEARCY, the old Sheriff of GRANVILLE COUNTY, N. C. He was educated at TRANSYLVANIA UNIVERSITY at Lexington, Kentucky, and about 1827 -1829 settled in TUSCALOOSA, ALABAMA. He married first, EVALINA [illegible], of an old Virginia and North Carolina family, who lived but a short time, dying in 1836; he then married a second time [illegible] [illegible] PEIRCE, a young artist-musician from PUTNEY, VERMONT, who had "come South" for a time. They were married in Tuscaloosa, Alabama, by whom he had five children; [illegible] EVALINA PEIRCE SEARCY (never married); JAMES THOMAS SEARCY (m. ANNIE REBECCA ROSS); [illegible] MARIA SEARCY (m. ROBERT T. [illegible]); REUBEN MARTIN SEARCY (killed in C. S. A.); GEORGE ALEXANDER SEARCY (m. first [illegible] [illegible], second [illegible] [illegible]).

DR. JAMES THOMAS SEARCY (Son of DR. REUBEN SEARCY and Great Grandson of REUBEN SEARCY the old SHERIFF of GRANVILLE COUNTY, N. C.) was married in TUSCALOOSA, ALA. Jan. 22, 1868 to one ANNIE REBECCA ROSS, and they were the parents of twelve (12) children.

The marriage of Dr. JAMES THOMAS SEARCY to ANNIE REBECCA ROSS, like so many marriages of members of a later generation, reunited the SEARCY FAMILY of GRANVILLE COUNTY, with other old families of that section. Annie Rebecca Ross was the daughter of ANN DAVIS SORSBY and WALTER [illegible] ROSS, who married the widow of JAMES [illegible]; and ANN DAVIS SORSBY was the daughter of ALEXANDER SORSBY and REBECCA WILLIAMS, daughter of MAJ. JOHN WILLIAMS; REBECCA was the sister of SALLIE WILLIAMS who married THOMAS [illegible], and of MARY ANN WILLIAMS who married WILLIAM [illegible]. ANNIE REBECCA'S uncle, [illegible] [illegible] SORSBY married ANN ELIZA HILL, daughter of GABRIEL HILL, the son of GREEN HILL and nephew of WILLIAM HILL who married MARY JONES, grand-daughter of old EDWARD JONES at whose home the first Court of Granville County, North Carolina, was held in 1746 (See p. 45). The twelve children of DR. JAMES THOMAS SEARCY (C.S.A.) were:

(1) REUBEN [illegible] SEARCY (2) WALTER ROSS SEARCY (3) JAMES THOMAS SEARCY (4) DR. [illegible] SORSBY SEARCY (5) ANNIE ROSS SEARCY (6) GEORGE HARRIS SEARCY (7) JOSEPH ALEXANDER SEARCY (8) [illegible] PEIRCE SEARCY (9) [illegible] [illegible] SEARCY (10) HARVEY BROWN SEARCY (11) EVELYN GRAY SEARCY (12) JULIA [illegible] SEARCY.

(1) DR. REUBEN THOMAS SEARCY attended the University of Virginia, and was a very promising young physician, at the time of his death, in Tuscaloosa, in 1882.

(2) WALTER ROSS SEARCY, married MISS LIZZIE DOUTHIT, of a prominent Texas family, her husband having settled in that State when a young man. For many years they resided in SMITH - VILLE, Texas, where Walter Ross Searcy was Mayor for many years. Latterly they located in the City of Dallas, where he was a leading Druggist. They had three children, MARY, ANABEL DOUTHIT and THOMAS JAMES SEARCY.

(3) JAMES THOMAS SEARCY, JR., born in 1872, married MATTIE HESTER, a descendant of the old GRANVILLE COUNTY Hester family, and had REUBEN HESTER and MARTHA ROSS SEARCY.

(4) BATTLE SORSBY SEARCY married MARY STRUDWICK NICHOLSON, and had two children, ELIZABETH STRUDWICK and BATTLE SORSBY SEARCY, JR. The father is a dentist of prominence.

(5) ANNIE ROSS SEARCY, born 1875, married WILLIAM SIMPSON KELLER, who was a half-brother of the famous HELEN KELLER, a world-known lecturer.

(6) DR. GEORGE HARRIS SEARCY became a prominent physician and married MARY PERSINGER of Nebraska. Dr. Searcy died in 1935, leaving a daughter HARRIET PERSINGER SEARCY, who married one GREER MURPHY.

(7) JOSEPH ALEXANDER SEARCY, born 1879, married NINA FOSTER, and had NINA ROSS SEARCY and JOSEPH ALEXANDER SEARCY, JR., of the U. S. Navy.

(8) ABBIE FITCH SEARCY, b. 1881, married HENRY ADAMS SNOW, and has three children, HENRY A. SNOW, JR., JAMES SEARCY SNOW and ANNIE ROSS SNOW. They live in TUSCALOOSA, Alabama.

(9) PETER BRYCE SEARCY, born in 1882, was named for DR. PETER BRYCE, one time Superintendent of the Alabama State Hospital. PETER BRYCE has never married. He is an artist of note, residing in Texas, where he has a large clientele. Only recently he has been widely mentioned as the artist who painted the picture depicting the beginning of Statehood, the centennial of which is being celebrated widely over the State this year (1945). By some current commentators this painting is fittingly called "The Transition", or the "Birth of a State". In 1933 this Great Great Grandson of REUBEN SEARCY (the old Sheriff) , based on research by this compiler, executed a beautiful map of "Colonial Granville County", the home of his ancestors, a copy of which, done in colors by the artist, may be seen in the Department of Archives and History at Raleigh, North Carolina. Another epic picture by SEARCY is "Law West of the Pecos", being a diaramic painting of Roy Bean, a famous West Texas Character, who was Justice of the Peace at a place on the Pecos River which he called LANGTRY, after the famous Lilly Langtry, who once visited him there and whom he idolized in his rough way.

(10) DR. HARVEY BROWN SEARCY, of Tuscaloosa, Alabama, stands at the head of the Medical profession in his State, and like his distinguished grandfather, by his civic work and intensive research has added luster to the SEARCY name as a physician. He married MARY EMILY FITTS. They had two children.

(11) EVELYN GRAY SEARCY, born in 1886, married DR. J. BROWN FARRIOR, and had seven children who bear the FARRIOR name, of course.

(12) JULIA DEARING SEARCY (1889-1919) married ESTES SNEDEGOR and had one daughter KATHERINE SNEDEGOR who married VINCENT NORTH, of SEATTLE, Washington. Thus the descendants of REUBEN SEARCY (the old Sheriff) scattered to the Pacific coast.

In an article by Nannie May Tillie in the North Carolina Historical Review (vol. 18 p. 339) which appeared in 1941, some interesting side lights are given on the career of REUBEN SEARCY of GRANVILLE COUNTY, including the story of his connection with so-called "election frauds" in GRANVILLE COUNTY, N. C. back in 1760. There can be no question but what the Sheriff "belonged to the court ring of Granville County" in those days and that they stood together. Not only Searcy, but dozens of others were dropped from the roll of Justices, and hailed before the Governor for their independent spirit and disregard of the edicts of His Royal Highness and the Governor who did his bidding. Among these also was the redoubtable ROBERT HARRIS, and JAMES YANCEY, the grandfather of the silver - tongued orator of the Confederacy, WILLIAM LOUNDES YANCEY, of South Carolina and Georgia. Usually when one was "on the carpet" the others were, and when, out of spite, one was thrown out of office, the others all quit in sympathy.

The SEARCY'S of TUSCALOOSA, headed by the grandson REUBEN were staunch Presbyterians, and aided in founding the old Church of that persuasion in Alabama. A recent brief sketch of the old Tuscaloosa First Presbyterian Church, it is interesting to note, shows the Grandson REUBEN also had his troubles, if the old minutes can be relied upon, since they show that DR. REUBEN SEARCY'S personal conduct was called in question at a meeting of the Session away back in about 1830, and a committee was appointed to "look seriously into the matter" and ascertain just why DR. SEARCY thus far strayed from the Presbyterian path of rectitude. The offense with which this grandson of the Granville REUBEN was charged, and for which he was "hailed before his elders" was that for some unknown reason he "attended a circus". Thus his love of the band-music and the tinkle of the tinsel and tamborines might have wrecked his placid and useful career in his young days, except it seems from traditional accounts, he had previously donated the land on which the church stood, when it was a few staunch souls trying to hold the small "congregation" together. That may have had something to do with settling the case, because we are told the good doctor died strong in the faith of his fathers.

(NOTE: The foregoing account of the SEARCYS may not be absolutely correct in all its details, and somewhere back in Granville County, Kentucky or Tennessee, the writer may have gotten mixed up a little, but it is presented with the thought that in the main it is correct and is worth preserving. It is set down in this book as worth preserving in the libraries of the country for the benefit of future generations- W.S.R.).

MORROW FAMILY. DANIEL MORROW and his widow ELIZABETH, both of whom left wills in GRANVILLE COUNTY, the first in 1817, and the last in 1836, lived on lands on the South side of Island Creek. This family was a segment of the family to which the writer's mother belonged in Tennessee, she being a MORROW. The family entered North Carolina, from PRINCE EDWARD COUNTY, Virginia, and located in various sections of the old North State, including BURKE, GRANVILLE, CASWELL, RUTHERFORD, IREDELL and MECKLENBURG. Some lived in WARREN at one time. Under "MECKLENBURG COUNTY" an attempt will be made to go into the family more fully.

HENDERSON FAMILY. In the space available it would be impossible to trace the entire HENDERSON FAMILY in all its ramifications. Besides there is nothing more tiresome to read than a lot of names all jumbled together in the name of "genealogy" and called a family history. Such accounts partake too much of dry statistics to be interesting. But the writer will take enough space to give the reader a pretty good general idea of the family of HENDERSONS who settled in what is now a part of the original GRANVILLE COUNTY. And I am afraid the account given will not comport with the statements that is to be found elsewhere, most of which appear to be founded upon unsupported family traditions.

SAMUEL HENDERSON was the ancestor of the GRANVILLE COUNTY HENDERSONS. He evidently came to what is now GRANVILLE (or VANCE) COUNTY, when it was EDGECOMBE, about 1740, maybe a little later, but not much later. His wife was ELIZABETH WILLIAMS, whom he is said to have married in HANOVER COUNTY. He had been SHERIFF of HANOVER COUNTY, Virginia, before coming to NORTH CAROLINA, and he became one of the early Sheriffs of GRANVILLE COUNTY, after it was organized. He was not born in HANOVER COUNTY, but in NEW KENT COUNTY, Virginia. From the various "family accounts" he and his wife ELIZABETH WILLIAMS had eleven children, as follows:

(1) MARY HENDERSON (b. 1734) married JOAB MITCHELL.
(2) ELIZABETH HENDERSON (b. 1738) married JOHN BECKHAM.
(3) ANN HENDERSON (b. 1739) married DANIEL WILLIAMS (Her Cousin).
(4) SUSAN HENDERSON (b. 1743) married REUBEN SEARCY .
(5) JOHN HENDERSON married SARAH HINTON (widow of SOLOMON ALSTON JR.)
(6) SAMUEL HENDERSON (b. 1748) married ELIZABETH CALLOWAY.
(7) THOMAS HENDERSON (b. 1752) married JANE MARTIN.
(8) PLEASANT HENDERSON (b. 1750) married SARAH MARTIN.
(9) WILLIAM HENDERSON (b. 1748) married LETITIA DAVIS (widow of JARED NELSON).
(10) NATHANIEL HENDERSON (b. 1736) married SARAH FRANKLIN (widow of SUGAR JONES).
(11) JUDGE RICHARD HENDERSON married ELIZABETH KEELING.

JUDGE RICHARD HENDERSON is perhaps the most famous of all of the children of SAMUEL HENDERSON and his wife ELIZABETH WILLIAMS, and it seems that he and his wife had SIX (6) children, as follows:

(1) FANNY HENDERSON who married the famous JUDGE SPRUCE McKAY, of SALISBURY, N. C.
(2) RICHARD HENDERSON (b. 1766).
(3) ARCHIBALD HENDERSON (b. 1768). (Clerk of GRANVILLE COUNTY).
(4) ELIZABETH HENDERSON married one of the MECKLENBURG COUNTY ALEXANDERS.
(5) LEONARD HENDERSON (b. 1772), a Distinguished JUDGE, of VANCE COUNTY.
(6) JOHN LAWSON HENDERSON (b. 1778) who it is said, never married.

As this story proceeds more will be said about several of the above named children and grand-children of SAMUEL HENDERSON. But, as to the origin of this family?

The acorn, from which this immediate family and its various branches sprange, was first planted, so far as American ancestry is concerned, in YORK COUNTY, VIRGINIA. And this applies both to SAMUEL HENDERSON and his wife ELIZABETH WILLIAMS, though this account will be held as near as can be to the HENDERSON family tree.

The family tradition seems to be that the first American ancestor of the HENDERSONS was one THOMAS HENDERSON who came to JAMESTOWN in 1707. This is not true, because there was no HENDERSON on that list. It is refuted by the statement that this THOMAS was the GRANFATHER of SAMUEL wgo was Sheriff of GRANVILLE COUNTY, N. C. in 1754-5, nearly 150 years later; an utter impossibility. Even the old records of YORK COUNTY, Virginia, are silent on the HENDERSON family, because shortly after the emigrant ancestor arrived - whatever his name - he settled on the "Eastern Shore" in ACCOMAC COUNTY, and later his descendants lived in both ACCOMAC and NORTHAMPTON, when the territory was divided. There the name HENDERSON, during the Seventeenth Century & long afterwards, was common. JOHN HENDERSON died leaving a will in NORTHAMPTON COUNTY, VIRGINIA, in 1721; GILBERT HENDERSON died in 1734; JACOB in 1754; another JOHN in 1756, and so on. SAMUEL HENDERSON left will in ACCOMAC in 1798, and a LEMUEL in 1797. These were descendants - some of them - of the original emigrant or emigrants. Other descendants came back over into YORK and settled across the river from YORK in NEW KENT COUNTY, long before HANOVER COUNTY was established. Among these was THOMAS HENDERSON, Carpenter, of the Lower Parish of Blissland, who married SARAH WILKINSON, on March 16, 1898, who, in all probability, was the father of SAMUEL HENDERSON, who later is found in HANOVER (cut off from New Kent) with his brothers and sisters.(p. 412 of St. Peter's Parish Register, New Kent County). On page 432 of the same record, appears this note: "THOMAS HENDERSON departed this life in February 1709". From the same records we have positive evidence of the following HENDERSONS:

JAMES HENDERSON who married JONE KING Feb. 14, 1726.
SUSANNA HENDERSON, daughter of THOMAS, a minor in 1722.
JANE HENDERSON, daughter of THOMAS baptised March 25, 1708.
THOMAS HENDERSON, whose wife was GRISSEL and who had a daughter URSULA HENDERSON born February 23, 1730.
JAMES HENDERSON who died in 1720.
SARAH HENDERSON and JOHN WILLIAMS were married in December 1711.
THOMAS HENDERSON allowed pay for making a horse block in 1728 at the church.
THOMAS HENDERSON paid by the vestry for making two horse blocks in 1728.
GRISETT HENDERSON appointed Sexton for the Church in 1747.
NOTE: DANIEL TAYLOR was the Minister of Blissland in 1727, and CAPT. GEORGE KEELING was a member of the Church Vestry.

In addition to the foregoing, on May 8, 1707, THOMAS HENDERSON was on a list of certain persons selected to help lay out a road, under the direction of COL. CHARLES FLEMING, and on the same list was a CAPT. WYATT, SAMUEL JORDAN, WILLIAM NORRIS and a certain JAMES MOSS. (The MOSS FAMILY became prominent in GRANVILLE COUNTY, N. C. long afterwards.)

Another item discloses that a certain JAMES HENDERSON did not arrive in the bounds of ST. PETER'S PARISH until sometime around 1713 or 1714, when he gave a bond (p. 160 and 161 of St. Peter's Parish Register), with one THOMAS JACKSON, as surety, to indemnify the Parish "from all manner of charges that might accrue from his coming" into said Parish. He may have simply moved from across the river in YORK COUNTY (Va.), or he may have come from the far side of CHESEPEAKE BAY, from Accomac or Northampton Counties. In all likelihood he may have been a brother of THOMAS HENDERSON who married SARAH WILKINSON March 16, 1698. (St. Peter's Parish Register, p. 412). The record further shows that a JAMES HENDERSON (perhaps the elder one, who made the bond) died August 15, 1720. (p. 433).

In the account of the WILLIAMS FAMILY we are told that DANIEL WILLIAMS, a brother of ELIZABETH, who married SAMUEL HENDERSON, married URSULA HENDERSON, a sister of SAMUEL, and in the above records from ST. PETER'S REGISTER it is shown that THOMAS HENDERSON and his wife GRISSELL had a daughter URSULA, who was born Feb. 23, 1730. This strongly suggests that THOMAS HENDERSON, her father, was a brother of SAMUEL, and, of course, another son of THOMAS HENDERSON, who according to the record died in 1709.

CAPT. GEORGE KEELING, who was a member of the vestry of old BLISSLAND PARISH in the days of THOMAS HENDERSON, was a man of some importance in the community, though far from being the "LORD KEELING" so fancifully pictured by the genealogists of the WILLIAMS and HENDERSON families. In 1704 he owned 1500 acres of land in NEW KENT COUNTY, VIRGINIA, (vol. 31 p. 222 Va. Mag. of Hist. & Biog.), and in 1708-9 was High Sheriff of the County. He came from YORK COUNTY to NEW KENT, sometime after 1695, for in that year he was plaintiff in a law suit he had instituted in the Courts there against EDWARD BREWER, in which one JOHN SMITH was a witness. (YORK COUNTY RECORDS for 1695 p. 192). The wife of COL. RICHARD HENDERSON, of GRANVILLE COUNTY, the famous promoter of "TRANSYLVANIA" was ELIZABETH KEELING, the step-daughter of JUDGE JOHN WILLIAMS, and of AGNES his wife, who is said to have been the widow of a LORD GEORGE KEELING. (See page 211 of this record). To further enhance the reader's interest and strengthen the evidence of the connection of these HENDERSONS with THOMAS of NEW KENT, some years ago Mrs. Hallie Lee (High) Royster, found the will of a GEORGE KEELING on record at HALIFAX. It had evidently been executed in what is now GRANVILLE or VANCE COUNTIES, but in what was then old EDGECOMBE COUNTY and recorded at the then county seat of PENFIELD, and later transferred to the HALIAX ARCHIVES. As CAPT. GEORGE KEELING, of New Kent was alive in 1727, he could possibly have been alive that late, and among the vanguard of migrants to what is now Granville County along about 1740, where he died, though it is known that some of his descendants moved to CAROLINE COUNTY (Va.) where a RICHARD KEELING was a prominent lawyer, and interemarried with the TYLER FAMILY, from YORK COUNTY, VIRGINIA. Certainly, in the light of all these facts, substantiated by the actual records, it is not hard to believe that a nephew of THOMAS HENDERSON, the carpenter, employed by CAPT. GEORGE KEELING and his fellow vestryman to build "two horse blocks for ye upper church" in 1727, should marry a grand-daughter of CAPT. KEELING over in North Carolina about 1763 - JUDGE RICHARD HENDERSON and ELIZABETH KEELING.

During the first or second decade after 1700 a new Parish was cut out of old ST. PETER'S on the upper side and called ST. PAUL'S, and a new county, called HANOVER was also erected at about or a little after said time (in 1720). (Southern Hist. Research Mag. Vol 1 p. 358). This automatically threw many of the ST. PETER'S PARISH members into the new Parish and the new County. Also some of them had been pushing farther West, anyway. JOHN DANIEL, who died in YORK COUNTY in 1724, left lands to his sons JOHN and JAMES in HANOVER COUNTY, which was then a "going concern", and the son JOHN married ANNE, a sister of ELIZABETH WILLIAMS who had married SAMUEL HENDERSON. John Daniel, like SAMUEL HENDERSON, died in GRANVILLE COUNTY, N. C. (p. 210 of this record). Some of the sons and daughters of THOMAS HENDERSON perhaps moved West from New Kent to HANOVER, where they acquired lands, as well as wives, and later children. The items below, taken from the records, apply to this family:

HENRY FOX, of KING WILLIAM COUNTY, Virginia, sold 1000 acres of land to SAMUEL HENDERSON, of HANOVER COUNTY, Virginia, July 14, 1730.

JAMES HENDERSON was living in ST. PAUL'S PARISH in 1715, and had his lands "processioned" that year.

WILLIAM HENDERSON was living in ST. PAUL'S PARISH (coterminus with HANOVER COUNTY) in 1731. Among his neighbors, shown by the procession list, were JOHN SYMES, JOHN HOGG, MILBURN HOGG, GEORGE BELL, DAVID BELL, JOHN COBBS and others. These same names ALL appear on similar lists for 1735, 1743. This same WILLIAM HENDERSON witnessed a deed to THOMAS BALLARD SMITH, with EDWARD HENDERSON, JR. (From York County, Va.), as shown by the Deeds of SPOTTSYLVANIA COUNTY (Va.) in 1734.

EDWARD HENDERSON, SR. (Suggested by the "JR" above mentioned) may have lived in SPOTTSELVANIA COUNTY.

SAMUEL HENDERSON and SAMUEL PRYOR (Perhaps the father of PHILLIP PRYOR, who was Sheriff of GRANVILLE COUNTY, after SAMUEL HENDERSON served) witnessed the will of CORNELIUS DABNEY in HANOVER COUNTY in 1717.

RICHARD HENDERSON (Claimed to have been the father of SAMUEL) does not appear on these records until 1735, 1738, 1739 and 1740 hen his accounts as Collector of the Parish levies is allowed and comments made thereon. Apparently RICHARD HENDERSON was a <u>brother</u> instead of the father of SAMUEL HENDERSON.

JOHN HENDERSON witnessed the will of HARRY BEVERLY in SPOTTSYLVANIA COUNTY in 1730. With BENJAMIN WOODSON, in 1745 he was appointed in ALBEMARLE to lay out the "Prison Bounds" in that county, which shows he had moved to ALBEMARLE COUNTY.

From the foregoing and other evidence from various sources this compiler has finally concluded that the father of SAMUEL HENDERSON, one time Sheriff of GRANVILLE COUNTY, N. C. was THOMAS HENDERSON, of NEW KENT COUNTY, Virginia, who married SARAH WILKINSON, March 16, 1698, in said County, and who "departed this life" in the month of February 1709;(St. Peter's Parish Register, pages 412 and 432); that THOMAS HENDERSON had been previously married and had several children by his first marriage and some by his second, and that SAMUEL HENDERSON was perhaps a child of the first marriage and born, perhaps, about 1795, or earlier, since he witnessed the will of CORNELIUS DABNEY in Hanover County as early as 1717, when he must have been a grown man at that time, and not merely a young boy in his teens.

Using this evidence as a basis, we are able to say with fair certainty that the children of THOMAS HENDERSON, of New Kent County were as follows:

(1) JOHN HENDERSON, of ALBEMARLE, whose wife was a BENNETT.
(2) THOMAS HENDERSON, Carpenter, of New Kent County, whose wife was GRISSEL.
(3) JAMES HENDERSON, who married JANE KING in New Kent County in 1726.
(4) SAMUEL HENDERSON who married ELIZABETH WILLIAMS and moved to N. C.
(5) WILLIAM HENDERSON, whose wife was probably SUSANNAH LOGAN.
(6) EDWARD HENDERSON, SR., of SPOTTSYLVANIA COUNTY.
(7) RICHARD HENDERSON, Collector of St. Mark's Parish, HANOVER COUNTY.
(8) SARAH HENDERSON married JOHN WILLIAMS , December, 1711.
(9) SUSANNAH HENDERSON (Her record not found after 1722).
(10) URSULA HENDERSON married DANIEL WILLIAMS.
(11) JANE HENDERSON (b. 1708) married WILLIAM TRAVILLIAN.

(1) JOHN HENDERSON, who moved with the WOODSONS to ALBEMARLE, was called JOHN HENDERSON, SR. He left many children, and owned lands there in 1745.

(2) THOMAS HENDERSON, Carpenter of NEW KENT, moved to LOUISA COUNTY, and died in 1768.

(3) JAMES HENDERSON lived and died in AUGUSTA COUNTY, Virginia.

(4) SAMUEL HENDERSON married ELIZABETH WILLIAMS and moved to GRANVILLE COUNTY, N. C.

(5) WILLIAM HENDERSON married SUSANNAH LOGAN and died in AUGUSTA COUNTY in 1770. He was the Great Grandfather of JAMES PINCKNEY HENDERSON, first Governor of the State of TEXAS.

(6) EDWARD HENDERSON, SR. of SPOTTSYLVANIA and ORANGE COUNTIES.

(7) RICHARD HENDERSON died in GOOCHLAND COUNTY in 1748, whither he had moved with the DANIEL and WOODSON families from HANOVER COUNTY.

(8) SARAH HENDERSON married JOHN WILLIAMS in 1711, and they were the parents of JUDGE JOHN WILLIAMS, famous Jurist, of N. C. who died in 1799.

(9) SUSANNAH HENDERSON was raised by a family named EPPERSON in New Kent County.

(10) URSULA HENDERSON married DANIEL WILLIAMS, who died in GRANVILLE COUNTY, N. C. in 1759 leaving a will in which he named his children, but not his wife.

(11) JANE HENDERSON, born in 1708 (p. 361 St. Peter's Par.) married WILLIAM TRAVILLIAN.

As can be readily seen this HENDERSON FAMILY was a large and interesting one, and the list given constitutes the ancestors of a group of people who, with their descendants, may be said to have remade the map of the Great West, especially, JUDGE RICHARD HENDERSON whose "TRANSYLVANIA" properly takes up much space in our Historic Annals, the son of SAMUEL HENDERSON and ELIZABETH WILLIAMS. The space available in this limited work will not permit the writer to give a full account of all of these sons and daughters, but enough will be set out below to apprise the reader in a general way of what became of their descendants, and the part that some of them have played in the development of the Nation, no comprehensive account having been heretofore given as to many of them.

----

(1) JOHN HENDERSON, SR., of ALBEMARLE COUNTY. Obviously he married a BENNETT, of a prominent family, though we have found no clue to her given or Christian name. The family of JOHN HENDERSON, SR. is mentioned in Wood's History of Albemarle County, and this account shows that he had purchased lands in that county as early as 1745. His children, according to data furnished this writer, were: (Numbered for convenience of the reader in following).

20. JOHN HENDERSON, JR. married FRANCES MOORE.
21. BENNETT HENDERSON married ELIZABETH LEWIS.
22. WILLIAM HENDERSON married REBECCA HUDSON.
23. ELIZABETH HENDERSON married DAVID CRAWFORD.
24. SUSAN HENDERSON married JOHN CLARK.
25. MARY HENDERSON married ____ BULLOCK.
26. HANNAH HENDERSON married ___BULLOCK.
27. FRANCES HENDERSON married JOHN THOMAS. He married (2) FRANCES LEWIS.

ELIZABETH LEWIS and FRANCES (the latter called ANN JEFFERSON LEWIS) LEWIS, who married BENNETT HENDERSON, were first cousins of PRES. THOMAS JEFFERSON, their mother, MARY RANDOLPH, being a sister of MR. JEFFERSON'S mother, and a daughter of ISHAM RANDOLPH. Their father, CHARLES LEWIS, was a brother of HOWELL LEWIS and his wife ISABELLA WILLIS, of GRANVILLE COUNTY, N. C., whose daughter MILDRED LEWIS married JOHN COBBS in that County in 1769.

This fact alone, irrespective of other data, should be enough to convince the most skeptical that the HENDERSONS of this tribe were of the same clan as those who migrated from HANOVER COUNTY, Va. to GRANVILLE COUNTY, N. C., the truth being that the father of BENNETT HENDERSON (JOHN HENDERSON, SR.) was a brother of SAMUEL HENDERSON, Sheriff of GRANVILLE COUNTY, and that BENNETT HENDERSON, whose wife was a niece of HOWELL LEWIS, was a first cousin of COL. RICHARD HENDERSON, of TRANSYLVANIA fame. The further fact that MARY and HANNAH HENDERSON, sisters of BENNETT and daughters of JOHN HENDERSON, SR. married BULLOCKS, puts the brand of HANOVER COUNTY origin and connections on this ALBEMARLE FAMILY of HENDERSONS, also; because it is well established that the BULLOCK FAMILY, of GRANVILLE COUNTY, like the HENDERSONS, came from HANOVER COUNTY, Virginia.

BENNETT HENDERSON (Son of JOHN HENDERSON, SR.) and his wife ELIZABETH LEWIS had the following list of interesting children:

30. JOHN HENDERSON married ANNA B. HUDSON.
31. WILLIAM HENDERSON.
32. SARAH HENDERSON married JOHN KERR.
33. JAMES HENDERSON. (Called JAMES PINCKNEY HENDERSON).
34. CHARLES HENDERSON.
35. ISHAM HENDERSON (Named for ISHAM RANDOLPH and ISHAM LEWIS, an uncle).
36. BENNETT HENDERSON married POLLY CROCKETT.
37. HILLSBORO HENDERSON.
38. ELIZA HENDERSON married JOHN H. BULLOCK.
39. FRANCES HENDERSON married THOMAS HORNSBY (Yorktown Family).
40. LUCY HENDERSON married JOHN WOOD.
41. NANCY HENDERSON married MATTHEW NELSON.

27. FRANCES HENDERSON (Dau. of JOHN HENDERSON, SR. and sister of BENNETT) married a certain JOHN THOMAS. After his wife's death JOHN THOMAS married (2) FRANCES LEWIS, a sister of ELIZABETH, the wife of BENNETT HENDERSON. In "Wood's History of Albemarle County" there is a somewhat sketchy account of this family of which the ancestor appears to have been one MICHAEL THOMAS, who patented lands in ALBEMARLE about 1745, near the same time that JOHN HENDERSON, SR. had settled there from SPOTTSYLVANIA and HANOVER. His children were MICHAEL, JOSEPH, JESSE, and a RALPH, EDWARD, JAMES and a daughter who married a CARROLL, who had a son JOHN CARROLL, mentioned in the elder THOMAS' will. The account then says that JOHN THOMAS came from AMHERST COUNTY to ALBEMARLE and was twice married (1) to FRANCES HENDERSON, and (2) to FRANCES LEWIS. He lived on IVY CREEK on lands given him by his second wife's father. By his first wife FRANCES HENDERSON he had children he had WARNER, NORBORN K., JAMES, ELIZABETH (m. a WOOD), and LUCY THOMAS, who married JAMES LEWIS. His son NORBORN K. THOMAS was head of the firm of N. K. THOMAS & CO., Commission Merchants at Richmond, Va. His children by the second marriage were CHARLES L., JOHN L., VIRGINIA and MARGARET THOMAS. One of these children by the first marriage had a son named ISHAM THOMAS who came to and settled in DALLAS, TEXAS, and who had a son, among others,named JAMES PINCKNEY THOMAS and another named JOHN THOMAS. To this writer, a son of the latter, declared that his grandfather was a nephew of JAMES PINCKNEY HENDERSON, the first Governor of Texas, after statehood. The records, of course, show he was in error, but the reference was to 33. JAMES HENDERSON, son of BENNETT HENDERSON and ELIZABETH LEWIS, whose name, in all probability was JAMES PINCKNEY HENDERSON. In fact, the late MRS. LUCY HENDERSON HORTON, of Tennessee, in her history of the HENDERSON FAMILY (She was of the GRANVILLE COUNTY, N. C. set), asserts that JAMES PINCKNEY HENDERSON, General in the War with Mexico, first Governor of the State of Texas, and UNITED STATES SENATOR in 1857, was the son of BENNETT HENDERSON and ELIZABETH LEWIS. This, and the fact that the descendants of JOHN THOMAS and FRANCES HENDERSON carried the name JAMES PINCKNEY down through several generations, shows that it was practically a family name, though the real ancestor of the GOVERNOR was WILLIAM HENDERSON, a brother of SAMUEL OF GRANVILLE, and JOHN HENDERSON, SR., of ALBEMARLE. In her account of JAMES PINCKNEY HENDERSON (son of BENNETT HENDERSON) Mrs. HORTON adopts the correct dates of the Texas Governor (1808-1858) but marries him off to MARGARET POLLARD, daughter of RICHARD, a descendant of COL. WILLIAM CABELL and MARGARET JORDAN, whereas it is a matter of common knowledge and history in Texas that GOV. JAMES PINCKNEY HENDERSON married FRANCES COX, daughter of a prominent PHILADELPHIA MERCHANT.

---

(5) WILLIAM HENDERSON (Son of THOMAS HENDERSON of NEW KENT COUNTY, Virginia, and the brother of JOHN HENDERSON, SR., of ALBEMARLE, and SAMUEL HENDERSON, of GRANVILLE COUNTY, N. C.) married, in all probability a LOGAN. Her name was SUSANNAH. While the writer thinks perhaps he could name several children, he is convinced after an extended research on the subject that WILLIAM HENDERSON and his wife SUSANNAH certainly had two sons:

(50) JAMES HENDERSON married VIOLET LAWSON.
(51) SAMUEL HENDERSON married JEAN.........

(51). SAMUEL HENDERSON. I find it more convenient to take up SAMUEL HENDERSON first. He left a will in AUGUSTA COUNTY, dated May 20, 1782, and proved October 15, the same year. His wife JEAN HENDERSON made her will in 1798, and same was proved in December 1800. She is described as of "Middle River". In his will SAMUEL names only six children, but in her will the widow is a bit more specific and names NINE. Doubtless her husband had settled with some of his heirs and omitted mention of them for that reason, whereas the mother saw fit to name each one with some kind of a bequest in her old age.

This compiler has long been of the opinion, without being able to present positive evidence that the HENDERSONS who settled first, in JEFFERSON COUNTY, TENNESSEE, and later in MONROE COUNTY, where MADISONVILLE, the County seat, was built on their lands, were the descendants of this SAMUEL HENDERSON of "Middle River" though there has been an insistent claim that they all came down from a "John Henderson, Sr.," of Virginia, through a son "John, Jr.," who, it is claimed, married a FRANCES MOORE. Mrs. Horton, in her account, gives a list of the children of this John Henderson, Jr., which does not contain the names of those Hendersons who came, first, to GREENE COUNTY, TENNESSEE, and later to JEFFERSON COUNTY. The children of SAMUEL HENDERSON, who died leaving a will in 1782, and who is said in the will to be of "Middle River", shows he had children:

(60) REBECCA HENDERSON
(61) SARAH HENDERSON
(62) FLORENCE HENDERSON
(63) DAVID HENDERSON (Left lands bought of SAMUEL GIVENS)
(64) ANDREW HENDERSON
(65) ALEXANDER HENDERSON (See later).
(66) JAMES HENDERSON (Left lands bought of JAMES THOMPSON)
(67) WILLIAM HENDERSON
(68) SAMUEL HENDERSON.

The following interesting notes are from the East Tennessee Records:

FEB. 2, 1785, SAMUEL HENDERSON, known to be the son of NATHANIEL HENDERSON and the grandson of SAMUEL HENDERSON, of GRANVILLE COUNTY, N. C. married LUCY RICKMAN, in Green County, Tennessee. Security on the bond was JAMES HENDERSON. Samuel Henderson had no brother JAMES and no cousin JAMES in North Carolina.

ANDREW HENDERSON was present at the meeting of the first Court for JEFFERSON COUNTY, Tennessee, when the county was organized July 23, 1792. In 1793 ANDREW HENDERSON was appointed administrator of the estate of John McWilliams in Jefferson County, Tennessee. At the sale of the effects of JESSE WALKER, Jan. 23, 1808, at Dandridge, Tennessee, ANDREW HENDERSON bought one Axe.

ROBERT HENDERSON (Feb. 14, 1798) deeded lands in Jefferson County, on the FRENCH BROAD RIVER to WILLIAM MORROW. Deed witnessed by JOHN HENDERSON.

JOHN HENDERSON was born in JEFFERSON COUNTY, Tennessee, in 1790, the son of a JOHN HENDERSON. He married DORCAS McSPADDEN. They lived and died in MONROE COUNTY.

ANDREW L. HENDERSON, another son of JOHN HENDERSON married MARGARET McSPADDEN. They also settled in MONROE COUNTY. They had a son JAMES M. HENDERSON, prominent in McMinn County (Tenn.) politics, and who was finally President of the First National Bank of Athens, Tenn. (See letter below.)

March 16, 1788, Samuel Wear married Sarah Bean, but Daniel Kennedy refused to issue the license until DANIEL HENDERSON signed the bond.

DAVID HENDERSON sought licnse the next day to marry JANE CARSON and DANIEL HENDERSON became the surety on that bond, also.

The compiler has found what he believes is a complete answer to the above puzzle. The genealogists who have heretofore written about it had SKIPPED A WHOLE GENERATION. (65) ALEXANDER HENDERSON (son of SAMUEL HENDERSON, of Middle River) was the ancestor of all these Hendersons. He first came from Virginia to Greene County (Territory South of the Ohio) and then with the Gentrys, Coons and other settlers, moved to Kentucky, where he died, leaving will in BOURBON COUNTY in October 1796, in which he named the following children, many of whom were still living at that time around DANDRIDGE, TENNESSEE:

(a) ROBERT HENDERSON (Rev. Robert).
(b) SAMUEL HENDERSON
(c) JAMES HENDERSON (witnessed the HENDERSON-RICKMAN marriage).
(d) JOSEPH HENDERSON
(e) ALEXANDER HENDERSON
(f) DAVID HENDERSON (m. JANE CARSON).
(g) DANIEL HENDERSON (Surety on marriage bonds above mentioned).
(h) GEORGE HENDERSON
(i) JOHN HENDERSON (His son JOHN mentioned as a grandson).
(j) FLORENCE HENDERSON (named for her aunt Florence).

A copy of the abstract of the will of ALEXANDER HENDERSON, from which the above account is taken, will be found on Ardry's Kentucky Records, at page 15. A letter reproduced in the Horton account from J. ANDREW HENDERSON to JOHN HENDERSON, from Virginia to the "Holston" and which was preserved by the ATHENS, TENNESSEE, Hendersons, dated Dec. 1, 1756 (an obvious error as to the date) strengthens the proof. I think this proof is now ample on the point involved.

---

(50) JAMES HENDERSON (Son of WILLIAM HENDERSON) married VIOLET LAWSON. She was the daughter of COL. HUGH LAWSON, of Lunenburg County, Virginia, a cousin of JOHN LAWSON, of ST. PETER'S PARISH, in Virginia. HUGH LAWSON in his latter years moved to North Carolina, and died and is buried at the old BAKER'S GRAVEYARD in Mecklenburg (Not Iredell or Rowan) County. He died about 1770, leaving a will dated in 1764, in which he mentioned two sons, HUGH LAWSON and ROGER LAWSON, four sons in laws, THOMAS IRWIN, GEORGE EWING, HUGH BARRY and JAMES HENDERSON (the husband of his daughter VIOLET); also his daughter MARY LAWSON, who became the wife of GENERAL JAMES WHITE, the founder of KNOXVILLE, TENNESSEE, and the mother of the Tennessee Jurist and statesman, JUDGE HUGH LAWSON WHITE. Thus, JAMES HENDERSON, who was the first cousin of JUDGE RICHARD HENDERSON, the founder of "Transylvania", was the brother in law of GEN. JAMES WHITE and his wife VIOLET was the aunt of HUGH LAWSON WHITE. Hugh Lawson White was the first cousin of LAWSON HENDERSON who married ELIZABETH CARRUTH in North Carolina, and the children of JUDGE WHITE were second cousins of JAMES PINCKNEY HENDERSON, the first Governor of Texas, United States Senator, etc., from the Lone Star State.

ROGER LAWSON, one of the sons of COL. HUGH LAWSON, married HANNAH THOMSON (No P in the name) daughter of REV. JOHN THOMSON, a contemporary and friend of the celebrated REV. SAMUEL DAVIES, one-time President of PRINCETON, UNIVERSITY, and a kinsman of the writer's wife. Rev. Thomson went to North Carolina some years before the REV. HUGH McADEN made his famous journey through the CAROLINAS and VIRGINIA, and preached the first PRESBYTERIAN sermon ever delivered on North Carolina soil, in what is now MECKLENBURG COUNTY, N. C. about one mile from the celebrated BEATTY'S FORD crossing of the CATAWBA RIVER, on the farm of his kinsman RICHARD BARRY under a "spreading oak tree". (Alexander's History of Mecklenburg County). Rev. JOHN THOMSON and COL. HUGH LAWSON are buried on the same plot of ground in what is and has always been called BAKER'S GRAVEYARD, near the banks of the limpid stream, long afterwards the scene of tense struggles between the liberty loving Americans and the Army of the Tory leader Cornwallis. Cowan's Ford is within two miles of BAKER'S GRAVEYARD. The writer has visited the place where HUGH LAWSON and REV. THOMSON are both buried in MECKLENBURG COUNTY, and NOT in ROWAN COUNTY, or IREDELL, as has been so often stated, erroneously.

JAMES HENDERSON died in 1783, and he was the owner of a large body of land along the South Fork of the Catawba River, then in LINCOLN, but now in GASTON COUNTY. In addition, before his death he had entered a large body of land along DUCK and STONE RIVER in Middle Tennessee. The writer has visited the grave of JAMES HENDERSON in what is now GASTON COUNTY, N. C. and has now on his desk as he writes a paper weight made from a small stone which had fallen from the high limestone wall surrounding the burial place. As further proof that this man was a cousin of JUDGE RICHARD and the other sons of SAMUEL HENDERSON, old ADAM SPRING, who married FANNIE HENDERSON, daughter of THOMAS HENDERSON (son of SAMUEL, of GRANVILLE COUNTY) is buried behind the same high stone wall on top of the mountain overlooking the swirling waters of the South Fork of the CATAWBA. At this point JAMES HENDERSON had built a dam and a mill, which, late in life he sold to ADAM SPRINGS.

The children of JAMES HENDERSON and his wife VIOLET LAWSON were as follows:

(70) JOHN HENDERSON.
(71) JAMES HENDERSON married MARGARET DICKSON, dau. of COL. JOSEPH DICKSON.
(72) WILLIAM HENDERSON
(73) LAWSON HENDERSON married ELIZABETH CARRUTH.
(74) LOGAN HENDERSON.
(75) KATHERINE HENDERSON (m. her cousin WILLIAM M. LOGAN).
(76) MARY HENDERSON
(77) MARTHA HENDERSON married ___ McKAY.

All of the above children except the son LAWSON HENDERSON and the daughter MARTHA moved to TENNESSEE with their mother VIOLET HENDERSON, about 1803.

(71) JAMES HENDERSON (Son of JAMES above) and his wife MARGARET DICKSON, settled on STONE RIVER near MURFREESBORO, TENNESSEE, sometime after 1800. Margaret was affectionately known in the settlements as "Aunt Peggy" Henderson. She and JAMES HENDERSON, JR. had the following children:

(80) VIOLET HENDERSON
(81) JOSEPH HENDERSON died young.
(82) MARGARET DICKSON (died in 1876) married DANIEL McKISSICK.
(83) BARRY HENDERSON
(84) ELIZABETH HENDERSON
(85) ISABELLA HENDERSON
(86) MATILDA HENDERSON
(87) JAMES HENDERSON III, accidentally shot when young.
(88) MARTHA HENDERSON.

(73) LAWSON HENDERSON married ELIZABETH CARRUTH, the daughter of WALTER CARRUTH. On the old marriage records and bonds of LINCOLN COUNTY, N. C. the writer found the following: "LAWSON HENDERSON married ELIZABETH CARRUTH, in LINCOLN COUNTY, JULY 25, 1798; JOHN DICKSON was surety on the marriage bond." These were the parents of the JAMES PINCKNEY HENDERSON who was the first Governor of the State of Texas, United States Senator, and Embassador to the Court of Saint James. He and FRANCES COX, whom he married, met in PARIS and LONDON and were later united. I consider the following a correct list of the children of LAWSON HENDERSON and his wife ELIZABETH CARRUTH:

(90) WALLACE ALEXANDER HENDERSON, M. D. (b. 1799, d. 1823).
(91) JOHN CARRUTH HENDERSON (1801-1833) married NANCY RILEY GAFNEY (Of Spartanburg).
(92) CHARLES COTESWORTH HENDERSON (1803-1869) married BARBARA GLENN BRYDEN, of N. Y.
(93) LAWSON FRANKLIN HENDERSON (1805-1868) m. ANN DUNAVANT, Chester, S. C.
(94) JAMES PINCKNEY HENDERSON (1808-1858) mar FRANCES COX. He was GOVERNOR OF TEXAS.
(95) HUGH LAWSON HENDERSON (1812-1837) died at Sea on way to SAVANNAH, GEORGIA.
(96) GEORGE WILLIAM HENDERSON (1814-1851) m. AMANDA M. MOORE (Spartanburg, S. C.).
(97) MARY GRAHAM HENDERSON (1815-1877) m. THOS. M. HERNDON (Died in New Orleans).
(98) LOGAN BARRY HENDERSON (1818-1844) died unmarried at MARSHALL, TEXAS.
(99) WALTER CARRUTH HENDERSON (1820-1850) Died unmarried, at CANTON, MISSISSIPPI.
(100) WALLACE ALEXANDER IRWIN HENDERSON (1827-1851) Died unmarried, CANTON, MISSISSIPPI.

(75) KATHERINE LOGAN and her husband WILLIAM M. LOGAN were the parents of CAPTAIN WILLIAM M. LOGAN, JR., who was in command of a contingent of troops in the famous battle of Independence in Texas at SAN JACINTO; another son, JAMES H. LOGAN served in the Texas Army and received lands for his services. Descendants live now at PORT ARTHUR, TEXAS.

DESCENDANTS OF SAMUEL HENDERSON, of GRANVILLE COUNTY. The following information in regard to the direct descendants of SAMUEL HENDERSON, of GRANVILLE COUNTY, is copied from material found in various places and from numerous accounts that have been written. The dates given in every instance have been copied from the same sources, and the writer is not sure that they are correct, since other dates pertaining to older members of the family have been found to be wrong in many cases. The numbers refer to the list of children inserted on page 221 of this record, which see.

(1) MARY HENDERSON, born in 1734, married JOAB MITCHELL. Children of this marriage were JACOB, SAMUEL, RICHARD, THOMAS, EDWARD, WILLIAM, RUTH, ELIZABETH, JELICO and SUSAN MITCHELL. MARY and JOAB MITCHELL moved first from GRANVILLE COUNTY to East Tennessee (or, what was afterwards called that), but later they moved to GRINDAL SHOALS on the PACOLET RIVER in South Carolina, where some of the other members of the HENDERSON FAMILY had settled. The name "JELICO" in the list of their children refers to ANGELICA MITCHELL, the wife of JUDGE ABRAM NOTT, a celebrated character in South Carolina History.

(2) ELIZABETH HENDERSON, said to have been born in 1738, married JOHN BECKHAM. They migrated from GRANVILLE COUNTY to GRINDAL SHOALS on the Pacolet River in South Carolina, whence JOAB MITCHELL and WILLIAM and JOHN HENDERSON had moved. The names of four of their children have been mentioned, JOHN, HENRIETTA, SUSAN and ELIZABETH. One account says that their " only son removed to Kentucky and the daughters all married and moved to the West". This, of course, would be JOHN BECKHAM, JR. John Beckham during the revolution in South Carolina was an active Whig. While MORGAN was encamped on GRINDALL SHOALS, Beckham kept him in constant motion and he did valuable service, says the Logan Manuscript, from which we draw. (Vol. III Joseph Habersham Chapter Publications pp. 38-39). On one occasion when closely pressed by the Light Horse of TARLTON, he plunged headlong down a fearful bank into the river and made his escape. The spot is still well known and often pointed out. It was on the old William Hodge Plantation, where John Beckham died and was buried long after the revolution. On this plunge John Beckham was accompanied by a companion named EASTERWOOD. It is said Beckham could have gotten away from the British on this occasion easier had he not stopped to light his pipe. He was an incessant smoker and swore he would light it before he budged a foot. When he gained the opposite bank he slapped his thigh, looked at his pursuers and shouted back at them "Shoot and be d_______d! " with his pipe still in his mouth.

(3) ANN HENDERSON, said to have been born in 1739, married DANIEL WILLIAMS, who was her cousin and the brother of GEN. JAMES WILLIAMS who lost his life at King's Mountain, and of HENRY, JOHN and JOSEPH WILLIAMS, of Caswell County. Their children: SAMUEL, DANIEL, JOSEPH, RICHARD, WILLIAM, DAVID, BETSY, NANCY, NUTTY and POLLY WASHER. After the death of her husband and cousin DANIEL WILLIAMS, the widow ANN HENDERSON WILLIAMS married ADAM POTTER, it is believed, in South Carolina; for it is known that she joined her sisters Mrs. Mitchell and Mrs. Beckham and her brothers John and William Henderson on the Pacolet River in the Grindal Shoals settlement. Though they married in South Carolina, perhaps, ADAM POTTER was a member of the GRANVILLE COUNTY POTTERS, and may have been a brother of ABRAHAM POTTER who died in Granville County in 1787, leaving THOMAS, ROBERT, POLLY and SALLY, with JOHN POTTER their guardian. See Granville County Court Records herein for that year.

(4) SUSAN HENDERSON, said to have been born in 1743, married REUBEN SEARCY (whose family came from HANOVER COUNTY, Va.) the old SHERIFF and CLERK of GRANVILLE COUNTY (pp. 217 to 220 herein) and had, as near as may be ascertained from all accounts examined: THOMAS, ASA, BENNETT, ROBERT, WILLIAM W., HENRIETTA, POLLY and ELIZABETH. THOMAS SEARCY married ANNE MARTIN, and they were the parents of DR. REUBEN SEARCY who settled in TUSCALOOSA, ALABAMA, becoming the ancestor of a numerous tribe heretofore reviewed; ASA SEARCY may have moved to TENNESSEE; BENNETT SEARCY went to Kentucky; ROBERT SEARCY settled in Tennessee, where he was the Second Grand Master of the Masonic Lodge of that Jurisdiction; WILLIAM W. (Washington) settled in GRANVILLE for "keeps" though his descendants went to Tennessee, and some of them to Texas; Polly and Henrietta have not been found in tracing, while ELIZABETH married a GRANVILLE County WHITE and her descendants (named WHITE) were numerous in Middle Tennessee. (See Acken's Tennessee Bible Records).

(5) JOHN HENDERSON was married on June 4, 1772 to SARAH HINTON, the widow of SOLOMON ALSTON, JR., and moved to the neighborhood of GRINDAL SHOALS, on the PACOLET RIVER in South Carolina. In August 1775, WILLIAM ALSTON, in behalf of the orphans of SOLOMON ALSTON, deceased, obtained a writ against JOHN HENDERSON, who married SARAH, the widow of SOLOMON ALSTON, for alleged mal practice in the administration of the estate of said Alston. The orphans named in the suit were LEMUEL ALSTON, HENRY ALSTON and CHARITY ALSTON; the executors to SOLOMON ALSTON were JOHN HENDERSON, JOSEPH JOHN WILLIAMS and WILLIAM ALSTON. Prayer granted. (Vol. 10, N. C. Records, p. 514.). CHARITY ALSTON, the daughter of SOLOMON, JR. and SARAH HINTON, married JAMES JONES, a grandson of EDWARD JONES, at whose home the County of GRANVILLE was formed in 1746, as shown by the records herein. GEN. WILLIAM HENDERSON, who before the revolution, had settled at GRINDAL SHOALS on the Pacolet in S. C., sold his planation there to his brother JOHN HENDERSON and moved over on the PEE DEE, and at his death his brother JOHN HENDERSON was made one of his Executors. The children of JOHN HENDERSON (who died at the age of 84 years) and his wife SARAH (HINTON) ALSTON were WILLIAM, JOSEPH, BETSY (m. FERNANDES) and SALLY (who married a HAILE). The son JOSEPH was the father of JANE HENDERSON (m. a DUKE) and of two other daughters who married respectively a WRIGHT and a WARE.

(6) SAMUEL HENDERSON accompanied his brother COL. RICHARD HENDERSON and his friend COL. RICHARD CALLOWAY with the Transylvanie contingent to the vicinity of BOONSBORO, Kentucky, in June, 1776. The romantic story of the capture of Elizabeth Calloway and Jemimah Boone by the Indians and their rescue by Daniel Boone and Samuel Henderson forms an interesting chapter in early Kentucky history and has been often repeated. Elizabeth Calloway was the eighth child of Col. Richard Calloway and his wife FRANCES WALTON and was born August 14, 1760. She married

SAMUEL HENDERSON on August 7, 1776, and is said to have become the first bride among all of the first settlers in Kentucky. SAMUEL HENDERSON and his wife ELIZABETH CALLOWAY, according to the family historians had only one child, FRANCES HENDERSON, who was born May 29, 1777, said to have been the fifth white child born in Kentucky, and the first child born of parents who were married in KENTUCKY. FRANCES HENDERSON became the wife of JAMES SMILEY GILLESPIE, and the same authorities claim there was only one son born of this union, named CHARLES JOSEPH GILLESPIE, who married MARY LILLIE CRABB, daughter of RALPH and MARY CRABB. CHARLES JOSEPH GILLESPIE and MARY CRABB had two daughters, MARY LILLIE GILLESPIE and FANNY HENDERSON GILLESPIE. Mary Lillie became the wife of William Willis Wiley Wood, and Fanny Henderson the wife of Gen. Anthony Street, of the Confederate States Army. The writer has been furnished with a note which says that JOSHUA CALLOWAY, supposedly the son of COL. RICHARD CALLOWAY and the brother of ELIZABETH CALLOWAY who married SAMUEL HENDERSON, was born in Virginia in 1757 and died in GEORGIA in 1816, and that he married ISABELLA GRAVES HENDERSON on January 29, 1778, and had five children: EUNICE (m. John Milner), MARY (m. MICAJAH WILLIAMSON, JR.), JOSHUA SAMUEL CALLOWAY, ISABELLA, and NANCY CALLOWAY (m. DANIEL HOLTZCLAW). Joshua Samuel Calloway was a minister.

CONTRADICTORY ACCOUNT. The foregoing account of the family of SAMUEL HENDERSON is contradicted by MRS. LUCY HENDERSON HORTON in her statements in regard to the matter, who says they had eight children: FRANCES, RICHARD, PLEASANT, ALFRED, SUSAN, BETSY, SALLY and DASCIA, who married an ESTILL. Mrs. Horton says also that SAMUEL HENDERSON was born February 6, 1746. Mrs. Blanch S. Bentley, of McMinnville, Tennessee, on page 144 of Acklen's Tennessee Tombstone Records, has the following information published, based on the markers in the old RIVERSIDE CEMETERY in McMinnville: "COL. SAMUEL HENDERSON, born Feb. 25, 1742 in GRANVILLE COUNTY, N. C., defender of BOONSBORO, KY. under DANIEL BOONE. Rescued from the Indians ELIZABETH CALLOWAY, whom he afterwards married, and Colonel in the Revolutionary War. Brother of JUDGE RICHARD HENDERSON of NORTH CAROLINA. In old age lived with his son, PLEASANT HENDERSON, in McMinnville. Died in 1816." As for the son PLEASANT, she quotes: "PLEASANT HENDERSON, born in GRANVILLE COUNTY, N. C.; son of SAMUEL HENDERSON and wife ELIZABETH CALLOWAY; married AGNES ROBARDS; died 1837". His wife Agnes, died in 1870. NOTE: After receiving this account direct from MRS. BENTLEY, the writer went to McMinnville and carefully examined the old graves that were marked, and did not find the grave of COL. SAMUEL HENDERSON. Mrs. Horton in her account says he died at WINCHESTER, which is some distance from McMinnville. To make these accounts still more confusing to the research working on page 213 of the Acklen Tombstone Records, where an effort is made to show where the several members of this Henderson family are buried, is this statement: "SAMUEL HENDERSON, son of SAMUEL HENDERSON (1700-1783), and his wife ELIZABETH WILLIAMS, lies buried in ROCKINGHAM COUNTY, N. C.". This last note, of course, necessarily applies to the SAMUEL HENDERSON (brother of Judge Richard Henderson) who married ELIZABETH CALLOWAY. He can't be buried, both in ROCKINGHAM COUNTY, N. C. and at WINCHESTER, TENNESSEE. The compiler is of the opinion that this (6) SAMUEL HENDERSON probably died at McMinnville (though his grave is not marked); that he & Elizabeth Calloway had several sons and daughters; that in addition to those named by Mrs. Horton, he MAY have had others, but that it is pretty safe to include those named in Mrs. Horton's list in the family chart.

(7) THOMAS HENDERSON, another son of SAMUEL HENDERSON and his wife ELIZABETH WILLIAMS of GRANVILLE COUNTY, is said to have been born March 19, 1752. (I wonder where these numerous Henderson genealogists found all of these birth and death dates. Very few of them agree with each other, and none of them seem to comport with the facts and dates I have found here and there in regard to the family, from the real records.). He married JANE MARTIN. They say she was the SISTER of Governor ALEXANDER MARTIN, of North Carolina, also of COL. JAMES MARTIN, of SNOW CREEK, N. C., of a ROBERT MARTIN, a THOMAS MARTIN and a SAMUEL MARTIN. (HUGH MARTIN, the father of GOV. ALEXANDER MARTIN married JANE HUNTER in 1731 and they lived in HUNTERTON, COUNTY, New Jersey, where ALEXANDER MARTIN was born in 1740. He was a younger brother of CAPT. SAMUEL MARTIN, of LINCOLN COUNTY, N. C. who lead his troops at COWPENS and was at KING'S MOUNTAIN with Col. CHRONICLE. - Historic Note). The children of THOMAS HENDERSON and JANE MARTIN were: ALEXANDER, SAMUEL (b. 1787), POLLY (m. a LACEY), JANE (m. KENDRICK), NATHANIEL, FANNY (m. ADAM SPRING), THOMAS, who died in 1831, aged 70 years. THOMAS HENDERSON and his wife JANE MARTIN lived in ROCKINGHAM COUNTY, N. C., where their son THOMAS HENDERSON was born, who married ANN, the daughter of DR. ERASMUS FENNER SR., and brother of DR. FENNER, of N. C. This son THOMAS established "The Raleigh Star", an early newspaper. He sold out and went to WEST TENNESSEE, and it is claimed that HENDERSON COUNTY in that State was named for him. He lived not far from or in JACKSON and his home was close to or at what is known as MOUNT PINSON, a noted land - mark in that part of the country. He and his wife had: RICHARD HENDERSON a West Pointer, killed in Florida in the Seminole War; CALVIN (no issue); WILLIAM F. HENDERSON (m. MARY McCORRY, of JACKSON, TENN.); THOMAS (a merchant in NEW ORLEANS) who became a Scourt with GEN. FORREST during the WAR BETWEEN THE STATES (he married three times) and his children were: SUSAN, THOMAS, WILLIAM and SAMUEL HENDERSON (died in New Orleans); another son of THOMAS HENDERSON, of JACKSON, TENNESSEE, was ALEXANDER HENDERSON, of the Mexican War, who settled near AUSTIN, TEXAS, and died at SEGUIN, near by, leaving two sons NATHANIEL and ALEXANDER HENDERSON; CORRINE HENDERSON, daughter of THOMAS HENDERSON and JANE MARTIN, of JACKSON, TENNESSEE, married JUDGE HENRY McCORRY, of that place.

(8) PLEASANT HENDERSON, son of SAMUEL HENDERSON and ELIZABETH WILLIAMS, of GRANVILLE, married SARAH MARTIN (said to have been the daughter of COL. JAMES MARTIN, of SNOW CREEK, N. C., presumably a brother of ALEXANDER, the GOVERNOR. It is said that he was a revolutionary soldier, and being an officer, was a member of the NORTH CAROLINA SOCIETY of the CINCINNATI. Their list of children were: JAMES MARTIN HENDERSON (b. 1787); WILLIAM HENDERSON (b. 1789); MAURICE HENDERSON (b. 1791); TIPPO L. (b. 1793); MARK (b. 1795); PLEASANT (b. 1802); ALEXANDER (b. 1807), and ELIZABETH JANE HENDERSON (b. 1798). The compiler has no further information in regard to this PLEASANT HENDERSON and his family, save and except the likelihood that he lived and died in GRANVILLE COUNTY, and that his children, named above, were probably born there, since he was living in the "HENDERSON DISTRICT" somewhere near the present town of HENDERSON in 1790.

(9) WILLIAM HENDERSON, son of SAMUEL HENDERSON and ELIZABETH WILLIAMS, supposed to have been born March 5, 1748, known in History as GEN. WILLIAM HENDERSON, of the American Revolution, some time prior to that great conflict, moved to PACOLET, in SOUTH CAROLINA, where he engaged in the mercantile business. At least one of his brothers and maybe two located in that section at about the same time, and two of his sisters also settled there, and the widow of one of his cousins, his sister ANN also came there and married as her second husband ADAM POTTER, as has been before stated. For several years and before his marriage, GEN. HENDERSON, lived on what was called SANDY RUN with his sister and brother in law JOHN BECKHAM. One of his father's sisters, JANE HENDERSON and her husband WILLIAM TRAVILLIAN also lived in the same settlement, so that the HENDERSONS, TRAVILLIANS, BECKHAMS, NOTTS and others made up a pretty fair community of kin folks along the PACOLET and around GRINDAL SHOALS. When he came there WILLIAM HENDERSON had secured quite a large grant of land, adjoining the HAYNIES and SIMS families, which, after his marriage to LETITIA DAVIS, the widow of JARED NELSON, in 1782, he sold to his brother JOHN HENDERSON. With his wife he moved over on the SANTEE RIVER, where he resided until his death, January 29th, 1788, according to the notice thereof which appeared in the "STATE GAZETTE" of South Carolina, on February 11th, following, which says that he "died on his plantation" on the Santee. He made JOHN HENDERSON, his brother, THOMAS SUMPTER, DOUGLAS STARK and PHILLIP PEIRSON, his executors. He bequeathed his brother JOHN a thousand acres of his land, perhaps in CAMDEN, where he lived, and to his daughter ELIZA MORIAH also a tract of land in CAMDEN DISTRICT. She is described as "his only child", (Dr. Archibald Henderson Vol. 1 Southern Historical Research Magazine, p. 232, etc.). Incidentally Dr. Henderson, in his very able article, states that his mother's name was MARY, instead of ELIZABETH WILLIAMS, otherwise in this account I am following his version. According to LUCY HENDERSON HORTON, who is a descendant of SAMUEL HENDERSON, the son of Gen. William's older brother, NATHANIEL, there were other children besides the daughter ELIZA MORIAH HENDERSON, including BETSY TAYLOR, ETHELRED HENDERSON and JOHN HENDERSON "who lived near DANDRIDGE, TENNESSEE". She says that JOHN HENDERSON, of DANDRIDGE, was the father of JAMES HENDERSON, who was in turn the father of JOHN B. HENDERSON, U. S. Senator from MISSOURI, who was born in PITTSYLVANIA COUNTY, Virginia. It is not improbable that this account may be correct, except that the JOHN HENDERSON, whom she says was the son of GEN. WILLIAM HENDERSON, of SOUTH CAROLINA, was in fact the son of ALEXANDER HENDERSON, who died in BOURBON COUNTY, Kentucky, heretofore mentioned, and the grandson of SAMUEL HENDERSON, of "Middle River", who was, in fact a first cousin of GEN. WILLIAM HENDERSON, of South Carolina. Mrs. Horton, assuming that she made this mistake, nevertheless, by quoting a statement from SEN. JOHN B. HENDERSON in regard to his father's family pieces out the names of the children of this JOHN HENDERSON, of DANDRIDGE, which, adding the information we already had, appears to have had children: JAMES HENDERSON (father of SEN. HENDERSON, of Missouri), THOMAS J. HENDERSON, SAMUEL HENDERSON, JOHN HENDERSON (m. DORCAS McSPADDEN), ANDREW L. HENDERSON (m. MARGARET McSPADDEN, ANNE HENDERSON, FANNY HENDERSON, (m. a LEWIS, and her descendants lived in MARIETTA, GEORGIA), and perhaps one or two other sisters. Thus we learn that SEN. JOHN B. HENDERSON was a nephew of JOHN and ANDREW HENDERSON, of MONROE COUNTY, TENNESSEE, on whose lands TELLICO (afterwards called MADISONVILLE) was built. To this list of the children of JOHN HENDERSON, of DANDRIDGE, might also be added the name of ETHELRED HENDERSON, the ancestor of WILLIAM ALBERT HENDERSON, of GRAINGER COUNTY, TENNESSEE. ELIZA MORIAH HENDERSON, the only child and daughter of GEN. WILLIAM HENDERSON, of SOUTH CAROLINA, married SIMON TAYLOR, a member of one of the really old and prominent families of COLUMBIA, SOUTH CAROLINA, who was a nephew of the original COL. THOMAS TAYLOR, of COLUMBIA and RICHLAND COUNTY.

(10) NATHANIEL HENDERSON, perhaps the oldest son of SAMUEL HENDERSON and his wife ELIZABETH WILLIAMS, said to have been born in HANOVER COUNTY, Virginia, in 1736, has an interesting lot of descendants. He appears to have been twice married. The writer hopes to be able to adequately and accurately portray them in this brief space. He first married the widow of CAPT. SUGAR JONES. She was SARAH FRANKLIN and was a relative of HON. JESSE FRANKLIN, who was Governor and who married a sister of COL. BENJAMIN CLEVELAND, of King's Mountain fame, long afterwards. SUGAR JONES was an intrepid Indian campaigner and the oldest son, I think, of EDWARD JONES, friend and contemporary of COL. WILLIAM EATON, of GRANVILLE, heretofore mentioned in these notes (both of them) and in the record of the first court of GRANVILLE COUNTY. By Mrs. JONES, NATHANIEL HENDERSON had one son, so the story goes, named NATHANIEL HENDERSON. (10) NATHANIEL married second a widow by the name of MORGAN, related in some way to the HART FAMILY, some of whom were connected with "The Transylvania Company" and COL. RICHARD HENDERSON. By this second marriage there were two children, SAMUEL HENDERSON (m. LUCY RICKMAN, in GREENE COUNTY, TENN., Feb. 2, 1785), and ELIZABETH HENDERSON who married a man named YOUNG. SAMUEL, the son, moved to HAWKINS COUNTY, TENNESSEE, with his father, NATHANIEL, and afterwards to KNOX COUNTY, though his father accompanied his brother JUDGE RICHARD HENDERSON and was for a time, at least in BOONSBORO with him in the hey-day of TRANSYLVANIA. His children (those of the son SAMUEL) were all born in KNOX COUNTY, but after their births, he and his family moved to what is now ST. LOUIS, Missouri and lived for a time, and after that in about 1817, returned to TENNESSEE, and settled in WILLIAMSON COUNTY, where he died. The children of SAMUEL HENDERSON and LUCY RICKMAN were ANN, LEVISA, MARY, MATILDA, ELIZABETH (m. JOHN STRICKLAND), SALLY, LUCY (m. THOMAS GILLESPIE) and DR. SAMUEL HENDERSON who married RACHEL JANE HUGHES. DR. SAMUEL HENDERSON, of WILLIAMSON COUNTY, was the father of LUCY HENDERSON, who married H. H. HORTON, and to whom we are indebted for many of the details of this account of SAMUEL HENDERSON and his interesting family. NATHANIEL HENDERSON, older son of NATHANIEL HENDERSON and his wife MRS. SUGAR JONES, died in EDGEFIELD DISTRICT, S. C. in 1803, leaving a will in which he named his children: RICHARD, THOMAS, WILLIAM, MARY, MARTHA, JOHN, NATHAN and ELI HENDERSON. The NATHANIEL HENDERSONS, father & son, both served in the Revolution, according to the family accounts. ELI HENDERSON was the father of AUGUSTINE HENDERSON, who was the father of HON. CHARLES HENDERSON, Governor of ALABAMA from 1914 to 1918. His mother was MILDRED HILL and his wife LAURA MONTGOMERY. JOHN HENDERSON (son of NATHANIEL and MRS. SUGAR JONES) married NANCY STALLWORTH, (whose sister JEMIMA married MARK TRAVIS) in ABBEVILLE DISTRICT, S. C., and they had a son THOMAS STALLWORTH HENDERSON, who came to Texas in a very early day and settled at OLD WASHINGTON on the BRAZOS. A distinguished son, HON. THOMAS STALLWORTH HENDERSON (second cousin of COL. WILLIAM BARRETT TRAVIS, son of MARK TRAVIS and JEMIMAH STALLWORTH) died in CAMERON, TEXAS, some ten years ago, a leading member of the Texas Bar.

(11) RICHARD HENDERSON (son of SAMUEL HENDERSON and his wife ELIZABETH WILLIAMS) was born in HANOVER COUNTY, VIRGINIA, April 20, 1735 (WHEELER vol 1 p. 102); he died at his home in GRANVILLE COUNTY, N. C., January 30, 1785. Thus he lived for FIFTY YEARS only, but left the impress of a remarkable career on the history of his country. He was about ten years of age when his father, SAMUEL HENDERSON, removed from HANOVER COUNTY, Virginia, to GRANVILLE COUNTY, North Carolina. Somewhere I have read that when his father was SHERIFF, his young son RICHARD was one of his deputies. He studied law, when young, in the office of his cousin (who, in fact, was his double cousin) JUDGE JOHN WILLIAMS, who was much older than himself, was admitted to the bar and later was appointed by the Governor a Judge of the Superior Court, and was serving in that capacity when the trouble with the "Regulators" arose in North Carolina. His cousin, JUDGE WILLIAMS, was serving in the same capacity at the same time, and both were forced to leave Hillsboro to avoid violence with the enraged "regulators". In company with JUDGE WILLIAMS (whose step-daughter became his wife), LEONARD HENLEY BULLOCK, WILLIAM JOHNSTON, JAMES HOGG, THOMAS HART, JOHN LUTTRELL, NATHANIEL and DAVID HART, when the CHEROKEE INDIANS offered their lands for sale (WHEELER Vol. 1, p. 103) he organized a company called "THE TRANSYLVANIA COMPANY", which bought up a large tract thereof, paying a fair consideration for the same, which included "a large portion of the present States of Tennessee and Kentucky" of which the Company took possession the 20th of April, 1775. Governor MARTIN, of North Carolina about the same time, declared the purchase illegal, but JUDGE HENDERSON and his "associates" proceeded to Kentucky, guided by the intrepid DANIEL BOONE, where the "State of TRANSYLVANIA" was duly organized, and a proprietary government set in motion. JAMES HOGG (of an old HANOVER COUNTY, VIRGINIA, family) was dispatched to the seat of GOVERNMENT of the nation, as an agent to effect a settlement with the Colonial Government, but who failed in his mission. Eventually Col. Henderson and his associates were granted a block of some 200,000 acres as a compromise, and the original tract accepted as a "purchase" by the Nation, notwithstanding it had been repudiated as a "fraud" when first consumated. According to WHEELER this 200,000 acres was granted by VIRGINIA, and later TENNESSEE made HENDERSON & CO. a similar concession in the Powell's Valley country. In 1779 JUDGE HENDERSON (Sometimes COLONEL HENDERSON) opened a land office at what is now known as NASHVILLE, for the sale of these compromise lands to settlers. In GRANVILLE COUNTY, Judge Henderson lived in the "NUT BUSH SECTION" neighbor to JUDGE WILLIAMS. He married ELIZABETH KEELING, step-daughter of JUDGE WILLIAMS, a lineal descendant of COL. LEONARD KEELING of Charles City County, Virginia, after whom he named one of his sons, a distinguished Judge on the North Carolina Bench. The children of JUDGE RICHARD HENDERSON and his wife ELIZABETH KEELING are given as follows: FANNY HENDERSON (b. 1764) who married JUDGE SPRUCE McKAY, of Salisbury; RICHARD HENDERSON (b. July 1766); ARCHIBALD HENDERSON (b. August, 1768); ELIZABETH HENDERSON (born in 1770) who married an ALEXANDER, from MECKLENBURG COUNTY; LEONARD HENDERSON (b. 1772, died in August 1833) married FRANCES FARRER, and left two sons and two daughters; JOHN LAWSON HENDERSON, (b. 1778) who left no children, according to the writer's information. An interesting story is that of FANNY HENDERSON, a duaghter of JUDGE LEONARD HENDERSON and the grand-daughter of JUDGE RICHARD HENDERSON. She married a DR. WILLIAM TAYLOR and they had a daughter LUCY WHITE TAYLOR, who married JOEL ADDISON HAYES, of NASHVILLE, TENNESSEE, whose son JOEL ADDISON HAYES, JR. married MARGARET HOWELL DAVIS, the daughter of PRESIDENT JEFFERSON DAVIS, of the SOUTHERN CONFEDERACY.

GRANVILLE COUNTY REGIMENT OF MILITIA
MUSTER ROLL OCTOBER 8, 1754.

(From Vol. 22, N. C. Colonial Records, page 379.)

COLONEL WILLIAM EATON in Command.
COL. WILLIAM PERSON, Lieutenant-Colonel.
MAJ. JAMES PAYNE.

Company Commanders in this Regiment were as follows:

1. CAPT. JOHN GLOVER.
2. CAPT. GEORGE JEFFREYS.
3. CAPT. RICHARD COLEMAN.
4. CAPT. DANIEL HARRIS.
5. CAPT. JOHN SALLIS.
6. CAPT. SUGAR JONES.
7. CAPT. BENJAMIN SIMS.
8. CAPT. ANDREW HAMPTON.

In the Company of CAPT. SUGAR JONES were the following persons, among others:

GEORGE WOOTEN
DANIEL WOOTEN
ATKINS McLEMORE
JEREMIAH WOOTEN
JAMES RAINWATER
THOMAS COOPER
JAMES RAY
WILLIAM UNDERWOOD
JOHN WOOTEN
JAMES WOOTEN.

In the Company of CAPT. ANDREW HAMPTON the following names appear on the roster, among others:

JOHN CLARK
JOHN JONES
LEONARD ADCOCK
JOHN ADCOCK
VALENTINE WHITE.

Among the signers of a PETITION from the GRANVILLE COUNTY residents in 1771 (Vol. 9 N.C. Colonial Records, pp. 95-96) were the following:

GROVES HOWARD
VALENTINE WHITE
DAVID HOWARD
FRANCIS HOWARD
CHRISTOPHER HUNT
WILLIAM WORTHINGTON
CUTHBURT HUDSON
ISAAC HEAD
RICHARDSON OWEN
THOMAS OWEN
JONATHAN KNIGHT
WILLIAM ALLEN
JAMES WILLIAMSON
ISAAC WHITE
BENJAMIN HOWARD
MARTHA KNIGHT
JOSIAH STOVALL
JOHN HART
JAMES LANGSTON

LINEAGE AND CONNECTIONS OF THE HENDERSON FAMILY OF GRANVILLE COUNTY, NORTH CAROLINA.

HENRY HENDERSON, near YORK RIVER in the County of KENT (NEW KENT), in VIRGINIA, Planter, died leaving a will dated MARCH 10, 1763, which was proved November 3, 1764, in which he left "all my plantations, lands and tenements near YORK RIVER, in VIRGINIA, and all other estate in VIRGINIA or ENGLAND" to his wife SUSANNA. (Vol. 12 Va. Mag. of Hist & Biog., page 179-180.)

THOMAS HENDERSON, of NEW KENT COUNTY, VIRGINIA, who married (as his second wife) SARAH WILKINSON, March 16, 1698 (St. Peter's Parish Register p. 412) and who was the father of SAMUEL HENDERSON and the grandfather of JUDGE RICHARD HENDERSON, of GRANVILLE COUNTY, N. C., may, or MAY NOT have been the son of the above HENRY HENDERSON. The wording of the will indicates that if he had any children by his wife SUSANNA they were very young and for that reason were left wholly, with all of his considerable property to the care and sole custody of his wife. As this will is copied from "VIRGINIA GLEANINGS IN ENGLAND" and furnishes no proof that the testator was even related to THOMAS HENDERSON save and except that he was living in NEW KENT COUNTY, where THOMAS HENDERSON resided, the one point it seems to establish is that the NEW KENT COUNTY HENDERSONS were of ENGLISH and not of SCOTTISH ORIGIN, as has been claimed. The "connections" of the HENDERSONS, as hereinafter shown, being with well known ENGLISH FAMILIES (some of them of WELCH extractions) further strengthens this point. The chart which follows will give a fair idea of these connections:

THOMAS FLEMING m. JUDITH TARLETON

Ch:

JOHN FLEMING (d. 1686).
TARLETON FLEMING
CHARLES FLEMING m. SUSANNA TARLETON.
URSULA FLEMING m. CAPT. GEO. KEELING
JUDITH FLEMING m. THOMAS WILKINSON.
SUSANNA FLEMING m. JOHN TARLETON

STEPHEN TARLTON m. SUSANNA BATES

Ch:

STEPHEN TARLETON
JOHN TARLETON m. SUSANNA FLEMING
SUSANNA TARLETON m. CHARLES FLEMING
JUDITH TARLETON m. JOHN WOODSON
CHARLES TARLETON
ELIZABETH TARLETON m. STEPHEN HUGHES

(JUDITH TARLETON who married THOMAS FLEMING was a sister of STEPHEN TARLETON who married MISS BATES).

CHARLES FLEMING m. SUSANNA TARLETON

Ch:

JOHN FLEMING m. MARY BOLLING. (1720).
TARLETON FLEMING m. HANNAH BATES
JUDITH FLEMING m.(1712) THOMAS RANDOLPH
SUSANNA FLEMING m. (1) JOHN BATES, and
(2) JOHN WOODSON.
URSULA FLEMING m. TARLETON WOODSON
ELIZABETH FLEMING m. SAMUEL JORDAN (1703)

CAPT. GEORGE KEELING m. URSULA FLEMING

Ch:

GEORGE KEELING
RICHARD KEELING
MARY KEELING m. JOHN WILLIAMS
URSULA KEELING m. THOMAS HENDERSON
(He m (2) SARAH WILKINSON)
SARAH WILKINSON was the daughter of THOMAS WILKINSON and JUDITH FLEMING.

THOMAS FLEMING and STEPHEN TARLETON were both of CAVALIER STOCK and came to VIRGINIA in the days of SIR GEORGE YEARDLEY.

The origin and identity of JOHN WILLIAMS who married MARY KEELING will be discussed under the "WILLIAMS FAMILY OF GRANVILLE COUNTY". The genealogists who have heretofore attempted to identify JOHN WILLIAMS claim that he was a native of WALES and came to VIRGINIA only a few years prior to 1700, which is a mistake. His father before him, with perhaps several brothers, and possibly his GRANDFATHER was in YORK COUNTY, VIRGINIA, early in the Seventeenth century.

THOMAS HENDERSON and THOMAS RANDOLPH, the latter of a prominent ENGLISH FAMILY, married first cousins. ISHAM RANDOLPH, his brother, had a daughter MARY who married CHARLES LEWIS of "Buckeye Land" in ALBEMARLE, and BENNETT HENDERSON, grandson of THOMAS HENDERSON, married their daughter ELIZABETH LEWIS.

CAPT. GEORGE KEELING, who married URSULA FLEMING was, in my opinion, the son of LEONARD KEELING (brother of ADAM) and the grandson of THOMAS KEELING (Ensign) who patented 100 acres in the County of ELIZABETH CITY, adjoining the land of HENRY SOUTHWELL (Southall) and WILLIAM MORGAN and the BACK RIVER, November 18, 1635. ADAM KEELING lived in NEW POQUOSON section of YORK COUNTY and married a daughter of JOHN MARTIN. LEONARD KEELING lived at JAMESTOWN at the "Governor's House" at one time, and was a prominent and influential member of the VIRGINIA COLONY (5 Va. Mag. of Hist. & Biog. p. 246.). The ADAM KEELING set populated LOWER NORFOLK for many generations, among them being COL. THOMAS KEELING, who owned land next to REV. WILLIAM WILKINSON, close kinsman of the NEW KENT WILKINSONS. The wife of REV. WILLIAM WILKINSON was NAOMY. (vol. 4 Va. Mag. of Hist. & BIOG. p. 201.). WILLIAM WILKINSON (brother of THOMAS) went to N. C. (See p. 185, this Book.

THOMAS HENDERSON OF NEW KENT

Married (1) URSULA KEELING
Married (2) SARAH WILKINSON

(1) JOHN HENDERSON
m. MISS BENNETT
Ch:

JOHN HENDERSON
m. FRANCES MOORE
BENNETT HENDERSON
m. ELIZABETH LEWIS
WILLIAM HENDERSON
m. REBECCA HUDSON
ELIZABETH HENDERSON
m. DAVID CRAWFORD
SUSAN HENDERSON
m. JOHN CLARK
MARY HENDERSON
m.___BULLOCK
HANNAH HENDERSON
m. ___BULLOCK
FRANCES HENDERSON
m. JOHN THOMAS

BENNETT HENDERSON who
m. ELIZABETH LEWIS
Had Ch.

JOHN HENDERSON m. HUDSON
WILLIAM HENDERSON
SARAH HENDERSON m JOHN KERR
JAMES PINCKNEY HENDERSON
CHARLES HENDERSON
ISHAM HENDERSON
BENNETT HENDERSON
HILLSBORO HENDERSON
ELIZA HENDERSON m. BULLOCK
FRANCES HENDERSON
LUCY HENDERSON m. JOHN WOOD
NANCY HENDERSON

(10) URSULA HENDERSON
m. DANIEL WILLIAMS
They had:

HENRY WILLIAMS
GEN'L JAMES WILLIAMS
JOHN WILLIAMS
JOSEPH WILLIAMS
DANIEL WILLIAMS m. ANN HENDERSON (cousin).

After the death of DANIEL WILLIAMS next above, his wife ANN moved to PACOLET in S. C. where she married as her second husband one ADAM POTTER

(7) RICHARD HENDERSON
m. POLLY WASHER
of
Hanover County, Va.
(d. 1749).

(3) JAMES HENDERSON
m. JOANE KING 1726.
(No record)

(2) THOMAS HENDERSON (d1768)
m. GRISSEL and had:

URSULA HENDERSON
GRISSET HENDERSON (son).

(6) EDWARD HENDERSON SR. of
SPOTTSYLVANIA CO. VA.
Had son:

EDWARD HENDERSON JR.

(9) SUSANNAH HENDERSON
Was still a minor in 1722. By LAST MARRIAGE

(11) JANE HENDERSON
m. THOMAS TRAVILLIAN
Of HANOVER COUNTY
and moved to PACOLET in S. C.

(8) SARAH HENDERSON
m. JOHN WILLIAMS in 1711.
Had:

JUDGE JOHN WILLIAMS
m. AGNES (BULLOCK) KEELING.
Had:

ELIZABETH KEELING
m. JUDGE RICHARD HENDERSON, and
AGATHA WILLIAMS
m. COL. ROBERT BURTON

AGNES BULLOCK was the daughter of RICHARD BULLOCK and wife CATHERINE; who died in GRANVILLE COUNTY in 1766.

(5) WILLIAM HENDERSON
m. SUSANNAH LOGAN
Ch:

SAMUEL HENDERSON m. JANE
JAMES HENDERSON
m. VILOET LAWSON

SAMUEL HENDERSON (wife JANE)
Had Ch.

REBECCA HENDERSON
SARAH HENDERSON
FLORENCE HENDERSON
DAVID HENDERSON
ANDREW HENDERSON
ALEXANDER HENDERSON (Ky & Tenn)
JAMES HENDERSON
WILLIAM HENDERSON
SAMUEL HENDERSON

ALEXANDER HENDERSON (To KY.)
(d. 1796)
and had

REV. ROBERT HENDERSON (TENN.)
SAMUEL HENDERSON
JAMES HENDERSON (TENN.)
JOSEPH HENDERSON
ALEXANDER HENDERSON
DAVID HENDERSON m. JANE CARSON
DANIEL HENDERSON (TENN).
GEORGE HENDERSON
JOHN HENDERSON (Ancestor of Madisonville, Tenn. Family.
FLORENCE HENDERSON.

JAMES HENDERSON m. VIOLET LAWSON and had:

JOHN HENDERSON
JAMES HENDERSON m. MARG. DICKSON
WILLIAM HENDERSON
LAWSON HENDERSON m. ELIZABETH CARRUTH
LOGAN HENDERSON
KATHERINE HENDERSON m. LOGAN.
MARY HENDERSON
MARTHA HENDERSON

LAWSON HENDERSON and ELIZABETH CARRUTH were parents of

HON. JAMES PINCKNEY HENDERSON
(First Governor of Texas).

(4) SAMUEL HENDERSON, OF GRANVILLE COUNTY, NORTH CAROLINA.
For His Children see p. 221 and also pages 227 to 230 inclusive

NOTE: In the year 1654, SKIMINO CREEK, which runs into the YORK RIVER not far from the present WILLIAMSBURG, VIRGINIA, was made the dividing line between YORK COUNTY and NEW KENT. If a person lived on the East side of SKIMINO he was in YORK COUNTY, but if on the West side he was in NEW KENT. In 1703 there were only 136 families living on the WEST SIDE and most of those were seated along the YORK RIVER and the SKIMINO, on account of the INDIAN situation, although BACON'S REBELLION had helped the situation. So it happens that the HENDERSONS, WILLIAMS, KEELINGS and other families were simply on the "other side of the creek" from YORK, though they were FROM YORK COUNTY.

JOHN WILLIAMS, the father of ELIZABETH WILLIAMS, who married SAMUEL HENDERSON in HANOVER COUNTY, Virginia, according to family tradition and in accord with accounts that have been published by genealogists, was not a native of WALES, born in 1679, as has been stated, but a native of YORK COUNTY, VIRGINIA, where the WILLIAMS FAMILY settled during the first half of the Seventeenth Century. He may have been born in 1679, though this would be in the face of the records which show that he was living on his plantation with his wife and family as late, or as early, as 1685-6. He was also the ancestor of JUDGE JOHN WILLIAMS of GRANVILLE COUNTY, North Carolina. These statements are based on the actual records of YORK COUNTY, VIRGINIA, and as the compiler writes these lines he has before him a photostatic copy complete of VOLUME VIII, of the YORK COUNTY RECORDS, from which the facts are drawn. This photostat is, of course, a complete and exact copy of every word that appears on the record and it has been checked carefully, not in a hot, uncomfortable vault, or a dusty room, but in the quiet, cool precincts of a home library, where the examination could be made leisurely and without hindrance or interference, a boon that in the days of LYON G. TYLER and R. A. BROCK could not be enjoyed. Modern machinery and contrivance has been employed to streamline this investigation and having also the advantage of the vast store of information such men gathered in their useful lives, gives the modern investigator and advantage they did not have and it is no detraction of them to say, with the limited facilities at their command, that they made a few mistakes and on rare occasions arrived at conclusions which by later discoveries turned out to be mistakes.

THE WILLIAMS FAMILY, doubtless of WELCH descent, settled on QUEEN'S CREEK in YORK COUNTY, Virginia, sometime prior to the year 1645. The rough sketch presented below will convey an idea of where they lived at that time.

QUEEN'S CREEK in YORK COUNTY, as this sketch indicates, extends inland from YORK RIVER in a Southerly direction from its mouth. Comparing the crude scale representing a distance of FIVE MILES it may be seen that SKIMMINO CREEK is about, and in some places less than that distance West of it. The latter constituted the line between NEW KENT and YORK COUNTIES. Here are the names of some of the families who lived on QUEEN'S CREEK and East of SKIMMINO in YORK COUNTY:

ABBOTT	COBBS	HARRISON	WALKER
ADAMS	COMINGS	HOWLE (HOWELL)	WATKINS
ADCOCK	COLLIER	KEELING	WEST
BARRON	COPELAND	LEWIS	WHEELER
BATES	CROSHAW	PINKETHMAN	WHITE
BELL	CUNNINGHAM	REYNOLDS	WILDE
BENNETT	DANIEL	SHIELDS	WILLIAMS
BURTON	DAVIS	SMITH	WILLIAMSON
BURWELL	DOSWELL	TAYLOR	WILLIS
CHESLEY	EATON	TAYLOR	UNDERWOOD
CLARKE	GRAVES	WADE	UTIE

All of the families named settled in YORK COUNTY during the first half of the 17th century. One generation after another toddled along. They intermarried and formed ties and alliances that have never been abandoned or dissolved. Show me the name on any record of any one of these families and I'll soon be able to prove to you they descend from and are related to some of the other families listed on this "QUEEN'S CREEK CLUB."

THE FIRST JOHN WILLIAMS. The compiler must, in all fairness, acknowledge his indebtedness to the inimitable BEVERLY FLEET, of Richmond, descendant of the intrepid HENRY, who has been called the "Virginia Daniel Boone" of the days of Lord Baltimore and Col. Claiborne, for the record of the first JOHN WILLIAMS, who came to YORK COUNTY and settled on QUEEN'S CREEK, at least as early as 1644-5. (See FLEET'S COLONIAL ABSTRACTS, Vol. 24 p. 90, for the records of BOOK 2, of York County, pages 138-139). The record follows:

> Nov. 5, 1639. SIR JOHN HARVEY, KNT., GOVERNOR, ETC., to SAMUEL WATKINS, deed to 250 acres in CHARLES RIVER (as YORK COUNTY was then designated), in the forest adjoining the land of JOHN UTYE extending from the head of KING'S CREEK, Westerly to the mayden swamp, and adjoining the lands formerly granted to the said SAMUEL WATKINS by patent due by assignment from JOSEPH CROSHAW, for transporting five persons. Signed, JOHN HARVEY.

One of the "five persons" transported by JOSEPH CROSHAW, referred to above was a certain JOHN DANIEL, an ancestor of that JOHN DANIEL who married ANNE, daughter of a later JOHN WILLIAMS, and the same JOHN DANIEL who left a will in GRANVILLE COUNTY, NORTH CAROLINA in 1763. SAMUEL WATKINS was the ancestor of THOMAS WATKINS, of SWIFT CREEK, whose daughter ELIZABETH married JAMES DANIEL, another member of the same family. UNITY, the daughter of JOSEPH CROSHAW, married LIEUT. COL. JOHN WEST, son of GOVERNOR and CAPT. JOHN WEST. But to continue with the record:

> June 10, 1644. SAMUEL WATKINS, of QUEEN'S CREEK, assigns the above 250 acres to JOHN BELL; part of which was due to JOHN BELL by deed of gift, and now the full patent is sold to him. Signed SAMUEL WATKINS. The witnesses to this assignment were GEORGE CLARKE and WILLIAM ROBERTS.

Then follows the following item:

> Oct. 1, 1645. JOHN BELL, of QUEEN'S CREEK, Planter, assigns to JOHN WILLIAMS the above 250 acres lying in HAMPTON PARISH, etc. This is signed by JOHN BELL.

Then follows a further and more particular description of the land which was thus sold to JOHN WILLIAMS in October, 1645, which description is dated April 20, 1642, saying it adjoined BRIERY SWAMP, the land of WILLIAM TAYLOR, the land of NICHOLAS COMINGS, the land of THOMAS GIBSON and another dividend belonging to SAMUEL WATKINS.

Still another interesting deed dated JUNE 10, 1641, reads as follows: "JOHN BELL, of QUEEN'S CREEK, Planter sells SAMUEL WATKINS his plantation and house in QUEEN'S CREEK, formerly purchased from WILLIAM REYNOLDS". GEORGE CLARK and WILLIAM W. ROBERTS, witnesses. From which it appears that one of the early comers to this QUEEN'S CREEK settlement and a possible and probable predecessor in title to the JOHN WILLIAMS land was this WILLIAM REYNOLDS. The part he plays and the role he takes in these family genealogies will be discussed later.

All of these families are interlocking and were then or later related to each other.

The name of the first JOHN WILLIAMS' wife we do not know. They had several children who settled with them on QUEEN'S CREEK, including JOHN, EDWARD, OBEDIAH, RICHARD and WILLIAM WILLIAMS. The SON JOHN was known as JOHN WILLIAMS, SR. He settled on the "EASTERN SHORE" of VIRGINIA, in ACCOMAC COUNTY, as did also JOHN DANIEL, a son of the immigrant, ROGER DANIEL. JOHN WILLIAMS (the son), SR. apparently had the following children:

(1) JOHN WILLIAMS (m. MARY KEELING).
(2) NATHANIEL WILLIAMS (In Accomac County in 1704).
(3) WILLIAM WILLIAMS (Minister of ST. PETER'S).
(4) RANDALL WILLIAMS
(5) LEWIS WILLIAMS (Of NEW KENT COUNTY).
(6) DANIEL WILLIAMS.
(7) SARAH WILLIAMS married WILLIAM DANIEL (Accomac County).
(8) MARY WILLIAMS married JOHN DANIEL

JOHN WILLIAMS, SR. (Son of the first JOHN WILLIAMS) eventually returned to YORK & NEW KENT COUNTIES. He died sometime after 1688, when he was named as an executor of the will of his son in law WILLIAM DANIEL in ACCOMAC. His widow settled on lands belonging to him along the PAMUNKY between NEW KENT and KING WILLIAM. She is known on the records thereafter as the "Widow Williams". Her son LEWIS WILLIAMS, or some of his descendants established what was known as the WILLIAMS FERRY, where GENERAL WASHINGTON crossed to visit with the CHAMBERLAINS and where he met the comely young widow MARTHA CUSTIS, long afterwards, whom he married.

As for (6) DANIEL WILLIAMS, he was a man of some importance and in accordance with a law passed requiring notice of trips being taken abroad we find this note in Vol. VIII of the YORK COUNTY (Va.) RECORDS:

> "At a Court held for YORK COUNTY, February 24, 1686, DANIEL WILLIAMS, JOSIAS STACEY and JOHN POINDEXTER did lett and publish their INTENTIONS of going for OLD ENGLAND, GOD WILLING."

(3) WILLIAM WILLIAMS was a Minister of ST. PETER'S PARISH and his name as such appears on the Church Register. He was also a school master and conducted a school in DENBEIGH PARISH

(1) JOHN WILLIAMS (who married MARY KEELING) probably died on his plantation on QUEEN'S CREEK, in YORK COUNTY, Virginia, sometime during the first decade of the Eighteenth century, as some of his children were born AFTER 1700, though all of them were born much earlier than the accounts given by the genealogists. One JOHN WILLIAMS, believed to have been a son of EDWARD WILLIAMS and a cousin of (1) JOHN, died in YORK COUNTY in 1697-8, without leaving a will and probably without children, though he had several brothers.

This JOHN WILLIAMS was a man of some prominence in the County, and while the records examined do not give his life history, they do give enough to show that he was one of those men whose name not infrequently appeared on the court and other records, and it is surprising how much such entries, scarce though they were, reveal of the man.

He was sued on one occasion by JOHN CONSTANT and after a hearing of the case, judgment was rendered against him for the payment of a judgment of four pounds Sterling, "which said JOHN WILLIAMS is ordered to pay". This was on November 24, 1688.

At a meeting of the YORK COUNTY COURT in February of the same year there was a suit pending between JOHN WILLIAMS, plaintiff, and WILLIAM CLOPTON, defendant, which was passed over to the next meeting of the court. This WILLIAM CLOPTON was an important personage, who owned considerable property, both in YORK and NEW KENT COUNTY, and the presence of litigation in the courts initiated against him by JOHN WILLIAMS indicates they were probably of about equal standing in the Colony at that period.

But one of the most interesting items on the YORK RECORDS grew out of a suit for assault and battery brought by JOHN WILLIAMS in 1688 against one WILLIAM WADE, in which WILLIAMS alleged that WADE had come to his plantation on QUEEN'S CREEK in York County, in his absence from home, and abused his wife. Unfortunately the record in this suit fails to mention the name of JOHN WILLIAMS' wife, bu I have no sort of doubt but what it was MARY. The record of the trial appears on page 104 of Vol 8 of the YORK COUNTY RECORDS. On March 26th a jury was empanelled by the Sheriff and returned and sworn, consisting of:

JOHN MILES	JOHN BATTEN	THOMAS BUCK
JOHN LANDERS	JOSEPH HIGTH	ROBERT ROBERTS
HUMPHREY MOODY	JOHN EATON	WILLIAM CLOPTON
HENRY LEE	ISAAC GODDING	GEORGE GLASSCOCK,

and, as the record says, "whoo upon their oaths returned their verdict that they find for the plaintiff 1000 pounds of tobacco and cask which said verdict is confirmed and ordered that the said WADE pay to the said WILLIAMS, the aforesaid summe of 1000 lbs of tobacco and cask and costs of suit,"etc.

In the trial of this lawsuit two witnesses appeared for JOHN WILLIAMS and gave their version of the unseemly conduct of WILLIAM WADE towards MRS. WILLIAMS. Wade had some horses in the tobacco house of JOHN WILLIAMS and when he appeared on the plantation Mrs. Williams had told him "Thee should turn them out!", whereupon, enraged he abused the lady in the absence of her husband, who had brought the suit. MARY BELL, aged about 19 years (one of the descendants, of course, of JOHN BELL who had sold the land on QUEEN'S CREEK to John Williams' father, more than thirty-five years previously) swore to the details on which the jury rendered its verdict, and declared that WADE had struck Mrs. Williams with a "tobacco sticke", etc. The other witness, ANN ABBOTT (a descendant of CHRISTOPHER ABBOTT, of QUEEN'S CREEK, whose deed Oct. 11, 1640, had been witnessed by WILLIAM WILLIAMS and JOHN BENNETT - Va. Col. Abs. 24)testified to still greater abuses by WADE of MRS. WILLIAMS, saying he "knocked her down and kicked her out of the house." In these deposition and in the trial of the case of WILLIAMS v. WADE no mention is made of children, and the conclusion seems reasonable that, when this cause was tried, JOHN WILLIAMS and his wife, had not been long married. This was in the fall of 1688. Between that date and the date of JOHN'S death, some twenty years later, their children were born.

They had the following children:

(10)	JOHN WILLIAMS	(b. about 1690)
(11)	SARAH WILLIAMS	(b. about 1692)
(12)	NATHANIEL WILLIAMS	(b. about 1695)
(13)	DANIEL WILLIAMS	(b. about 1697)
(14)	JOSEPH WILLIAMS	(b. about 1699)
(15)	ANNE WILLIAMS	(b. about 1702)
(16)	MARY WILLIAMS	(b. about 1703)
(17)	ELIZABETH WILLIAMS	(b. about 1705)

This is the traditional list of their children as it has appear in different accounts of the family. Of each of the above named children there are records available on which we have drawn, but since JOHN WILLIAMS (wife MARY KEELING) left no will listing the names of his children the traditional list must be accepted as approximately correct. That there were other children is hardly possible, though it could be; but if so, they have not been identified as belonging on the list. I have often been tempted to believe that there was another son named ZADOCK WILLIAMS (killed in Kentucky by the Indians) whose parentage I could not find, but have concluded he did not belong, at least in the generation with this set.

In attempting to set down inteligently an account of the above eight children of JOHN WILLIAMS and his wife MARY KEELING this compiler finds it necessary to dig up facts about JUDGE JOHN WILLIAMS, of GRANVILLE COUNTY and his family, and the BURTONS, his descendants. Under MARY WILLIAMS facts about the GRAVES FAMILY, of Granville County; under ANNE WILLIAMS data relating to the DANIEL FAMILY, the HARRISON FAMILY, of GRANVILLE COUNTY and something about the HAMPTON FAMILY. (16) SARAH WILLIAMS, I believe, I have not facts about, but ELIZABETH, her sister, was the one who married SAMUEL HENDERSON, of HANOVER COUNTY, VA., who has already been covered herein.

(10) JOHN WILLIAMS (son of JOHN WILLIAMS and his wife MARY KEELING) who was probably the oldest son and child, according to the St. Peter's Parish Register (p. 419) was married in December, 1711, to SARAH HENDERSON, the daughter of THOMAS HENDERSON and his first wife URSULA KEELING. (See Chart p. 231). They were the parents of JUDGE JOHN WILLIAMS, born in NEW KENT or HANOVER COUNTY, Virginia, perhaps about 1715, who moved to GRANVILLE COUNTY, North Carolina, where he died in 1799. JOHN WILLIAMS (father of JUDGE JOHN WILLIAMS) died in HANOVER COUNTY, VIRGINIA, in 1735, intestate, and JOHN TYLER (husband of FRANCES GRAVES) and THOMAS PROSSER gave bond for administration on his estate. JOHN TYLER belonged to an old YORK COUNTY family, and one of his nephews, WILLIAM TYLER, had married ELIZABETH KEELING, a relative of both JOHN WILLIAMS and his wife. There being no will, of course, no children are mentioned, and no record this compiler has ever found, mentions children other than

JUDGE JOHN WILLIAMS, of GRANVILLE COUNTY, North Carolina. On page 163 Mr. WHEELER, the Historian says of him: "JOHN WILLIAMS was a native of HANOVER COUNTY, Virginia. In April, 1770, for some real or imaginary cause, while attending court at HILLSBORO (N. C.) he was seized by the Regulators and beaten by them. He was one of the first judges under the State Constitution in 1777, with SAMUEL SPENCER and SAMUEL ASHE. He was a member of the Continental Congress in 1778. His early education was defective, as he was raised to the trade of a house carpenter. But he was eminently distinguished for his sound judgment and plain common sense. He died in October, 1799". JUDGE RICHARD HENDERSON and JUDGE JOHN WILLIAMS were not only first cousins, but double cousins, as the mother of JUDGE WILLIAMS was the aunt of JUDGE HENDERSON, and SAMUEL HENDERSON (father of the JUDGE) was the uncle of JUDGE WILLIAMS and the brother of his mother. JUDGE WILLIAMS, however, was several years the senior of his cousin RICHARD HENDERSON, who studied law in his office, when a young man, when, he, himself, had been practicing law for some years; and also, the wife of JUDGE RICHARD HENDERSON was the step daughter of JUDGE WILLIAMS, she being ELIZABETH KEELING, the daughter of AGNES BULLOCK and her first husband KEELING, also a relative of both the HENDERSONS & the WILLIAMS family.

AGNES BULLOCK, who first married GEORGE KEELING, a grandson perhaps of CAPT. GEORGE KEELING, of NEW KENT COUNTY, and second, JUDGE JOHN WILLIAMS, was a sister of LEONARD HENLEY BULLOCK and a daughter of RICHARD BULLOCK, the latter having died leaving a will in GRANVILLE COUNTY, N. C. in 1766, his children being SARAH (m. SIMS), AGNES, WILLIAM (m. TAYLOR), ZACHARIAH, NATHANIEL, JOHN and LEONARD HENLEY BULLOCK. The BULLOCKS, like the HENDERSONS and WILLIAMS came to GRANVILLE COUNTY (N. C.) from HANOVER and NEW KENT COUNTIES. The name BULLOCK appears very frequently on the St. Peter's Parish Register. According to MR. WHEELER, JUDGE WILLIAMS and his wife AGNES had only one child born to them, whose name was AGATHA (named for AGATHA KEELING, daughter of GEORGE KEELING JR.), who married COL. ROBERT BURTON, an account of whose family will follow the WILLIAMS FAMILY HISTORY. The town of WILLIAMSBORO, seven miles West of the town of HENDERSON, N. C., was the home of JUDGE JOHN WILLIAMS, (then in GRANVILLE COUNTY, but now in VANCE). About 1740 the WILLIAMS and HENDERSON and other families began to settle there and the place was called NUTBUSH. On the old county records there was a NUTBUSH DISTRICT which surrounded it. After the death of JUDGE WILLIAMS in 1799, his son in law, COL. ROBERT BURTON named the place WILLIAMSBORO, in his memory. Col. Burton fell heir to the Williams property there. The finest race track in the State of North Carolina was located in this community, and many of the State's most prominent leaders resided there.

---

(11) SARAH WILLIAMS (born about 1784) was one of the older children of JOHN WILLIAMS and his wife MARY KEELING. Her name is on the list of children commonly accepted by the family as correct, but this compiler has found no recognizable record as to what became of her.

---

(12) NATHANIEL WILLIAMS was born about 1695, probably in YORK COUNTY, VIRGINIA, or in the lower part of New Kent County on the West side of SKIMMINO CREEK. In 1733 NATHANIEL WILLIAMS, JOHN WILLIAMS and JOHN WINGFIELD witnessed a deed in HANOVER COUNTY, Virginia, from GEORGE MATLOCK, SR. to GEORGE MATLOCK, JR., and also a deed from JOHN MATLOCK to his daughter MARY, then the wife of BENJAMIN JOHNSON. Evidently NATHANIEL at that date (1733) was living in HANOVER COUNTY. The family genealogists ascribe to NATHANIEL WILLIAMS five children:

(20) ROBERT WILLIAMS
(21) ELIZABETH WILLIAMS
(22) JOHN WILLIAMS
(23) NATHANIEL WILLIAMS
(24) JOSEPH WILLIAMS

(20) ROBERT WILLIAMS, son of (12) NATHANIEL WILLIAMS, was known in PITTSYLVANIA COUNTY, VIRGINIA, where he spent the latter part of his life, as COL. ROBERT WILLIAMS, and was a COLONEL in the REVOLUTION from PITTSYLVANIA. The following account is taken from Maude Carter Clements' History of PITTSYLVANIA COUNTY, Virginia: "ROBERT WILLIAMS and his brother JOSEPH WILLIAMS settled in NORTH CAROLINA prior to the Revolution, and married sisters, SARAH and REBECCA LANIER, the daughters of THOMAS LANIER, an early Justice of LUNENBURG COUNTY (Va.), who later moved to NORTH CAROLINA. SARAH LANIER and ROBERT WILLIAMS were married OCTOBER 10, 1774 in GRANVILLE COUNTY, N. C., and moved to PITTSYLVANIA COUNTY to live, settling near SANDY CREEK, of BANNISTER RIVER. Here he practiced his profession of law and served as Commonwealth Attorney for both PITTSYLVANIA and HENRY COUNTIES. He died in 1790." He left no will, but in 1799, some nine years after his death there was a division of his estate, in which the children, then living were mentioned. This list of children is not in agreement with the list that appears on the chart of the family gotten up by some genealogist, which is evidently wrong, since it says that a daughter POLLY married HON. MATTHEW CLAY, M. C. This POLLY was the daughter of COL. JOSEPH WILLIAMS, instead of COL. ROBERT.

The children of (20) COL. ROBERT WILLIAMS, as gathered from the division of his estate in 1799 were:

(a) COL. JOHN WILLIAMS, whose wife was ELIZABETH and to whom was allotted 617 acres of land, including the Manor plantation on SANDY CREEK.

(b) NATHANIEL W. WILLIAMS, who received 1,540 acres, beginning on the line of one JOHN WHITE and taking in the mill.

(c) SARAH WILLIAMS, who was the wife of MICAJAH WATKINS (harking back to SAMUEL WATKINS of QUEEN'S CREEK in YORK COUNTY, Virginia), who received two tracts of land, one of 240 acres and another of 1,156 acres. (The genealogical account says she married JAMES CHALMERS, of Halifax County, Virginia). She could have been twice married, but MICAJAH WATKINS, her husband, was living in 1799 when the estate of Col. Robert Williams was divided.

(d) PATSY WILLIAMS, 279 acres, the balance of the land of the Manor Plantation, 147 acres the mill tract and 168 acres on Cascade Creek. PATSY WILLIAMS married JOHN HENRY, of Woodlawn, who was a descendant of the HENRY FAMILY, of ACCOMAC COUNTY, Virginia, where NATHANIEL WILLIAMS was listed on the Quit Rent Rolls in 1704, he being a Great Uncle of Col. Robert Williams.

(e) FANNIE WILLIAMS, who received three tracts of land, one of 200 acres, one of 296 acres and one of 790 acres.

From the CLEMENTS HISTORY of PITTSYLVANIA, p. 153, the following note relating to the identity of JOHN HENRY, who married PATSY WILLIAMS is taken:

> "Another HENRY FAMILY of PITTSYLVANIA COUNTY, was that of JAMES HENRY, of ACCOMAC COUNTY, who owned large bodies of land there. The list of tithables for 1777 showed that he paid taxes on 19,000 acres of land at that time. JAMES HENRY is said to have been a grandson of ALEXANDER and JEAN ROBERTSON HENRY, grandparents of PATRICK HENRY; he married SARAH SCARBOROUGH and had sons JOHN, CHARLES and probably others. JOHN HENRY was settled on the PITTSYLVANIA lands which lay in the Eastern part of the county, and he called his home "WOODLAWN". The house is standing today and the interior woodwork is elaborately carved. The garden laid off in terraces, is called a "falling garden".

HUGH HENRY, who married MARY DONELSON, sister of COL. JOHN DONELSON, was also from this ACCOMAC COUNTY family and a brother of JAMES HENRY, the father of JOHN of WOODLAWN, who married PATSY, the daughter of COL. ROBERT WILLIAMS.

---

(21) ELIZABETH WILLIAMS. The compiler has been unable to find any identifying record of this daughter of NATHANIEL WILLIAMS. An ELIZABETH WILLIAMS is listed by the family genealogist as a daughter of COL. ROBERT WILLIAMS, and an account of her family, but the compiler believes that she was ELIZABETH, a cousin, daughter of HENRY WILLIAMS and grand-daughter of DANIEL, who lived in CASWELL COUNTY (See p. 196).

---

(22) JOHN WILLIAMS (son of (12) NATHANIEL WILLIAMS) was known as COL. JOHN WILLIAMS. He was a COLONEL in the REVOLUTION from HILLSBORO, N. C. according to one account. He was a first cousin of COL. JAMES WILLIAMS, who was killed at KING'S MOUNTAIN and also a first cousin of JUDGE JOHN WILLIAMS of GRANVILLE COUNTY. He was not a lawyer. He married ELIZABETH WILLIAMSON, a member of a prominent North Carolina and Virginia family. The family genealogist has confused him with his cousin the Judge, as to dates, and says that he died in 1799, which is error, as he left will in CASWELL COUNTY in 1805, which was probably the year of his death. (See p. 196.) In his will he mentions his wife BETSY and children DUKE, BETSY GRAVES and HENRIETTA SIMPSON. DUKE WILLIAMS was the son MARMADUKE, who was a member of Congress from North Carolina, who married the widow of a HARRIS, who had been AGNES PAYNE. I have been unable to find a correct list of the children of COL. JOHN WILLIAMS prepared by any genealogical account, but have concluded after investigating the entire record available that COL. JOHN WILLIAMS and his wife ELIZABETH WILLIAMSON had the following children:

(f) ROBERT WILLIAMS (b. 1768)
(g) JOHN WILLIAMS (d. in CHATHAM COUNTY N. C. 1816)
(h) MARMADUKE WILLIAMS (d. in ALABAMA 1850).
(i) GEORGE WILLIAMS (d. CHATHAM COUNTY N. C. 1833).
(j) ELIZABETH WILLIAMS m. AZARIAH GRAVES

FROM WHEELER'S HISTORY: MARMADUKE WILLIAMS was born in CASWELL COUNTY, N. C. on April 6, 1772, and married AGNES (PAYNE) HARRIS, a widow in 1798. In 1802 he was elected to the State Senate, and the next year elected to Congress to succeed his brother, ROBERT WILLIAMS who was appointed by President Jefferson, Governor of MISSISSIPPI. He remained in Congress until 1809. In 1810 he moved to ALABAMA, settled in TUSCALOOSA COUNTY, and was a delegate from that county to the Convention which formed the Constitution for that State. In 1832 he was elected a Judge of TUSCALOOSA COUNTY. ALABAMA. He died October 29, 1850.

(f) ROBERT WILLIAMS, who served in Congress from North Carolina and served as Governor of the Territory of Mississippi, was born in PRINCE EDWARD COUNTY, Virginia, in the year 1768. His father, COL. JOHN WILLIAMS came to what is now PRINCE EDWARD COUNTY in 1748 and settled on lands adjoining JAMES DANIEL, a brother of JOHN DANIEL who had married ANNE WILLIAMS, his father's sister. Their names appear on the tax lists together in 1748-1749 and at other times later. (See Bell's Sunlight on the Southside).

ELIZABETH WILLIAMSON, the wife of COL. JOHN WILLIAMS, of CASWELL COUNTY, North Carolina was the daughter of JOHN WILLIAMSON, of NEW KENT COUNTY, Virginia, and his wife REBECCA CHAMBERLAINE, and the sister of THOMAS WILLIAMSON (b. 1708) who married JUDITH FLEMING, daughter of TARLETON FLEMING. (Bell's Old Free State Vol. ii p. 376). THOMAS RANDOLPH, of TUCKAHOE, was her uncle by marriage. The father of COL. JOHN WILLIAMS (NATHANIEL) was born about 1695 and was married by 1715-16, and in 1735 his son JOHN WILLIAMS had moved to GOOCHLAND COUNTY, Virginia, and where in MARCH of that year a suit was brought against him by JOHN DANIEL, which resulted in Daniel having to give a peace bond. The Flemings, Williams and Daniels had moved to Goochland, and from there JAMES DANIEL, who had been Sheriff of Goochland, moved with JOHN WILLIAMS down into AMELIA, which was later erected into PRINCE EDWARD COUNTY. COL. WILLIAMS moved to North Carolina and settled in what was then Orange County (now Caswell) sometime between 1768 and 1772. GEORGE WILLIAMS and JOHN WILLIAMS, sons of COL. JOHN WILLIAMS of CASWELL COUNTY, moved down into CHATHAM COUNTY, where they both died. (See p. 199). Both of them married into the CRUTCHFIELD FAMILY, from SPOTTSYLVANIA COUNTY. HENRY CRUTCHFIELD died in CHATHAM in 1787 leaving will. He was related to STAPLETON CRUTCHFIELD and these CRUTCHFIELDS were kin of the DANIEL FAMILY from YORK COUNTY.

---

(23) NATHANIEL WILLIAMS (Son of NATHANIEL) married, and is said to have had three children. There is some indications that he moved to LOUISIANA, where his nephew the HON. ROBERT WILLIAMS, former Governor of Mississippi died and was buried on his plantation near the town of MONROE, in 1836. Nathaniel Williams is credited with two sons, ROBERT and NATHANIEL WILLIAMS and a daughter ELIZABETH, who is said to have married a man named BALDWIN.

---

(24) JOSEPH WILLIAMS. This paragraph and the data that follows has reference to the JOSEPH WILLIAMS, son of NATHANIEL WILLIAMS. He may be identified more particularly as the "SHALLOW FORD" Joseph Williams, who was the ancestor of the WILLIAMS FAMILY OF TENNESSEE, particularly those who settled and lived at KNOXVILLE. From what is known as the "LOGAN MANUSCRIPT", published in Vol. III of the Joseph Habersham Chapter D. A. R. of Georgia, page 111 appears the following note, which refers to this particular JOSEPH WILLIAMS:

> MAJ. JOSEPH WILLIAMS, a cousin of COL. JAMES WILLIAMS, killed at KING'S MOUNTAIN, was the youngest son of NATHANIEL WILLIAMS, who emigrated from Wales (sic) to HANOVER COUNTY, Va. JOSEPH lost his father when he was 15 years old, and was taken care of by a namesake, and kinsman, JOSEPH WILLIAMS, a merchant of WILLIAMSBORO, Granville County, N. C. JOSEPH WILLIAMS settled at the SHALLOW FORD of the YADKIN before the Revolution, and died in August, 1827, his widow surviving until 1832. The following is a letter from his son ALEXANDER WILLIAMS, of GREENVILLE, TENNESSEE, written June 28, 1845, this being the postscript:
>
> "I expect I received a letter from the same gentleman you speak of, from Baltimore, MR. LYMAN C. DRAPER, who wishes to know something of my father, and particularly as to the battle between the WHIGS and TORIES fought near SHALLOW FORD of the YADKIN, at which battle my father headed and commanded the WHIGS. It is a little singular, history has never named this battle, although nearly 100 Tories were killed and only one Whig lost his life. A. W."

From the postscript of the above letter it will be observed that MAJOR JOSEPH WILLIAMS (son of NATHANIEL) was partly, if not mostly, raised at WILLIAMSBORO in GRANVILLE COUNTY, N. C. by his cousin, a JOSEPH WILLIAMS. This JOSEPH WILLIAMS (the cousin) was the son of DANIEL WILLIAMS and his wife URSULA HENDERSON. (See Henderson Chart p. 232). This store at WILLIAMSBORO (then called NUTBUSH) was for a time known as the WILLIAMS & BURTON store, the BURTON being either COL. ROBERT BURTON, son in law of JUDGE JOHN WILLIAMS, or his father HUTCHINS BURTON. This information discloses therefore that there were TWO JOSEPH WILLIAMS, prominent merchants in this section of North Carolina; the JOSEPH, of GRANVILLE (Now VANCE) at NUTBUSH or WILLIAMSBORO, and the MAJ. JOSEPH WILLIAMS, merchant at the SHALLOW FORD, on the YADKIN.

Since this MAJ. JOSEPH WILLIAMS of "Shallow Ford" was a brother of COL. ROBERT WILLIAMS, later of PITTSYLVANIA COUNTY, VIRGINIA, it is clear that they were the two partners in business, COL. ROBERT WILLIAMS owning an interest in the store on the Yadkin before he married SARAH LANIER (daughter of THOMAS LANIER, of GRANVILLE COUNTY) and moved back to Virginia and established himself as a lawyer in PITTSYLVANIA COUNTY. MAJ. JOSEPH WILLIAMS, his brother,married REBECCA LANIER, sister of SARAH. But what further complicates this entangling relationship of these two brothers to the family of THOMAS LANIER is the fact that SARAH LANIER before she married COL. ROBERT WILLIAMS, had married COL. JOSEPH WILLIAMS, of GRANVILLE COUNTY, the merchant of NUTBUSH or WILLIAMSBORO, who died, and upon his death, she married, as the widow WILLIAMS, COL. ROBERT WILLIAMS. Whether COL. JOSEPH WILLIAMS, the merchant of NUTBUSH and his wife SARAH LANIER left children by their marriage, has not been ascertained. On page 237 is given a list of the children of COL. ROBERT WILLIAMS and SARAH LANIER.

NOTE OUT OF PLACE: HON. MARMADUKE WILLIAMS , son of COL. JOHN WILLIAMS, of CASWELL COUNTY, N. C., was twice married. His first marriage was to EDY HARRIS in 1790, who was the mother of CHRISTOPHER HARRIS WILLIAMS, the father of JOHN SHARP WILLIAMS, of MISSISSIPPI. (p. 197).

(24) JOSEPH WILLIAMS. (This was MAJ. JOSEPH WILLIAMS, the merchant of SHALLOW FORD, on the YADKIN). In the marriage bond of JOSEPH WILLIAMS and REBECCA LANIER in GRANVILLE COUNTY, with JOHN HENDERSON as the bondsman, he is called JOSEPH WILLIAMS, JR. The bond is dated September 11, 1772. They were probably married when he was living in GRANVILLE COUNTY and employed in the store of WILLIAMS & BURTON at NUTBUSH, and his cousin, JOSEPH the merchant, being then living and much the oldest, was perhaps known as JOSEPH WILLIAMS SR. In CLEMENT'S History of PITTSYLVANIA COUNTY, Joseph Sr. is designated as COLONEL, which title was later conferred on JOSEPH JR., following the revolution, or before its close. (See p. 216 for the record of the marriage bond referred to).

The SHALLOW FORD, where JOSEPH WILLIAMS was in business, was evidently in ROWAN COUNTY at that time, if not now. The WILLIAMS STORE in addition to being called at the SHALLOW FORD must have been on a little stream called "PANTHER CREEK" also. It is described in one place as "on the old Shallow Ford road, out of WINSTON-SALEM". Anyway we picked up what purports to be an old family BIBLE RECORD of the children of COL. JOSEPH WILLIAMS and his wife REBECCA LANIER, which gives a list of their children with dates of birth, etc., and which names, dates & other data seems to harmonize with the names of the known descendants and children gathered from other sources, histories, etc., and which is copied below:

(30) ROBERT WILLIAMS born July 12, 1773.
(31) JOSEPH WILLIAMS born Oct. 12, 1775.
(32) JOHN WILLIAMS born Jan. 29, 1778.
(33) NATHANIEL WILLIAMS born Aug. 10, 1783.
(34) LEWIS WILLIAMS born Feb. 1, 1786.)
(35) THOMAS WILLIAMS born Feb. 1, 1786) Twins.
(36) REBECCA WILLIAMS born March 22, 1788.
(37) STERLING WILLIAMS born March 10, 1791 (d. May 6, 1792).
(38) FANNY WILLIAMS born April 20, 1796.
(39) ALEXANDER WILLIAMS
(40) NICHOLAS LANIER WILLIAMS born Feb. 4, 1800.

Here are a few brief facts about the above children of COL. JOSEPH WILLIAMS, the SHALLOW FORD merchant:

(30) ROBERT WILLIAMS (b. July 12, 1773) is said by one writer to have been born in CASWELL COUNTY, N. C. But he was NOT a "Member of Congress from North Carolina" as has been stated by some of the genealogists. That ROBERT was his first cousin and the son of COL. JOHN WILLIAMS, and was born in PRINCE EDWARD COUNTY, Virginia in 1768. This ROBERT WILLIAMS came to TEXAS as a pioneer in a very early day and some of his descendants are still living in that State.

(31) JOSEPH WILLIAMS is said to have married SUSAN TAYLOR and was perhaps the JOSEPH who was Clerk of SURRY COUNTY, N. C. The genealogists give him three children, SUSAN, REBECCA and JOHN T. WILLIAMS.

(32) JOHN WILLIAMS (b. Jan. 29, 1778) was the distinguished JOHN WILLIAMS, who settled in KNOXVILLE, TENNESSEE, and married MALINDA WHITE, daughter of GEN. JAMES WHITE, on whose lands the original town of KNOXVILLE was built. He was a distinguished member of the bar of the State of Tennessee, United States Senator, a Judge, and Minister at one time to GUATEMALA. His brother THOMAS LANIER WILLIAMS was also a distinguished Tennessee lawyer. The following statement is copied from a widely quoted TENNESSEE History:

> "Col. John Williams was one of the pioneer lawyers of East Tennessee, but his career as a politician eclipsed his legal career. He served as a member of the General Assembly, as a United States Senator, and was sent as minister to Guatemala by President Adams. He was a brother of THOMAS L. WILLIAMS who rather excelled him as a lawyer. He was most courtly and fascinating in his manners, and although not an eloquent speaker, possessed a wonderful personal magnetism."

From various sources, including the WHITE FAMILY BIBLE we know that COL. JOHN WILLIAMS, of Knoxville, Tennessee, had the following children:

50. JOSEPH LANIER WILLIAMS
51. JOHN WILLIAMS
52. REBECCA LANIER WILLIAMS d. y.
53. JAMES WHITE WILLIAMS d. y.
54. MARGARET WILLIAMS m. JUDGE RICHARD MUMFORD PEARSON.

(33) NATHANIEL WILLIAMS, about whom no information has been identified.

(34) LEWIS WILLIAMS. The following sketch is from page 1115 of the Congressional Directory, Biographical section:

> "LEWIS WILLIAMS, a representative from North Carolina, born in Surry County, N. C. February 1, 1786; was graduated from the University of North Carolina in 1808; member of the House of Commons 1813-1814; elected to the Fourteenth, and to the thirteen succeeding Congresses and served from March 4, 1815 until his death; received the title of "Father of the House"; died in Washington, D. C., February 23, 1842; interment in PANTHER CREEK CEMETERY, in SURRY COUNTY, NORTH CAROLINA."

(35) THOMAS LANIER WILLIAMS was a twin of Hon. Lewis Williams, and with his brother U. S. Senator JOHN WILLIAMS practiced law and carved out a career in TENNESSEE.

(13) DANIEL WILLIAMS (Son of JOHN WILLIAMS and his wife MARY KEELING) was born, as near as can be estimated about 1697. He married URSULA HENDERSON, who was the daughter of THOMAS HENDERSON and his wife by his first marriage, URSULA KEELING, daughter of CAPT. GEORGE KEELING, of NEW KENT and his wife URSULA FLEMING. URSULA KEELING was a sister of MARY KEELING who married JOHN WILLIAMS and was the aunt of DANIEL WILLIAMS. DANIEL WILLIAMS settled in NUTBUSH DISTRICT in GRANVILLE (Now VANCE) COUNTY somewhere around 1740. He died leaving a will in GRANVILLE COUNTY dated in 1759 in which he mentioned the following children:

(60) HENRY WILLIAMS
(61) JAMES WILLIAMS
(62) JOHN WILLIAMS
(63) JOSEPH WILLIAMS
(64) DANIEL WILLIAMS.

(60) HENRY WILLIAMS died in CASWELL COUNTY in 1796, leaving a will in which he named his several children (See page 196)

(61) JAMES WILLIAMS was the Col. JAMES WILLIAMS who lead his men and was killed at the battle of KING'S MOUNTAIN. An abstract of his will in CASWELL COUNTY will also be found on page 196 giving a complete list of his children.

(62) JOHN WILLIAMS. I am uncertain about the identity of this particular JOHN WILLIAMS but believe him to be the JOSEPH JOHN WILLIAMS of GRANVILLE COUNTY whose name is mentioned several times in the GRANVILLE COUNTY records. In this I may be mistaken. (SEE NOTE BELOW).

(63) JOSEPH WILLIAMS. This is the COL. JOSEPH WILLIAMS merchant of NUTBUSH and partner in the firm of WILLIAMS & BURTON at what is now WILLIAMSBORO. He married SARAH LANIER, the daughter of THOMAS LANIER, who, after his death, married his cousin COL. ROBERT WILLIAMS, of PITTSYLVANIA COUNTY, Virginia, an eminent lawyer. POLLY, daughter of JOSEPH m. HON. MATTHEW CLAY.

(64) DANIEL WILLIAMS, who married his first cousin ANN HENDERSON, the daughter of SAMUEL HENDERSON and his wife ELIZABETH WILLIAMS. They had (according to a family genealogist) the following children: SAMUEL, DANIEL, JOSEPH, RICHARD, WILLIAM, DAVID, BETSY, NANCY, NUTTY and a POLLY WASHER WILLIAMS. After the death of her first husband, ANN (HENDERSON) WILLIAMS married on the PACOLET, in SOUTH CAROLINA, one ADAM POTTER. No children mentioned by this last marriage. (See page 227 herein).

(13) DANIEL WILLIAMS was living in HANOVER COUNTY, Virginia, as late as 1735, for in an old, old record book in that county this writer found that on September 2, 1735, DANIEL WILLIAMS sold to WILLIAM GOOCH land that had been granted to him in 1734, lying in ST. MARTIN'S PARISH in HANOVER COUNTY.

---

(14) JOSEPH WILLIAMS (Son of JOHN WILLIAMS and his wife MARY KEELING) was born in YORK COUNTY, Virginia, about 1699.

Doubtless JOSEPH WILLIAMS, like the other members of this family, lived for a time in HANOVER COUNTY, Virginia, but as early as 1749 he was living in LUNENBURG COUNTY, which as it was then constituted took in a lot of Territory, and his name appears next to that of COL. WILLIAM RANDOLPH on the tythe list for that year. (Bell's Sunlight on the South Side). In the year 1764, he was living in what is now MECKLENBERG COUNTY, VIRGINIA, and his lands, consisting of 795 acres joined the lands (1029 acres) belonging to THOMAS WILLIAMSON'S orphans, one of whom (ELIZABETH) had married his nephew COL. JOHN WILLIAMS, of Caswell County, N. C. This writer is not sure of the names of all his children, but from an examination of these old records he thinks he was the father of the following:

(70) JOSEPH WILLIAMS
(71) NATHANIEL WILLIAMS
(72) LAZARUS WILLIAMS
(73) JOHN WILLIAMS, JR.
(74) THOMAS WILLIAMS (d. 1783).
(75) BENJAMIN WILLIAMS
(76) RICHARD WILLIAMS (d. 1769)
(77) ISAAC WILLIAMS

Possibly daughters.

DANIEL, JONES, DAVID, LEWIS, GILES and a number of other persons of the name of WILLIAMS appears on these same tax records contemporaneously with JOSEPH and his children, most of whom, it may be assumed were probably cousins of the children of JOHN WILLIAMS and his wife MARY KEELING, but it is impossible to positively identify each one and place him where he belongs. Some may belong on this list and some may be on the list that do not belong there, but I am quite sure that (71) NATHANIEL (73) JOHN belong, and am pretty sure the others do.

NOTE: That the JOSEPH WILLIAMS whose name appears so frequently on the records of MECKLENBERG COUNTY, VIRGINIA RECORDS, was a son of JOHN WILLIAMS and his wife MARY KEELING is bourn out by the circumstance that a JOHN WILLIAMS, son of GEN. JAMES WILLIAMS of KING'S MOUNTAIN fame, left a will in that county in 1794, in which he is described as "Of District 96, S. C." and in it refers to "My Uncle, CAPT. JOHN WILLIAMS" of the same place. This also shows that (62) JOHN WILLIAMS son of DANIEL WILLIAMS and URSULA HENDERSON removed to 96 District in South Carolina. The records of MECKLENBERG COUNTY (Va.) reflect the presence in that section of many members and many descendants of the WILLIAMS FAMILY of YORK COUNTY, Virginia, and of other families with which they were connected, including the WILLIAMSONS, CRUTCHFIELDS, BURTONS and others into which they married.

(15) ANNE WILLIAMS (Daughter of JOHN WILLIAMS and wife MARY KEELING) is believed to have been born about 1701-2 in YORK COUNTY, VIRGINIA. She married JOHN DANIEL, who was born in York County also. JOHN DANIEL moved from YORK COUNTY to HANOVER, then to GOOCHLAND COUNTY, and lived for a time with cousins by the name of DANIEL in CAROLINE COUNTY, Virginia; he finally moved to GRANVILLE COUNTY, NORTH CAROLINA, where he died leaving a will in which he named his children in 1762. For an abstract of this will and the names of their children see page 212 of this book. Their children were JAMES DANIEL, JOHN WILLIAMS DANIEL, SARAH DANIEL who married JOHN HARRISON, MARTHA DANIEL who married BARBER and ELIZABETH DANIEL who married CHRISTOPHER DUDLEY. James Daniel died in GRANVILLE COUNTY in 1785 leaving a will and naming his children; JOHN WILLIAMS DANIEL died in WARREN COUNTY, N. C. in 1808 leaving a will; JOHN HARRISON (the ancestor of the numerous HARRISON FAMILY of GRANVILLE COUNTY) died in HALIFAX COUNTY, Virginia, in 1761, and CHRISTOPHER DUDLEY left will in HALIFAX COUNTY, N. C. The HARRISON, DANIEL and other allied families descended from ANNE WILLIAMS and her husband JOHN DANIEL will be taken up separately herein.

(16) MARY WILLIAMS (Daughter of JOHN WILLIAMS and wife MARY KEELING) born about 1702-3 in YORK COUNTY, Virginia, married HENRY GRAVES, a member of an old YORK COUNTY FAMILY, which came originally from ACCOMAC COUNTY on the "EASTERN SHORE" of VIRGINIA, and which was very highly connected, including a relationship with CAPT. JOHN WEST, Governor of Virginia, and a younger brother of LORD DELAWARE who first settled at "WESTOVER" on the JAMES RIVER. In writing the story of the GRAVES FAMILY the writer finds it necessary to review a great deal of material accumulated about the early families in YORK COUNTY in order to show their connections. Members of this GRAVES FAMILY were numerous in GRANVILLE COUNTY, and they, like the HENDERSON and WILLIAMS FAMILIES lived for a time in HANOVER COUNTY, VIRGINIA. The name of HENRY GRAVES and his wife MARY (WILLIAMS) appears on the records of HANOVER COUNTY, VIRGINIA, in the year 1734-5, and they probably came to GRANVILLE COUNTY, N. C. about the same time as the HENDERSONS and others came there, somewhere around 1740 to 1745. Nobody appears to have the correct or positive date of their advent into North Carolina.

This GRAVES FAMILY will be taken up separately under its own heading, as one of the interesting old families of GRANVILLE COUNTY, NORTH CAROLINA.

(17) ELIZABETH WILLIAMS (Daughter of JOHN WILLIAMS and wife MARY KEELING) married one SAMUEL HENDERSON, and an account of this family has already been presented in this work, so that it will not be necessary to go into it again.

THE BURTON FAMILY OF GRANVILLE COUNTY

One of the most interesting as well as prominent persons who was identified with the History of Colonial GRANVILLE COUNTY, was COL. ROBERT BURTON. The following brief but accurate mention of him is made on page 517 of the CONGRESSIONAL DIRECTORY (1774-1911):

> ROBERT BURTON was a Delegate from NORTH CAROLINA; born in MECKLENBURG COUNTY, VIRGINIA, OCT. 20, 1747; moved to GRANVILLE COUNTY, N. C. in 1775; served in the Revolutionary Army, and attained the rank of COLONEL; sat in the Continental Congress in 1787-1788; member of the Commission which established the boundary line between North Carolina, South Carolina and Georgia in 1801; died in GRANVILLE COUNTY, NORTH CAROLINA, MAY 31, 1825.

COL. ROBERT BURTON married AGATHA WILLIAMS, the only daughter of JUDGE JOHN WILLIAMS and AGNES BULLOCK, the widow of GEORGE KEELING, in GRANVILLE COUNTY, North Carolina, on OCTOBER 12, 1775. (Va. Mag. of Hist. & Biog. p. 55, Vol. 28).

THE BURTON FAMILY to which COL. ROBERT BURTON belonged came from YORK and ACCOMAC COUNTY, VIRGINIA, and later settled in HENRICO COUNTY (See p. 20 of this Book). They were related to the HUNT FAMILY, which also had its representatives in GRANVILLE COUNTY, in the person of MEMUCAN HUNT and his family (Page 74).

WILLIAM HUNT, of CHARLES CITY COUNTY, Virginia, married TABITHA EDLOE of an early Virginia migration, and had GEORGE, JOHN, WILLIAM and MARY HUNT. MARY HUNT married May 15, 1695, ROBERT MINGE, by whom she had daughters TABITHA and MARTHA MINGE. TABITHA MINGE (whose grandmother was AMADEA HARRISON, a daughter of ROBERT HARRISON of QUEEN'S CREEK in YORK COUNTY, Virginia) married HUTCHINS BURTON. HUTCHINS BURTON was the son of NOEL HUNT BURTON and his wife JUDITH ALLEN. The children of NOEL HUNT BURTON and JUDITH ALLEN were HUTCHINS, JOHN, JOSIAH, ROBERT, BENJAMIN and an ALLEN BURTON. The children of the son HUTCHINS BURTON and TABITHA MINGE were JOHN BURTON who married MARY GORDON (parents of HUTCHINS GORDON BURTON, Governor of N. C.), HUTCHINS BURTON, NOEL HUNT BURTON, ROBERT BURTON (m. AGATHA WILLIAMS), JAMES MINGE BURTON, MARTHA BURTON and MARY BURTON.

ANOTHER WILLIAMS NOTE: COL. JOSEPH WILLIAMS, the merchant of NUTBUSH DISTRICT in GRANVILLE COUNTY, N. C. was the first husband of SARAH LANIER, daughter of THOMAS LANIER, who afterwards married COL. ROBERT WILLIAMS of PITTSYLVANIA COUNTY, VIRGINIA, a cousin of her first husband by whom she had several children listed at the top of page 237. But by her first husband, COL. JOSEPH WILLIAMS of NUTBUSH, GRANVILLE COUNTY, she had a daughter POLLY WILLIAMS, born JUNE 16, in the year 1770, who on December 4, 1788 married HON. MATTHEW CLAY, of HALIFAX COUNTY, Virginia, who was a revolutionary soldier and a member of CONGRESS. Her oldest son, CLEMENT C. CLAY moved to KNOXVILLE TENNESSEE and later to HUNTSVILLE, ALABAMA, where he became a UNITED STATES SENATOR, and his son Hon. C. C. CLAY also became a UNITED STATES SENATOR from ALABAMA and a member of the CONFEDERATE CONGRESS from that STATE.

AGATHA WILLIAMS, daughter of JUDGE JOHN WILLIAMS, of GRANVILLE COUNTY, N. C. and his wife AGNES (BULLOCK) KEELING, according to the family BIBLE was born OCTOBER 6, 1757, and died in 1831. ROBERT BURTON and AGATHA his wife had the following children:

1. HUTCHINS BURTON b. DEC. 9, 1777, died 1811.
2. FRANK N. W. BURTON born MAY 2, 1779.
3. ROBERT H. BURTON born JULY 22, 1781. (JUDGE in BUNCOMB COUNTY) p. 194.
4. AGNES BURTON born APRIL 11, 1783; died 1796.
5. ALFRED M. BURTON born SEPT. 9, 1785.
6. JAMES MINGE BURTON born DEC. 31, 1786.
7. AUGUSTINE BURTON born MARCH 31, 1789, died 1828.
8. HORACE A. BURTON, born FEB. 25, 1791.
9. FANNIE H. BURTON born JULY 1, 1793.
10. ELIZA W. BURTON born OCT. 1, 1795.
11. JOHN WILLIAMS BURTON, born OCT. 31, 1798.

5. ALFRED M. BURTON married ELIZABETH FULLINWIDER in 1811.

6. JAMES MINGE BURTON married (1) PRUDENCE ROBARDS, daughter of JAMES ROBARDS and wife MARY (relative of the first husband of RACHEL DONELSON, wife of ANDREW JACKSON); he married (2) MARTHA JOHNSON (daughter of JAMES and JANE JOHNSON); married (3) CATHERINE LOVE (daughter of EDWARD and LUCY LOVE); married (4) MARTHA GILBERT, June 22, 1824.

3. JUDGE ROBERT H. BURTON married POLLY FULLINWIDER, sister of his brother's wife.

2. FRANK N. W. BURTON married LAVINIA B. MURFREE.

11. J. WILLIAMS BURTON married SUSAN LYNE (Daughter of HENRY and LUCY LYNE), in 1819.

8. HORACE A. BURTON married MARGARET WILLIAMS (Daughter of WILLIAM WILLIAMS and his wife ELIZABETH WILLIAMS in 1825.

FRANK N. W. BURTON, son of COL. ROBERT BURTON was the Executor of his Grandfather, JUDGE JOHN WILLIAMS.

AGNES BULLOCK, widow of GEORGE KEELING, and later wife of JUDGE JOHN WILLIAMS had by her first husband, KEELING, daughters ELIZABETH KEELING, who married JUDGE RICHARD HENDERSON; ANNE KEELING who married THOMAS SATTERWHITE in 1772, and FRANCES KEELING, who married a RIDLEY.

THOMAS SATTERWHITE and his wife ANNE KEELING were the parents of EDWIN, HORACE, PEGGY & NANCY SATTERWHITE.

FRANCES KEELING and her husband RIDLEY were the parents of JAMES, ROBERT, FRANCES and POLLY RIDLEY.

THE GRAVES FAMILY OF GRANVILLE

In his will in CASWELL COUNTY in 1805 COL. JOHN WILLIAMS mentions only three of his children (p. 196) though he had at least SIX (See p. 237, in which the name of his daughter HENRIETTA SIMPSON was omitted by error). BETSY, or ELIZABETH, married AZARIAH GRAVES. This AZARIAH GRAVES. AZARIAH GRAVES was a grandson of HENRY WHITE GRAVES and his wife MARY WILLIAMS and MARY WILLIAMS was the aunt of COL. JOHN WILLIAMS of CASWELL COUNTY, N. C. and the sister of his father NATHANIEL WILLIAMS.

The lineage and family history of the GRAVES FAMILY of GRANVILLE, CASWELL and CHATHAM Counties, NORTH CAROLINA is very interesting and dates back to one THOMAS GRAVES who came to VIRGINIA and settled in ACCOMAC and NORTHAMPTON COUNTIES, before the latter County was erected out of the former. He is said to have arrived in VIRGINIA before 1630, and appears to have had at least THREE CHILDREN:

(1) RICHARD GRAVES
(2) RALPH GRAVES
(3) ANN GRAVES.

The descendants of RICHARD GRAVES were perhaps as numerous as those of his brother RALPH GRAVES, but this compiler has not attempted to identify and follow them. Their names on the record are accounted for as his descendants, when they do not apparently belong with those of his brother RALPH. Doubtless there were many of them in NORTH CAROLINA, among them, doubtless being THOMAS GRAVES of SPOTTSYLVANIA COUNTY, Virginia, who is known to have come there & who was NOT a descendant of RALPH.

ANN GRAVES, daughter of THOMAS GRAVES and sister of RICHARD and RALPH GRAVES became the wife of the celebrated REV. WILLIAM COTTEN, of ACCOMAC COUNTY, VIRGINIA, whose sister married CAPT. WILLIAM STONE, who became GOVERNOR OF MARYLAND. VERLINDA COTTEN, the daughter of REV. WILLIAM COTTEN married THOMAS BURDETT and eventually settled in CHARLES COUNTY, MARYLAND, where GOV. THOMAS STONE sought refuge in his old age after a hectic career in Maryland Politics and a narrow escape from the wrath of the second or third LORD BALTIMORE and his crowd. The BURDETTS and HARRISONS of MARYLAND intermarried and the name VERLINDA is perpetuated in both families.

DANIEL. I want to make a correction in the note on page 213 about the DANIEL FAMILIES OF GRANVILLE COUNTY. All that is said in that note is correct except that the JAMES DANIEL who married ELIZABETH WOODSON was NOT SHERIFF OF GOOCHLAND. The SHERIFF of GOOCHLAND was still another JAMES DANIEL (my wife's ancestor) who married JEAN KELSO. All of his sons except one moved to GREENE COUNTY, GEORGIA, and all THREE of his sons married CUNNINGHAMS and one of his daughters married SAMUEL CUNNINGHAM. There were in fact FIVE or SIX JAMES DANIELS in GOOCHLAND, AMELIA and PRINCE EDWARD and I will attempt to identify all of them when I take up the story of the DANIEL FAMILY in its proper place in this book.

LIEUT. JOHN WEST, son of the GOVERNOR, and said to have been the first white child of ENGLISH parentage born in the COLONY OF VIRGINIA, was a brother in law of the first RALPH GRAVES (son of THOMAS and brother of ANN who married REV. WILLIAM COTTEN). They both married daughters of the emigrant JOSEPH CROSHAW, who patented considerable land in YORK COUNTY and along QUEEN'S CREEK. In one account of JOSEPH CROSHAW (Vol 2 W.& M. p. 270, first series) it is said that he married at least three times (1) the widow FINCH, (2) ANNE HODGES and (3) MARGARET, the widow of DANIEL TUCKER. His children were by his first wife. They were: (1) BENJAMIN CROSHAW, (2) JOSEPH CROSHAW, (3) RACHEL CROSHAW who married RALPH GRAVES, (4) MARY CROSHAW who married MR. HENRY WHITE and (5) UNITY CROSHAW who married Lieut. Col. JOHN WEST.

RALPH GRAVES (the first) died MAY 9, 1667. He and his wife RACHEL CROSHAW, according to the account mentioned, had four children:

(6) ANN GRAVES
(7) RALPH GRAVES
(8) WILLIAM GRAVES
(9) MARY GRAVES.

RACHEL (CROSHAW) GRAVES, after the death of her husband, married second one RICHARD BARNES, by whom she probably had children who married into the COTTEN FAMILY, some of whom came to NORTH CAROLINA.

(8) WILLIAM GRAVES, son of RALPH and RACHEL may have been an ancestor of some of the GRAVES FAMILY in SPOTTSYLVANIA COUNTY. This fact has greatly complicated the lineage of some of the members of this family and has almost run some of the genealogists crazy in trying to straighten them out. This compiler has kept his eye on the RALPH GRAVES set, because he has been sue from the beginning that they were the GRANVILLE set.

---

(7) RALPH GRAVES (son of RALPH GRAVES and RACHEL CROSHAW, and nephew of LIEUT. COL. JOHN WEST and also of HENRY WHITE, of QUEEN'S CREEK in YORK COUNTY) married his first cousin, UNITY WHITE, daughter of HENRY WHITE and his wife MARY CROSHAW. Thanks to the unwavering courtesy and benevolent generosity of my friend HON. BEVERLY FLEET, tireless genealogical antiquarian, of RICHMOND, VIRGINIA, I do not have to depend on "family genealogists" for verification of this alliance between the GRAVES, CROSHAW and WHITE families. The following order of the YORK COUNTY, (Virginia) Court appears in the proceedings of said court on MARCH 26, 1688, on page 105 of Vol. VIII of the YORK COUNTY RECORDS and contains much information relating to the relationships in question:

> "WHEREAS, JOSEPH WHITE and WILLIAM WHITE, sons of HENRY WHITE, late deceased, and WILLIAM DAVIS, as marrying MARY, one of the said daughters, and RALPH GRAVES, as marrying UNITY, one other of the said daughters of the said HENRY WHITE, setting forth by their petition to this Court that the said HENRY WHITE, by his last will and testament did make COL. JOHN WEST and BRYAN SMYTH the executors, and did give and bequeath unto his daughter REBECCA WHITE thirty pounds of tobacco and a certaine part of his estate as may appear by a division of the said estate amounting to forty-eight pounds, forty-one shillings and eight pence Sterling and One Thousand Eight Hundred and THIRTY POUNDS of tobacco, and in cattell 4 cowes under ten yeares old, 2 steers three years old, two steer yearlings, 1 heifer cowe calfe. And in case the said REBECCA dye under age and before marriage then her part to bee equally divided amongst the surviving children. And now, it appearing to this Court that the said REBECCA WHITE dyed under age and before marriage, it is therefore ordered that COL. JOHN WEST, the surviving executor of the said HENRY WHITE do forthwith pay unto the said JOSEPH and WILLIAM WHITE, WILLIAM DAVIS and RALPH GRAVES as aforesaid, the sum of Thirty Pounds Sterling, * * given by said will and also all other the estate * * both money, tobacco and cattell according to the age above mentioned and sett down in the said division and according to the true intent of the said HENRY WHITE'S written will, etc."

Further proceedings of interest in this connection is shown on pages 27 and 28 of the same record above quoted in 1687, where a deed is recorded from JOSEPH WHITE to EDMUND JENNINGS to property on ST. ANDREWS CREEK in York County, including a tract of land on which there was a mill. This deed is interesting on account of the names of the witnesses who were REV. ROWLAND JONES (minister of BRUTEN PARISH and kinsman of GIDEON MACON and the GOOCH FAMILY of GRANVILLE COUNTY), JOHN GAILOR and WILLIAM SHERWOOD (Distinguished early lawyer of YORK and JAMES CITY COUNTY). The wife of JOSEPH WHITE, who signed the deed with him was MAGDALENE.

NOTE - DANIEL WILLIAMS. I have found another copy of an abstract of the will of DANIEL WILLIAMS, of GRANVILLE COUNTY (other than the one previously mentioned) in which, in addition to the sons HENRY, JOHN, JAMES, JOSEPH and DANIEL (who married ANN HENDERSON) there there appears the names of two daughters: MARY WILLIAMS who married a MITCHELL, and MARIA WILLIAMS who married a man named GOODMAN. On page 227 there is a note which says that MARY HENDERSON, daughter of SAMUEL HENDERSON married a JOAB MITCHELL, His brother probably married MARY.

From the records of the YORK COUNTY COURT quoted on the preceding page that on MARCH 26, 1688 (7) RALPH GRAVES was living and that at that time his wife was UNITY WHITE. Unity's sister, REBECCA WHITE, was then deceased and she had died while a minor, unmarried. Sometime prior to the date of the order (we do not know just how long or how many years) their sister MARY WHITE had become the wife of WILLIAM DAVIS, who likewise shared in the HENRY WHITE estate, under his will, the date of which is not given. The WHITES, like the CROSHAWS and GRAVES lived on QUEEN'S CREEK (see page 233) as well as the PINKETHMANS.

(7) RALPH GRAVES and his wife UNITY must have had a handfull of children, but the "family genealogist) always enterprising, could find but one, certainly, and he was named RALPH, who for convenience and identification will be given the number (10). His brothers and sisters, if he had any, are unaccounted for. I have an idea that he had several and that their children and grandchildren have helped very much to clutter up the GRAVES FAMILY history. (10) RALPH GRAVES may have been in his 'teens about the time his grandfather HENRY WHITE passed away and his aunt REBECCA died and brought on a redistribution of the WHITE PROPERTY.

(10) RALPH GRAVES married MARY PINKETHMAN. We have no record of just when they were married. When WILLIAM PINKETHMAN died leaving a will in 1712, he mentioned his "daughter MARY, wife of RALPH GRAVES". (Vol 6 Tyler p. 121). At the time of his death WILLIAM PINKETHMAN was Sheriff of YORK COUNTY. He was the son of TIMOTHY PINKETHMAN who died in 1672 and who had a tobacco warehouse and mill at SKIMMINO "on York River", on the line of YORK and NEW KENT COUNTY. In 1685 WILLIAM PINKETHMAN witnessed the will of JOHN DANIEL in YORK COUNTY, grandfather of the JOHN DANIEL who married MARY WILLIAMS and left will in GRANVILLE COUNTY, N. C. (p. 212 herein). WILLIAM PINKETHMAN had three daughters and it is interesting to note the names of his FOUR sons in laws: (10) RALPH GRAVES who married MARY PINKETHMAN; WILLIAM EATON, father of COL. WILLIAM EATON, of GRANVILLE COUNTY, N. C. (p. 43 of LOST TRIBES); who married the daughter SARAH EATON, and DANIEL TAYLOR, Sarah's second husband, Minister of BLISSLAND PARISH in 1727, when CAPT. GEORGE KEELING (of SKIMMINO CREEK) was on the Vestry; another son in law was ROBERT COBBS, who married REBECCA PINKETHMAN (his first wife) and was the grandfather of GENERAL ALLEN and COL. WILLIE JONES, of HALIFAX COUNTY. From this it can be seen that (10) RALPH GRAVES was brother in law to four distinguished men, as well as the Great Nephew of LIEUT. COL. JOHN WEST. The genealogist claims that (10) RALPH GRAVES married a second wife named ELIZABETH, but identifies no children by this marriage.

The children of (10) RALPH GRAVES and his wife MARY PINKETHMAN were:

(20) WILLIAM GRAVES
(21) HENRY GRAVES (b. about 1700) married MARY WILLIAMS.
(22) RICHARD GRAVES
(23) RICHARD CROSHAW GRAVES
(24) UNITY GRAVES married WILLIAM HILLIARD
(25) ELIZABETH GRAVES married a STONE (Perhaps from Maryland STONES).

(21) HENRY GRAVES (son of RALPH GRAVES and MARY PINKETHMAN) married MARY WILLIAMS, a daughter of JOHN WILLIAMS and his wife MARY KEELING, of YORK COUNTY, VIRGINIA. They may have been married in YORK COUNTY, or possibly in HANOVER, where the old record shows they were living in 1734-5. In setting down an account of this set the enterprising genealogist ran wholly out of dates. He says the oldest brother (20) WILLIAM GRAVES died in 1758, and also that (22) RICHARD GRAVES (Of NEW KENT COUNTY Va.) had children born in 1756 and 1758, which we think was mighty late. CAPT. JOHN WILLIAMS GRAVES (whom we think unquestionably was one of the sons of HENRY GRAVES and his wife MARY WILLIAMS) appears on the tax list of CASWELL COUNTY (which serves as the 1790 census) about 1784-5, and he must have died about 1787 in GRANVILLE COUNTY. For abstract of his will see page 213. RALPH, HENRY and MARY GRAVES lived in the ABRAHAM PLAINS District of GRANVILLE (listed in 1790 census), while HENRY GRAVES, JR. is listed down in the GOSHEN District, below. This was because, perhaps, one of the CHESLEY DANIELS, of GOSHEN DISTRICT - LEONARD DANIEL - had married his sister, MARY ANN GRAVES, as later a CHESLEY DANIEL married AGNES WILLIAMS. (See page 215).

The children of HENRY GRAVES and his wife MARY WILLIAMS, some of them, possibly, were born in YORK COUNTY, VIRGINIA, while doubtless some of them were born in HANOVER where they resided contemporaneously with SAMUEL HENDERSON and his brothers and sisters, before they came to NORTH CAROLINA. The HENRY GRAVES JR. of GOSHEN DISTRICT, was probably the son of the HENRY GRAVES (son of HENRY and wife MARY WILLIAMS), while the MARY GRAVES, who was living in GRANVILLE, and is listed as the head of a family was perhaps his grandmother MARY (WILLIAMS) GRAVES, who could have been living at that time, although nearly or about 85 years of age.

The children of (21) HENRY GRAVES and his wife MARY WILLIAMS were:

(30) HENRY GRAVES (Of GRANVILLE COUNTY)
(31) JOHN WILLIAMS GRAVES m. MARY JONES.
(32) WILLIAM GRAVES
(33) BARZILLA GRAVES
(34) MARY GRAVES married a BARNETT.
(35) RACHEL GRAVES married JOHN CHRISTMAS.
(36) ELIZABETH GRAVES married REV. JOSHUA COFFEE.
(37) RALPH GRAVES.

(30) HENRY GRAVES (probably known as Sr.) was doubtless the father of HENRY GRAVES JR. of the GOSHEN DISTRICT and of MARY ANN GRAVES who married LEONARD DANIEL; also, I surmise he was the father of a RALPH GRAVES and a RACHEL GRAVES, who with HENRY GRAVES witnessed the will of (32) WILLIAM GRAVES, April 24, 1786 in GRANVILLE COUNTY. (See page 213).

(35) RACHEL GRAVES married JOHN CHRISTMAS, who was a descendant of the old YORK COUNTY FAMILY of DOCTORIS WILLIAM CHRISTMAS and probably the father of WILLIAM CHRISTMAS, noted first "City Planner" who laid out WARRENTON and RALEIGH.

(31) JOHN WILLIAMS GRAVES married MARY JONES. He is listed as a tax payer in CASWELL COUNTY, which list was used as a basis for the UNITED STATES CENSUS, though the list so used was several years old. CAPT. GRAVES left will in GRANVILLE COUNTY (p. 213) but only named a part of his children. He was perhaps married more than one time, MARY JONES being his last wife by whom he had children. After his death the widow MARY married CAPT. JOHN WILLIAMS GRAVES' first cousin, COL. [illegible] WILLIAMS DANIEL, of WARREN COUNTY, formerly of GRANVILLE and of the NUTBUSH DISTRICT. In his will CAPT. GRAVES mentions only three sons, JOHN, RALPH and WILLIAM GRAVES but from the will of COL. DANIEL it appears he had at least two other children, probably by his last marriage, JONATHAN and FRANCES.

The compiler believes that the children of CAPT. JOHN WILLIAMS GRAVES consisted of the following:

(40) JOHN WILLIAMS GRAVES JR.
(41) RALPH GRAVES
(42) WILLIAM GRAVES
(43) JONATHAN GRAVES
(44) FRANCES GRAVES married TRIGG.

(32) WILLIAM GRAVES (Son of HENRY GRAVES and MARY WILLIAMS) married MARY, and died in GRANVILLE COUNTY, N. C. in 1786, leaving the following children, all of whom are mentioned in the abstract of his will on page 213 herein: MARY (m. HESTER), ELIZABETH (m. MONTAGUE), NANCY, HENRY GRAVES, WILLIAM GRAVES, [illegible] GRAVES, NATHANIEL GRAVES, ANNA GRAVES and MARTHA GRAVES.

(33) BARZILLA GRAVES (Son of HENRY GRAVES and MARY WILLIAMS) married, but the name of his wife is not known, though he apparently lived in CASWELL COUNTY and had at least the following children:

(45) THOMAS GRAVES
(46) SOLOMON GRAVES
(47) BAZILLA GRAVES
(48) AZARIAH GRAVES

(The above names of children of BARZILLA GRAVES are taken from the CASWELL COUNTY Tax List, but they are identified as his children, though he may have had others, especially one or more daughters).

Mr. WHEELER, in his "Sketches" says that the GRAVES FAMILY came from JAMES CITY County to CASWELL COUNTY, N. C. about 1742. Some of them MAY have been living in JAMES CITY COUNTY, since that county and YORK put together are only about the size of a pocket handkerchief and adjoin each other, but we have already presented the evidence showing that they were originally of YORK COUNTY. But we think the proof further shows that HENRY GRAVES who married MARY WILLIAMS came to North Carolina from HANOVER more directly.

(48) AZARIAH GRAVES, grandson of HENRY GRAVES and MARY WILLIAMS, married ELIZABETH WILLIAMS, daughter of COL. JOHN WILLIAMS of CASWELL COUNTY, an abstract of whose will appears herein (p. 196). AZARIAH GRAVES represented CASWELL COUNTY in the STATE SENATE from 1805 to 1811. His son CALVIN also served in the SENATE from CASWELL and in 1840 to 1842 served as SPEAKER of that body. Among the children of AZARIAH GRAVES and his wife ELIZABETH WILLIAMS were the following:

(49) REV. ELIJAH L. GRAVES
(50) BARZILLA GRAVES (b. March 12, 1802).
(51) HON. CALVIN GRAVES (b. January 1804).
(52) JOHN WILLIAMS GRAVES
(53) GEORGE GRAVES
(54) ______ GRAVES (Dau.) m. JOHN E. TUCKER.
(55) HENRY L. GRAVES

(50) BARZILLA GRAVES (b. 1802) moved to GEORGIA. He was one of the Trustees of of the UNIVERSITY OF GEORGIA and served as a member of the STATE SENATE in that State afterwards. In the fall of 1851 he moved to ALABAMA, from RANDOLPH COUNTY, GA. where one of his children was born in 1845.

(51) JOHN WILLIAMS GRAVES married a MISS RAY and moved WEST.

(52) REV. HENRY L. GRAVES moved to TEXAS and became the first PRESIDENT of BAYLOR UNIVERSITY at OLD WASHINGTON-ON-THE-BRAZOS. In his declining years he settled at BRENHAM, TEXAS, where he married a widow, one of the daughters of CAPT. SAMUEL LUSK, who had come out from WARREN COUNTY, TENNESSEE, in an early day. She was a sister of CAPT. PAT LUSK who was a member of what is known in Texas as the MIER EXPEDITION to Old Mexico.

---

(36) ELIZABETH GRAVES (Daughter of HENRY GRAVES and wife MARY WILLIAMS) married REV. JOSHUA COFFEE, a son of PETER COFFEE, of PRINCE EDWARD COUNTY, Virginia, and they were the parents of COL. JOHN COFFEE, of TENNESSEE, one of ANDREW JACKSON'S Generals in the early wars and at NEW ORLEANS. GEN. JOHN COFFEE married MARY DONELSON, daughter of JOHN DONELSON (brother in law of ANDREW JACKSON) and had nine children, as follows: (1) MARY COFFEE married ANDREW HUTCHINS; (2) JOHN D. COFFEE married NARCISSA BRAHAN; ELIZABETH GRAVES COFFEE (named for her grandmother, a daughter of HENRY GRAVES and MARY WILLIAMS); ANDREW JACKSON COFFEE, married ELIZABETH HUTCHINS ; (5) ALEXANDER D. COFFEE, married twice; (6) RACHEL JACKSON COFFEE married A. J. DYAS; KATHERINE HARRIET COFFEE; (8) EMILY COFFEE; (9) WILLIAM COFFEE who married VIRGINIA MALONE.

REV. JOSHUA COFFEE had a brother PETER COFFEE, who moved to GEORGIA, who was the father of another GEN. JOHN COFFEE, contemporaneous with the one in TENNESSEE and who was equally famous as a trail blazer and INDIAN FIGHTER. PETER COFFEE of PRINCE EDWARD CO. VA. was the ancestor

(15) ANNE WILLIAMS (Daughter of JOHN WILLIAMS and MARY KEELING) married JOHN DANIEL, who died leaving a will in GRANVILLE COUNTY, an abstract of which is shewn herein on page 212. JOHN DANIEL was born on QUEEN'S CREEK in YORK COUNTY, VIRGINIA. In order to give the reader an idea of the DANIEL FAMILY it is necessary to go back again to the same old neighborhood in YORK COUNTY from whence came the various other families mentioned in the HENDERSON and WILLIAMS family history. To me the facts unfolded in my investigation of these families sound like a veritable fairy tale. Nearly all of them started among the CAVALIERS who flocked to VIRGINIA when OLIVER CROMWELL "took over" in England and in a generation or two developed into liberty-loving Americans, took root in the soil of this new country and became the ancestors of a race of people of the purest Anglo-Saxon type, who have played important roles in the establishment of American culture and American ideals unequaled in any other part of the world.

This compiler does not "go very strong" on the coat of arms type of genealogy, but believes a family does mighty well to keep or find and accumulate a record of facts showing its original ancestor in this country, if it is really of the old stock. The stereotyped or tin-can genealogical tables that trace (?) families back to "William the Conqueror", King Ogg, the much maligned "Stuarts" and all that sort of rot are not worth the time it takes to copy them. In the days of all those "Visitations" one finds quoted so often in so-called ENGLISH references, people were just as vain and ambitious to connect with the much vaunted "nobility" as they are today, and a lot of those tables were pure "bunk". All this as a preface to what I am about to say about the origin of the DANIEL FAMILY.

Any good history of ENGLAND will probably contain the name and some reference to the celebrated SAMUEL DANIEL, Poet, Jurist and erstwhile "hanger on" at the Court of St. James, away back in the decades preceding the rise of CROMWELL. He was a HISTORIAN of some note, an essayist and a kind of "Royal Troubadour" to the reigning dignitaries. The family to which he belonged was "seated" at TAUNTON, ENGLAND, a town of some little consequence in DORSETSHIRE, not so very far out of BRISTOL. It is an old town. I suppose at one time it was just a castle with some be-booted overlord with a title. Anyway an old note says there was a ROGER DANIEL on the Dombsday Book, or whatever that was. Maybe the DANIEL FAMILY of Taunton came from his family, if he had one. Somebody has tried to make them out JEWS, from FRANCE, who originated from "Daniel in the Lion's Den". Pure rot. In my files I have the material that will convince any reasonable person that the ROGER DANIEL who settled in VIRGINIA before 1650 belonged to a family of the name from BRISTOL, ENGLAND, which came there from TAUNTON. That is all I can prove, but that is all I want to prove. I am descended from those DANIELS on the maternal side. They were the DANIEL who lived in GRANVILLE COUNTY, N. C.

ROGER DANIEL came to VIRGINIA with his "known kinsman" MILES CARY, from BRISTOL, in ENGLAND. The "quote" is from the "VIRGINIA CARYS" one of the really fine genealogical works of the last century and absolutely dependable, so far as the author could go with the lights before him, but anyway it is the last word so far as the CARY FAMILY is concerned. Just how ROGER DANIEL was related to MILES CARY we will never know. If there is a record it is in ENGLAND and I don't ever intend to hunt for it. I don't care. But that a son of ROGER DANIEL married ANNE CARY, one of the daughters of MILES CARY the emigrant I am quite sure. The book does not give this. It says she "probably never married ". The author had no record and no facts on which to base any other statement. Three hundred years is hard to bridge with scant material, when one wants to be absolutely accurate. The first CARYS and their kinsmen the DANIELS located in WARWICK COUNTY. Later generations of both families shifted around a bit, but usually where there was a member of one of the families, a member of the other would show up. This happend in PRINCE EDWARD COUNTY, Va., where JAMES DANIEL settled and died in 1763. I Quote:

> WILLIAM CARY: "The immigrant's youngest son, "the miller" was established on a plantation his father had acquired on the North end of MULBERRY ISLAND at the mouth of SKIFF'S CREEK. His grandson (WM. CARY,JR.) responding to the lure of a broader boundary, migrated to new lands in PRINCE EDWARD, where his descendants have since been seated."—Virginia Carys p. 128.

ROGER DANIEL (and his wife, whoever she was) were the parents of the following children, at least one and possibly more of whom were born in ENGLAND:

(1) THOMAS DANIEL, died in YORK COUNTY in 1679.
(2) JOHN DANIEL, died in ACCOMAC (NORTHAMPTON) Co. Va. in 1666.
(3) HUGH DANIEL married MARY BILLINGTON.
(4) DARBY DANIEL married ANNE CARY.
(5) ROGER DANIEL (b. in ENGLAND).
(6) WILLIAM DANIEL (Of NEW KENT COUNTY).

(2) JOHN DANIEL, of ACCOMAC and NORTHAMPTON COUNTY, Virginia, married ELIZABETH. He died in 1666, and after his death his widow married as his third wife THOMAS HARMONSON of an old EASTERN SHORE family. Children:

(10) WILLIAM DANIEL married SARAH WILLIAMS
(11) JOHN DANIEL married MARY WILLIAMS
(12) ELIZABETH DANIEL married JOHN BATES.

(10) WILLIAM DANIEL died leaving a will in ACCOMAC COUNTY, dated in 1688 in which he mentions two sons and his wife SARAH; witnessed by JOHN WILLIAMS, SR.

The two sons of (10) WILLIAM DANIEL (Of ACCOMAC COUNTY, VA.) whose will was dated in 1688, but not probated until 1692, were

(20) ALEXANDER DANIEL married JANE COLLINS
(21) JAMES DANIEL, married ANNE PARKER.

The (21) JAMES DANIEL who married ANNE PARKER died in GOOCHLAND COUNTY, VIRGINIA, intestate in the year 1734. He left no will but his wife ANNE was made administratrix of his estate and RICHARD PARKER was one of her bondsmen.

He had three sons, RICHARD, WILLIAM and JAMES DANIEL. This last named son, JAMES DANIEL was the one who married ELIZABETH WOODSON, daughter of BENJAMIN WOODSON, who is mentioned in this volume in the notes on pages 213 and 242.

---

(11) JOHN DANIEL who married MARY WILLIAMS, daughter of JOHN WILLIAMS SR. and sister of JOHN WILLIAMS who married MARY KEELING, was the grandfather of the JOHN DANIEL who died and left a will in GRANVILLE COUNTY, N. C. in 1763 shown herein on page 212.

The last will and testament of (11) JOHN DANIEL is dated JANUARY 5, 1685-6, in YORK COUNTY, VIRGINIA, and appears on the records of that county. It was proved MAY 24, 1689, and the abstract I have provides:

1. To my son JOHN, all lands, houses, etc., but if JOHN should died without issue, to son WILLIAM; if he should die without issue to eldest daughter (not named, but her name was ELIZABETH); but if she should die without issue to youngest daughter MARY.
2. To daughter MARY two silver spoons.
3. To god-son GEORGE BATES, a cowe and calfe.
4. Wife (not named, but her name was MARY) Executrix.
5. If my wife dies, my loving friends MR. BENJAMIN BUCK and MR. EDWARD BRUCE to look after my children.

Witnesses: MARY BRUCE and WILLIAM PINKETHMAN.*

The probate of the foregoing will was granted to BARRENTINE HOWIE (HOWELL) who, between the death of the testator and the time the will was presented for probate had married MARY DANIEL, the executrix and widow. It is likely that the will had b een withheld from probate for about two years and that JOHN DANIEL died shortly after the will was written, about 1686-7.

* WILLIAM PINKETHMAN was the father-in-law of RALPH GRAVES and the grandfather of HENRY GRAVES who married MARY WILLIAMS; he was also the grandfather of COLONEL WILLIAM EATON (see page 43) of GRANVILLE COUNTY.

From this will it will be ascertained that the children of (11) JOHN DANIEL and his wife MARY WILLIAMS were:

(30) JOHN DANIEL married ANN BATES
(31) WILLIAM DANIEL married SARAH WILLIAMS*
(32) MARY DANIEL died young.
(33) ELIZABETH DANIEL married CRUTCHFIELD.

Following herewith is an abstract of the will of (30) JOHN DANIEL, as same appears in VOL. 16 of the YORK COUNTY ORDERS, WILLS, ETC., page 274. Dated November 12, 1722. Probated May 18, 1724:

Will of JOHN DANIEL, of BRUTON PARISH, York County, Virginia:

Item: To eldest son JOHN DANIEL, one-half of that tract of land in HANOVER COUNTY that I lately bought of JOHN BRYANT, where he is now lately seated, or this plantation in YORK COUNTY where I now live, which one of them he shall make choice of; and the remainder, after son JOHN hath made choice, I give to my son WILLIAMS DANIEL.

Item: To son JAMES DANIEL, the other half of the land in HANOVER COUNTY.

Item: To son JOHN DANIEL, my negro man named TOM, with bed and all necessaries he carried with him to keep house in HANOVER COUNTY.

Item: To son JAMES DANIEL, a negro woman JENNIE and increase, etc. He to be bound to a trade that he shall choose, by my Executors.

Item: To son WILLIAMS DANIEL, a negro boy named WILL.

Item: To daughter SARAH BARKSDALE, negro woman MOLL and her increase.

Item: To daughter HANNAH DANIEL, a negro boy named TOM.

Item: To sister ELIZABETH CRUTCHFIELD, fifty shillings.

Executors: Son JOHN DANIEL and friend, JAMES BATES.

Witnesses: JOHN HUMPHREYS, ROBERT WHITECHURCH and MARTHA GRANGER.

So, the children of (30) JOHN DANIEL and his wife ANN BATES, were:

(34) JOHN DANIEL (He married ANNE WILLIAMS)
(35) WILLIAMS DANIEL (He married ELIZABETH WATKINS).
(36) JAMES DANIEL (He married JEAN KELSO).
(37) SARAH DANIEL (She married a BARKSDALE).
*(38) HANNAH DANIEL (She married JAMES LEWIS).

*HANNAH DANIEL was a minor and after the death of her father she chose TARLETON FLEMING as her guardian. He had married her father's first cousin, HANNAH BATES.

NOTES ON SOME ALLIED CONNECTIONS OF THE DANIEL FAMILY.

THE BATES FAMILY. The first BATES to arrive in VIRGINIA, so far as any record I can find is concerned, was JOHN BATES, who was a "servant" of ABRAHAM PERSEY, who at one time was the wealthiest man in the JAMESTOWN settlement. JOHN BATES is mentioned as early as 1626. JOHN BATES became a "merchant", and must have been a man of parts. ABRAHAM PERSEY died in 1626 and left a will, in which one of the "overseers" named by him was the REV. GREVILLE POOLEY, who had courted CYCELY JORDAN, the early VIRGINIA GLAMOUR GIRL, who had no less than five husbands and who sued her for breach of promise. It so happens that the genealogy of the BATES FAMILY, the descendants of JOHN became intimately related to the JORDAN family afterwards, just as they also intermarried with the WOODSONS. The ancestress of the WOODSONS is said to have been a SARAH WINSTON. That there is some foundation for this claim is partly supported in reason by the fact that when JOHN BATES died in 1666 in BRUTEN PARISH, YORK COUNTY, the witness to his will was WILLIAM WINSTON (BOOK 4, p. 165 YORK COUNTY). Fairfax Harrison, in his admirable story of the SKIMINO HARRISONS, says that JOHN BATES was born about 1598 and died in 1666 and that he was a resident of MIDDLETOWN (BRUTEN) PARISH at the time of his death. This writer has puzzled over the obvious connection of the BATES FAMILY with the DANIEL FAMILY for many years and has at last ferreted out the facts. The name of the wife of JOHN BATES will never be known, perhaps, but reasoning the matter from all angles it is not improbable that SARAH WINSTON (whom it is claimed was the wife of DR. JOHN WOODSON) may have had a sister who married JOHN BATES and that they were both sisters of the WILLIAM WINSTON who witnessed the will of BATES in 1666. If so, the connection between the BATES and WOODSONS dates back to 1620 when DR. JOHN is supposed to have arrived in Virginia. ROGER DANIEL, the ancestor of the DANIEL FAMILY is believed to have come along not long afterwards, say about 1630 or 1635. I have raked up only two children for JOHN BATES and his wife, whoever she may have been. They were:

(1) GEORGE BATES (born about 1625).
(2) SUSANNA BATES married STEPHEN TARLTON.

The children of STEPHEN TARLTON (shown in Chart on page 231) were STEPHEN, JOHN (m. SUSANNA FLEMING), SUSANNA (m. CHARLES FLEMING), JUDITH (m. JOHN WOODSON), CHARLES, and ELIZABETH, who married STEPHEN HUGHES.

The name of the wife of (1) GEORGE BATES is said to have been MARY.

(1) GEORGE BATES (and his wife MARY) had children:

(3) JAMES BATES (1650-1723)
(4) JOHN BATES (1755-1719) m. ELIZABETH DANIEL.

(4) JOHN BATES and his wife ELIZABETH DANIEL (Sister of JOHN DANIEL who married ELIZABETH WILLIAMS) had the following children:

(5) GEORGE BATES (Called "My God-son GEORGE BATES" in will of JOHN DANIEL in 1685-6)
(6) JAMES BATES m. SARAH ....
(7) ANN BATES married JOHN DANIEL (Will 1723-4)
(8) HANNAH BATES married TARLTON FLEMING
(9) JOHN BATES JR. married SUSANNA FLEMING.

The brothers JAMES and JOHN BATES both became QUAKERS under the preaching of the famous THOMAS STORY and it was at the home of JOHN BATES on SKIMINO that STORY held one of his first meetings in VIRGINIA. JOHN BATES and his wife ELIZABETH DANIEL entertained STORY though they were not Quakers, but STORY in his account says that at this meeting "both JOHN BATES and his wife were convinced of the truth".

(5) GEORGE BATES. Of him we have no record other than the mention made of him in the will of his uncle JOHN DANIEL in 1685.

(6) JAMES BATES and his wife SARAH (maiden name unknown) were the parents of HANNAH BATES who married SAMUEL JORDAN. SAMUEL JORDAN belonged to a QUAKER family of NANSEMOND or Isle of Wight County and they had a regular QUAKER WEDDING. They were married on JAN. 3, 1738.*

---

* NOTE: Among the nineteen persons (All QUAKERS, of course), who are listed among those who attended the wedding of HANNAH BATES to SAMUEL JORDAN on January 3, 1733, was a certain SAMUEL WALLACE. This wedding took place in YORK COUNTY on SKIMINO CREEK. There was a family of WALLACES who lived in YORK and ELIZABETH CITY COUNTY to which this SAMUEL must have belonged. This SAMUEL WALLACE was NOT from PENNSYLVANIA, but belonged to the family of WALLACE that lived on BACK RIVER in NEW POQUOSON in YORK or ELIZABETH CITY COUNTY which was established there by the REV. JAMES WALLACE in the 17TH CENTURY. SAMUEL WALLACE moved to PRINCE EDWARD COUNTY, Virginia and settled on BUFFALO CREEK where he patented lands and married ESTHER BAKER, a daughter of CALEB BAKER. in 1772 he moved to CHARLOTTE COUNTY. His son CALEB BAKER WALLACE was born in 1742 and in 1782 father and son moved to KENTUCKY, where CALEB BAKER WALLACE became a distinguished JUDGE on the Kentucky Bench. In 1775 CALEB BAKER WALLACE was appointed an Executor of the will of JAMES CUNNINGHAM, of CHARLOOTE COUNTY. Three of his wife's brothers married daughters of REV. JOHN THOMPSON, who died in MECKLENBURG COUNTY, N. C. in 1753.

(6) ANN BATES married JOHN DANIEL (See children page [illegible])

(7) HANNAH BATES married TARLTON FLEMING. TARLTON FLEMING was the son of CHARLES FLEMING and his wife SUSANNA TARLTON, son of STEPHEN TARLTON and SUSANNA BATES. This writer has never been able to find a complete list of the children of TARLTON FLEMING and HANNAH BATES, but below is given the names of those we have found ascribed to them from different sources:

(10) TARLTON FLEMING married MARY BERKELEY.
(11) ELIZABETH FLEMING married JOSIAS PAYNE, JR.
(12) JUDITH FLEMING married (1730) THOMAS WILLIAMSON.

MARY BERKELEY who married TARLTON FLEMING JR. was the daughter of EDMUND BERKELEY and JUDITH RANDOLPH, sister of THOMAS MANN RANDOLPH and ANNE CARY and daughter of WILLIAM RANDOLPH the son of THOMAS RANDOLPH and his wife JUDITH FLEMING; the latter a daughter of CHARLES FLEMING and his wife SUSANNA TARLTON (daughter of STEPHEN TARLTON and SUSANNA BATES).

JOSIAS PAYNE, JR. who married ELIZABETH FLEMING, daughter of TARLTON FLEMING, was the son of JOSIAS PAYNE and grandson of GEORGE PAYNE who married MARY WOODSON. MARY WOODSON was the sister of JOHN WOODSON who married JUDITH TARLTON (daughter of STEPHEN TARLTON and SUSANNA BATES). JOSIAS PAYNE JR. had a sister ANNE PAYNE who married WILLIAM HARRISON in 1765. JOSIAS PAYNE JR. moved from GOOCHLAND or PITTSYLVANIA COUNTY, VA. to the WATAUGA valley in TENNESSEE, and afterwards to the vicinity of NASHVILLE.

(8) JOHN BATES, JR. (brother in law of JOHN DANIEL will 1685) married SUSANNAH FLEMING. She was a sister of TARLTON FLEMING and the daughter of CHARLES FLEMING and SUSANNA TARLTON. She was the grand-daughter of STEPHEN TARLTON and SUSANNA BATES. Her sister URSULA FLEMING married TARLTON WOODSON, and after the death of her first husband JOHN BATES JR. of YORK COUNTY, she married JOHN WOODSON, a brother of TARLTON WOODSON. My information is that SUSANNA FLEMING and her first husband JOHN BATES, JR. had the following children:

(15) CHARLES BATES
(16) GEORGE BATES
(17) JOHN BATES
(18) JAMES BATES
(19) FLEMING BATES

(19) FLEMING BATES married SARAH JORDAN, daughter of BENJAMIN JORDAN, of NANSEMOND COUNTY, VIRGINIA, son of THOMAS JORDAN of CHUCKATUCK, and was the father of

(20) EDWARD BATES married MISS HARRISON
(21) ELISHA BATES married MISS HARRISON
(22) MARY BATES married RATCLIFFE
(23) SARAH BATES married RATCLIFFE
(24) THOMAS FLEMING BATES m. CAROLINE MATILDA WOODSON.

(24) THOMAS FLEMING BATES and his wife CAROLINE WOODSON (Daughter of CHARLES WOODSON and grand-daughter of TARLETON WOODSON and URSULA FLEMING) had the following children:

(25) EDWARD BATES, U. S. Attorney General.
(26) FREDERICK BATES
(27) JAMES WOODSON BATES
(28) TARLETON BATES
(29) GEORGE BATES (Gov. of Missouri).
(30) CHARLES BATES
(31) FLEMING BATES
(32) URSULA BATES m. FRANCIS KENNINGTON.

(18) HON. JAMES BATES, son of JOHN BATES, JR. and SUSANNA FLEMING, was a prominent member of the Assembly and the Conventions from GOOCHLAND COUNTY, who married SUSANNA HIX of HICKS, and had two sons who fought in the revolution, from HALIFAX COUNTY, VIRGINIA. They were:

(33) CAPT. FLEMING BATES (1747-1785)
(34) JOHN BATES.

SUSANNA FLEMING, who married JOHN BATES JR., after his death married JOHN WOODSON and moved to GOOCHLAND COUNTY and settled, and they had children JOHN, ROBERT, JOSIAH, STEPHEN, JUDITH and ELIZABETH WOODSON. JOHN WOODSON was the brother of TARLTON WOODSON and they were the sons of JOHN WOODSON who married JUDITH TARLTON and grandson of STEPHEN TARLTON and his wife SUSANNA BATES. JOHN WOODSON who married JUDITH TARLTON was the son of ROBERT WOODSON and his wife ELIZABETH; and ROBERT is supposed to have been one of the two sons of DR. JOHN WOODSON and his wife SARAH WINSTON. As stated before, JOHN BATES, the ancestor of the BATES FAMILY may also have married a WINSTON.

It will be seen that the wife of JOHN BATES, SR. (son of GEORGE BATES, son of JOHN, the emigrant) was ELIZABETH DANIEL, daughter of JOHN DANIEL and grand-daughter of ROGER DANIEL, the "known kinsman" of MILES CARY, the immigrant from BRISTOL, ENGLAND. Thus, it is shown that ELIZABETH DANIEL, her father JOHN and her grandfather ROGER DANIEL were the direct ancestors of all of the members of the BATES FAMILY shown above, from JOHN BATES JR. on down.

JOHN DANIEL (father of JOHN DANIEL who married ANN WILLIAMS, who died in GRANVILLE COUNTY, N. C. in 1763) was a first cousin of JOHN BATES JR., second cousin to HON. JAMES BATES of ALBEMARLE and to FLEMING BATES, father of the distinguished family of MISSOURI and ARKANSAS.

(34) JOHN DANIEL (Son of JOHN DANIEL and ANN BATES) married ANNE WILLIAMS, and his wife was a sister of ELIZABETH WILLIAMS who married SAMUEL HENDERSON, the ancestors of the HENDERSONS of GRANVILLE COUNTY, N. C. The children of JOHN DANIEL and his wife ANNE WILLIAMS are mentioned in JOHN'S will in GRANVILLE COUNTY, an abstract of which is given on page 212 herein. They were:

(40). JOHN WILLIAMS DANIEL
(41). JAMES DANIEL
(42). SARAH DANIEL married JOHN HARRISON.
(43). MARTHA DANIEL married a BAKER.
(44). ELIZABETH DANIEL married CHRISTOPHER DUDLEY.

(40) JOHN WILLIAMS DANIEL, on the first MONDAY in MAY, 1786, was appointed on a committee with JOHN MASON and PLEASANT HENDERSON by the County Court of GRANVILLE COUNTY to run the line between GRANVILLE and WARREN COUNTY (See page 210 herein). JOHN WILLIAMS DANIEL lived in WARREN COUNTY when he made his will May 22, 1809, in which he mentioned the following devisees:

1. My beloved wife MARY DANIEL the use of my estate both real and personal during her natural life and after her death -
2. To my son ZADOCK DANIEL, my land and plantation whereon I now live, together with my two negroes, DAVE and JERRY.
3. To my daughter MARTHA VAUGHAN my two negroes LUKE and LUCY and $50 in cash.
4. To my daughter MARY STAMPER, my negroes PHEBE, JINNY and GRACY and their increase.
5. To my step-son JONATHAN GRAVES $100.00.
6. To my step-daughter FRANCES TRICE, a box of furniture and my cubbard and old negroes SAM and NANCY.
7. My son ZADOCK and son-in-law WILLIAM STAMPER.
Witnesses: JAMES BULLOCK, FRANCIS TUCKER and WILLEY SMITH.

The husband of his daughter MARTHA DANIEL was VINCENT VAUGHAN, a fact gleaned from other sources than the will, and this name harks back to SKIMINO CREEK and NEW KENT COUNTY, where, on the Quit Rent Rolls of 1704 we find the name of VINCENT VAUGHAN, probably the grandfather or possibly the Great Grandfather of this particular VINCENT VAUGHAN.

The ZADOCK DANIEL family genealogist tells us, as does the will itself, that JOHN WILLIAMS DANIEL had been twice married. That his second wife MARY was the widow of JOHN WILLIAMS GRAVES (See abstract of his will herein p. 213), and that her maiden name was JONES. This genealogist fails to disclose the name of his first wife, whom he must have married before 1768 (as ZADOCK DANIEL was born that year) or the names of any children by his first marriage except ZADOCK. A comprehensive account of the descendents of ZADOCK DANIEL has been furnished us, including his numerous children by his wife ELIZABETH LEWIS, but no reference is made to the fact that ZADOCK DANIEL married a second wife in his old age by whom he had at least two children. An account of these will be given under WAKE COUNTY NOTES.

---

(41) JAMES DANIEL. His wife, at the time his will was written in GRANVILLE COUNTY in 1785, was SARAH. There is no mention of anything indicating that she was a second wife. His children were, according to his will he had the following children:

(50) JOHN DANIEL
(51) WILLIAM DANIEL
(52) REUBEN DANIEL m. ELIZABETH HARRISON, DEC. 12, 1781.
(53) RICHARD HARRISON
(54) JOSEPH DANIEL
(55) MARY DANIEL m. DAVID ROYSTER JAN. 11, 1775.
(56) ANN DANIEL

At the time this will was written RICHARD, JOSEPH and ANN DANIEL were probably minors, because there is a clause in the will which reads: "For each child, when they come of age a bed and furniture.

The will also mentions "my son in law EDMUND SMITH". The WILLEY SMITH who witnessed the will of his brother JOHN WILLIAMS DANIEL was probably a son of this EDMUND SMITH, and the inference from the will is that the daughter who married EDMUND SMITH is not mentioned in the will by name.

MARY DANIEL, the daughter who married DAVID ROYSTER, at the time this will was made in 1785 had three children, who are mentioned in the will: LUCY, POLLY and REBECCA ROYSTER, the testator's grandchildren.

(52) REUBEN DANIEL who married ELIZABETH HARRISON was, of course, marrying his first cousin, the daughter of JOHN HARRISON and his wife SARAH DANIEL. The family genealogist has furnished the following account of their children: (1) SOPHIA DANIEL (married SMITH), JESSE DANIEL (m. MARIA SMITH), JENNIE DANIEL (m. a WELLS), RICHARD (married a MORROW, and moved to Tennessee and later to ALABAMA), ELIZABETH (m. an UNDERWOOD), NANCY (m. a HICK), MARTHA (m. a GALLAGHER), SARAH DANIEL married AMOS LILES (1789-1863).

In order to make these numerous connections plain to the ready I shall now switch back again, this time from the DANIEL to the HARRISON FAMILY, prominent in GRANVILLE COUNTY.

THE QUEEN'S CREEK (YORK COUNTY, VA.) HARRISONS.

THE HARRISON FAMILY of GRANVILLE COUNTY, NORTH CAROLINA were of the QUEEN'S CREEK HARRISONS in YORK COUNTY, VIRGINIA.

JOHN HARRISON, who married SARAH DANIEL (p. 250) was the ancestor of the GRANVILLE COUNTY HARRISONS. His wife SARAH DANIEL was the daughter of JOHN DANIEL who married ANNE WILLIAMS, sister of ELIZABETH WILLIAMS who married SAMUEL HENDERSON. Her parents, JOHN DANIEL and ANN BATES lived somewhere between QUEEN'S CREEK and SKIMINO CREEK in YORK COUNTY, Virginia. (See map and list on page 233 herein).

JOHN HARRISON, who married SARAH DANIEL did not live in GRANVILLE COUNTY, but in HALIFAX COUNTY, Virginia, where he died in 1861. Before his death sometime he had settled there among his wife's kinfolks, the DANIEL, BATES and some of the WILLIAMS families. JOHN WILLIAMS DANIEL, his wife's brother, was named as one of the executors of his will and at that time may havd been living in HALIFAX COUNTY.

In order to establish the line of descent of JOHN HARRISON, the compiler will first attempt to show that he was NOT a descendant of what is called the JAMES RIVER HARRISONS, as these HARRISONS who descend from the first BENJAMIN HARRISON (1630) are popularly called. Numerous "family genealogists" have tried in vain to connect JOHN HARRISON (who married SARAH DANIEL) with the latter family. They refused to concede that he was not so descended, and several accounts have been PUBLISHED and are to be found in public libraries and volumes, in which such erroneous contention is adhered to, in spite of the fact that there is positively no basis for such claims. It is not improbable that there may have been a remote connection between the JAMES RIVER HARRISONS and those who settled on QUEEN'S CREEK in YORK COUNTY, but if so, it dates back to ENGLAND somewhere and is too distant to be considered here or to be of interest to this writer. My friend GEN. FRANCIS BURTON HARRISON, of VIRGINIA, co-laborer with his late brother, HON. FAIRFAX HARRISON in compiling the "SKIMINO HARRISONS" is unquestionably the best authority now living on this subject. I have pumped him dry in my bothersome efforts to connect these two families, in vain. He knows more about the JAMES RIVER HARRISON antecedents than the members of that family knows, and I am impressed with the ideas he has advanced as to whom the ancestors of the first BENJAMIN HARRISON were. In fact, I believe that in his famous "FOOTNOTES" in the VIRGINIA MAGAZINE OF HISTORY & BIOGRAPHY, particularly Vol. 53 p. 21 (January, 1945) he has found the real solution, (which is referred to and quoted from on page 99 herein).

To aid the claimants to JAMES RIVER HARRISON descent, this writer presents herewith an interesting CHART of that family, showing the MAIN DESCENDANTS ONLY of that line for the first SIX GENERATIONS. If the ancestor you claim is not among them you simply DO NOT BELONG.

(First Generation) B E N J A M I N H A R R I S O N (Died ca. 1645)

(Second) BENJAMIN HARRISON (1645-1712) — PETER HARRISON (No Issue)

(Third) BENJAMIN HARRISON (1673-1710) Of WESTOVER — HENRY HARRISON No male issue — NATHANIEL HARRISON Of WAKEFIELD

(Fourth) BENJAMIN HARRISON (Berkeley) m. ANNE CARTER ... — NATHANIEL HARRISON Of BRANDON — BENJAMIN HARRISON m. SUSANNA DIGGES

(Fifth) BENJAMIN HARRISON The "Signer" had: — NATHANIEL HARRISON (d. young); DIGGES HARRISON (d. young); BENJAMIN HARRISON m. EVELYN BYRD — NATHANIEL HARRISON had BENJ. MUMFORD HARRISON — BENJ. HARRISON

(Sixth) BENJAMIN HARRISON; WILLIAM H. HARRISON; CARTER B. HARRISON — BENJAMIN HARRISON (1747-1759); PETER COLE HARRISON

GEORGE EVELYN HARRISON — WILLIAM BYRD HARRISON

(FIFTH) CARTER HARRISON m. SUSAN RANDOLPH — NATHANIEL HARRISON m. ANN GILLIAM — HENRY HARRISON m. ELIZ AVERY — CHARLES HARRISON m. CLAIBORNE — ROBERT HARRISON

(SIXTH)
CARTER HARRISON had: ROBERT CARTER HARRISON; PEYTON HARRISON; RANDOLPH HARRISON; CARTER H. HARRISON
NATHANIEL HARRISON had: EDMUND HARRISON; BENJAMIN HARRISON; NATHANIEL HARRISON; JOHN HARRISON (Died in COLLEGE)
HENRY HARRISON had: HENRY HARRISON; PEYTON HARRISON
CHARLES HARRISON: AUGUSTINE HARRISON; CHARLES HARRISON; BENJ. H. HARRISON
ROBERT HARRISON: TWO SONS BUT IDENTITY Uncertain

According to the will of JOHN HARRISON, of HALIFAX COUNTY, VIRGINIA, in the year of 1767, he had sons JAMES, JOHN, RICHARD, ISHAM and ANDREW HARRISON. A study of the subjoined CHART of the male members of the BENJAMIN HARRISON family through the first SIX GENERATIONS will disclose, that aside from the young JOHN HARRISON (son of NATHANIEL HARRISON, of the fifth generation) there was not a male member of that Harrison family who bore any of these names. In the "REIDS and THEIR RELATIVES", a reputable genealogical work, which this writer has no desire to discredit, a THOMAS HARRISON, who is claimed to have been a descendant of the BENJAMIN HARRISON family is classed as a revolutionary soldier. There is not a THOMAS HARRISON anywhere in the JAMES RIVER HARRISONS for the first SIX GENERATIONS, so, the writer of the "REIDS" book is bound to be mistaken.

JOHN HARRISON, who married SARAH DANIEL, was born, lived a long life, begat a numerous family and died nearly twenty years before the revolutionary war got well under way. He was contemporaneous with about the FOURTH or not later than the FIFTH generation of the JAMES RIVER HARRISONS.

SIX OF THE EARLIEST HARRISONS IN VIRGINIA.

This compiler is satisfied from his investigations that all of the HARRISONS in NORTH CAROLINA came originally from VIRGINIA. GEN. FRANCIS BURTON HARRISON in a series of important articles in the Virginia Magazine of History & Biography, called "FOOTNOTES" has given an authentic account of the SIX HARRISONS known to have been the first in Colonial Virginia, which briefly stated were as follows:

1. RICHARD HARRISON, Master's Mate, who came to VIRGINIA in 1603 on a voyage with CAPT. BARTHOLOMEW GILBERT, a nephew of SIR WALTER RALEIGH. They probably landed on the "EASTERN SHORE" of Virginia, in what is now ACCOMAC or NORTHAMPTON COUNTY. This was three years before the first emigrants arrived in VIRGINIA. Most of the party, including RICHARD HARRISON, were killed by the INDIANS, and HENRY SUITE thereupon took his course home for ENGLAND. This RICHARD is identified by GEN. FRANCIS BURTON HARRISON as a probable uncle of JOHN HARRISON, who in 1622-3 was Acting Governor of the BERMUDAS.

2. ENSIGN JAMES HARRISON lived in VIRGINIA from the time of his arrival in 1618 until his death, MARCH 22, 1622. He first entered Virginia as one of CAPT. JOHN MARTIN'S "people" and was sent out by MARTIN with Ensign Rossingham to trade for corn with the INDIANS of the "EASTERN SHORE". His wife was ANNE OLIFF, and after the death of ENSIGN JAMES HARRISON his widow ANNE (OLIFF) HARRISON became the wife of the famous JUSTINIAN COOPER.

3. HARMON HARRISON, according to CAPT. JOHN SMITH, came to Virginia in 1608 on CHRISTOPHER NEWPORT'S third Voyage. It is believed that he died of fever or some ailment. It is established that HARMON HARRISON was a brother of JEFFREY HARRISON, Mariner, who died leaving a will proven in LONDON in 1605. No proof of the date of his death, but it is surmised that he died unmarried and without children because of his disappearance from the records of the Colony, shortly after his arrival in the country. HUGH BLAIR GRIGSBY advanced the theory that HARMON HARRISON may have been the father of BENJAMIN HARRISON of the Council. More will be said about HARMON HARRISON later in the notes.

4. ANNE HARRISON, the wife of ENSIGN JAMES HARRISON who became the wife of JUSTINIAN COOPER. The will of JUSTINIAN COOPER shows they left no surviving children.

5. LIEUT. GEORGE HARRISON lived in VIRGINIA for SIX years and died there in 1624, having arrived there in 1618. He was a son of WILLIAM HARRISON and a brother of SIR. JOHN HARRISON, of LONDON. He settled on the Easterly side of CHIPOAKES CREEK in what is now SURRY COUNTY, and directly opposite to MARTIN'S BRANDON. BENJAMIN HARRISON, of the COUNCIL, owned land also on the "Upper Chippoakes" near by the same place. One would naturally think they may have been brothers, but from all accounts they were NOT, though their relationship is possible in some degree. In a dispute with CAPT. RICHARD STEPHENS in 1624 he received a slash between the garter and the knee & shortly thereafter died. A jury decided that he died a natural death and not from the wound thus received.

6. RALPH HARRISON died in what is now ELIZABETH CITY COUNTY sometime between APRIL in 1623 and FEB. 16th of the following year. He had, it seems, previously been living in the EAST INDIES before 1609. Nothing further appears to be known about him, so far as his residence in Virginia is concerned.

From 1624 for the next six years, or until 1630, no person of the name of HARRISON is known to have been living in VIRGINIA.

FROM "THE SKIMINO HARRISONS" (p. 5). We know that RICHARD HARRISON (1600-1664), the immigrant, was born in ST. NICHOLAS PARISH in the town of COLCHESTER, ESSEX, but when and under what circumstances he came to VIRGINIA we do not know. The earliest record of him in Virginia is of his paying tithes in 1634 in respect of a patent of land on QUEEN'S CREEK, in MIDDLETOWN (afterwards BRUTON) PARISH, YORK COUNTY. His plantation lay within the limits of SKIMINO HUNDRED and for nearly two hundred years the name SKIMINO spelled HOME to his family. His estate shows he was a man of substance, and in addition to himself and his wife ELIZABETH HENCOTT he brought into the Colony eight persons.

THE FIRST HARRISONS OF QUEEN'S CREEK. So far as the actual records show RICHARD HARRISON was the first of the name to settle on QUEEN'S CREEK in YORK COUNTY, VIRGINIA. His wife was ELIZABETH BESOUTH and JAMES BESOUTH, a brother of ELIZABETH HARRISON arrived in VIRGINIA and settled in the same general neighborhood about the same time. In 1635 he witnessed a deed by Capt. JOHN UTI , of UTIMARIA, with EDWARD MAJOR. JAMES BESOUTH lived until 1681.

In 1645 a certain JOHN HARRISON, designated as a "close kinsman" of RICHARD HARRISON, above, was living there on QUEEN'S CREEK and bought two Indians.

RICHARD HARRISON'S "close kinsman" DR. JEREMY HARRISON settled near him, also on QUEEN'S CREEK, according to the "SKIMINO HARRISONS" page 6. He had been in the East Indian service. He married a MISS WHITEGRAVE. The available records about him fail to show any evidence that he left any children or descendants. One writer in TYLER'S MAGAZINE, Vol. 6, declares that he was a brother of JOHN HARRISON, mentioned above.

JEREMY HARRISON and JOHN HARRISON were sons of a HENRY HARRISON who may have been in Virginia contemporaneously with RICHARD HARRISON.

ROBERT HARRISON (1612-1668) also settled first in MIDDLETOWN (BRUTON) PARISH and latterly in YORK-HAMPTON Parish in York County and in 1650 married ELIZABETH COMINS, daughter of NICHOLAS COMINS and his wife ELEANOR (who may have been a HARRISON). After the death of NICHOLAS COMINS, his widow ELEANOR married FRANCIS WHEELER. Many of the HARRISONS in NORTH and SOUTH CAROLINA were descended from this ROBERT HARRISON, including COL. ROBERT BURTON, whose grandmother was AMADHA HARRISON, his daughter.

NICHOLAS HARRISON. This was DR. NICHOLAS HARRISON, who also owned lands on QUEEN'S CREEK and in 1653 made his last will and testament and gave all of his estate to his mother, DOROTHY HARRISON. It was a nuncupative will and was sworn to by JANE PARSONS and ELIZABETH CHAMBERS. This Dr. NICHOLAS HARRISON was a ship's doctor, but at the time of his death was designated as a "planter of York County". Obviously, he died without children and may never have been married.

CAPT. THOMAS HARRISON was another one of the name who settled on QUEEN'S CREEK in YORK County. He is supposed to have been a seaman and Master of the Ship "HONOUR", which belonged to COL. WILLIAM PRYOR, a member of the Court of YORK COUNTY and who was otherwise prominent. On JAN. 11, 1641/2 he bought 200 acres in the Parish and County of York from CAPT. WILLIAM BROCAS and DANIEL DICKINSON for 4000 pounds of tobacco. He and CAPT. THOMAS HARWOOD and RICHARD BENNETT, Esq. are each remembered in the will of COL. WILLIAM PRYOR which was admitted to record in York County on January 25, 1646. Col. Pryor, in his will, also mentions his brother in law, JASPER CLAYTON and his daughters MARGARET and MARY PRIOR, leaving to the former "my whole part of the ship HONOUR" commanded by CAPT. THOMAS HARRISON. The following interesting item is taken from William & Mary Magazine Vol. 25:

> "WHEREAS, FRANCIS WHEELER, of LONDON, Merchant, bound for Virginia, on the Ship "HONOUR" with CAPT. THOMAS HARRISON, he (FRANCIS WHEELER) being servant (in the service)of MR. JOHN WHITE, of LONDON, Grocer, WHEELER & WHITE, appoint ANTHONY STANFORD, factor for WILLIAM ALLEN, a Merchant, agent to trade goods in the event WHEELER should die." Date, SEPT. 16- 1645. *
>
> Another item dated JAN. 20, 1646:
>
> "Tobacco to be delivered to WILLIAM ALLEN, merchant in LONDON by CAPT. WILLIAM BROCAS, ESQ. and wife MARY, to THOMAS HARRISON, Master of the ship HONOUR". *

* FRANCIS WHEELER married ELEANOR COMINS (after the death of NICHOLAS COMINS) and became the step-father of ELIZABETH COMINS the wife of ROBERT HARRISON; and CAPT. WILLIAM BROCAS sold lands in YORK COUNTY to CAPT. THOMAS HARRISON. COL. ROBERT BURTON, of GRANVILLE COUNTY, whose mother was TABITHA MINGE, was the grandson of MARY HUNT who married ROBERT MINGE son of JAMES MINGE and AMADHA HARRISON (Daughter of ROBERT HARRISON and ELIZABETH COMINS), and after the death of ROBERT MINGE she married WILLIAM ALLEN, whose sister JUDITH ALLEN married NOEL HUNT BURTON, grandfather of COL. ROBERT BURTON.

Considering the above, we have listed the following HARRISONS who settled on QUEEN'S CREEK in YORK COUNTY:

1. RICHARD HARRISON (1630)
2. JOHN HARRISON (1645)
3. JEREMY HARRISON (1645)
4. ROBERT HARRISON (1650)
5. NICHOLAS HARRISON, M. D. (1653)
6. CAPT. THOMAS HARRISON

In listing the above HARRISONS we have given the dates where they are shown on the records, though it is patent that some of them were there much earlier. And we have omitted the mention of TWO OTHER HARRISONS who MAY have been residing in the same locality at the same time:

7. HARMON HARRISON, who came to VIRGINIA in 1608 on CHRISTOPHER NEWPORT'S third Voyage, and whose name disappears from the records and who "is believed to have died of fever or some ailment". The mere disappearance of his name from the records does not establish it as a fact that he died. His brother, WILLIAM, lived until 1634. He may have lived even longer, but the fact that he was not mentioned in WILLIAM'S will may mean that he was <u>then</u> dead. The testator, WILLIAM, when he made his will, mentioned his OWN SON, WILLIAM, with an expression of doubt "if living, or his heirs". If he did not know whether his eldest son was alive, doubtless he was equally ignorant as to brother HARMON'S being alive or deceased.

8. BURR HARRISON. (Hope the professional genealogists will throw a fit!). The name, on the records of LANCASTER COUNTY in 1654, is spelled BOUR, but I have no sort of doubt but what it was the old NORTHERN NECK BURR or "BUR" as he sometimes signed it himself. (Pages 51 and 69 Vol. 22 VIRGINIA COLONIAL ABSTRACTS by BEVERLY FLEET, for Lancaster County.)

It is not the theory of the compiler that all of the EIGHT HARRISONS who settled in YORK COUNTY, VIRGINIA, most of them owning lands and living on QUEEN'S CREEK, were brothers. It is his theory that there is a strong probability that they were all more or less related to each other. From what has been said in the preceding page (253) there is strong evidence of a very close relationship between ROBERT HARRISON and CAPT. THOMAS HARRISON. Charts of the first three generations of the families of ROBERT HARRISON and RICHARD HARRISON have been furnished the writer by GEN. FRANCIS BURTON HARRISON, of Charlottesville, Virginia, which show:

RICHARD HARRISON (1620-1664) married ELIZABETH BESOUTH, and emigrated to Virginia about 1634-5. He died about 1664. Will lost because of disappearance of the record book. The supervisors of his will were ROBERT HARRISON and JAMES BESOUTH. This is a very strong indication that ROBERT and RICHARD HARRISON were brothers, as JAMES BESOUTH is known to have been his brother in law. RICHARD HARRISON had these children:

(1) JOHN HARRISON (1646-1690) m. MARY HALL.
(2) WILLIAM HARRISON (1650-1713-19) m. MARY HUBBARD.
(3) JAMES HARRISON (1658-1703?) m. (1) ANNE (2) JANE BURLEY.
(4) ANNE HARRISON m. JOHN KENDALL (1638-1702)
(5) ELEANOR HARRISON (b. 1655) m. WILLIAM WALTER.

(1) JOHN HARRISON and MARY HALL had children: MARY HARRISON m. JOHN HUBBARD, and RICHARD HARRISON (1680-1722). His will mentions JOHN KENDALL and sister MARY HUBBARD.

(2) WILLIAM HARRISON and wife MARY HUBBARD (Dau. of MATTHEW HUBBARD) was the ancestor of the "SKIMINO HARRISONS", and had four children: WILLIAM HARRISON married ANN RATCLIFFE (his dates 1680-1722); JOHN HARRISON (alive 1727) possibly moved to SURRY COUNTY; THOMAS HARRISON (living in 1710); SAMUEL HARRISON (living in 1715.). JOHN HARRISON (who was alive in 1727) married MARY.... MRS. MARY (HUBBARD) HARRISON was living in 1709 when she gave a power of attorney to or in connection with land bought by WILLIAM JORDAN (York County Records), and in 1714 FLORANCE McCARTY bought a tract of land from JOHN HARRISON and his wife MARY. This JOHN was the son of (2) WILLIAM HARRISON.

(3) JAMES HARRISON (1658-1703) m (1) ANNE (2) JANE BURLEY, widow of GEORGE BURLEY, but so far as is known, had no children. Nothing shown after 1703 about him.

(4) ANNE HARRISON (m. JOHN KENDALL, who left will in 1702 and only mentions one son, RICHARD KENDALL. In 1711 RICHARD KENDALL served on a jury in YORK COUNTY.

(5) ELEANOR HARRISON married WILLIAM WALTER. No further information, except that long afterwards a WALTERS FAMILY was intimately connected with the HARRISONS of PITTSYLVANIA COUNTY, Virginia, who may or may not have been of this same tribe.

ROBERT HARRISON (1613-1668) was aged 45 years in 1658. His wife was ELIZABETH COMINS (Or CUMMINGS as I find it on the YORK RECORDS), the daughter of NICHOLAS COMINS and his wife ELEANOR, who after his death married FRANCIS WHEELER. From all accounts it appears that this was the elder FRANCIS WHEELER, father of another FRANCIS WHEELER, a London Merchant. ELIZABETH COMINS who married ROBERT HARRISON about 1650 had one brother NICHOLAS COMINS, whose wife was named ELIZABETH. According to FRANCIS BURTON HARRISON'S chart, ROBERT HARRISON and his wife ELIZABETH COMINS had the following children:

(1) NICHOLAS HARRISON (1652-1697) n. m.
(2) ROBERT HARRISON m. SARAH.
(3) JAMES HARRISON (1661-1695) died s. p.
(4) AMATHA HARRISON (1650-17___) m. JAMES MINGE.
(5) FRANCES HARRISON m. THOMAS SHANDS.

The following additional information comes from a different source, and adds a daughter ELIZABETH HARRISON to the above list, in what purports to be the will of ROBERT HARRISON. It gives no further information about either NICHOLAS or JAMES HARRISON, but does give the following:

(2) ROBERT HARRISON was a builder and erected the brick prison or jail in YORKTOWN and perhaps the CUSTOM HOUSE located there.

(4) AMATHA HARRISON was mentioned as the grand-child of MRS. ELEANOR WHEELER in her will in 1660, together with her son NICHOLAS COMINS. And AMATHA HARRISON, after having been previously married once or twice, finally married JAMES MINGE, the Clerk of CHARLES CITY COUNTY, VIRGINIA, and they were the parents of a ROBERT MINGE, who married MARY HUNT, daughter of WILLIAM HUNT and TABITHA EDLOE. This last marriage produced TABITHA MINGE, who married HUTCHINS BURTON, who was the father of COL. ROBERT BURTON, of GRANVILLE COUNTY, NORTH CAROLINA. HUTCHINS BURTON moved from VIRGINIA to GRANVILLE COUNTY, where he had a tragic ending (See p. 20 of this volume).

(5) FRANCES HARRISON married THOMAS SHANDS, the father of WILLIAM who patented lands in SURRY COUNTY, VA. in 1722 and married ELIZABETH ROBERTS, daughter of JOHN ROBERTS, of SURRY COUNTY, who left a will in 1740. They had one son named WILLIAM SHANDS. This WILLIAM SHANDS died leaving a will in SURRY COUNTY, VIRGINIA in 1759, in which is named sons THOMAS, JOHN and WILLIAM SHANDS, and THREE daughters, whose Christian names are omitted, but who married respectively, one a man named STUART, another a NATHANIEL MITCHELL, and another a certain CHRISTOPHER GOLIGHTLY.

NOTE: IT appears MOST obvious that, considering the data above presented, ROBERT and RICHARD HARRISON were brothers, and there is also a very strong indication that CAPT. FRANCIS WHEELER'S presence connects them with CAPT. THOMAS HARRISON mighty close. Follow the line.

SOME DESCENDANTS OF (42) SARAH DANIEL AND JOHN HARRISON

JOHN HARRISON, who married SARAH DANIEL, died in HALIFAX COUNTY, VIRGINIA, as has been heretofore stated in the year 1761. The witnesses to his will were JOSEPH COLLINS, FRANCIS LUCK and one THOMAS GREENWOOD, and the Executors were JOHN CHISUM (CHISHOLM) and JOHN WILLIAMS DANIEL his brother in law. From the will and from other reliable sources, the children of JOHN HARRISON and SARAH DANIEL were as follows:

100. JAMES HARRISON (b. JULY 20, 1748) m. ELIZABETH HAMPTON. (x)
101. JOHN HARRISON.
102. ANDREW HARRISON
103. RICHARD HARRISON (b. MARCH 18, 1752) m. ANN PATILLO. *
104. ISHAM HARRISON (b. 1750) m. AMY GILLIAM
105. MARY HARRISON m. a COOPER.
106. MARTHA HARRISON m. a COOPER
107. ELIZABETH HARRISON m. REUBEN DANIEL (See p. 250).
108. NANCY ANN HARRISON m. WILLIAM DANIEL**

*ANN PATILLO was the daughter of REV. HENRY PATILLO the noted pioneer NORTH CAROLINA minister and teacher.

**WILLIAM DANIEL who married NANCY ANN HARRISON was the Great Great grandfather of this compiler.

(x) ELIZABETH HAMPTON was the sister of the first COL. WADE HAMPTON, who served in the American Revolution.

---

100. JAMES HARRISON (These numbers are merely for identification and to be used in references in other parts of the account) married ELIZABETH HAMPTON, a daughter of ANTHONY HAMPTON who was masacred by the Indians in the upper part of South Carolina, and who was a sister of Col. Wade Hampton, as stated above. The best and most reliable account this compiler has been able to find of their children is as follows:

200. JOHN HAMPTON HARRISON (1777-1828) m. JEMIMAH JENKINS.
201. HARRIET HARRISON (b. 1778) m. SAMUEL EARLE.
202. LOUISE JANE HARRISON (b. 1780) m. (1) JOHN WRIGHT (2) a WILSON.
203. JAMES HARRISON (b. 1782) m. SARAH EARLE.
204. CLARISSA HARRISON (b. 1784)
205. RICHARD HARRISON m. CATHERINE SLOAN
206. ISHAM HARRISON (b. 1789) m. HARRIET KELSEY.
207. THOMAS HARRISON (b. 1790) m. HANNAH EARLE
208. ELIZABETH HARRISON (b. 1792) m. ROWLAND THURMOND.
209. MARY V. HARRISON m. EARL HARRIS.
210. BENJAMIN HARRISON (1796-1812).
211. HENRY HARRISON (1798-1808).

---

101. JOHN HARRISON
102. ANDREW HARRISON

JAMES HARRISON, who married SARAH EARLE was the grandfather of DR. THOMAS PERRIN HARRIS, of the English Department of the North Carolina State College of Agriculture and Engineering of the University of North Carolina, in 1943, in a letter to this compiler, makes the following interesting observations in regard to the history of JOHN and ANDREW HARRISON, who were two of the sons of JOHN HARRISON and SARAH DANIEL:

> "My grandfather HARRISON appears in all his records to be scrupulously careful. Here is what he wrote of his uncles, JOHN and ANDREW:
>
> 'ANDREW never married, died a young man in GRANVILLE'.
>
> 'JOHN married, died in the employ of LAMAR and WILLIAMS at a place now or lately called Huntsville near the Shallow Ford on Yadkin, Surry county, N. C.'
>
> "The account continues about grandfather's father:
>
> 'JAMES married ELIZABETH HAMPTON, whilst in the employ of the same firm, in their store at GRAY BYNUMS on Town Fork branch of DAN RIVER, two miles from Stokes, C. H., N. C.' ".

103. RICHARD HARRISON and his wife ANNE PATILLO (Dau. of Rev. HENRY PATILLO) according to the best authority available, had these children:

220. JOHN HARRISON (b. 1776)
221. JANE HARRISON (b. 1779) m. CHRISTOPHER COLLINGTON (See p. 254)
222. BETSY HARRISON m. JAMES MOSS
223. MARY HARRISON m. THOMAS WOODRUFF — GR. GR. Grandson of BENNET HARRISON of QUEEN'S CREEK.
224. HENRY HARRISON (b. 1782).
225. RICHARD HARRISON (b. 1787) m. a widow CRUMP who was ANN MOORE.
227. SARAH PATILLO HARRISON married ANDREW BANKY.

NOTE: A JAMES PATILLO HARRISON (b. 1789) m. SALLIE LANDRON in LUNENBURG CO. Va. 1807.

LETTER FROM GEN. FRANCIS BURTON HARRISON, OF VIRGINIA.

612 Rugby Road, Charlottesville, Va.
October 23, 1942.

Worth S. Ray, Esq.
Box 1111, Austin, Texas.

My Dear Mr. Ray:

I have this morning received your very kind and most interesting letter, and it gives me great pleasure to enter into a correspondence with one whose ancestors three hundred years ago lived as near neighbors of my own in York County, Virginia.

First, let me offer several suggestions in explanation of the Harrisons of Skimino. This was undertaken by my brother and myself as a memorial to our father who died in 1904. The material for the biographies of the three generations back of us was collected by me from family letters which I assembled for the purpose from various members of the family.

The genealogical research in XVII and XVIII (centuries) records was done for me by a professional genealogist, our cousin, the late Wilson Miles Cary, who had been living in London and had made considerable investigation of the records there at my request for the English provenance of our Queen's Greek Harrisons. (Skimino was the name of the Quaker Meeting house which they attended after the middle of the XVIII century. I wanted my brother to call the stock the "Harrisons of Queen's Creek".)

We became rather impatient with the length of W. Cary's research in the English records and decided to go ahead without waiting for full proof of the theories then in hand - hence several mistakes, as we later discovered, in the early genealogy.

These I will indicate as follows:

(a) There is no proof that Richard Harrison of Queen's Creek, came from St. Nicholas Parish, Colchester - although I have for many years been living in England myself and have indulged in much research. I have today no idea whence Richard Harrison came.

(b) There is no proof of the names of the wives of the first three Harrisons (Richard I, William I and William II) of Queen's Creek - they are mere surmises and tho' possibly correct, are not justified in our book.

My brother felt so chagrined over this (when we were better informed) that he declined to distribute the rest of the copies of the Harrisons of Skimino. When I came back from Europe last year, my sister in law and I decided to complete the distribution of this book and this has been done to several libraries throughout the country. After all, it was really a biographical work, and the genealogy was only incidental to it.

As for the Harrison items on the genealogy, I am satisfied that they are scrupulously accurate and to be entirely relied on from say 1650 downwards.

So far as I know, of the three sons left by Richard I, Harrison, of Queen's Creek (who died 1664) and the three sons of his brother (?) Robert Harrison who moved about 1664 from Queen's Creek to the site of the property now known as "Ringside" in York County and died there in 1668, there were no MALE descendants in the third generation except in my own line. I should much like to be corrected if inaccurate in this point - or any other statement I may venture to offer you.

Your opinion that these men Richard I and Robert were of the third generation in Virginia is of extreme interest to me at the present moment, since I am engaged in writing a "footnote" on the six or seven Harrisons known to have been in Virginia up to 1624 when the Charter was revoked. So far as I have been able to ascertain, none of them left descendants in Virginia. If you can tell me otherwise I shall not only be exceedingly grateful but take pleasure in giving you due appreciation in my article.

If Richard I and Robert of Queen's Creek were of the third generation, and born and brought up in Virginia, that would explain why they could not sign their own names!

As for Benjamin I, Harrison, the immigrant and founder of the family of James River Harrisons, I shall be able to publish no proof of his English provenance unless those who are still working on the records for me in England can gather further information. Conditions nowadays over there are, as you can well imagine, exceedingly difficult. One lady who was doing some work for me last year in Norfolk has been bombed out three times. It takes months to get answers to ordinary questions sent to England. All I could do in an article on Benjamin (I) at present is to sum up the information in hand and indulge in "speculations". My only excuse for offering even a speculation at this time would be that I am getting pretty old myself!

It would not surprise me to find relationship between the Harrisons of Queen's Creek and those of Brandon, since my great grandfather Harrison, of Lynchburg, a century ago used to tell his children that he was "related to the best people on the South side of the James" - but naturally I have never cared to make use of so vague a statement and have always denied stoutly any such relationship as (to) the Harrisons.

The other Harrison families in lower tidewater to which you make reference are of course of great interest to me, but I cannot make even fairly intelligent comment on them without a good deal of research. When I left occupied France last year, I was allowed as a special courtesy from the German High Command to bring out one suit case of my papers. I naturally chose my English notes, since I knew I could recapture those relating to Virginia from the records over here.

Please forgive the length of this letter and believe me, very glad to be in touch with you, and I should be most grateful for any further information you can give me about my ancestors of Queen's Creek. I am much entertained by your description of the rush of Harrisons all over the country to get on the band-wagon of Brandon and Berkeley. As I have been living abroad for thirty years, I assumed that people had all become Democrats over here.

Sincerely yours,
FRANCIS BURTON HARRISON.

GEN. FRANCIS BURTON HARRISON (Governor General of the Philipines in the administration of Woodrew Wilson) is a descendant of RICHARD HARRISON (1620 -1664) of QUEEN'S CREEK in YORK COUNTY, VIRGINIA. In one of his "Footnotes" (51 Va. Mag p. 160) Gen. Harrison makes public for the first time in 1943 an abstract of the will of a JEFFREY HARRISON, proved in LONDON, Dec. 17, 1605, in which he mentioned his mother SUSANNA and the following brothers and sisters:

(1) WILLIAM HARRISON
(2) ROBERT HARRISON
(3) HARMON HARRISON
(4) THOMASINE CLERE
(5) ANN REYNOLDS.

(1) WILLIAM HARRISON (called the oldest brother in the will) left will in LONDON also on May 5, 1634. In his will he mentioned his own children, WILLIAM, TOBIAS, SUSAN and MARY and his wife MARY. He also mentioned his two sisters ANN REYNOLDS and THOMASINE CLERE and his brother ROBERT; also leaving a bequest to "my brother's children, ROBERT and MARTHA."

(3) HARMON HARRISON is identified as the HARMON who came to VIRGINIA in 1608, and who is supposed to have died shortly after, leaving no issue.

(4) THOMASINE HARRISON had married MR. CLARE or CLEARE, Master of a ship called the "GIFT OF GOD", which belonged partly to JEFFREY HARRISON, her brother, and which is mentioned frequently in the very early Colonial records. In 1623 the "GIFT OF GOD" was under a charter to EDWARD BENNETT of VIRGINIA and was still under the command of CAPT. CLAIRE, her husband.

(5) ANN HARRISON in 1605 was married to WILLIAM REYNOLDS, named in the JEFFREY HARRISON will as his executor. At that time he had a son NICHOLAS REYNOLDS, called the "nephew" of the testator.

We find WILLIAM REYNOLDS living on QUEEN'S CREEK in YORK COUNTY, VIRGINIA, as early as 1641.

We know that HARMON HARRISON came to VIRGINIA in 1608. He, also, possibly lived in this neighborhood in YORK.

The YORK COUNTY records show a family of CLEARE living in the county as late as 1687. (Vol. VIII York Records).

ANN HARRISON lived on QUEEN'S CREEK, the wife of WILLIAM REYNOLDS.

ROBERT HARRISON lived on QUEEN'S CREEK at least as early as 1645, when he had a dispute with JOHN UNDERWOOD. (Vol. II, York Records, p. 49).

RICHARD HARRISON lived on QUEEN'S CREEK (apparently a brother of ROBERT,) as early as 1634 when he paid tithes.

Dr. NICHOLAS HARRISON also lived there until his death in 1653. (See page 253).

CAPT. THOMAS HARRISON, who bought lands in this same settlement is mentioned as early as 1640.

Deed, JUNE 10, 1641. John Bell of Queen's Creek, planter, sells SAMUEL WATKINS his plantation and house in QUEEN'S CREEK, formerly purchased from WILLIAM REYNOLDS. Witnesses were George Clarke and William Roberts. (Vol. 1 York Records). This was apparently the same lands, or a part of them, which was afterwards sold by John Bell to John Williams, ancestor of the family that afterwards married into the DANIEL and HENDERSON FAMILIES of GRANVILLE COUNTY, NORTH CAROLINA.

The truth of the matter is that the mere fact that certain members of a family are never mentioned on the public records does not mean they have ceased to exist or never existed. There were many more families named HARRISON in York County than have ever been found on the records. To say they never existed and were NOT there does not make sense. Non-contemporaneous records establish that they MUST have been there, in order to account for so many who appeared to have once been there represented.

TO ILLUSTRATE: In 1645 ROBERT HARRISON and JOHN UNDERWOOD were directed by the YORK COUNTY COURT to "agree upon a division of a cropp" of tobacco. Some fifty years later an ANDREW HARRISON married a grand-daughter of JOHN UNDERWOOD. Who was that ANDREW HARRISON? Was he of no relation to ROBERT HARRISON? Considering the custom and complex of these early families to intermarry with their oldest associated families and their cousins, an almost universal practice among them, a negative answer would not make sense or sound reasonable. So far as the records show ROBERT HARRISON had no son or grandson named ANDREW, or "any male descendants of the name of HARRISON after the THIRD GENERATION." But he could have had a cousin ANDREW HARRISON, the son of a BROTHER, who in turn, had a son ANDREW. That is probably what happened.

That RICHARD and ROBERT HARRISON were brothers is almost conclusively proven by the fact that ROBERT HARRISON was one of supervisors of RICHARD HARRISON'S will in 1664, with RICHARD'S brother in law JAMES BESOUTH, and the further fact that when ROBERT HARRISON, son of ROBERT died his legatees were his "loving friend RICHARD KENDALL and his heirs". This RICHARD KENDALL was the son of JOHN KENDALL and ANNE HARRISON, the daughter of RICHARD. As ROBERT HARRISON was born in 1613 and RICHARD seven years later in 1620, one can see also that these two brothers represented only a piece of a family. Sons and daughters may have been born before ROBERT and also between ROBERT and RICHARD. Who were these missing sons and daughters, and who were the parents? Without actual proof the evidence is convincingly strong that they were the sons of ROBERT, the brother of JEFFREY HARRISON and of HARMON HARRISON, and of MRS. ANN (HARRISON) REYNOLDS, the wife of WILLIAM REYNOLDS, of QUEEN'S CREEK. So, after familiarising himself with the extant records of all the HARRISONS in Virginia at this period, and their numerous activities, he concludes that:

ROBERT HARRISON and his wife MARY had children:

(1) GEORGE HARRISON "Mariner", d. 1634.
(2) ROBERT HARRISON (1613-1668)
(3) SAMUEL HARRISON
(4) RICHARD HARRISON
(5) MARTHA HARRISON

(1) GEORGE HARRISON made his will Nov. 17, 1630, in which he mentions his brother RICHARD HARRISON. Other legatees were GERALD PINSON, ROBERT COLSON, PETER HOLLOWAY and WILLIAM ALLISON. The will shows he had been in the service of the EAST INDIA COMPANY.

(2) ROBERT HARRISON (See pages 253-254).

(3) SAMUEL HARRISON. I have found no record of SAMUEL HARRISON, but have a record of another SAMUEL, whom I am quite sure must have been his son. He died in GLOUCESTER COUNTY (Va.) in FEB. 1703-4 without leaving a will. His wife was SARAH HUNT, the daughter of WILLIAM HUNT who died in GLOUCESTER in 1688. (ROBERT MINGE, a grandson of ROBERT HARRISON (1613-1668) married MARY HUNT, daughter of a WILLIAM HUNT, probable son of this WILLIAM). The will of THOMAS PINSON (Of GLOUCESTER) in 1697, mentions two sons of SAMUEL HARRISON: WILLIAM HARRISON and SAMUEL HARRISON, JR. In 1744 two grandchildren of SAMUEL HARRISON and his wife SARAH HUNT were JOSEPH and PRISCILLA HARRISON.

(4) RICHARD HARRISON (1620-1664) See pages 253-254.

(5) MARTHA HARRISON. Mentioned in the will of her Uncle, WILLIAM HARRISON in 1634. No further record.

CAPT. THOMAS HARRISON of the ship HONOUR, owned by COL. WILLIAM PRYOR, was obviously a very close kinsman of the children of ROBERT HARRISON and his wife MARY named in the above list. I am inclined to the view that he was a cousin of ROBERT, JEFFREY and HARMON HARRISON and that he was also the brother of ELLENER HARRISON who was the wife of COL. WILLIAM PRYOR. In fact, in the abstract of COL. PRYOR'S will in YORK COUNTY, he is called "brother in law" but GEN. FRANCIS BURTON HARRISON who has gone to much trouble to investigate the matter, declares that in the ENGLISH VERSION of the will, which he examined, it is revealed that this is a mistake, due to a misplaced comma. CAPT. THOMAS HARRISON'S dates are 1590-1678, which would make him a contemporary of MRS. PRYOR and of the parents of ROBERT and RICHARD HARRISON. I regret very much my inability to give a list of his children. It appears that he died leaving a will in which their names are mentioned. Among them was a JOHN HARRISON, who died before his father. This JOHN HARRISON left a son JOHN, who was Master of a vessel riding in JAMES RIVER on May 15, 1706 and whose name appears on a petition presented to the council by a number of other seamen for some purpose. (Executive Journals of Virginia). A later CAPT. THOMAS HARRISON who patented lands in SURRY COUNTY with one JOHN SCOTT on ATCHAMOWSOCK SWAMP falling into the NOTTOWAY RIVER, whom I have not positively identified at this writing may have been a grandson also. He was apparently one of the PRINCE GEORGE and BRUNSWICK COUNTY HARRISON ancestors, his daughter ANN HARRISON having married one of the HAMBLINS from YORK COUNTY.

HARMON HARRISON. It is the writer's deliberate conclusion after working for some years on this HARRISON FAMILY, that HARMON HARRISON, son of SUSANNA, and brother of JEFFREY HARRISON, who came to JAMESTOWN on CHRISTOPHER NEWPORT'S third voyage in 1608-9, did NOT die of disease, that he survived the Indian troubles (perhaps because of being absent from the Colony at the time), that he married and left children and that he was the ancestor of a large number of the HARRISON FAMILIES of VIRGINIA who have been so much trouble to the genealogists for the past hundred years or more. He was the ancestor of JOHN HARRISON who married SARAH DANIEL, who settled in and finally died, leaving a will in the County of HALIFAX in VIRGINIA, an abstract of which is on page 255. He married a sister of ANDREW HILL, whose son ANDREW was in NORFOLK in 1638 and 23 years old at that time. Their children were: (*)

1. JOHN HARRISON m. MYLBOROUGH HILL
2. THOMAS HARRISON
3. JAMES HARRISON
4. ANDREW HARRISON
5. HANNAH HARRISON m. JAMES HILL
6. WILLIAM HARRISON
7. THOMASINE HARRISON m. RICHARD WHITEHEAD.
8. ELIZABETH HARRISON m. JOHN HILL.

(*) What the writer is trying to do is to explain, as near as he can, from whence came the numerous families who settled in GRANVILLE COUNTY, NORTH CAROLINA, and what became of them, and in this instance, where the Harrisons came from. He knows their ancestry was from the South side of the JAMES RIVER and that they were related to the HARRISONS of QUEEN'S CREEK in YORK COUNTY. The records to be drawn upon are very scant. The only record of HARMON HARRISON has already been repeated. The names of his children and grand-children are simply the work of deduction BASED UPON THE FEW SCANT RECORDS available. Pure reason and common sense has been employed. The hard-boiled genealogist is expected to reject it all and many of them at the same time will adopt as the Gospel truth material that has not a grain of sense to it, when subjected to the light of pure reason. I can prove in hundreds of instances that they are wrong, and challenge any of them to DISPROVE these records(?).

Here I shall quote from the "Harrisons of Skimino, page 16:

> "In 1768 the Harrisons of Skimino became Quakers, and by the marriage of William Harrison, fourth of the name, with Margaret Jordan, there was blended in the blood of his descendants an inheritance of the vigorous and manly character of the Jordans of Nansemond and the Bates of Skimino, who, since 1660 had been leaders among the Friends in Virginia."

WILLIAM HARRISON, the first (son of RICHARD HARRISON) married MARY, who was the daughter of either MATTHEW HUBBARD or his wife's second husband, JEROME HAM. She may have been MARY HAM. This first WILLIAM'S dates are 1750-1719.

WILLIAM HARRISON, the second (1675-1727) married ANNE RATCLIFFE.

WILLIAM HARRISON, the third, (1705-1771) married MARGARET BUCK.

WILLIAM HARRISON, the fourth, (1740-1819) married in 1765, MARGARET JORDAN, referred to in the above quotation.

RICHARD HARRISON was contemporaneous with the children of HARMON HARRISON named on the preceding page (1620-1664). Both were of the second generation. Therefore, the WILLIAM HARRISON "fourth of the name" who brought the QUEEN'S CREEK HARRISONS into the QUAKERS, was of the SIXTH GENERATION.

I shall now take up one of my "fragments" from the actual records:

WILLIAM BRESSIE, or BRESSEY, was a QUAKER, who had settled early on LAWNE'S CREEK, on the plantation of CHRISTOPHER LAWNE in ISLE OF WIGHT COUNTY. In 1674 he was one of the overseers of the will of MAJ. NICHOLAS HILL. He was a planter in ISLE OF WIGHT County in 1671. He bought lands from SAMUEL HASWELL on February 9, 1658. (Isle of Wight Book 1 p. 21). His wife, SUSANNA JONES, was the sister of REV. ROWLAND JONES, minister of BRUTON PARISH in "Middletown Plantation" where the QUEEN'S CREEK HARRISONS lived.

He probably died sometime about 1700, as his will was proved in Isle of Wight County, June 9, 1701 (Vol. 7, W & M p. 254). Some provisions of his will were:

Certain lands to his brother, WILLIAM HARRISON.

Certain lands to "my kinsman" JOHN HARRISON (Son of JOHN HARRISON, deceased, and his wife MELBOROUGH.)

JOHN HARRISON to be allowed timber off certain lands to construct a dwelling house, etc.

JOHN JORDAN, son of THOMAS JORDAN, lately deceased.

Quaker Meeting House at LEVY'S NECK.

My wife SUSANNA, my copper still, and after her decease to JOHN HARRISON and WILLIAM HARRISON.

From Page 217 of the Valentine Papers: WILLIAM BRESSIE of the UPPER PARISH of ISLE OF WIGHT County, Planter, and SUSANNAH, his wife, give to WILLIAM YARRETT, JOHN GRAVES, FRANCIS WREN, EDWARD PAYNE, THOMAS TOOKE and HENRY WIGGS and the rest of the Servants of God frequently called QUAKERS one house built by the said people in the place called LEVY NECK old field, near the Creek Side, with ground sufficient for a graveyard and what more may be thought fit, with free egress and for the said people through the said BRESSIE'S land. Recorded in Isle of Wight Court by JOHN PITT, Clerk.

From page 215 of the Valentine Papers: FRANCIS BRESSEY of ISLE OF WIGHT COUNTY, son of HUGH BRESSEY of the same County, Planter, marriage to ELIZABETH WIGGS, daughter of HENRY WIGGS (See above). Witnesses were John Scott, Blackabee Terrell, WILLIAM HARRISON, Joan Scott, MARTIN HARRISON, George Wiggs, Sarah Wiggs and KATHERINE SCOTT. July 15, 1715.

From same Page: HUGH BRESSEY and SARAH BRESSEY were witnesses to the marriage of MATTHEW JORDAN, of NANSEMOND COUNTY to SUSANNAH BRESSEY, widow of ISLE OF WIGHT COUNTY, March 17, 1702.

From page 658 Valentine Papers: MATTHEW JORDAN, of ISLE OF WIGHT COUNTY received a deed to 100 acres in the County aforesaid, known as LONG NECK, being part of 1050 acres, from WILLIAM HARRISON, devised to him by WILLIAM BRESSEY of said Parish and County. December 23, 1713. On December 28th following SUSANNAH JORDAN, wife of MATTHEW JORDAN and the widow of WILLIAM BRESSEY releases her dower to lands held by WILLIAM HARRISON. Same Page.

We are told that WILLIAM HARRISON (the second) married ANNE RATCLIFFE (Skimino Harrisons p. 15); that the third WILLIAM (1705-1771) and his wife MARGARET MAUPIN had a son WILLIAM (the fourth) who married MARGARET JORDAN, and that this last WILLIAM had a sister ELIZABETH HARRISON who married WILLIAM RATCLIFFE, and that two of the sons of WILLIAM RATCLIFFE and ELIZABETH HARRISON married daughters of the fourth WILLIAM HARRISON and his wife MARGARET JORDAN. The RATCLIFFE family were QUAKERS at the time the second WILLIAM HARRISON (1650-1719) married ANNE RATCLIFFE, if the following record is correct:

Page 738 Valentine Papers (Friends Meeting Records): RICHARD JORDAN, son of THOMAS JORDAN of Chuckatuck deceased, marriage to REBECCA RATCLIFFE, daughter of RICHARD RATCLIFFE of TRAVESCOE NECK, married in the house of her father, the sixth month (JUNE) in the year 1706. The witnesses were JOHN JORDAN, brother ROBERT JORDAN, brother JAMES JORDAN, MARGARET JORDAN, mother, MARY JORDAN, MARGARET JORDAN, RICHARD RATCLIFFE, ELIZABETH RATCLIFFE, mother, RICHARD RATCLIFFE, brother, JOHN RATCLIFFE, brother, WILLIAM SCOTT and others.

On page 258 of BODDIE'S 17TH CENTURY ISLE OF WIGHT we are told that JOHN HARRISON was married to a sister of WILLIAM BRESSIE, a QUAKER, who was an overseer of the will of NICHOLAS HILL, and that SARAH LUCK was a sister of JOHN JENNINGS who married one of the daughters of MAJ. NICHOLAS HILL, and owned lands adjoining JOHN HARRISON in ISLE OF WIGHT COUNTY November 6, 1719.

The foregoing items (on this and the page preceding) are set out somewhat in detail by the compiler to show certain things in connection with the HARRISONS who descended from HARMON HARRISON.

The will of WILLIAM BRESSEY discloses that there was an older JOHN HARRISON, then perhaps long deceased (1700), whose wife was MELBOROUGH or MYLBOROUGH. As his son WILLIAM HARRISON was a "brother" of the old QUAKER and contemporaneous with him, he was married and had, perhaps grown sons by 1658, when BRESSEY bought lands from SAMUEL HASWELL in that year.

The notes show that both WILLIAM HARRISON and JOHN HARRISON must have married sisters of WILLIAM BRESSIE, and further show that WILLIAM HARRISON was alive in 1713 when he sold 100 acres of his inherited lands (from BRESSIE) to MATTHEW JORDAN.

The JOHN HARRISON who married MYLBOROUGH HILL could not have been JOHN, the son of RICHARD, (1648-1690) who married MARY HALL, of course and had one lone daughter MARY, who married JOHN HUBBARD and a son RICHARD who died in 1722 unmarried.

The WILLIAM HARRISON who married a BRESSEY and was "called brother" in BRESSEY'S will was certainly not the WILLIAM (1650-1719) aho married MARY HUBBARD or MARY HAM, and became the ancestor of all of the "Skimino Harrisons".

If what is pointed out so far was ALL the evidence we would not have a peg to stand on. The material evidence is the part that discloses the relationship between these WILLIAM BRESSEY HARRISONS and those of QUEEN'S CREEK in YORK COUNTY, which may not be brushed aside or ignored.

JOHN JORDAN, son of THOMAS JORDAN, lately deceased, is a legatee under the will. He was a brother of MATTHEW JORDAN, who in 1702 married the widow SUSANNAH BRESSEY, the sister of REV. ROWLAND JONES. Also a brother of ROBERT JORDAN, grandfather of MARGARET JORDAN who married the fourth WILLIAM HARRISON of QUEEN'S CREEK.

In other words JOHN HARRISON (son of HARMON HARRISON?) had two sons, JOHN and WILLIAM HARRISON who married sisters of WILLIAM BRESSEY, the QUAKER of LEVY NECK. In one sense they were brother's in law of REV. ROWLAND JONES, minister of BRUTON PARISH. That brought them mighty close to QUEEN'S CREEK.

They were co-legatees with the JORDANS of Nansemond and CHUCKATUCK.

They were certainly step-sons of MATTHEW JORDAN, great uncle of MARGARET JORDAN, who married the fourth WILLIAM HARRISON of QUEEN'S CREEK.

They were in the same family circle with the RATCLIFFES who married into the JORDANS and the HARRISONS of LEVY NECK as well as the HARRISONS of QUEEN'S CREEK, all of whom were QUAKERS.

They had a brother (evidently) named MARTIN HARRISON, or else MARTIN was a son of either JOHN or WILLIAM (the sons of JOHN and MYLBOROUGH HARRISON. Thus we are able to present from the RECORDS the names of at least two and maybe THREE sons of JOHN HARRISON, son of HARMON HARRISON, alive in ISLE OF WIGHT COUNTY in 1700, 92 years after the ancestor first came to VIRGINIA. *

---

* THESE BRESSEY HARRISONS, although so little is said of them on the records were men of substance and importance and the echo of their lives reverberated in GRANVILLE COUNTY in its Colónial days. JOHN HARRISON (JR) was called "my kinsman", and WILLIAM HARRISON "my brother" in the BRESSEY will in 1701. BODDIE tells us that JOHN married a sister of William Bressie. WILLIAM HARRISON may have married a sister of SUSANNAH, his wife. If so he was in fact a brother in law of REV. ROWLAND JONES of BRUTON PARISH.

REV. ROWLAND JONES, of BRUTON PARISH had a son ORLANDO JONES. He had several sisters, one of whom married WILLIAM BRESSIE, as stated. ORLANDO JONES married MARTHA MACON. MARTHA MACON was the sister of GIDEON MACON, who married PRISCILLA JONES, daughter of EDWARD JONES (p. 43 this book), and among the children of GIDEON MACON and his wife PRISCILLA JONES was the distinguished HARRISON MACON.

5. HANNAH HARRISON, whom I believe to have been a daughter of HARMON HARRISON and have placed as such, married JAMES HILL, a brother of MELBOROUGH, who married JOHN HARRISON. She was perhaps a younger child of the family, for she was living in 1680 in Perquiman's Precinct in North Carolina then, when she and her husband attended the wedding of CHRISTOPHER NICHOLSON & ANN ATWOOD at the house of FRANCIS TOMES (THOMAS?). Hinshaw's Quaker Genealogy Vol. 1. They had a daughter named HANNAH HILL who married JAMES PERISHO, and another daughter who married JOHN PIERCE (See p. 126 "Index" this volume).

6. WILLIAM HARRISON and 2. THOMAS HARRISON, sons of HARMON HARRISON were, in my opinion, the ancestors of most of the HARRISONS who lived in ST. ANDREWS PARISH in BRUNSWICK COUNTY, Virginia, MEHERRIN PARISH, GREENSVILLE COUNTY, and later in NORTH CAROLINA. In my files are oodles of data tending to substantiate this statement, including the will of at least one HARMON HARRISON and his wife SARAH and another HARMON HARRISON, son of a BENJAMIN.

7. THOMASINE HARRISON, daughter of HARMON HARRISON married RICHARD WHITEHEAD, of ABBINGDON PARISH, Gloucester County, as witness the following notes, from Book No. 7, Rappahannock County Deeds pp. 161-162:

> NOV. 23, 1682 : THOMASINE WHITEHEAD, wife of MR. RICHARD WHITEHEAD, GENT., of ABBINGDON PARISH, Gloucester County, Virginia, appoints her loving friends, MR. DANIEL GAINES, EDMUND CRASK, and MR. JAMES HARRISON, of Rappahannock County, Virginia, Gents, or either of them, her true and lawful attorney to acknowledge in RAPPAHANNOCK COUNTY her release to dower on 2000 acres of land in the freshes of of Rappahannock River near a muddy creek formerly bought by my husband of Mr. JOHN and GEORGE MOTT and now sold to GEORGE CONNOR, of WARE PARISH, Gloucester County. Witnesses were Samuel Orrill and MARY Whitehead. Recorded in Rappahannock, County, Virginia, November 24, 1682.
>
> NOV. 23, 1682: MR. RICHARD WHITEHEAD, GENT. of ABBINGDON PARISH, Gloucester County, appointed his loving friend MR. JAMES HARRISON, of Rappahannock County, Virginia, his power of attorney to acknowledge in his stead a deed of conveyance of land lying in Rappahannock County, Virginia, to THOMAS CONNOR, of Ware Parish, Gloucester County. (Said Thomas Connor paid 12,000 pounds of tobacco for this land).

Other records show that GEORGE MOTT mentioned with his brother JOHN in the first note above, died, and shortly afterwards his widow (about 1683-4) married MR. JAMES HARRISON, GENT, to whom RICHARD WHITEHEAD gave the power of Attorney, along with his wife THOMASINE. This JAMES HARRISON was a grandson of HARMON HARRISON, and RICHARD WHITEHEAD had married his AUNT, THOMASINE HARRISON.

3. JAMES HARRISON (Son of HARMON) married, but the name of his wife is, of course unknown. This compiler has concluded that he had three sons:

10. THOMAS HARRISON
11. GEORGE HARRISON (d. 1713).
12. ANDREW HARRISON (d. 1686) m. THOMASINE WHITEHEAD, daughter of MR. RICHARD WHITEHEAD, of GLOUCESTER and his wife THOMASINE HARRISON (Dau. of HARMON HARRISON).

4. ANDREW HARRISON (Son of HARMON) married, but the name of his wife is, of course unknown. He also had three sons, whose names were:

13. JAMES HARRISON (d. 1712) m. the widow of GEORGE MOTT.
14. JOSEPH HARRISON (Of Westmoreland County in 1655).
15. ANDREW HARRISON (d. in ESSEX County 1718) "aged and infirm". His wife was ELLENER. (possibly ELLENER LONG, sister of RICHARD LONG).

---

15. ANDREW HARRISON was the grandfather of JOHN HARRISON, who married SARAH DANIEL, and who died in HALIFAX COUNTY, VIRGINIA, in 1761, the father of the HARRISONS who lived in GRANVILLE COUNTY, NORTH CAROLINA.

Following is an abstract of the will of 15. ANDREW HARRISON, the son of ANDREW, son of HARMON HARRISON, from the ESSEX COUNTY WILL BOOK 3, page 84; dated APRIL 28, 1718 and proved NOV. 18, 1718:

> Being grown aged and at this time very sick and weak; wife ELEANOR, Executrix; son ANDREW and son in law GABRIEL LONG my trustees and overseers. Have already settled three of my children, viz: WILLIAM, ANDREW and ELIZABETH on lands on which they now live; son WILLIAM, 270 acres; son ANDREW 200 acres, and daughter ELIZABETH 200 acres. Have put in the hands of WILLIAM STANNARD money to buy negroes for the use of my wife during her lifetime, and at her decease to daughter MARGARET LONG'S three youngest sons, GABRIEL, RICHARD & WILLIAM as soon as they shall reach 21 years. Personalty after wife's death to my 4 children, WILLIAM, ANDREW, ELIZABETH and MARGARET.

The witnesses to 15 ANDREW HARRISON'S will were JOHN ELLETT or ELLIOTT, WILLIAM DAVIDSON and MARY DAVIDSON. The testator was of ST. MARY'S PARISH in ESSEX COUNTY. He was the father of

1. ANDREW HARRISON of SPOTTSYLVANIA and ORANGE COUNTY, Virginia.
2. WILLIAM HARRISON, of CAROLINE COUNTY.
3. ELIZABETH HARRISON who married THOMAS MUNDAY in September, 1810.
4. MARGARET HARRISON who married GABRIEL LONG.

1. ANDREW HARRISON (Son of ANDREW HARRISON who died in 1718) on August 10, 1708, gave bond in ESSEX COUNTY COURT as the guardian of ELIZABETH BATTAILE (D. B. 13 p. 128), and on January 2, 1710, ANDREW HARRISON and ELIZABETH, his wife, deeded land which was bequeathed by the said ELIZABETH'S father, JOHN BATTAILE. By which we know that the wife of ANDREW HARRISON, JR. was ELIZABETH BATTAILE, daughter of CAPT. JOHN BATTAILE, of ESSEX County, Virginia, who was CAPTAIN of Rangers against the Indians in 1692 and in the same year a member of the House of Burgesses from ESSEX COUNTY. Capt. John Battaile's wife was ELIZABETH SMITH, daughter of MAJ. LAWRENCE SMITH, of YORK COUNTY, VIRGINIA, commander of the garrison at the falls of the Rappahannock in 1676, who was recommended for a commission as a member of the Governor's Council, but who died before receiving the same. His son JOHN SMITH, of YORK COUNTY, succeeded to the honor.

1. ANDREW HARRISON and his wife ELIZABETH BATTAILE had the following children:

30. BATTAILE HARRISON (Will in AMHERST CO. 1775).
31. LAWRENCE HARRISON married CATHERINE (Of ORANGE COUNTY in 1754).
32. CHARLES HARRISON (In Orange County 1738). Wife SARAH.
33. JOHN HARRISON (married SARAH DANIEL).

The space available in this work will not permit an excursus into all of the ramifications of this set of HARRISONS, descendants of HARMON HARRISON. Their history is absorbingly interesting. LAWRENCE HARRISON, brother of JOHN who married SARAH DANIEL, resided at one time (1750) with the QUEEN'S CREEK HARRISONS in YORK COUNTY, where his first child, COL. BENJAMIN HARRISON was born. (He had nine children). Col. Benjamin Harrison of this family moved to KENTUCKY, and HARRISON COUNTY in that State was named for the LAWRENCE HARRISON family. The son ROBERT had two daughters CYNTHIA and ANN, and the town of CYNTHIANA, KENTUCKY was named for them.

2. WILLIAM HARRISON, the second son of ANDREW OF ESSEX (will 1718), lived in CAROLINE COUNTY, where he is said to have died in 1742. He had a son COL. BENJAMIN HARRISON who married PRISCILLA CARY, daughter of HUGH CARY, of ESSEX (Quit Rent Rolls 1704) who was intimate with and bought lands in Cumberland County, Virginia, from HENRY CARY, father of Hon. ARCHIBALD CARY of "Ampthill" in Chesterfield, who was the father in law of THOMAS MANN RANDOLPH.

Lest somebody complains that authorities are not cited throughout to support these statements, the writer's files are replete with statements from the records bearing out the several relationships set forth. There were other families besides the HARRISONS who came to GRANVILLE COUNTY and I cannot appropriate all the space to this one.

JOHN HARRISON and SARAH DANIEL had five sons, JAMES, JOHN, ANDREW, RICHARD and ISHAM. The names of the children of the first four have been given (p. 255).

104. ISHAM HARRISON, according to a descendant, married AMY GILLIAM and had the following children:

1. ANDREW W. HARRISON (b. 1780) m. ELIZABETH RODGERS.
2. LEMUEL RICHARD HARRISON (b. 1792) m. JUDITH WOOD.
3. LUCY HARRISON m. BENJAMIN GOODE
4. NANCY HARRISON m. MR. GEORGE.
5. PRISCILLA HARRISON married MR. ALLEN.

2. LEMUEL RICHARD HARRISON and his wife JUDITH WOOD had one son (Of which the descendant knows), though he probably had others, whose name was

10. ISHAM HARRISON, who married (1) MARGARET MINERVA HUMPHREYS
(2) LAURA ANNEAR.

By his first marriage, ISHAM HARRISON had two children:

10a. PINCKNEY HARRISON
10b. CHARLOTTE ELIZABETH HARRISON married WILLIAM GARNEY BURR.

By his second marriage ISHAM HARRISON had five children:

10c. LEMUEL HARRISON
10d. ALBERT HARRISON
10e. EFFIE HARRISON m. CLAYTON SNYDER, of CHRISTOPHER, ILLINOIS.
10f. ELPHIN HARRISON m. WILLIAM SEEBER, of CHRISTOPHER, ILLINOIS.
10g. ELLA HARRISON m. HON. FRANK SPILLER, ATTY., of BENTON, ILLINOIS.

WILLIAM GARNEY BURR (b. 1846) was still living in 1943, aged 97 years, at the town of LAREDO, TEXAS, with two children, JAMES GUY BURR and MINNIE MAY BURR, our informant.

SOME DESCENDANTS OF JAMES HARRISON AND ELIZABETH HAMPTON

Herewith are given some of the descendants of JAMES HARRISON and ELIZABETH HAMPTON, a list of whose twelve children are set forth on page 255 herein.

200. JOHN HAMPTON HARRISON was born January 22, 1772 and died May 22, 1837. He was a member of Congress from South Carolina, according to one report, which is not bourn out by the Congressional Records, however. He married JEMIMAH JENKINS and had the following children:

1. JOHN HAMPTON HARRISON married MARIA BENSON.
2. JAMES HARRISON married a BERRY.
3. CLARISSA HARRISON, married SAMUEL THOMPSON
4. ELIZABETH HARRISON married SAMUEL GERARD HALE
5. HARRIET HARRISON married McCLANAHAN. (SAMUEL G. McCLANAHAN).

I am informed that JEMIMAH JENKINS was the son of a THOMAS JENKINS and his wife JEMIMAH WILLIAMS, daughter of OWEN WILLIAMS, an ENGLISHMAN who settled in VIRGINIA in an early day, apparently in CULPEPPER COUNTY.

203. JAMES HARRISON (1782-1866) married SARAH EARLE (1791-1844), May 29, 1806, and they had the following children:

10. ELIZABETH HAMPTON HARRISON (b. 1810) married JUDGE JOSEPH NEWTON WHITNER in 1830.
11. WILLIAM HENRY HARRISON (1813-1861)
12. ELIAS EARLE HARRISON (1816-1843)
13. JAMES WASHINGTON HARRISON (1817) married MARY J. BENSON in 1840.
14. FRANCES HARRISON (1821-1822).
15. SAMUEL EARLE HARRISON (1823-1845)
16. FRANCIS EUGENE HARRISON (1826-1878) married MARY EUNICE PERRIN.

16. FRANCIS EUGENE HARRISON and his wife MARY EUNICE PERRIN had the following children:

20. FRANCIS EUGENE HARRISON, JR. (1862-1931)
21. THOMAS PERRIN HARRISON (b. Oct. 11, 1866).
22. JANE WARDLAW HARRISON (b. May 25, 1866.
23. LEWIS CLARKE HARRISON (1868-1911).
24. WILLIAM HENRY HARRISON (1870-1929)

21. THOMAS PERRIN HARRISON married ADELIN LAKE LEFTWICH, January 9, 1894, and had:

25. JANE LEFTWICH HARRISON (b. Sept. 10, 1895).
26. THOMAS PERRIN HARRISON, JR. (b. May 9, 1897).
27. FLORENCE LEFTWICH HARRISON (b. Sept. 4, 1901).
28. LEWIS WARDLAW HARRISON, (b. Sept. 28, 1903.

Dr. THOMAS PERRIN HARRISON, JR. is a member of the faculty of the University of Texas, and married a daughter of JUDGE GORDON BOONE, of Corpus Christi, Texas, a life long friend of this compiler. They have a son THOMAS PERRIN HARRISON III born May 17, 1943. This information was obtained from DR. THOMAS PERRIN HARRISON, SR. of RALEIGH, and from my old comrade in arms and at the bar, JUDGE BOONE, both the proud grandfathers.

---

206. ISHAM HARRISON (7th child and fourth son of JAMES HARRISON and ELIZABETH HAMPTON) married HARRIET KELLEY and had the following children:

30. ANN ELIZA HARRISON m. DR. BAYLESS EARLE. (To WACO, TEXAS).
31. LAURA HARRISON m. JUDGE WILLIAM H. JACK (Of Texas).
32. JAMES E. HARRISON m. (1) MARY EVANS (2) HENRIETTA M. CARTER.
33. LOUISA JANE HARRISON (b. 1817) m. HON. WELLS THOMPSON.
34. DR. JOHN H. HARRISON (d. 1840.)
35. DR. RICHARD HARRISON married three times, died WACO, TEXAS 1876.
36. GEN. THOMAS HARRISON (Of Texas).
37. WILLIAM K. HARRISON (b. 1825) never married.
38. HARIET HARRISON m. WILLIAM B. EVANS and died 1876.
39. DR. MOSES K. HARRISON, surgeon C. S. A. (d. 1894).
40. ELIZABETH HARRISON m. JOHN T. BARRON.
41. MARY VIVIAN HARRISON (Called "WINDE") married MATTHEW CLAY.*

The data on the family of 206 ISHAM HARRISON is based on statements in a letter by RICHARD H. HARRISON, a great grandson of ELIZABETH HAMPTON HARRISON, grandson of ISHAM HARRISON and HARRIET KELLEY, and a son of JAMES E. HARRISON and his first wife MARY EVANS.

NOTE: The marriage of MARY V. HARRISON to MATTHEW CLAY, of ALABAMA reunited two old GRANVILLE COUNTY, NORTH CAROLINA, families. MATTHEW CLAY, whom she married was the son of a MATTHEW CLAY, who in turn was the son of MATTHEW CLAY, of PITTSYLVANIA COUNTY, VIRGINIA, who married POLLY WILLIAMS, the only daughter of JOSEPH WILLIAMS, of GRANVILLE COUNTY (Nut Bush District), merchant, and SARAH LANIER, daughter of THOMAS LANIER. After this JOSEPH WILLIAMS died, his widow SARAH married another JOSEPH WILLIAMS, merchant of "SHALLOW FORD, a cousin of her first husband and the ancestor, by SARAH, of U. S. Senator JOHN WILLIAMS, of TENNESSEE.

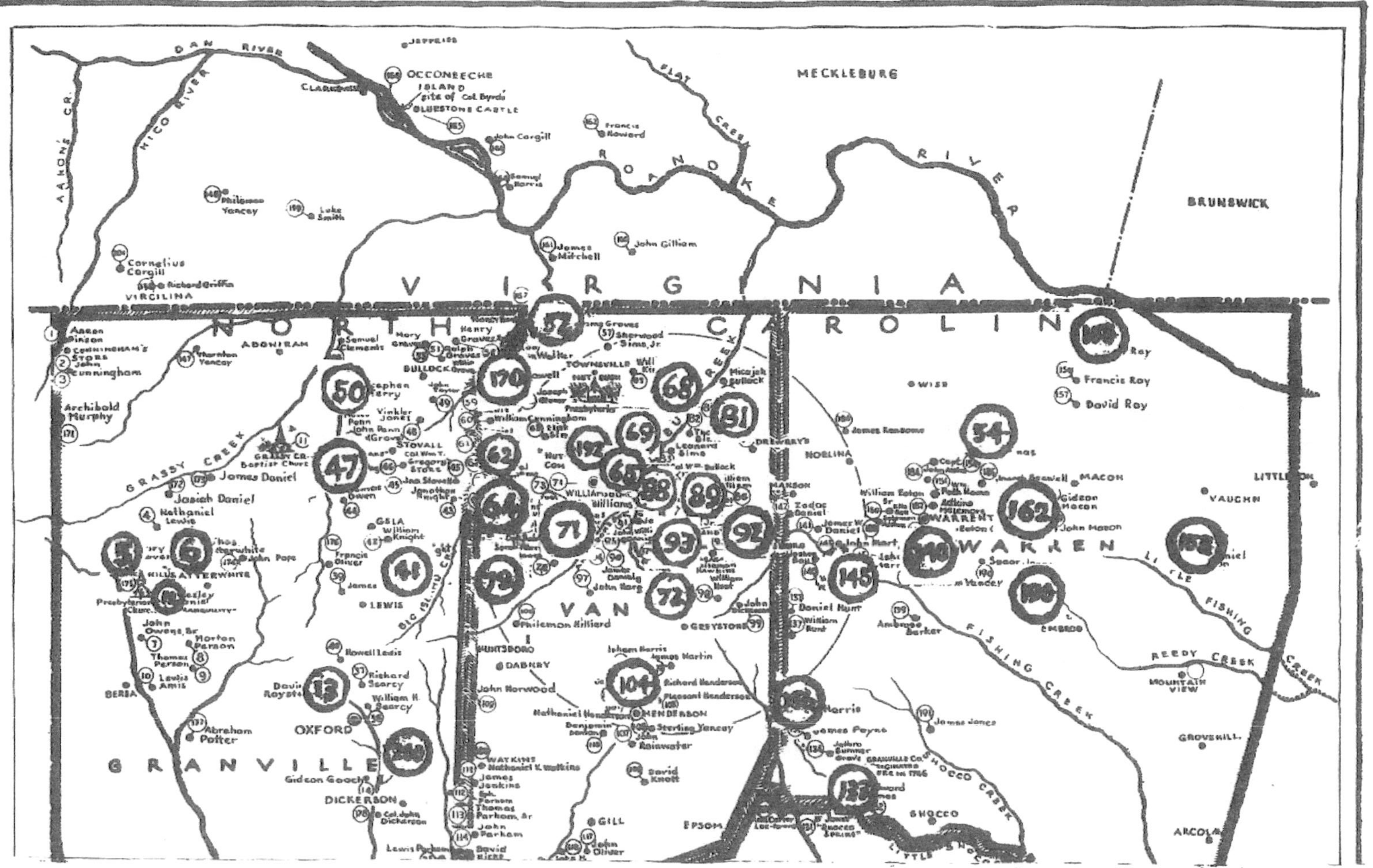
DAN RIVER
HICO RIVER
AARON'S CR.
OCCONEECHE ISLAND site of Col. Byrds' BLUESTONE CASTLE
MECKLEBURG
FLAT CREEK
ROANOKE RIVER
BRUNSWICK
John Cargill
Francis Howard
Samuel Harris
Philemon Yancey
Luke Smith
James Mitchell
John Gilliam
Cornelius Cargill
Richard Griffin
VIRGILINA
VIRGINIA
NORTH CAROLINA
Aaron Pinson
CUNNINGHAM'S STORE
John Cunningham
Archibald Murphy
Thornton Yancey
ADONIRAM
Samuel Clements
BULLOCK
TOWNSVILLE
Micajah Bullock
Sherwood Sims, Jr.
Vinkler
John Penn
STOVALL
Jonathan Knight
GRASSY CREEK
James Daniel
Josiah Daniel
Nathaniel Lewis
John Pope
KILLIS ATTERWHITE
John Owens, Sr.
Norton Person
Thomas Person
Lewis Amis
BEREA
Abraham Potter
OXFORD
GRANVILLE
Gideon Gooch
DICKERSON
Col. John Dickerson
GELA
William Knight
Francis Oliver
James
LEWIS
BIG ISLAND CR.
Howell Lewis
Richard Searcy
William H. Searcy
David Royster
WILLIAMSBORO
Leonard Sims
DREWRY'S
NORLINA
James Ransome
WISE
Francis Roy
David Roy
Roy
MACON
Gideon Macon
John Macon
WARRENTON
WARREN
LITTLETON
VAUGHN
LITTLE FISHING CREEK
FISHING CREEK
REEDY CREEK
MOUNTAIN VIEW
GROVEHILL
ARCOLA
EMBRO
Ambrose Barker
Zodac Daniel
James W. Daniel
John Hunt
Daniel Hunt
William Hunt
MANSON
VANCE
Philemon Hilliard
John Harg
GREYSTONE
HUNTSBORO
DABNEY
John Norwood
Isham Harris
James Martin
Richard Henderson
Pleasant Henderson
HENDERSON
Nathaniel Henderson
Sterling Yancey
John Rainwater
David Knott
WATKINS
Nathaniel K. Watkins
James Jenkins
Thomas Parham, Jr.
John Parham
David Kittrell
GILL
John Oliver
EPSOM
Harris
James Payne
James Jones
SHOCCO CREEK
SHOCCO
SHOCCO SPRINGS

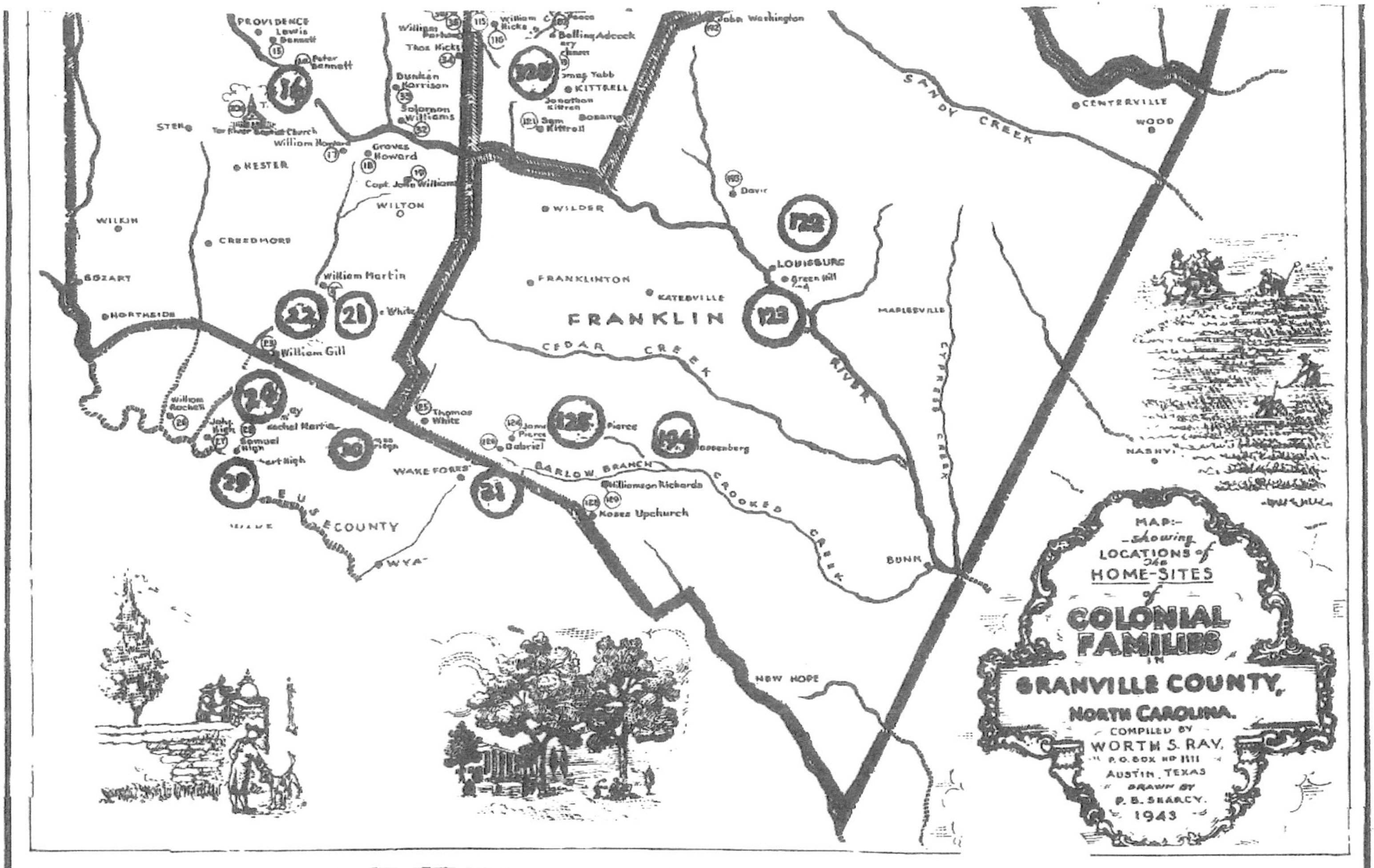

MAP:—
showing
LOCATIONS of
the
HOME-SITES
of
COLONIAL
FAMILIES
IN
GRANVILLE COUNTY,
NORTH CAROLINA.
COMPILED BY
WORTH S. RAY,
P. O. BOX NO 1111
AUSTIN, TEXAS
DRAWN BY
P. B. SEARCY,
1943

THE PETER BRYCE SEARCY MAP OF COLONIAL GRANVILLE COUNTY; PAGE 266 FOR KEY.

"KEY" TO THE SEARCY MAP OF COLONIAL GRANVILLE COUNTY.

(5) HENRY GRAVES, JR.	(72) HUTCHINS BURTON
(6) THOMAS SATTERWHITE	(79) THOMAS LANIER
(12) CHESLEY DANIEL	(81) RICHARD BULLOCK
(13) DAVID ROYSTER	(88) JOHN DANIEL
(16) PETER BENNETT	(89) REUBEN SEARCY
(21) VALENTINE WHITE	(92) PHILEMON HAWKINS
(22) ERASTUS GILL	(93) SAMUEL HENDERSON
(24) JAMES RAY	(104) RICHARD HENDERSON
(29) HARBERT HIGH	(120) JONATHAN KITTRELL
(30) THOMAS HARRISON	(122) "SPELLING" JOHN ALLEN
(31) THOMAS RAY	(123) GREEN HILL
(41) JOHN KNIGHT	(125) PHILLIP PIERCE
(47) JOHN PENN	(133) EDWARD JONES
(50) STEPHEN TERRY	(136) WEST HARRIS
(52) JOHN WILLIAMS GRAVES	(140) WILLIAM EATON
(54) WILLIAM CHRISTMAS	(145) ISHAM HARRISON
(62) DANIEL MORROW	(153) NATHANIEL MACON
(64) DANIEL WILLIAMS	(155) CHRISTMAS RAY
(65) MEMUCAN HUNT	(162) GIDEON MACON
(68) JOHN BOYD	(190) SUGAR JONES
(69) JOHN SIMS	(194) NICHOLAS MASSENBURG
(71) JUDGE JOHN WILLIAMS	(200) SAMUEL BENTON

---

(5) HENRY GRAVES, JR. On page 244 it will be seen that the compiler has identified this HENRY GRAVES, JR. as the son of HENRY GRAVES and the grandson of the HENRY GRAVES who married MARY WILLIAMS, the aunt of JUDGE RICHARD HENDERSON and of JUDGE JOHN WILLIAMS, of GRANVILLE COUNTY. From the SEARCY MAP it will be noticed that HENRY GRAVES, JR. lived in the GOSHEN DISTRICT not far from (12) CHESLEY DANIEL. LEONARD DANIEL, a nephew of CHESLEY, married MARY ANN GRAVES, his sister. HENRY GRAVES, SR., his father, lived in the upper part of the Eastern area of the present GRANVILLE COUNTY in the ISLAND CREEK DISTRICT. RALPH GRAVES, his uncle, also lived in that part of the county. RALPH GRAVES, of YORK COUNTY, VIRGINIA, who married UNITY WHITE, was the Great Great grandfather of HENRY GRAVES, JR. of GRANVILLE COUNTY.

---

(6) THOMAS SATTERWHITE was a native of YORK COUNTY, VIRGINIA, where so many of the old families of GRANVILLE COUNTY, NORTH CAROLINA, originated. He married a step-daughter of JUDGE JOHN WILLIAMS, the daughter of his wife AGNES by her first husband MR. KEELING. In the will of AGNES WILLIAMS, the relict of JUDGE JOHN WILLIAMS in 1802 in GRANVILLE COUNTY, she mentions HORACE and EDWIN and PEGGY and NANCY SATTERWHITE as her grandchildren. These were the names of four of the children of THOMAS SATTERWHITE, who had married her daughter, who was also a half-sister of AGATHA WILLIAMS who married COL. ROBERT BURTON. (See page 213).

The SATTERWHITE FAMILY seems unquestionably to have had its VIRGINIA origin in YORK and GLOUCESTER COUNTIES. In 1646 and 1647 the name of MARSHALL SATTERWHITE appears as confessing judgments in the YORK COUNTY court, and in JULY, 1687, MICHAEL SATTERWHITE of Mop Jack Bay (in GLOUCESTER, confessed an indebtedness in YORK COUNTY. In 1742 THOMAS SATTERWHITE gave a quit claim for certain negroes to PETER RICE in YORK COUNTY. (Page 2313 Valentine Papers).

MANN SATTERWHITE and WILLIAM SATTERWHITE, from VIRGINIA, settled in KENTUCKY; THOMAS SATTERWHITE (revolutionary soldier) settled in NORTH CAROLINA and married a MISS KEELING, and another SATTERWHITE settled on BROAD RIVER in GEORGIA and left a numerous family, whose daughter MILDRED m. JOHN H. WHITE, whose ancestors were related to UNITY WHITE (m. RALPH GRAVES) and became the ancestress of MAJ. GEORGE W. LITTLEFIELD, the noted Texas Cattle Baron and Philanthropist, of Austin, Texas.

(12) CHESLEY DANIEL. This CHESLEY DANIEL married JUDITH CHRISTIAN. He was the son of JAMES DANIEL, who was the Sheriff of ALBEMARLE COUNTY, VIRGINIA, in 1754, and whose wife was JENNIE HICKS. JAMES DANIEL, the old SHERIFF of ALBEMARLE was the son of a ROBERT DANIEL, who was SHERIFF OF MIDDLESEX COUNTY, Virginia, in 1689; and he in turn was the son of a CAPT. WILLIAM DANIEL, of MIDDLESEX, and his first wife DOROTHY.

JAMES DANIEL (Sheriff of ALBEMARLE) married JENNIE HICKS on NOV. 11, 1725, and his will in ALBEMARLE COUNTY in 1761 named the following children:

1. MARGARET DANIEL (1728-1734)
2. CHESLEY DANIEL (b. Jan. 6, 1731).
3. RUTH DANIEL (1733-1760).
4. ABRAHAM DANIEL (b. 1735).
5. JAMES DANIEL (b. 1738).
6. JANE DANIEL (b. 1740).
7. LEONARD DANIEL (b. 1741).
8. SUSANNAH DANIEL (b. 1743).
9. JOSIAH DANIEL (b. 1745).
10. JOHN DANIEL (b. 1747).
11. MARY DANIEL (b. 1749).
12. MERCY DANIEL (b. 1752).

2. CHESLEY DANIEL was the subject of this note and the one who moved to and settled in GOSHEN DISTRICT of GRANVILLE COUNTY and called his home "TRANQUILITY". He was the father of BEVERLY DANIEL who was ATTORNEY GENERAL of NORTH CAROLINA and is buried in the City Cemetery at RALEIGH, North Carolina. CHESLEY DANIEL died in NORTH CAROLINA in 1814. He and JUDITH CHRISTIAN had the following children:

20. JAMES DANIEL (1762-1841) m. ANN VENABLE.
21. JOHN GRANVILLE DANIEL m. SUSAN WATKINS.
22. WOODSON DANIEL m. ELIZABETH MILTON.
23. BEVERLY DANIEL (d. in RALEIGH).
24. MARTHA DANIEL married GEORGE DANIEL (1736).
25. JUDITH CHRISTIAN DANIEL m. DAVID HUGHES (moved to Georgia).
26. GANO DANIEL (Twin of JUDITH C.)
27. SUSAN DANIEL m. JOHN WATKINS in 1798.
28. ELIZABETH DANIEL m. SAMUEL G. HOPKINS.
29. MARY DANIEL (Said to have married a KEY - to TENN.)

20. JAMES DANIEL and his wife ANN VENABLE had a daughter ANN V. DANIEL who married DR. SAMUEL VENABLE WATKINS, and they had a daughter MARGARET ELIZABETH WATKINS who married WILLIAM MORTON (Called "MOTON") and were the parents of HON. W. S. MORTON, of Farmville, Virginia, who has rendered much aid in assembling this material.

10. JOHN DANIEL (b. 1747), the son of CHESLEY DANIEL and JUDITH CHRISTIAN, married ELIZABETH MORTON in 1772, lived in CHARLOTTE COUNTY, Virginia, and died in 1802, leaving a will in which he named his children:

30. SAMUEL DANIEL
31. JOSEPH MORTON DANIEL
32. JANE DANIEL m. STEPHEN BEDFORD.
33. AGNES DANIEL m. WOODSON.
34. CHESLEY DANIEL married NANCY SIMS(?)
35. JOHN DANIEL m. (1) MARTHA SIMS (2) LUCY MURPHY, of N. C.
36. JAMES DANIEL, a Minister.
37. ELIZABETH DANIEL m. Rev. JOHN MATTHEWS.
38. MARTHA DANIEL
39. NANCY DANIEL
40. SUSANNAH DANIEL
41. PAULINA DANIEL
42. FRANCES VENABLE DANIEL.

35. JOHN DANIEL who married LUCY MURPHY was the ancestor of the NORTH CAROLINA DANIELS who married into the WORTH FAMILY.

4. ABRAHAM DANIEL was the father of seeveral children, including LEONARD DANIEL who married a daughter of HENRY GRAVES SR., mentioned on the preceding page.

9. JOSIAH DANIEL, another son of JAMES DANIEL of ALBEMARLE COUNTY, moved to GRANVILLE COUNTY, N. C. and died leaving a will there in 1811, an abstract of which, giving the names of all his children will be found set out herein on page 213.

MR. W. S. MORTON, of PRINCE EDWARD COUNTY, VIRGINIA, gives an account of this CHESLEY DANIEL family that makes him the son of another JAMES DANIEL, who was the Sheriff of GOOCHLAND COUNTY, some ten years earlier, and whom he says married ELIZABETH WOODSON. He is mixed up in the matter. First, the Sheriff of GOOCHLAND was not the JAMES who became afterwards the SHERIFF OF ALBEMARLE, and the JAMES DANIEL who married ELIZABETH WOODSON was NOT the Sheriff of GOOCHLAND. The Sheriff of GOOCHLAND was JAMES DANIEL who married JANE KELSO and who died in PRINCE EDWARD COUNTY, VA. In his account Mr. MORTON gives to JAMES DANIEL (Of Goochland) the same children named in the will of the ALBEMARLE JAMES DANIEL in 1961. (See p. 213).

(13) DAVID ROYSTER. The ROYSTER FAMILY came originally from Eastern Virginia. In the year 1744 JOHN ROYSTER owned lands in GLOUCESTER COUNTY next to a patent to lands taken out by WILSON CARY; and in 1768 JOHN ROYSTER deeded lands to ROBERT PLEASANTS of "Curles" lands that had previously belonged to the estate of JOHN WILLIAMS (p. 77 D. B. 1767-1774 of Henrico County). The family was intimate with the PLEASANTS family, from CHARLES CITY COUNTY and with the FLEMING family mentioned in the notes pertaining to GRANVILLE COUNTY PEOPLE herein. JACOB ROYSTER, whose wife was PATTY, with his brother WILLIAM ROYSTER lived in MECKLENBURG COUNTY, probably on the South Side of the ROANOKE, and was well to do, and he and his brother and THOMAS ANDERSON were assessed 65 tithes by CORNELIUS CARGILL for Cumberland Parish in 1750, apparently having something to do with the lands of COL. WILLIAM BYRD. All three of them may have been overseers of COLONEL BIRD'S island properties on the ROANOKE. JACOB ROYSTER, the father of (13) DAVID left will at BOYDTON, Mecklenburg County, it is said, which was probated in 1798. His children were:

1. JACOB ROYSTER
2. DENNIS ROYSTER
3. DAVID ROYSTER
4. JOHN ROYSTER
5. PATTY ROYSTER
6. FRANKEY ROYSTER
7. MARY ROYSTER
8. SUSAN ROYSTER
9. SARAH ROYSTER married a WILKINS.

3. DAVID DANIEL (the same as (13) on the Searcy Chart), married MARY DANIEL, daughter of JAMES DANIEL and his wife SARAH, of GRANVILLE COUNTY, who left will in 1785 (p. 212). They had the following children:

10. JETHRO ROYSTER married (1) RUTH MASON (2) MARTHA STAINBACK.
11. DAVID ROYSTER married SUSAN SIMS.
12. SARAH ROYSTER married HARRELL WIGGINS
13. NANCY ROYSTER lived in KENTUCKY.
14. POLLY ROYSTER died in 1816 in KENTUCKY.
15. LUCY ROYSTER married her cousin SMITH.
16. REBECCA ROYSTER died before 1798.

3. DAVID ROYSTER, according to one family genealogist, died after 1810. He was a school teacher in MECKLENBURG COUNTY, Virginia, and in WARREN and GRANVILLE COUNTIES in North Carolina. He moved to HENDERSON COUNTY, KENTUCKY, and later to SHELBYVILLE, TENN. (Bedford County).

11. DAVID ROYSTER, moved to RALEIGH, N. C. and was living there in 1800. In one book he is referred to at that period as the "old cabinet maker" causing this compiler to believe it possible that the reference was to his father. At any rate, one DAVID, believed by the family to have been 11, the son, had the contract for all woodwork in the State Capitol and all the desks and chairs in the Senate and House. Most of the woodwork was limited to the furniture, as the building - still standing - is built of stone, exclusively. He married SUSAN SIMS, the daughter of ELISHA SIMS, said to have been "of Warren County" though it is known he lived for a while in the "NUTBUSH SECTION" of the present VANCE - then GRANVILLE, near the other members of the SIMS family. 11. DAVID ROYSTER and his wife SUSAN SIMS had the following children:

20. WILLIAM HOWARD ROYSTER married MARY STEPHENS.
21. SARAH SANDERS ROYSTER
22. JAMES DANIEL ROYSTER (1807-1890) Paper Mfg.
23. MADISON BULLOCK ROYSTER m. MARTHA TERRY
24. LEONARD HENDERSON ROYSTER
25. IRENA NICHOLS ROYSTER
26. ELISHA SIMS ROYSTER
27. ZACHARIAH ROYSTER
28. ADELINE SUSAN ROYSTER
29. MARY DANIEL ROYSTER
30. DAVID ROYSTER married SARAH WOMBLE in 1849.
31. AMANDA MALVINA ROYSTER, m. WILLIAM HENDERSON HIGH.

22. JAMES DANIEL ROYSTER, paper Manufacturer of RALEIGH, married MARY ASHLEY, and had at least two sons, to whom he gave the unusual names of VERMONT CONNECTICUT ROYSTER and ARKANSAS DELAWARE ROYSTER. They composed the firm of A. D. ROYSTER & BRO., Candy Manufacturers, of Raleigh, N. C. VERMONT CONNECTICUT ROYSTER married HALLIE LEE HIGH, daughter of WILLIAM HENDERSON HIGH, and grand-daughter of ALEXANDER MARTIN HIGH (1793-1876) and his wife ELIZABETH KIFF RAY. MRS. HALLIE LEE (HIGH) ROYSTER was still living in RALEIGH in 1936, and some of the valuable material she furnished in letters is appended herewith as throwing much light on these various connections.

20. WILLIAM HOWARD ROYSTER married MARY STEPHENS and had seven children, SUSAN, DAVID, JOHN C., SARAH, LEONARD HENDERSON, *WILLIAM BURT and MARY HOWARD ROYSTER.
*WILLIAM BURT ROYSTER married JULIA E. TUTT, and had the following children:

32. FRANCIS BROOKS ROYSTER married KATE WARREN.
33. JULIANA ADELINE ROYSTER married JAMES LITTLEJOHN BUSBEE.
34. EDITH (ISABELLE) ROYSTER married ZEBULON VANCE JUDD.

MRS. JUDD is a prominent resident of AUBURN, ALABAMA and a leader in the National D. A. R.

SOME NOTES RELATING TO THE ROYSTERS, DANIELS, HIGHS and BULLOCKS
FROM LETTERS BY MRS. HALLIE LEE (HIGH) ROYSTER, 1936.

My father was WILLIAM HENDERSON HIGH, who married AMANDA MALVINA ROYSTER, the twelfth child and youngest of the twelve children of DAVID ROYSTER, JR. and SUSAN SIMS. My father was born March 14, 1820 and my mother in 1826. They were married March 20, 1849. My father was a son of ALEXANDER MARTIN HIGH and his wife ELIZABETH KIFF RAY. There were NINE children. Two died in infancy, namely, MYRA MARTIN, the eldest, died aged two, from swallowing a grain of corn which lodged in her throat and killed her. NICK MARRIOT HIGH, the fourth child, died aged 18 months from membranous croup. The second child was WILLIAM HENDERSON HIGH, JR. (my brother Billy), next ELIZABETH KIFF HIGH (sister Bettie; then REBECCA WARREN HIGH (called Beck), HALLIE LEE HIGH, ALEXANDER HIGH, ZADOCK HIGH, GAVIN DHU HIGH and GEDDY HILL HIGH.

All but the last two are named for Pa's people; GAVIN for old GAVIN HOGG (Pa's friend), and the DHU to add to the Scotch name, GAVIN. GAVIN HIGH was four when named and objected to the "HOGG", so Pa put the DHU in. Sister Bettie was named for Pa's mother, ELIZABETH KIFF RAY HIGH; BECK was called REBECCA WARREN for Aunt REBECCA NORWOOD (George's mother), who was the sister of my father. Pa's grandmother was RACHEL MARTIN, daughter of WILLIAM MARTIN. Maybe the MARTIN woman, second wife to LEONARD HENLEY BULLOCK was kin to me too. It seems that I am kin to everybody.

ELIZABETH KIFF RAY, who married ALEXANDER MARTIN HIGH (Son of (29) HARBERT HIGH on the Searcy Map) was the daughter of JAMES RAY, a Revolutionary Soldier. We have the SIMS and DANIEL LINE. I also have the HIGH and MARTIN side also fixed, and the RAY FAMILY on Pa's side. My oldest sister BETTIE was named for his mother, ELIZABETH KIFF RAY. My eldest sister, REBECCA WARREN HIGH was named for Pa's sister, REBECCA WARREN HIGH, who married first JAMES T. MARRIOTT and second GEORGE WASHINGTON NORWOOD.

I have been trying to find the marriage bond of DAVID ROYSTER and SUSAN SIMS, but so far I am not able to do so. The date and place as handed down to us was 1802 and they were married in WARREN COUNTY. All the marriage bonds here of Warren do not include the bond. Nor have I been able to find the marriage bonds of WILLIAM SIMS and BETSY HOWARD, daughter of WILLIAM HOWARD, nor of SALLIE HOWARD who married ELISHA SIMS. They have not been found up at the State Library so far.

I cannot understand why H. U. SIMS is not willing to accept JOSEPH JOHN ALLEN'S names, that his mother OLIVE SIMS, daughter of WILLIAM HOWARD SIMS, and WILLIAM SIMS' grandson, and great grandson of JOHN SIMS and ANN HENLEY. THURSTON ALLEN, son of JOSEPH JOHN ALLEN lives at LOUISBURG. THURSTON ALLEN has an auto plant (1936) right at the bridge as you go to LOUISBURG from RALEIGH. He lives in a beautiful old place (No. (122) on the Searcy Map) that his father owned and it is out in the country. I have been there several times. JOSEPH JOHN ALLEN was the "Speller" and no fool. His brother, who was killed in the war (C.S.A.) is the bronze soldier depicted on the top of the Confederate Monument on the Capitol Square here in Raleigh, facing HILLSBORO STREET. ZACHARIAH SIMS, brother of SUSAN SIMS who married DAVID ROYSTER JR. is said to have settled in Alabama.

GEN. R. F. HOKE and FINIS RAY are descended from RICHARD BULLOCK through AGATHA the daughter of AGNES. AGNES married JUDGE JOHN WILLIAMS and their daughter AGATHA married ROBERT BURTON, uncle of the HUTCHINS GORDON BURTON who was Governor of NORTH CAROLINA.

I'll copy here some data that I got lately:

Here are some land transfers at OXFORD, in GRANVILLE COUNTY:
In 1756 and 1760 JAMES DANIEL bought land from JOHN SEARCY, JR. Book C page 483.
In 1760 JAMES DANIEL bought lands from ROBERT JONES JR. Book C p. 546.
In 1760 JOHN WILLIAMS DANIEL bought land from WILLIAM SEARCY. Book C p. 561.
In 1762 -63 JAMES DANIEL bought land from RICHARD BULLOCK. Book F p. 424.
In 1779-80 JAMES DANIEL bought land from RICHARD HENDERSON. Book O p 202.
From NUTBUSH SECTION in 1778 JAMES DANIEL took the oath of allegiance; also JOHN W. DANIEL and CHESLEY DANIEL.
Items from the Old BURTON STORE LEDGER at WILLIAMSBORO:
Account of JAMES DANIEL: 1784, to sundries L110 -14-3
1785, Feb. 12, by cash L 171 -14 -3.

Here are som GRANVILLE COUNTY MARRIAGE BONDS, I found:
1759. JOHN BULLOCK and SOPHRONIA McMULLEN.
1760. Nathaniel Bullock and MARY HAWKINS (Len. H. Bullock, Sec.)
1763. Leonard H. Bullock and Fannie Hawkins (Thomas Lowe, Sec.)
1771. John Bullock and Catherine Lewis (William Bullock, Sec.)
1772. James Bullock and Mary Phillips, Sept. 30. (Wm. Phillips, Sec.)
1791. Frances Bullock m. William Boyd, April 28 (L. Potter, Sec.)
1796. George Bullock married Mary Freeman (Oct. 25) PETER MANN, Sec.
1783. Charles Bullock, Nov. 12, a bondsman.
1797. James Cozart James married FRANCES HOWARD, Oct. 19.
1772. JAMES DANIEL married SALLIE COOK, Nov. 30. (William Cook, Sec.).

Will of JOHN HOWARD in WARREN COUNTY:
Dated 1771; proved 1774. JOHN HOWARD names the following children: JULIUS, THOMAS, JOHN, JAMES, MARTIN and SARAH HOWARD. And this:

COUNTY OF BUTE, PROVINCE OF N. C. "I, JOHN HOWARD, give to my son JULIUS certain real property, he to pay ten pounds, the land on LONG BRANCH". NUTBUSH, Granville County, June, 1765. God Save the KING.

These notes from Mrs. Hallie Lee (High) Royster continued over to the next page:

"TRANQUILITY", the home of CHESLEY DANIEL was ten miles Northwest from OXFORD. Where JAMES DANIEL lived is now (was afterwards) known as the TURNER PLACE. The BULLOCKS owned several thousand acres of land North of this point.

REUBEN SEARCY was the son in law of SAMUEL HENDERSON.

SAMUEL HENDERSON sold the 800 acres to JOHN SIMS in 1750 on NUTBUSH CREEK.

The GILLIAM PLACE was bought by HENRY T. WATKINS in 1855, according to JOHN B. WATKINS, his grandson, of HENDERSON, North Carolina.

"HARRIS POND" was where ISHAM HARRIS lived South of JAMES DANIEL. It became the MABRY PLACE, as STEPHEN MABRY married MISS HARRIS about 1870.

Mr. Watkins (of Henderson) says: "There was another set of DANIEL that lived West of OXFORD in 1760, who have descendants in OXFORD today. They were cousins of my CHESLEY DANIEL who died in 1814.

NAT B. DANIEL (great uncle of John B. Watkins) was the son of NATHANIEL CHESLEY DANIEL who died between 1797 and 1802.

In HALIFAX COUNTY (continues Mrs. Hallie Lee Royster) I found this will on page 141 (in a record book, number not given, and date forgotten):

Will of GEORGE KEELING leaves to GEORGE KEELING, ELIZABETH KEELING, ANN KEELING, AGATHA KEELING and FRANCIS KEELING, his property.

RICHARD BULLOCK'S wife was ANN HENLEY. LEONARD HENLEY BULLOCK was the son and was the RICH Bullock, so FINIS RAY says.

Uncle JIM ROYSTER'S family records were given to a man (whose name I have forgotten, who was going to get the estate of NATHANIEL CARPENTER (Aunt MARY ASHLEY ROYSTER'S uncle) out of Chancery in LONDON, ENGLAND. It is still there, so VERNON, JIM and HUBERT all said. VERNON was in EUROPE in 1880 and they told him it was there, but it would take a great deal of money and time to get it out. Aunt MARY ROYSTER'S mother (ASHLEY) was a MARTHA CARPENTER, and I believe they said she was this DR. CARPENTER'S sister. He was "keeper" or some such thing, of the Port of Virginia, and on a trip to or from EUROPE was drowned.

PARISH SIMS married KEZIAH.

WILLIAM SIMS married RACHEL WALKER.

M. W. SIMS wrote a letter from Texas, dated "BRYAN, Sept. 3, 1905, addressed to Mrs. V. C. Royster (Hallie Lee High Royster), Raleigh, N. C. in which he said: "I cannot go beyond my grandfather and grandmother. My father's family is all I can give complete. My father was the third son and fifth child of PARISH SIMS and his wife Keziah. I send you a letter from THETUS W. SIMS, M. C. from Tennessee, who is of our family".*

The letters from which the foregoing notes are taken were signed by

MR. HALLIE LEE (HIGH) ROYSTER
(Mrs. V. C. Royster)
RALEIGH, N. C.

---

* Up to 1911 three members of the SIMS family have been members of the United States Congress according to the Congressional Directory. They were ALEXANDER DROMGOOLE SIMS from S. C. born in BRUNSWICK COUNTY, VA. June 11, 1803; LEONARD HENLEY SIMS, from SPRINGFIELD, Missouri, a member of the 29th Congress, born in North Carolina, and THETUS WILLRETTE SIMS, a member of the Congress for several terms, from Tennessee, who was born in WAYNE COUNTY, in that State, April 25, 1852. The latter is the one mentioned in Mrs. Royster's letter from M. W. SIMS, of Bryan, Texas.

---

(16) PETER BENNETT, who lived on HAW RIVER in the Southern part of the present GRANVILLE COUNTY, below OXFORD, was the son of RICHARD BENNETT who left a will in GRANVILLE COUNTY, dated in 1783 and proved in 1786, in which he mentioned his wife ANNE and several children, including "PITTER". Space available here will not permit a "study" of this family and a presentation of the material that might establish the identity of this family with the BENNETTS of VIRGINIA and NORTHAMPTON COUNTY, in which the name WILLIAM appears, as it does in this family. The presence of the name BARTLETT in the BENNETT family and the same name in the SEARCY family, as well as a BENNETT SEARCY indicates a possibly relationship between these two families, also. These BENNETTS "belonged" somewhere in the important BENNETT FAMILY tree, but just where is yet to be determined.

---

(21) VALENTINE WHITE was a descendant of the WHITES OF QUEEN'S CREEK in YORK COUNTY, Virginia, and was related to the RALPH GRAVES family, kin of the WILLIAMS and DANIEL and HENDERSON tribes. In 1748 and 1749 VALENTINE WHITE was voting for BURGESS in BRUNSWICK COUNTY, Virginia, but by 1754 he had settled in GRANVILLE COUNTY and joined the militia, being a member of the Company of CAPT. ANDREW HAMPTON, in COL. WILLIAM EATON'S REGIMENT. Doubtless he had a son of the same name, who could have been the Valentine White who belonged to the Company of CAPTAIN JONATHAN KITTRELL more than twenty years later. The names THOMAS, VALENTINE, MARK, GEORGE, JOHN, WILLIAM, ISAAC and LUKE WHITE appear in this GRANVILLE COUNTY, FAMILY, on the old records. One of these WHITES married a daughter of old JEREMIAH BLOOMER, of WILKES COUNTY, North Carolina, and moved to South Carolina and GEORGIA and had a VALENTINE and a BLOOMER WHITE. The descendants of BLOOMER WHITE in each generation carried the name VALENTINE on down through Alabama, Mississippi and into TEXAS, where a life long friend of the compiler, DR. E. VALENTINE WHITE became and is now serving as Dean of the Texas College for Women, at Denton, Texas.

The name MANN WHITE found its way into this family, through the intermarriage of several WHITES with the MANN FAMILY, just as the name MANN found its way into the SATTERWHITE FAMILY, of GRANVILLE COUNTY. MILDRED SATTERWHITE, of MISSISSIPPI married first a JOHN WHITE and after her first husband's death married his plantation overseer, FLEMING LITTLEFIELD. Both the Littlefields and WHITES came on into Texas and went full-tilt into the ranching and cattle business and accumulated fortunes. Their descendants are numerous there today.

There were a great many members of this WHITE FAMILY in COLONIAL GRANVILLE COUNTY and some idea of the number of them may be gleaned from the following record of marriages that are to be found in the old books:

March 13, 1786: COLEMAN REED WHITE married SELAH BRADFORD in Granville County, N. C.
February 7, 1797. PHILLIP WHITE married ANN MANN in Granville County, N. C.
October 24, 1799. JOSEPH WHITE married NANCY MANN in Granville County, N. C.
1827. ANN MANN WHITE married JORDAN B. MOSS in Granville County, N. C.
September 26, 1812. COLEMAN REED WHITE married POLLY COLE in Granville County, N. C.
October 4, 1839. FRANCES ASBURY WHITE married REUBEN J. MOSS, in Granville County, N. C.
December 19, 1821. EDWARD WHITE married MARY HAGOOD, in Warren County, N. C.
September 7, 1833. EDWARD WHITE married MARY WILLIAMSON HILLIARD in Warren County, N. C.
November 26, 1830. NANCY ANN NELSON WHITE married ELIAS JENKINS, in Granville County, N. C.
March 20, 1811. POLLY WHITE married JOHN M. VINCENT, in Granville County, N. C.
1836. WILLIAM G. V. WHITE (probably VALENTINE) married MIRANDA V. HESTER in Granville County, N. C.
November 30, 1825. JOHN WHITE married NIXEY COLE (daughter of JOHN and SUSAN COLE) in Granville County, N. C.

COLEMAN and PHILLIP WHITE and JACOB and ISAAC VINCENT appear on the first Census of Granville County in 1790.

In the days of VALENTINE WHITE's first appearance on the records of GRANVILLE COUNTY, N. C. people moved about a great deal, and it is startling to find a VALENTINE WHITE of some prominence in AUGUSTA COUNTY, VIRGINIA, from the Chalkley Records. In 1782 around Staunton Valentine White was a Captain of Patrollers; in 1785 he was a deputy Sheriff under William Bowyer, and somewhere I have a note copied from the same records showing that he was at one time City Marshall of Staunton, Virginia. That he was the same VALENTINE WHITE is possible, or at least one of the same persons of the name who lived in GRANVILLE is suggested by a deed executed in October, 1801 by ARCHIBALD MANN and LEWIS MYERS, of Bath County to LEONARD FISHER, which was witnessed by VALENTINE WHITE and JOHN BIRD, JR.

---

(22) ERASTUS GILL. ERASMUS GILL (evidently the same person) married SARAH NEWSOME in DINWIDDIE COUNTY, Virginia, JUNE 8, 1786. On the records of WAKE COUNTY there is a marriage bond between one WORMLEY ROSE RAY and NANCY GILL (Daughter of ERASMUS or ERASTUS RAY) dated December 24, 1813. Both the RAYS and the GILLS lived near the falls of the Nuse in the upper part of Wake and the lower part of GRANVILLE COUNTY in what was called the "NEWLIGHT DISTRICT" of Wake County and not far from the WAKE FORREST section. They properly belong in the WAKE COUNTY Chapter of this work. However, many of the RAYS of this family settled in GRANVILLE COUNTY, and the late C. D. RAY, whom the compiler met on some of his visits to OXFORD, was of this family, coming down through WORMLEY ROSE RAY and NANCY GILL. His brother ERASMUS GILL RAY was for several years a neighbor of the compiler in DALLAS, TEXAS, prior to his death a few years ago.

---

(24) JAMES RAY, who lived in WAKE COUNTY belonged to the family of RAYS mentioned in the GILL paragraph above. He is said to have been a revolutionary soldier. His will and data pertaining to his family will be presented more at length in the Chapter on WAKE COUNTY which will appear later on in the "LOST TRIBES OF NORTH CAROLINA".

---

(29) HERBERT HIGH (pronounced HARBERT) has already been touched upon in the notes of his Great Grand-daughter HALLIE LEE (HIGH) ROYSTER. He was the father of her grandfather ALEXANDER MARTIN HIGH. The HIGH FAMILY also belongs mainly to WAKE COUNTY and will be taken up in the WAKE COUNTY CHAPTER of this work.

---

(30) THOMAS HARRISON also belongs to WAKE COUNTY, and the HARRISONS of WAKE will be mentioned more at length in the Chapter on that County.

---

(41). JOHN KNIGHT was from VIRGINIA and was related to the WATKINS and WOODSON families. He was a son of JONATHAN KNIGHT who married JUDITH WOODSON daughter of JOSEPH WOODSON & ELIZABETH MADDOX February 24, 1757, and JONATHAN KNIGHT was the son of JOHN KNIGHT and his wife ELIZABETH WOODSON, daughter of ROBERT WOODSON and his second wife RACHEL WATKINS. (I am accepting the version of the Woodson Family genealogists on this, which is perhaps correct) This (41) JOHN KNIGHT had a brother WILLIAM KNIGHT, who was a minister, and who lived and was perhaps born in GRANVILLE COUNTY, who moved to BEDFORD COUNTY, TENNESSEE, where he established what was and still is known as the old "Knight Camp Ground" South of Duck River. His wife was ELIZABETH MAUPIN of an old Virginia family from around WILLIAMSBURG. WILLIAM KNIGHT had a son OBEDIAH WOODSON KNIGHT, who went to Texas, married one of the TENNESSEE HUGHES family from around NASHVILLE and left the prominent KNIGHT FAMILY pioneers of the City of Dallas.

THE PENN AND TAYLOR FAMILIES OF GRANVILLE COUNTY NORTH CAROLINA.

(47) JOHN PENN (One of the "Signers" on behalf of North Carolina) was related to the TAYLOR, PENDLETON and LEWIS FAMILY. His mother, CATHERINE TAYLOR was the daughter of CATHERINE PENDLETON and JOHN TAYLOR. CATHERINE PENDLETON was the daughter of PHILLIP PENDLETON, according to my information.

JOHN TAYLOR, the grandfather on his mother's side of JOHN PENN, died in GRANVILLE COUNTY and his will (W. B. 1, p. 275) dated March 16, 1780, is on record in the county. The father of JOHN PENN, who married CATHERINE TAYLOR, was MOSES PENN.

Following were the children of JOHN TAYLOR and his wife CATHERINE PENDLETON:

1. EDMUND TAYLOR married ANNE LEWIS
2. JOHN TAYLOR married a MISS LYNNE
3. WILLIAM TAYLOR married an ANDERSON
4. JOSEPH TAYLOR married FRANCES ANDERSON
5. ISABELLA TAYLOR married a HOPKINS
6. ELIZABETH TAYLOR married (1) JAMES LEWIS (2) WILLIAM BULLOCK.
7. JAMES TAYLOR married ANNE POLLARD.
8. MARY TAYLOR married MR. PENN.
9. PHILLIP TAYLOR married MARY WALKER
10. CATHERINE TAYLOR married MOSES PENN

: Parents of (47) JOHN PENN.

JOHN PENN, through his connection with the TAYLOR FAMILY, was distantly related to PRESIDENT ZACHARY TAYLOR and the HON. JEFFERSON DAVIS, President of the Confederate States. I have often seen and heard this statement repeated and have called for information to substantiate the claim, which has been furnished. In substance, abbreviated as far as possible, I present this information below:

JAMES TAYLOR (Of Carlisle, England) settled on CHESAPEAKE BAY (probably in YORK COUNTY, Virginia, about 1640. He died in 1698 and is buried in KING WILLIAM COUNTY. He was twice married, first to FRANCES, second to MARY GREGORY.

By his first wife he had:

1. JANE TAYLOR.
2. JAMES TAYLOR born March 14, 1674, married MARTHA THOMPSON.
3. SARAH TAYLOR married ROBERT POWELL.

By his second wife he had:

4. JOHN TAYLOR (died in infancy).
5. ANN TAYLOR married GEORGE EASTMAN.
6. MARY TAYLOR m. (1) HENRY PENDLETON (2) EDWARD WATKINS.
7. EDMUND TAYLOR (b. 1690)
8. ELIZABETH TAYLOR (b. 1684 with 5.ANN, a twin).
9. JOHN TAYLOR (b. 1696) m. CATHERINE PENDLETON.

2. JAMES TAYLOR (oldest son of JAMES TAYLOR I, of Carlisle, England, was one of the earliest surveyors in VIRGINIA. He is said to have located 10,000 acres of land in the Counties of HANOVER, SPOTTSYLVANIA and ORANGE and moved on this land. He died in 1729. His eldest child, FRANES TAYLOR married AMBROSE MADISON and was the grandmother of the PRESIDENT JAMES MADISON. The third child and oldest son, JAMES TAYLOR III was the ancestor of a large family and moved to NEWPORT, KY.

The fourth child and second son was ZACHARY TAYLOR (1707-1768), the father of the gallant LIEUT.-COL. RICHARD TAYLOR, of Revolutionary fame, and who made the first trip down the Ohio and Mississippi from Pittsburg to New Orleans, through the Indian country, in 1769 in company with his brother HANCOCK TAYLOR, ABRAHAM HAPSTONSTALL and BARBOUR, all from ORANGE COUNTY, Virginia. ZACHARY TAYLOR married ELIZABETH LEE, established Meadows Farm plantation and acquired 26 slaves. HANCOCK LEE was mortally wounded by the Indians in 1744, but RICHARD TAYLOR lived to a ripe old age. ZACHARY TAYLOR had four children:

10. HANCOCK TAYLOR married his cousin ALICE CHEW.
11. ELIZABETH TAYLOR married CAPT. THOMAS BELL.
12. RICHARD TAYLOR married SARAH DABNEY STROTHER
13.

SARAH DABNEY STROTHER was the sister of WILLIAM DABNEY STROTHER, who was killed at GUILFORD COURTHOUSE. Her husband RICHARD TAYLOR was a graduate of WILLIAM & MARY COLLEGE and moved to KENTUCKY in 1785, where their son ZACHARY TAYLOR (b. in Virginia) grew to manhood, & afterwards became PRESIDENT OF THE UNITED STATES, after serving his country in the Revolution.

In a note in one genealogical account we are told that "JOHN TAYLOR of CAROLINE died September 19, 1763,"and that "JOHN TAYLOR, son of JAMES TAYLOR I, who married CATHERINE PENDLETON, was the ancestor of COL. JOHN TAYLOR, whose daughter married FRANCIS LIGHTFOOT LEE." The only way we can account for this statement, knowing that JOHN TAYLOR who married CATHERINE PENDLETON died in GRANVILLE COUNTY, N. C., is that his son JOHN "married a MISS LYNNE" must have been the "COL. JOHN TAYLOR of CAROLINE".

It is of interest to note that PRESIDENT JAMES MADISON married DOLLY PAYNE, who is said to have been born just over the line from GRANVILLE COUNTY at PAYNE'S TAVERN, Person County.

(50) STEPHEN TERRY was a revolutionary soldier, the son of ZACHARIAH TERRY, and the grandson of the old surveyor JAMES TERRY who moved from PITTSYLVANIA COUNTY, Virginia, in 1755 to CASWELL COUNTY, N. C. At least to that part of ORANGE which is now CASWELL. STEPHEN and JAMES TERRY lived in ISLAND CREEK DISTRICT in GRANVILLE COUNTY in 1790, at approximately the spot indicated on the SEARCY MAP. During the revolutionary war STEPHEN TERRY had returned to and was living in PEYTONSBURG, HENRY COUNTY, VIRGINIA, a supply post for Virginia troops in the revolution. He died sometime prior to October 16, 1797, when his will was proven, in which he named his wife SARAH TERRY and the following children:

1. NATHANIEL TERRY
2. JAMES TERRY
3. WILLIAM TERRY
4. JOHN TERRY
5. ANNE TERRY
6. ELIZABETH TERRY
7. RHODA TERRY

These TERRYS were from VIRGINIA and were related to the DICKERSON family, some of whom also came from VIRGINIA and settled in GRANVILLE COUNTY. JAMES TERRY, the grandfather of STEPHEN TERRY with his brothers BENJAMIN and NATHANIEL were surveyors in what is now PITTSYLVANIA COUNTY, Virginia. These TERRYS had lived in HANOVER and NEW KENT COUNTIES before coming to what is now HALIFAX and PITTSYLVANIA. NATHANIEL died in HALIFAX CO. VA. in 1778, and among a long list of children he had a daughter NANCY TERRY who married HERRYMAN GREEN (from Westmoreland County, Va.), and had a son THOMAS JEFFERSON GREEN who married FRANCES KEELING BURTON, who was born at "NINE OAKS" in N. C. in 1797. FRANCES KEELING BURTON was the daughter of JAMES MINGE BURTON, a brother of COL. ROBERT BURTON who married AGATHA WILLIAMS the daughter of JUDGE JOHN WILLIAMS of GRANVILLE COUNTY. JAMES MINGE BURTON married ELIZABETH RIDLEY and they were the parents of JOHN BURTON, ROBERT BURTON, BROMFIELD BURTON, FRANCES KEELING BURTON (who married THOMAS JEFFERSON GREEN in N. C.) and MARTHA BURTON.

---

(52) JOHN WILLIAMS GRAVES. There were several persons of this name, all related in some degree, the name coming into the family from the ancestor JOHN WILLIAMS, of QUEEN'S CREEK in YORK COUNTY, VIRGINIA. Nearly every generation of the descendants carried the name in the list of children and there were so many that they become confusing and difficult to identify. The wife of the first one of the name was MARY JONES (according to family tradition) and after his death she married her late husband's first cousin JOHN WILLIAMS DANIEL who left will in WARREN COUNTY in 1808. (See pages 244-245 for the GRAVES FAMILY notes).

---

(54) WILLIAM CHRISTMAS. THOMAS RAY, of NEW POQUOSON, in YORK COUNTY, VIRGINIA, the direct ancestor of this compiler, married MARY CHRISTMAS. MARY (sounds like MERRY) CHRISTMAS was my ancestress. She was a daughter of DOCTORIS WILLIAM CHRISTMAS who left will in YORK COUNTY in 1655. The CHRISTMAS FAMILY of WARREN COUNTY (and GRANVILLE) were descendants of this YORK FAMILY. DRURY CHRISTMAS probably came to Colonial Granville County with his kinsman CHRISTMAS RAY (See page 209 herein). His will was proven in what is now WARREN COUNTY in the year 1785, in which he named two sons JESSE and WILLIAM CHRISTMAS. DRURY was a brother of JOHN CHRISTMAS who died in 1782, leaving children THOMAS, SARAH, REBECCA and MIDDLETON CHRISTMAS. From a "Guide to the Old North State" (Federal Writer's Project, 1939) is taken the following items:

> WARRENTON and WARREN COUNTY were founded in 1779 and named for General Joseph Warren * who fell at BUNKER HILL. The town was laid out in that year by WILLIAM CHRISTMAS. The only building then on the site was a granary where grain was collected to finance the revolution, through there was a settlement nearby at the junction of SHADY GROVE and HALIFAX stage roads. - page 476.
>
> The town (RALEIGH, N. C.) was laid out by WILLIAM CHRISTMAS in APRIL, 1792 with UNION (Now CAPITOL) SQUARE reserved for the Statehouse. The four parks were named for the first three Governors under the Constitution and for ATTORNEY GENERAL ALFRED MOORE. The streets were named for the eight districts, each identified by the name of its principal city, for the commissioners and for other prominent citizens. In pursuance of instructions the commissioners built a brick statehouse "large enough for both houses of the assembly", and upon its completion (1794) Raleigh was taunted with being a "city of streets without houses". - page 234.

---

(62) DANIEL MORROW. Daniel Morrow is another one of the compiler's kinsmen, his mother having been SARAH LAVINIA MORROW of this family of ISLAND CREEK DISTRICT. This particular arm of his mother's family came down out of PRINCE EDWARD COUNTY, VIRGINIA, some of them going as far as MECKLENBURG and the upper part of SOUTH CAROLINA. They will be mentioned more in detail in the MECKLENBURG SECTION of this work, later on.

(64) DANIEL WILLIAMS married URSULA HENDERSON, a daughter of THOMAS HENDERSON and the sister of SAMUEL HENDERSON who married his sister ELIZABETH WILLIAMS (See page 221 and the account of the HENDERSON and WILLIAMS FAMILIES as shwon herein). Just when DANIEL WILLIAMS first came to GRANVILLE COUNTY is not definitely known, but he died in 1759 leaving a will in which he mentioned his children, but did not give the name of his wife. His son DANIEL married his first cousin ANN HENDERSON, sister of JUDGE RICHARD HENDERSON and the daughter of SAMUEL HENDERSON. After the death of DANIEL HENDERSON, JR. his widow moved to the PACOLET in SOUTH CAROLINA, where she married ADAM POTTER as her second husband. DANIEL WILLIAMS, the first, may have lived for a time in BRUNSWICK COUNTY, Virginia, for on the records there is a deed from THOMAS DENTON to DANIEL WILLIAMS in 1752 (Book 5 p. 259).

(65) MEMUCAN HUNT was the first Treasurer of NORTH CAROLINA, and was called "MUKE" hunt by his familiars. He was also a member of the Provincial Congress of North Carolina. His old home in WILLIAMSBORO was sold by one of his sons to the "rich" HAMILTON FAMILY, who named it "BURNSIDE" after their English home. The family genealogist has only furnished us with the names of two of his sons:

(1) WILLIAM HUNT
(2) DR. THOMAS HUNT

(1) WILLIAM HUNT was the father of a son named MEMUCAN HUNT, born in GRANVILLE COUNTY, who emigrated to Texas and became Secretary of the Navy of the REPUBLIC of TEXAS in the cabinet of SAM HOUSTON. This MEMUCAN HUNT married a MISS HOWARD, of another GRANVILLE COUNTY family, who after his death in Texas, married two other husbands, I am informed. In the course of his career in Texas this younger MEMUCAN HUNT became Minister from the Republic of Texas to the United States and he was also one of the Commissioners who ran the boundary line between Texas and the United States. In the year 1845, while living in GALVESTON, TEXAS, MEMUCAN HUNT was defeated as a delegate to the annexation convention by RICHARD BACHE, who was a grandson of DR. BENJAMIN FRANKLIN.

(2) DR. THOMAS G. HUNT, another son of (65) MEMUCAN HUNT, married BETTY DUKE, a daughter of GREEN DUKE and his wife ELIZABETH WADE, and they were the parents of eight children, one of whom was DR. JAMES ANDERSON HUNT, who was born in GRANVILLE COUNTY, N. C., December 22, 1808, and who died at CALDWELL, BURLESON COUNTY, TEXAS, in 1892. He was a BINGHAM student and received his medical education at TRANSYLVANIA UNIVERSITY in Kentucky. He married ANNA ADAIR BRIDGES at Harrodsburg, Kentucky, in 1838, the daughter of JUDGE JOHN L. BRIDGES and his wife NANCY ADAIR, daughter of GOV. JOHN ADAIR. DR. JAMES ANDERSON HUNT and his wife ANNA ADAIR BRIDGES had the following children:

10. WILLIAM HUNT
11. ELIZA HUNT
12. CATHERINE HUNT
13. ANNA HUNT
14. MARIAN HUNT
15. ISABELLA HUNT
16. HENRY HUNT
17. CALLIE HUNT
18. JOHN HUNT
19. BEN HUNT
20. ROWAN HUNT

19. BEN BRIDGES HUNT (Son of DR. JAMES ANDERSON HUNT) was born at HARRODSBURG, KY. February 19, 1857, and died at CALDWELL, TEXAS, in 1904. He married LAURA BELL PARKS and had the following children: JAMES DUDLEY HUNT, MABEL HUNT, WALLIE HUNT, BEN BRIDGES HUNT, HORACE HAMILTON HUNT, EDITH HUNT, GLADYS HUNT, WARREN WOOD HUNT, LAURA BELL HUNT and ALMA HUNT. BEN BRIDGES HUNT II, of this family is an attorney and writer of note and a commentator on current world events who is widely read and quoted, a personal friend of the writer and his neighbor in the City of AUSTIN, TEXAS.

DR. THOMAS G. HUNT (son of the original MEMUCAN HUNT of Granville County) migrated to Texas and settled at GAY HILL in the present WASHINGTON COUNTY, not far from the present town of BRENHAM, where he died in the first half of the nineteenth century, and is buried, a fact that perhaps few members of the HUNT family know.

The above account is substituted for the one on page 74, which is badly printed.

(68) JOHN BOYD came to GRANVILLE COUNTY and settled in the upper part of GRANVILLE COUNTY near the BULLOCKS and HAWKINS family. His home before coming to GRANVILLE COUNTY was within the bounds of CUMBERLAND PARISH in what was then LUNENBURG COUNTY, or possibly MECKLENBURG. The vestry of the Parish at its first meeting appointed LEWIS DELONEY, WILLIAM HOWARD and JOHN BOYD in 1749 to "fix on some convenient place near the fork of the ROANOKE to erect a Chapel and make report to the next vestry." (Bell's Cumberland Parish p. 35).

On the records of LUNENBURG COUNTY dated OCTOBER 15, 1749, appears the will of one MARY LAWSON (W. B. 1, p. 36) in which she mentions the names of eight children, among them being "JOHN BOYD and wife MARGARET", from which it appears that, if this is the same JOHN BOYD who later moved to GRANVILLE COUNTY, his wife was MARGARET LAWSON, who, according to the will of her mother had brothers TRAVIS, JOHN, WILLIAM & DAVID LAWSON.

In Lunenburg County there were several other members of this BOYD FAMILY, including ALEXANDER, RICHARD and ROBERT BOYD. The HAWKINS family lived there also, as well as in NUTBUSH, in North Carolina. The daughter of JOHN BOYD of GRANVILLE was the wife of GOVERNOR WILLIAM HAWKINS, and NANCY HAWKINS married WILLIAM HAWKINS in MECKLENBURG COUNTY, VIRGINIA, in December (the 24th) 1803. (Cumberland Parish Register p. 316).

(69) JOHN SIMS, of NUTBUSH DISTRICT, GRANVILLE COUNTY, NORTH CAROLINA, like the SEARCYS, GRAVES, WILLIAMS, BULLOCKS and a number of other families who have been mentioned in these notes, came from HANOVER and NEW KENT COUNTY, VIRGINIA.

The compiler is indebted to his friend, HON. HENRY UPSON SIMS, former President of the AMERICAN BAR ASSOCIATION, and to his cousin MRS. ZEBULON JUDD, of Auburn, Alabama, for the information about the SIMS FAMILY here presented. JUDGE SIMS, as everyone should know, is a leading member of the bar of BIRMINGHAM, and has painstakingly prepared a history of the SIMS FAMILY published exclusively for the family. In a letter to the writer dated September 10, 1943, he gives the following abstract of the genealogy of JOHN SIMS of GRANVILLE COUNTY:

1. CAPT. GEORGE SYMES, of Somersetshire, England, married DOROTHY EVERARD and settled in ANTIGUA, in the BRITISH WEST INDIES, about 1672. They had a son

2. GEORGE SYMES, who came to VIRGINIA when about 16 years of age, and settled in ISLE OF WIGHT COUNTY. This GEORGE SYMES, of ISLE OF WIGHT County appears to have been the father of at least two sons:

(10) ADAM SYMES (oldest son). See later.
(11) JOHN SYMES (of HANOVER and NEW KENT COUNTIES, Va.)

11. JOHN SYMES or SIMS, of Hanover and New Kent Counties, married about 1705, MARY RICE, of a prominent HANOVER COUNTY FAMILY, the daughter of THOMAS RICE. MARY RICE is said to have been the aunt of REV. DAVID RICE, an early VIRGINIA MINISTER and teacher. JOHN SIMS and his wife MARY RICE were the parents of a large family of children, including six or seven sons, one of whom was (69) JOHN SIMS, who married SARAH BULLOCK, daughter of RICHARD BULLOCK, about 1734, and moved to GRANVILLE COUNTY, N. C.

MRS. ZEBULON JUDD, of AUBURN, ALABAMA, mentioned above, in a letter to the compiler in 1943, says:

> "I have a photostatic copy of the will of JOHN SIMS who located in GRANVILLE COUNTY, North Carolina about 1750, having previously (circa 1734) married SARAH, daughter of RICHARD BULLOCK. They were probably married in Hanover County, Virginia. The Saunders, Bullock, Gilliam, Brown, etc., families of Granville intermarried."

MRS. JUDD then gives us the names of the following descendants of JOHN SIMS and his wife SARAH BULLOCK. JOHN SIMS died in 1769 in GRANVILLE COUNTY and left the following children, who are named in his will:

20. WILLIAM SIMS married ELIZABETH HOWARD
21. ELISHA SIMS married SARAH HOWARD
22. LEONARD SIMS married SARAH SWEPSON (His name was LEONARD HENLEY SIMS)
23. AGNES SIMS
24. DORCAS SIMS
25. SARAH SIMS
26. SUSANNA SIMS
27. MARY SIMS
28. LUCRETIA SIMS
29. EUPHRATES SIMS

20. WILLIAM SIMS and his wife ELIZABETH HOWARD had the following children:

30. DORCAS SIMS
31. ELIZABETH SIMS
32. BETHANY SIMS
33. MARY (POLLY) SIMS
34. SARAH (SALLY) SIMS
35. REBECCA SIMS
36. WILLIAM HOWARD SIMS
37. JOHN SIMS
38. ALFRED SIMS
39. JARRETT SIMS

MARTIN SIMS may have been a son of ELISHA SIMS, who was the son of JOHN SIMS, of GRANVILLE. Martin Sims married Anna Jane Howard, January 20, 1782, as shown by the marriage records of GRANVILLE, and she must have been a daughter of JULIUS HOWARD, who was the brother of ELISHA SIM'S wife. MARTIN SIMS was in FRANKLIN COUNTY, GEORGIA, in 1802, and died there APRIL 7, 1822. See Vol. 1 Historical Collections of Georgia D. A. R., page 288. But MARTIN SIMS may have been descended from the ADAM SYMES line. - Extract from a letter from Hon. Henry Upson Sims, to the compiler in 1943.

MARTIN SIMS does not appear among the children of ELISHA SIMS and wife SARAH HOWARD as furnished by MRS. ZEBULON JUDD, which appears on the page following.

21. ELISHA SIMS and his wife SARAH HOWARD had the following children:

40. JOHN SIMS
41. HERBERT SIMS
42. ZACHARIAH SIMS (Settled in GEORGIA).
43. ELISHA SIMS (Moved to TENNESSEE).
44. GUILFORD SIMS
45. IRENA SIMS
46. THIRIA SIMS
47. MAHALA SIMS
48. SUSAN SIMS married DAVID ROYSTER, JR.
49. SAUNDERS (?) SIMS
50. LEONARD HENLEY SIMS

50. LEONARD H. SIMS moved to ALABAMA and settled in COURTLAND in 1822, where he ran a manufacturing business, improving cotton gins; he being an inventive genius. He married, evidently in his later years a widow WASHINGTON, from PULASKI, Tennessee, to which place she returned after the death of Leonard Sims. By this marriage LEONARD H. SIMS had two daughters ELIZABETH SIMS and PRUDENCE SIMS.

22. LEONARD HENLEY SIMS and his wife SARAH SWEPSON had children:

51. JOHN SIMS married NANCY HENDRICKS
52. RICHARD SIMS married REBECCA DROMGOOLE.*
53. SWEPSON SIMS
54. LEONARD HENLEY SIMS married ELIZABETH VAUGHAN in 1804.
55. THOMAS SIMS
56. JOSEPH SIMS (Had only 1 child, JAMES SIMS).
57. HENRY SIMS married SALLY BURT in 1813. *
58. JENNIE SIMS married her cousin JEFFERSON SIMS.
59. SUSANNA SIMS married a BURT and had 19 children.
60. SARAH (SALLIE) SIMS.

* Both HENRY and RICHARD SIMS married cousins.

---

(10) ADAM SIMS, the older brother of JOHN SIMS of NEW KENT and HANOVER COUNTY, and an uncle of JOHN SIMS of GRANVILLE COUNTY who married SARAH BULLOCK is the ancestor in an excellent genealogy called "Adam Symes and His Descendants" by Mrs. Jane Morris, of Little Rock, Arkansas - Dorrance & Co., Philadelphia, 1938, to which the writer's attention was called by Judge Sims of Birmingham and his cousin Mrs. Judd, of Auburn. Judge Sims writes:

> ADAM SYMES, oldest son of GEORGE of BRUNSWICK COUNTY, was born about 1709 and died about 1763, and had a son named BARTLETT SIMS in North Carolina.
>
> CAPT. GEORGE SYMES of ANTIGUA had a younger brother WILLIAM SIMS, who came to NEW KENT COUNTY, VIRGINIA (direct from England) about 1698, and had a couple of grants of land in VIRGINIA. He had a son named THOMAS, who lived in SPOTTSYLVANIA COUNTY, VIRGINIA; and a lease made by one Thomas Grayson to one Thomas Turner on January 27, 1737, will be found in Volume 1 of a reprint of Virginia County Records, Spottsylvania County, on page 46, witnessed by "IGNAT'S" and PETER SYMES; which would indicate that IGNATIUS SIMS was a son of THOMAS, because the same volume shows that Thomas had a son Thomas & a son PETER. *

BARTLETT SIMS, IGNATIUS SIMS AND REV. MARTIN SIMS OF TEXAS

The two notes last above from JUDGE SIMS were the result of research conducted by the compiler in an effort to discover the identity of an IGNATIUS and a BARTLETT SIMS, both of whom were early pioneers in Texas. In this effort the information contained in the notes wasmost hekpful. In HENRY COUNTY, VIRGINIA, among those taking the oath of allegiance in 1776-77 were both IGNATIUS and BARTLETT SIMS and a MATTHEW SIMS; also an ELIJAH CHISUM or CHISHOLM. On the deed records of HAWKINS COUNTY, TENNESSEE in 1791, BARTLETT SIMS sold lands to ELIJAH CHISHOLM. in a "History of Columbus, Miss." among those who lived there prior to 1821 was a HANCOCK CHISHOLM, a BARTLETT SIMS and a REV. MARTIN SIMS, who afterwards died in Columbus at the ripe age of 95 years. Then at WARRENTON, the county seat of WARREN COUNTY, GEORGIA, synonymous with WARREN COUNTY, N. C. we found the will of a BARTLETT SIMS, SR. (who may well have been the son of ADAM, born in 1709 in BRUNSWICK COUNTY, Virginia) who named his wife CATHERINE, his son BARTLETT SIMS, JR. (executor) and "My sons and daughters". One of those sons may have been REV. MARTIN SIMS.

BARTLETT SIMS came to Texas in 1822, being one of the "Old Three Hundred", the first of the Austin Colonists, and he was a surveyor and Indian fighter of historic interest. He was a member of the General Council of the Provisional Government in 1835. His wife was a CURTIS.

IGNATIUS SIMS settled in GRIMES COUNTY. His wife was NANCY PANKEY. They left sons RICHARD, WILLIAM, and JOHN and several daughters.

(71) JUDGE JOHN WILLIAMS has already been accounted for on pages 235 and 236 in the general outline of the WILLIAMS FAMILY. He was the son in law of RICHARD BULLOCK and the father in law of COL. ROBERT BURTON who married his only child and daughter, AGATHA WILLIAMS. I have an abstract of his will in GRANVILLE COUNTY proved in 1799 in which there are the names of several legatees, including ROBERT BURTON and others, but it is not clear that those mentioned are his children. The accepted tradition that seems to prevail in his family and among the descendants that he and his wife AGNES (BULLOCK) KEELING had only the one child seems correct. As has been stated before, he and JUDGE RICHARD HENDERSON were not only cousins, but what is called double cousins.

---

(72) HUTCHINS BURTON married TABITHA MINGE, the daughter of ROBERT MINGE and MARY HUNT (b. May 15, 1695). ROBERT MINGE was the son of the old Surveyor and Clerk of James City County, JAMES MINGE who married AMADEA HARRISON, daughter of ROBERT HARRISON of YORK COUNTY, VIRGINIA. After the death of ROBERT MINGE, his widow married WILLIAM ALLEN, who was the father of SAMUEL ALLEN, whose daughter MARTHA ALLEN married WILLIAM DANIEL, the son of WILLIAMS DANIEL, of YORK COUNTY, Virginia, and the nephew of JOHN DANIEL and his wife ANNE WILLIAMS. For the details of these intermarriages see the WILLIAMS FAMILY, DANIEL FAMILY and the BURTON FAMILY in this volume. NOEL HUNT BURTON was the father of HUTCHINS BURTON and his name very frequently occurs on the records of GOOCHLAND and MECKLENBURG COUNTIES. The first BURTONS of this family are said to have settled on the "Eastern Shore" of Virginia, in ACCOMAC COUNTY. (Vol. 2 Tyler p. 277). The following interesting land sale is taken from the records of GOOCHLAND COUNTY:

> JOHN BULLOCK and AGNES BULLOCK, of GOOCHLAND COUNTY, to JOSEPH WOODSON, 375 acres in GOOCHLAND COUNTY, bounded by land of NOEL BURTON, JOSIAH HATCHER and others. Dated February 4, 1763. (Vol 8, p. 411).

The NOEL BURTON mentioned in this item was NOEL HUNT BURTON, the father of HUTCHINS BURTON and the grandfather of COL. ROBERT BURTON. He had married JUDITH ALLEN, a sister of WILLIAM ALLEN the step-father of TABITHA MINGE who married his son HUTCHINS BURTON. On page 344 of the "Guide to the Old North State (1939) is the following item under a description of the town of HENDERSON in the present VANCE COUNTY:

> On the South side of Main Street is a long lane leading to CEDAR WALK (private), hidden from view by a few of the cedars that gave the place its name. It was built in 1750 by HUTCHINS BURTON for a boarding school, and called BLOOMING HOPE. Burton hanged himself ffrom the attic stairwell and visitors testify to the presence of his ghost. The house is two stories high with a central door flanked by pilasters. The wing at the left, a later addition, has a fine dentiled cornice, the detail of which resembles the work at BURNSIDE and Prospect Hill.

BURNSIDE, mentioned in the above paragraph, has reverence to the old MEMUCAN HUNT home, not so far distant, which was so named by PATRICK HAMILTON, the wealthy Englishman, who had bought it from DR. THOMAS HUNT. In 1760 BURNSIDE had been the home of MEMUCAN HUNT, the first State Treasurer. (See page 274.)

---

(73) THOMAS LANIER (1722-1805) was the son of NICHOLAS LANIER, who appears to have lived in PRINCE GEORGE COUNTY, Virginia, and the grandson of JOHN LANIER who was under sixteen years of age in 1660. On page 98 of the Index section of this work, appears an outline of the entire Lanier family, which see.

The wife of THOMAS LANIER was ELIZABETH HICKS.

THOMAS LANIER died leaving a will in GRANVILLE COUNTY, from which the names of his children are taken:

1. ROBERT LANIER (b. in 1742)
2. MOLLIE LANIER (b. in 1744)
3. SARAH LANIER (b. in 1748)
4. BETTIE LANIER (b. 1750)
5. PATSY LANIER (b. in 1754)
6. REBECCA LANIER (b. in 1757)
7. THOMAS LANIER (b. in 1760)
8. SUSANNA LANIER (b. in 1763)
9. LEWIS LANIER (b. in 1765)
10. FANNY LANIER (b. in 1767)
11. WILLIAM LANIER (b. in 1770)

JOSEPH WILLIAMS (son of DANIEL WILLIAMS m. URSULA HENDERSON) married 3. SARAH LANIER, June 3, 1766; Robert Lanier, security. Orange County Records.

ROBERT WILLIAMS (a cousin of JOSEPH) married SARAH WILLIAMS (widow of JOSEPH, October 10, 1774. DUNCAN CAMPBELL security. Orange County Records.

JOSEPH WILLIAMS (BROTHER of ROBERT, next above) married 6. REBECCA LANIER, on September 11, 1772, with JOHN HENDERSON security on the bond.

These marriage bonds are not from GRANVILLE, but from ORANGE COUNTY, N. C.

THE BULLOCKS OF GRANVILLE

By the Assistance of
HUGH BUCKNER JOHNSTON, OF WILSON, N. C.

(NOTE: Mr. JOHNSTON has furnished the compiler with most of the material for this sketch, but he is not to be held responsible for the CONCLUSIONS of the compiler in assembling the relationships)

(81) RICHARD BULLOCK. In an effort to ferret out the American ancestry of RICHARD BULLOCK of GRANVILLE COUNTY, N. C., the compiler is once again relegated to YORK COUNTY, VA. and its environs, which had already furnished the bulk of the antecedents of the many old Granville County families who have been reviewed in these sketches. The relationships that apparently sprung up for the first time, as reflected by the Granville records, were in fact a mere renewal of old relationships and old connections that were made in the very earliest years of the Colony of Virginia. What Mrs. Jane Morris, of Little Rock, has said in her "Adam Symes and his Descendants" (1938) and what has come from the pen of Mr. W. M. Creasey through his "Bullocks and Allied Families", has all been read and considered in this deductive sketch, but the author has reached the conclusions here recorded, based upon, not only what has already been written, but what is reflected by the records and the more dependable traditions brought to his attention considered in connection with what such writers have said. Mr. Johnston, who is a stickler for accuracy and documentation in all that he writes, is due our thanks for the many citations and items in this sketch.

The ancestor of RICHARD BULLOCK of GRANVILLE COUNTY, N. C., this writer has concluded, was CAPT. HUGH BULLOCK, who, in December 1631, was a Burgess and Member of the Assembly for the Colony of Virginia, from York County. (Colonial Virginia Register, p. 32). On March 12, 1634, he patented 2550 acres of land on the POCOSON RIVER (Back Creek or Back River) in York County; (Nugent). His wife, apparently, was MARY, for it seems that about 1637, he and his wife MARY deeded to "William Bullock, of London, gentleman", his corn mill, saw mill and plantation in Virginia", the inference being that he had returned to London at that time, and that "William Bullock, gentleman" was his son, probably the eldest. On March 29, 1628, he was the owner of the ship "ENDEAVOR", (Virginia Colonial Court Records, p. 169.). He was in England in the Spring of 1632, but was back in Virginia and present at the meeting of the Council on February 8, 1634. (Ibed p. 201.)

From all of which it appears that HUGH BULLOCK was a planter, merchant, Councilor and a man of considerable importance; that he was a ship owner, as were many other merchants and planters in that day and time. His home was apparently down towards BACK RIVER in what is and was then called POCOSON, or NEW POCOSON in York County, in which part of the county GOV. JOHN WEST owned considerable areas of land, and who long afterwards perhaps bought this same 2550 acres from the heirs of HENRY WHITE, together with the mill and other hereditaments. (Vol. 8 York Records 1677).

The children of CAPT. HUGH BULLOCK and his wife MARY, of YORK COUNTY, VIRGINIA, were apparently the following:

1. WILLIAM BULLOCK, the "Pamphleteer".
2. RICHARD BULLOCK
3. THOMAS BULLOCK
4. JAMES BULLOCK

WILLIAM BULLOCK, the first son, was imported in 1638 to CHARLES CITY COUNTY, VIRGINIA, according to GREER'S IMMIGRANTS. *

On January 25, 1624, he was living at MULBERRY ISLAND in WARWICK COUNTY, having come to VIRGINIA in the "JONATHAN". (Hotten).

October 10, 1624 he was a witness. (Virginia Colonial Court, p. 24).

WILLIAM BULLOCK was the author of a very rare pamphlet on VIRGINIA, issued in 1649, which he styled "Virginia Impartially Examined, etc." (Cyc. of Va. Biog. Vol. 1, p 102.)

As the eldest son, WILLIAM BULLOCK, succeeded largely to the property and interests of his father CAPT. HUGH BULLOCK, including of course, his lands, his mills, his mercantile business and trade, and his shipping interest, including the ownership, perhaps of one or more vessels plying between Virginia and England. He was a man of the World and necessarily made numerous trips back and forth between the Colony and England. A will of a WILLIAM BULLOCK, of ESSEX, Gent., was made when he was about to leave London for Virginia (date of execution not stated, so that it may have been 20 years or more before the date of its probate) which was proven May 16, 1650, in which is mentioned his wife ELIZABETH, a son ROBERT and a daughter named FRANCES.

---

*NOTE: One of the most misleading things in Virginia research are these "transported" dates affixed to early Virginia emigrants. He could not have been imported in 1638 and at the same time have been "living at Mulberry Island" in 1624, except that on a return trip out of the country and back again, somebody obtained his "right" perhaps by purchase, to fifty acres of land which was selected in CHARLES CITY COUNTY. This does not mean that William Bullock was imported to Charles City County; nor does it mean that he was imported in 1638. It means that was the year the land was obtained. The immigrant may have arrived in the Colony twenty-five years earlier. Sometimes they were here fifty years before the right was claimed. In many instances they had been dead and buried for a long time.

On family genealogist has stated that the wife of WILLIAM BULLOCK, of WARWICK was an ANNE TAYLOR and that he had sons EDWARD, ZACHARIAH, JOHN and ROBERT, but for this we have found no supporting evidence. There was a THOMAS TAYLOR in Warwick who had a daughter named ANNE, but unfortunately the "Virginia Carys" disclose proof that she married the emigrant MILES CARY, and there are no evidences of another ANNE of the right vintage. All agree that there was a son ROBERT, which we are going to accept. So, WILLIAM BULLOCK had a son:

10. ROBERT BULLOCK.

10. ROBERT BULLOCK, son and heir of WILLIAM BULLOCK, of WARWICK COUNTY, VIRGINIA, on March 13, 1671, brought suit against COL. PETER JENNINGS, guardian of JOHN MATTHEWS, the orphan of COL. MATTHEWS, over the title to 5000 acres of land in WARWICK COUNTY; same being lands left by his father, as a member of the Council and General Court of Virginia. (Virginia Colonial Court pp. 326, 343); on April 8, 1671 this land was awarded ROBERT BULLOCK by the Court (Ibid p. 249). 10. ROBERT BULLOCK left no will.

---

3. RICHARD BULLOCK (second son of CAPT. HUGH BULLOCK) was in Virginia as early as 1632 (William & Mary Vol. 1 (1) p. 165.) Notwithstanding this established fact the busy importation recorders say:

In 1641 Richard Bullock was imported to Lower Norfolk County.

In 1654 Richard Bullock was imported to York County.

He is reputed to have died in Surry County in 1703, leaving a will and his wife was perhaps MARY, who owned lands there the following year.

---

3. THOMAS BULLOCK, believed to have been another son of HUGH BULLOCK, was living in Lower Norfolk County in 1640 and was then 28 years of age, from which we figure he was born about 1612. He died in Isle of Wight County about 1695, leaving three sons, WILLIAM, JOHN and THOMAS BULLOCK. 3 THOMAS BULLOCK was the ancestor of the Isle of Wight County Bullocks, who overflowed into North Carolina and whose descendants are all mixed up now with their GRANVILLE COUNTY cousins, so that it is hard to identify them.

This 3. THOMAS BULLOCK died without leaving a will and on AUGUST 9, 1695, his estate was appraised in Isle of Wight County by JACOB DARDEN, SIMON EVERETT and WILL MURFREE. His son THOMAS BULLOCK only the day previously - AUG. 8, 1695 - had helped to appraise the estate of HENRY ALLEN, whose widow MARY he had married. The son THOMAS left a will in the Lower Parish of ISLE OF WIGHT, January 25, 1709-10 (W. B. 2 p. 529). See also BODDIE'S 17TH CENTURY pages 622 and 625.

---

4. JAMES BULLOCK, the fourth son of CAPT. HUGH BULLOCK, married MARTHA and lived and died in BRUTON PARISH, in York County, Virginia. His wife MARTHA died in 1671, and his own estate was inventoried and spread on the York County records in 1681. No children of this couple are known, though there may have been many of them.

---

10. ROBERT BULLOCK, son of WILLIAM BULLOCK and grandson of CAPT. HUGH BULLOCK, was the ancestor of the GRANVILLE COUNTY BULLOCKS. He was evidently not a man with a large and numerous family, otherwise somewhere on the records the names of his sons would have appeared in connection with the business of settling up his estate, etc. I am convinced that he had only one son, even as his father before him, and that he was

<u>20. RICHARD BULLOCK</u> (Of New Kent County).

20. RICHARD BULLOCK, of NEW KENT COUNTY, VIRGINIA, is known on the records of St. PETER'S PARISH as RICHARD BULLOCK, SR. After his death in 1702, his son RICHARD BULLOCK, JR. became RICHARD BULLOCK SR..

RICHARD BULLOCK, SR. and RICHARD BULLOCK, JR., were processioners in ST. PETER'S PARISH on May 4, 1689 (St. Peter's Parish Register by Chamberlayne, p. 21). Richard Bullock, Jr. would not have been named a processioner unless he was a grown man at the time (1689), hence the Junior RICHARD was born around 1670, when his grandfather had the suit in Warwick against Judge Peter Jennings, over his patrimony. Knowing this much by common sense deduction, one only needs to anylize the Parish Records to gain an idea of the members of this family.

20. RICHARD BULLOCK had two sons:

21. RICHARD BULLOCK
22. EDWARD BULLOCK.

These two sons of RICHARD BULLOCK SR. of NEW KENT COUNTY, with the establishment of ST. PAUL'S PARISH and the erection of HANOVER COUNTY near the beginning of the Eighteenth Century, moved with their children and the WINSTONS, SIMS, HENDERSONS, WILLIAMS, DICKERSONS, TERRYS and others further West and took up lands in the new Parish and the new County. Somewhere in YORK, JAMES CITY, KING and QUEEN or NEW KENT they came in contact with the HENLEY FAMILY. LEONARD HENLEY, son of REYNOLDS HENLEY had married into the YORK COUNTY RICHARDSONS and had MAJ. RICHARDSON HENLEY, of "Merry Oaks" in JAMES CITY COUNTY. The BULLOCKS also joined the HENLEYS.

It is the opinion of the writer that practically all of the members of the BULLOCK FAMILY of New Kent and Hanover Counties stem from 20. RICHARD BULLOCK (son of 10. ROBERT BULLOCK, son of 1. WILLIAM BULLOCK of WARWICK COUNTY, son of CAPT. HUGH BULLOCK, of YORK County, Virginia), and that 22. EDWARD BULLOCK was the father of RICHARD BULLOCK, who settled in NUTBUSH DISTRICT, in GRANVILLE COUNTY, about 1750 to 1753, he having disposed of his plantation, mercantile business and other property in HANOVER COUNTY, on August 28th of the latter year (D. B. A page 525 of Hanover County, Virginia).

Only the most fragmentory records of the BULLOCKS can be found in the old vestry book of St. Peter's Parish. Enough only to whet the appetite of the seeker after information about them and enough to show that there were apparently only two sons of 20. RICHARD BULLOCK residing in that county. To ascertain the names of the probable children of these two sons, it is necessary to consider not only the names of the BULLOCKS who appear on the records of NEW KENT COUNTY, but also those who are mentioned long afterwards in HANOVER. There is nothing more obvious than that both 21. RICHARD and 22, EDWARD, lived in HANOVER COUNTY, coming there from NEW KENT, probably before the county was erected. The name of the wife of 20. RICHARD BULLOCK is wholly unkhown, and the name of the wife of his son, RICHARD BULLOCK, JR. was KATHERINE or KATE. The whole set up suggests that she may have been a HENLEY, though there is not a scintilla of proof. His nephew, RICHARD, is known to have married an ANNE HENLEY, but what her relationship was to COL. LEONARD HENLEY we are unable to determine. LEONARD HENLEY had four sons, RICHARDSON, LEONARD, TURNER and WILLIAM HENLEY. The younger LEONARD married ELIZABETH AYLETT in 1779. Doubtless COL. LEONARD HENLEY had daughters, but they are not mentioned. (William & Mary 5, p. 33 et seq.). The name of the wife of 22. EDWARD BULLOCK was SARAH, whose family name before marriage has not been found.

---

21. RICHARD BULLOCK and his wife KATHERINE had the following children:

25. EDWARD BULLOCK JR.
26. JOHN BULLOCK married AGNES WOMACK.
27. DAVID BULLOCK
28. KATHERINE BULLOCK
29. JAMES BULLOCK
30. LEWIS BULLOCK

22. EDWARD BULLOCK and his wife SARAH had the following children:

*31. RICHARD BULLOCK, JR. married ANNE HENLEY
32. WILLIAM BULLOCK,
33. EDWARD BULLOCK
34. MICAJAH BULLOCK
35. DOROTHY BULLOCK
36. ZACHARIAH BULLOCK
37. JOHN BULLOCK
38. POLLY BULLOCK
39. ANNE BULLOCK
40. SARAH BULLOCK.

The records on which we rely indicate that both 21 RICHARD and 22 EDWARD BULLOCK and their children owned lands in LOUISA and GOOCHLAND COUNTIES, after leaving NEW KENT. They were outstanding citizens and unquestionably related to many of the old families of these counties. The records show they were unquestionably related to the WINSTONS, as the casual reader can understand after a glance at the records. As late as 1853 GRANVILLE BULLOCK was named as the husband of MARY C. WINSTON, daughter of JOSEPH WINSTON, of LOUISA COUNTY.

* This was RICHARD BULLOCK, ancestor of most of the BULLOCKS of GRANVILLE COUNTY.

BULLOCK FAMILY RECORDS FROM NEW KENT COUNTY, VIRGINIA.

Richard Bullock, Sr. and Richard Bullock Jr. were processioners in St. Peter's Parish on May 4, 1689. (The Vestry Book and Register of St. Peter's Parish, New Kent and James City Counties, Virginia, by C. G. Chamberlayne, Richmond, 1937, page 21.)

Katherine Bullock, daughter of Richard Bullock, was born before 1697. (Same authority cited above, page 342.)

Dorothy Bullock, daughter of Edward Bullock and wife Sara, was born before 1697.
_______ Bullock, daughter or son of Edward Bullock and wife Sara, was born before 1697.

*RICHARD BULLOCK, daughter of EDWARD BULLOCK and wife SARA, was baptised on April 66, 169____.

_______ Bullock, daughter or son of Edward Bullock and wife Sara, was baptized on June 4, 1704.

The last four items above appear on pages 342, 343 and 345, of Chamberlayne's St. Peter's Parish Register, above cited.

* This was RICHARD BULLOCK, who settled in GRANVILLE COUNTY.

31. RICHARD BULLOCK, JR., son of 22. EDWARD BULLOCK, by 1753, on account of the death of his uncle 21 RICHARD, had dropped the "JR." in his name, since there was no further necessity therefor in business transactions. He was born sometime between 1690 and 1700 and had become a prosperous merchant in HANOVER. As has been stated before, it was in that year, (1753) that he sold out his plantation and property in that county. The purchasers were THOMAS BALLARD SMITH, ABRAHAM VENABLE (ancestor of the Venables later in GRANVILLE COUNTY, N. C. and relatives of the WATKINS tribe), CHARLES SMITH, RICHARD YANCEY (relative of JAMES YANCEY, one time Sheriff of GRANVILLE) and WILLIAM RICE (whose sister MARY, or his aunt, married JOHN SIMS, of HANOVER, whose son JOHN married SARAH, the daughter of RICHARD BULLOCK). The list of the children of 31. RICHARD BULLOCK, of GRANVILLE COUNTY, given in MRS. MORRIS' "ADAM SYMES AND HIS DESCENDANTS" is adopted by the compiler as perhaps the nearest correct of any that has been submitted, and the writer believes IT IS CORRECT. She says that RICHARD BULLOCK came from HANOVER COUNTY, VIRGINIA, and settled on NUTBUSH CREEK (Between the town of DREWERY and NUTBUSH CREEK) in 1754; that he sold out in HANOVER COUNTY on account of INDIAN troubles with which they were then threatened; that he made his will in GRANVILLE on October 27, 1764, which was probated at the November Court in 1766, and that he had the following children:

50. SARAH BULLOCK married JOHN SIMS.
51. ANNE BULLOCK married HENRY VANDIKE.
52. AGNES WILLIAMS married (1) GEORGE KEELING, son of LORD KEELING, and (2) in 1757, JUDGE JOHN WILLIAMS.
53. ZACHARIAH BULLOCK, never married, moved to S. C.
54. WILLIAM BULLOCK, m. ELIZABETH TAYLOR widow of JAMES LEWIS (p. 272).
55. JOHN BULLOCK m. MARY MITCHELL (1759).
56. SUSANNA BULLOCK m. WILLIAM SYMES, of ADAM SYMES SR. To GEORGIA.
57. AGATHA BULLOCK married JOHN NUCKLES, moved to S. C.
58. NATHANIEL BULLOCK, m. Aug. 12, 1760, MARY HAWKINS.
59. LEONARD HENLEY BULLOCK married FANNIE HAWKINS 1st SUSAN MARTIN 2nd.

Mrs. Morris says that the mother of these children was "ANN HENLEY, the daughter of LEONARD HENLEY," a question we have discussed on the preceding page.

SOME BULLOCK FAMILY RECORDS FROM HANOVER AND OTHER VIRGINIA COUNTIES.

Robert Searcy died in Hanover County, Virginia in 1733 leaving a will in which he mentions his wife Susan and his daughter Susan. This will was witnessed by EDWARD BULLOCK, JR., THOMAS HAWKINS and ANN BULLOCK. - From "Small Book" Record of Hanover County. (p. 217 also).

RICHARD BULLOCK (wife KATE) owned lands in ST. MARTIN'S PARISH, HANOVER COUNTY on June 7, 1734, adjoining Capt. Isaac Winston and Samuel Goodman (Vol. 1733-35 p. 69, Records of Hanover County.).

Deed from VINKLER COBB to John Humber of land in St. Paul's Parish, HANOVER COUNTY, adjoining WILLIAM WINSTON, EDWARD BULLOCK, James Wade, Thomas Glass and ROBERT BULLOCK, and formerly belonging to JOHN BROWN. December 5, 1734. (Vol. 1733-35 Hanover Records, p. 159).

EDWARD BULLOCK on OCTOBER 28, 1730, and THOMAS RICE (father in law of JOHN SIMS who married SARAH BULLOCK) had 1200 acres of land surveyed on Cubb Creek in HANOVER (McIlwaine's Executive Journals of Virginia Vol. 4 p 230.).

EDWARD BULLOCK'S lands were ordered processioned in St. Paul's Parish, Hanover County, March 14, 1708-9, and on Sept. 12, 1711 and Feb. 10, 1719. On Feb. 14, 1707-8 EDWARD BULLOCK was added to JOHN WHITE'S PRECINCT. (St. Paul's Par. Register). An EDWARD BULLOCK'S lands were ordered processioned March 27, 1736. (Ibid p. 290.) This shows EDWARD BULLOCK was in HANOVER by 1707-8.

RICHARD BULLOCK'S lands were ordered processioned March 14, 1708-9, and on the same dates applicable to EDWARD'S above, and as late as 1739. (Ibid). On February 1, 1723 RICHARD BULLOCK was ordered to keep JOHN BAKER for twelve months and to be paid therefor 350 pounds of tobacco. (Ibid p. 103). March 23, 1743, RICHARD BULLOCK was a freeholder in ST. Paul's Parish and his lands were to be processioned (Same p. 310.)

JAMES BULLOCK'S lands were to be processioned and he was an overseer of the orphans of ROBERT BROOKS, February 17. 1715 (Ibid p. 249) also the same in 1718-19.

DAVID BULLOCK was a processioner of NATHANIEL ANDERSON'S lands, March 23, 1743. And 24 pounds of tobacco were to be paid to him for levy last year as patroller, October 6, 1746. and his lands were also to be processioned as late as 1751. (St. Paul's Register pp. 193 and 321.).

JOHN SIMS patented lands in HANOVER COUNTY, Feb. 4, 1729, which he sold to ISAAC WINSTON, Sept. 8, 1732 and this appears to have been part of a tract of 1736 acres patented by WINSTON later on both sides of BEAVER DAM Creek, adjoining the lands of RICHARD BULLOCK, JR., JOHN WHITLEY, JOSEPH TERRELL and others. (Va. Land Office Register Vol. 14, p. 471.)

RALPH GRAVES, TARLTON WOODSON JR. and JOHN BULLOCK were witnesses to the will of MARY FARRAR, of St. James Northam in GOOCHLAND COUNTY, February 1, 1756. MARY had first married a WOODSON and then a FARRAR (Vol. 7 p. 186 Goochland County Records.)

To his daughter, 52. AGNES BULLOCK (then AGNES WILLIAMS), RICHARD BULLOCK left one shilling, Sterling. Mrs. Morris, in her book, says "She married GEORGE KEELING, son of LORD KEELING". Being a "family genealogist" of the type, she runs true to form and goes "strong" on Lords and Earls, as well as "Coats of Arms". The "Lord Keeling" of her story was CAPTAIN GEORGE KEELING, of New Kent County, prominent among the descendants of the cavaliers, but just High Sheriff of the County and a member of the Vestry of BLISSLAND and ST. PETER'S PARISH. Her statement, however dressed up it may be, indicates the identity of the first husband of AGNES BULLOCK, as the son of the old New Kent Sheriff. He was the GEORGE KEELING who lived at "NINE OAKS" in GRANVILLE COUNTY and was the son of the Sheriff.

After the death of GEORGE KEELING of "Nine Oaks" Agnes Bullock married JUDGE JOHN WILLIAMS. Mrs. Morris says "Judge and Colonel John Williams". He was not COL. JOHN WILLIAMS. Colonel John Williams lived in CASWELL COUNTY and died in 1805. See will on page 196. She gives us the following light on the children of AGATHA BULLOCK and her two husbands:

1. THOMAS KEELING died unmarried.
2. FRANCES KEELING in 1770 married BROMFIELD RIDLEY.
3. ANNIE KEELING married CAPT. THOMAS SATTERWHITE.
4. ELIZABETH KEELING married JUDGE RICHARD HENDERSON in 1763.
5. AGATHA WILLIAMS (b. her 2nd marriage) m. COL. ROBERT BURTON.

53. ZACHARIAH BULLOCK never married. He moved to South Carolina. On February 14, 1748, he bought lands in GRANVILLE COUNTY, N. C. from SAMUEL HENDERSON, with JOHN and WILLIAM BULLOCK as witnesses. (This writer is of the opinion that the purchaser of the land in question was the elder ZACHARIAH, son of EDWARD and <u>brother</u> of RICHARD (not his son), on account of the date, which was SIX YEARS before RICHARD BULLOCK had left HANOVER COUNTY, VIRGINIA, and only fourteen years after the estimated date of his marriage to ANNE HENLEY. Also that the witnesses JOHN and WILLIAM BULLOCK were of this older generation, and not the sons of RICHARD and ANNE HENLEY. Obviously this does not make sense, so we are left in doubt as to WHICH Zachariah it was who "went to South Carolina" and "never married".)

---

54. WILLIAM BULLOCK (Son of RICHARD BULLOCK and ANNE HENLEY) married (1) UNITY WRIGHT, and (2) ELIZABETH TAYLOR, daughter of COL. JOHN TAYLOR (p. 272) who was the widow of JAMES LEWIS, son of CHARLES LEWIS of the BYRD and brother of HOWELL LEWIS. His wife UNITY died in 1760 in VIRGINIA. By his first marriage he had:

(a) ELIZABETH BULLOCK m. WILLIAM KENNON, JR., in 1771.
63 (b) JOHN BULLOCK m. March 11, 1771, CATHERINE LEWIS, son of JAMES.
By second marriage:
(c) FRANCES BULLOCK married WILLIAM BOYD.
(d) ELIZABETH BULLOCK (?) m. JAMES MARTIN (p. 215)
62 (e) WILLIAM (BILLY) BULLOCK (1773-1829) m. LUCY MARTIN BULLOCK.

LUCY MARTIN BULLOCK and NANCY BULLOCK were the daughters of LEONARD HENLEY BULLOCK.
JAMES LEWIS died in LUNENBURG CO. VA. 1764 (W. B. 2, p. 230, and left children, MARY, CATHERINE, JAMES, JOHN and CHARLES LEWIS.

---

62. WILLIAM (BILLY) BULLOCK who married his cousin LUCY MARTIN BULLOCK and became the son in law as well as nephew of LEONARD HENLEY BULLOCK had an interesting list of ten children, as follows:

64. SUSANNAH BULLOCK m. (1) DR. DAVIS (2) DAVID JIGGETTS.
65. ELIZABETH BULLOCK (b. 1795) m. RICHARD INGE. To ALABAMA.
66. WILLIAM H. BULLOCK m. PANTHEA BURCHETT. Moved to ALABAMA.
67. JOHN BULLOCK of "CEDAR WALK" m. SUSAN COBB.
68. RICHARD BULLOCK (b. 1801) m. MARY P. HUNT. Went to AUSTIN, TEXAS.
69. LUCY BULLOCK m. NICHOLAS MERIWETHER LEWIS, of MILTON.
70. FANNIE ANN BULLOCK m. DR. JOHN TAYLOR HUNT, of STOVALL.
71. EMILY BULLOCK, died young.
72. MARY AGNES BULLOCK, died young.
73. JAMES MADISON BULLOCK (b. Sept. 9, 1815) m. SALLIE A. LEWIS

73. JAMES MADISON BULLOCK was shot from ambush in 1864. He left no children.
68. RICHARD BULLOCK. See below.

---

68. RICHARD BULLOCK, married MARY P. HUNT, a sister of JOHN TAYLOR HUNT, and perhaps a daughter of the First Treasurer of North Carolina, HON. MEMUCAN HUNT (She may have been a grand-daughter) and went to AUSTIN, TEXAS. There RICHARD BULLOCK and his wife established and conducted what is known in Texas History as the old "BULLOCK TAVERN". The Bullock Tavern, in the days of MIRABEAU LAMAR and SAM HOUSTON was the gathering place for the early day notables and the meeting place of the Congressmen and Senators of a REPUBLIC. One of the rare stories in Texas History revolves around a controversy between RICHARD BULLARD and the French Ambassador, which came near precipitating a breach of international importance between two countries.

67. JOHN BULLOCK (son of WILLIAM BULLOCK and LUCY MARTIN BULLOCK) was born JUNE 12, 1799 and died in 1866. He was of "CEDAR WALK" near the town of HENDERSON, in the present VANCE COUNTY, the old home of HUTCHINS BURTON (See page 277). In 1824 he married SUSAN COBB, the daughter of REV. JESSE COBB. 63. JOHN BULLOCK was an older brother of RICHARD BULLOCK who married MARY P. HUNT and settled in AUSTIN, TEXAS; the proprietor of the old BULLOCK HOTEL or TAVERN (See below). JOHN BULLOCK and his wife SUSAN COBB had eleven children, as follows:

75. LUCY OLIVIA BULLOCK married THOMAS GREGORY.
76. WILLIAM COBB BULLOCK m. FRANCES CATHERINE DANIEL.
77. JOHN L. BULLOCK, never married.
78. JAMES ALEXANDER BULLOCK married CATHERINE TAYLOR.
79. ANNIE ELIZA BULLOCK married (1850) HENRY THOMAS WATKINS.
80. EDWARD FAISON BULLOCK, died young.
81. GEORGE BULLOCK
82. ALFRED BULLOCK died aged about 20 years.
83. RICHARD AUSTIN BULLOCK (1841-1927) m. BELLE BURNS BULLOCK.
84. JESSIE EDWIN BULLOCK.
85. WALTER BULLOCK married JUDITH CHRISTIAN WATKINS.

FRANCES CATHERINE DANIEL, who married WILLIAM COBB BULLOCK, was the daughter of NATHANIEL CHESLEY DANIEL of "OAKWOOD" near the town of STOVALL, and the grand-daughter of CHESLEY DANIEL and his wife JUDITH CHRISTIAN. She and WILLIAM COBB BULLOCK were the parents of ANNIE CHESLEY BULLOCK who married JOHN BULLOCK WATKINS SR., son of HENRY THOMAS WATKINS and his wife 79. ANNIE ELIZA BULLOCK, had a son JOHN BULLOCK WATKINS. (See Notes of HALLIE LEE HIGH ROYSTER on pages 269-270 herein).

THE OLD BULLOCK HOTEL OR TAVERN IN AUSTIN, TEXAS, OF 1839-40.

This old hostelry was presided over and was the early home of 68. RICHARD BULLOCK and his wife MARY P. HUNT, both from GRANVILLE COUNTY, NORTH CAROLINA, and the NUTBUSH DISTRICT; It is of intense historical interest to both TEXANS and descendants of GRANVILLE COUNTY, NORTH CAROLINIANS. In later years it was supplanted by what was then considered a magnificent business structure, in which was located the banking institution in which another famous NORTH CAROLINA - TEXAS personality was employed; one SYDNEY PORTER, better known to the world as "O. HENRY". The tragic story of his unfortunate entanglement with the law, while employed in this bank, his flight to Mexico, his return for trial and his final conviction, precedes his final rise to fame and fortune as the father of the modern American SHORT STORY. Only in the last three years of World War Second was the old bank building torn down and a new and modern structure erected thereon, which is now on the busiest corner in town, occupied by a famous chain department store. This book is published by a firm located directly across the street from the site of the old BULLOCK TAVERN.

---

66. JOHN BULLOCK (son of RICHARD BULLOCK and his wife ANNE HENLEY) married MARY MITCHELL on November 12, 1759, at OXFORD. The notation relating to this couple says they "lived in ORANGE COUNTY, North Carolina", which covers a wide range for that date. The probabilities are they lived in what is now CASWELL or PERSON Counties, more likely the former.

56. SUSANNAH BULLOCK (Daughter of RICHARD BULLOCK and his wife ANNE HENLEY) married WILLIAM SIMS and moved to WARREN COUNTY, GEORGIA, with her husband's brother BARTLETT SIMS. WILLIAM and BARTLETT SIMS were the sons of ADAM SYMES, SR., of BRUNSWICK COUNTY, VIRGINIA, who was a son or grandson of the first AMERICAN EMIGRANT, GEORGE SYMES, of ANTIGUA. Before moving to GEORGIA, however, WILLIAM SIMS and his wife SUSANNAH BULLOCK settled for a time in Johnston County, North Carolina.

The will of BARTLETT SIMS, SR., brother of WILLIAM SIMS who married SUSANNAH BULLOCK was found by this writer on the records of WARREN COUNTY, GEORGIA, a few years ago, dated May 20, 1802, in which he devises to BARTLETT SIMS, JR. and his unnamed brother, the "land where my two sons live", and then mentions "my sons and daughters" without naming them, and making BARTLETT SIMS, JR. his executor. This will was witnessed by FRANK BECK and ALEXANDER SNELLINGS, obviously of the SNELLINGS family of GRANVILLE who lived in the Fishing Creek District in 1788.

BARTLETT SIMS, JR. appears to have been the BARTLETT SIMS who moved first to COLUMBUS MISSISIPPI, and then to TEXAS (See note herein on page 278), and whose fame as a laugher was a by-word in Texas pioneer days. He was a giant in both strength and size, weighed over 300 pounds and was more than six feel tall.

---

57. AGATHA BULLOCK (Daughter of RICHARD BULLOCK and his wife ANNE HENLEY) married JOHN NUCKOLS and moved to SOUTH CAROLINA. One son, ZACHARIAH NUCKOLS was born before 1764, because he is mentioned in the will of his grandfather, RICHARD BULLOCK.

---

58. NATHANIEL BULLOCK (Son of RICHARD BULLOCK and his wife ANNE HENLEY) received the old home plantation on NUTBUSH, after the death of his mother ANNE(HENLEY)BULLOCK. He was born in 1738, and married MARY HAWKINS, daughter of PHIL. HAWKINS and sister of PHILEMON HAWKINS, of GRANVILLE COUNTY, August 12, 1760. There is one account which states that he married a second time, one ELIZABETH BRANTLEY, daughter of THOMAS BRANTLEY, but this was obviously a son named NATHANIEL, who perhaps moved to SOUTH CAROLINA and later to GEORGIA. Only three sons of NATHANIEL BULLOCK and his wife MARY HAWKINS are known, though there may have been several others. They were:

100. NATHANIEL BULLOCK
101. HAWKINS BULLOCK
102. JAMES BULLOCK

100. NATHANIEL BULLOCK (Son of NATHANIEL BULLOCK and MARY HAWKINS) married before 1804, ELIZABETH BRANTLEY, daughter of THOMAS BRANTLEY, of CHATHAM COUNTY, N. C. His widow was living in 1822, and he had died between that time and 1815, in SOUTH CAROLINA. So far as known there was only one son:

103. GEORGE WASHINGTON BULLOCK

102. GEORGE WASHINGTON BULLOCK is said to have been born in GEORGIA in 1804, and to have moved to INDIANA, where he died in 1840, leaving one son ABSALOM JASPER BULLOCK, whose descendants reside in that State. He married MARY DEAVENPORT, daughter of AUGUSTINE DAVENPORT, JR. and his wife JENNIE BASS of RANDOLPH COUNTY, N. C. The Davenports lived in ROWAN COUNTY and more will be said about them in the ROWAN COUNTY section of this work.

101. HAWKINS BULLOCK (Son of NATHANIEL BULLOCK and his wife MARY HAWKINS) was born in GRANVILLE COUNTY, N. C. and died near LEXINGTON, in OGLETHORPE COUNTY, GEORGIA, on NOVEMBER 1, 1833. He served in the revolution and was awarded bounty lands in what was then WILKES COUNTY, GEORGIA. March 12, 1789, he married FRANCES ROY GORDON, of an old VIRGINIA FAMILY, the daughter of ALEXANDER GORDON. Their children (taken from the family Bible) were:

110. JOHN GORDON BULLOCK, b. January 3, 1790.
111. MARY WYATT BULLOCK b. Nov. 10, 1791.
112. ALEXANDER GORDON BULLOCK b. Feb. 13, 1797.
113. NATHANIEL H. BULLOCK b. Dec. 10, 1798.
114. WILLIAM GORDON BULLOCK b. Sept. 27, 1802.
115. LOUISE NANCE BULLOCK b. Dec. 31, 1804.
116. FRANCIS ROY BULLOCK b. Dec. 12, 1806.
117. RICHARD HENLEY BULLOCK b. Oct. 21, 1810.
118. HAWKINS SHERMAN BULLOCK b. Dec. 23, 1812.

Deaths: HAWKINS BULLOCK, SR. d. Nov. 1, 1833.
FRANCIS ROY GORDON BULLOCK d. July 17, 1837.
JOHN GORDON BULLOCK d. April 4, 1835.

MARRIAGES: Hawkins Bullock and Frances Roy Gordon March 12, 1789.
George A. Gordon and Susannah Bullock April 11, 1811.
Richard R. Sims and Mary Wyatt Bullock Oct. 5, 1813.
Alexander Gordon Bullock and Milly Sorrells, Feb. 1, 1818.
Nathaniel H. Bullock and Betty Colbert Jan. 3, 1820.
William Gordon Bullock and Elener Sorrells Nov. 6, 1823.
Hiram Hampton and Frances Roy Bullock Dec. 28, 1826.
Richard Henley Bullock and Mary H. R. Griffeth Jan. 21, 1836.

Bible owned by MR. N. C. BULLOCK, of DANIELSVILLE, Madison County, GEORGIA.

102. JAMES BULLOCK (Son of NATHANIEL BULLOCK and his wife MARY HAWKINS) died about 1783 leaving a will in GRANVILLE COUNTY (Old's Abstracts of North Carolina Wills). JAMES HAWKINS was security on the marriage bond of his son JOSHUA BULLOCK when he was united in marriage to ANNE CASH, on June 21, 1781.

JAMES BULLOCK and his wife had the following children:

1. SARAH BULLOCK
2. JEREMIAH BULLOCK
3. JOSHUA BULLOCK m. ANNIE CASH.
4. CHARLES BULLOCK
5. SAMUEL BULLOCK
6. JAMES BULLOCK m. MARY PHILLIPS 1792.
7. GEORGE BULLOCK m. MARY FREEMAN Oct. 25, 1796.
8. PRISCILLA BULLOCK married COOK.
9. NANCY BULLOCK.

(From OLDS Abstracts of N. C. Wills).

---

59. LEONARD HENLEY BULLOCK was the executor of the will of his father RICHARD BULLOCK, who married ANNE HENLEY. He was born in 1736 and died in 1797. In 1769 he was Sheriff of GRANVILLE COUNTY. He first married FANNIE HAWKINS, daughter of PHIL.HAWKINS and a sister of PHILEMON HAWKINS and of MARY HAWKINS, the latter the wife of his brother NATHANIEL BULLOCK. After the death of his first wife he married SUSAN MARTIN, who was then the widow of GOODLOE. LEONARD HENLEY BULLOCK was associated with his brother in law JUDGE JOHN WILLIAMS and with HON. RICHARD HENDERSON in their "Transylvania" enterprise, and is said to have been the General Manager of the TRANSYLVANIA LAND CO., probably the same as "HENDERSON & CO.". His children married into the LYNES, TAYLORS and LEWIS' all of whom were kin-folks. His children were:

120. FANNIE BULLOCK who married JAMES LYNE.
121. SUSAN BULLOCK who married JOHN "BRANDY" TAYLOR, 1784.
122. LUCY MARTIN BULLOCK married 62. WILLIAM(BILLY) BULLOCK.
123. NANCY BULLOCK married (f) JAMES BULLOCK.
124. AGNES BULLOCK married DR. JOHN HARE.
125. RICHARD (BIG DICK) BULLOCK married ANN MARIA MARTIN

ANNIE BULLOCK, daughter of "BIG DICK" BULLOCK, married COL. ARCHIBALD HENDERSON.

---

63. JOHN BULLOCK (Son of WILLIAM BULLOCK and UNITY WRIGHT) m. CATHERINE LEWIS, daughter of JAMES LEWIS and ELIZABETH TAYLOR, by whom he had at least one son (f) JAMES BULLOCK, who married LUCY MARTIN BULLOCK, daughter of LEONARD HENLEY BULLOCK.

(f) JAMES BULLOCK and his wife LUCY MARTIN BULLOCK, who were first cousins, had the following children:

130. CATHERINE LEWIS BULLOCK, m. JOSEPH SIMS (To TENN.)
131. LEONARD HENLEY BULLOCK (never married).
132. FANNY LYNE BULLOCK m. MACON GREEN of WARREN COUNTY.
133. JAMES BULLOCK m. (1) ANN DORTCH (2) MARTHA THORPE.
134. ANN HARRIET BULLOCK married NATHANIEL CHESLEY DANIEL

134. ANN HARRIET BULLOCK and NATHANIEL CHESLEY DANIEL were the Great Grand-parents of JOHN BULLOCK WATKINS, JR.. of Henderson, Vance County.

SOME OF THE DESCENDANTS OF 3. THOMAS BULLOCK, SON OF CAPT. HUGH BULLOCK

3. THOMAS BULLOCK was another one of the sons of CAPT. HUGH BULLOCK of YORK COUNTY, VIRGINIA, and a brother of WILLIAM BULLOCK (the pamphleteer) ancestor of the GRANVILLE COUNTY BULLOCKS. He died in ISLE OF WIGHT COUNTY, VA. in 1695, leaving three sons:

10. THOMAS BULLOCK m. MARY ALLEN
11. WILLIAM BULLOCK
12. JOHN BULLOCK

The above three sons were contemporaneous with ROBERT BULLOCK, the father of RICHARD BULLOCK, SR. of NEW KENT COUNTY. Their children were cousins "once removed" of RICHARD and EDWARD BULLOCK of HANOVER COUNTY, EDWARD BULLOCK and his wife SARAH being the parents of RICHARD BULLOCK, of GRANVILLE COUNTY, N. C., who married ANNE HENLEY.

10. THOMAS BULLOCK, who married MARY ALLEN (the widow of HENRY ALLEN) step-daughter of STEPHEN POWELL (Boddie's 17th Century Isle of Wight p. 610), was apparently the ancestor of many of the BULLOCKS of ISLE OF WIGHT, while his brothers 11. WILLIAM and 12. JOHN were perhaps the progenitors of the BULLOCKS in EDGECOMBE COUNTY, who will be considered in the chapter relating to EDGECOMBE COUNTY in this work.

C A P T. H U G H B U L L O C K
and wife M A R Y
O F Y O R K C O U N T Y, V A.

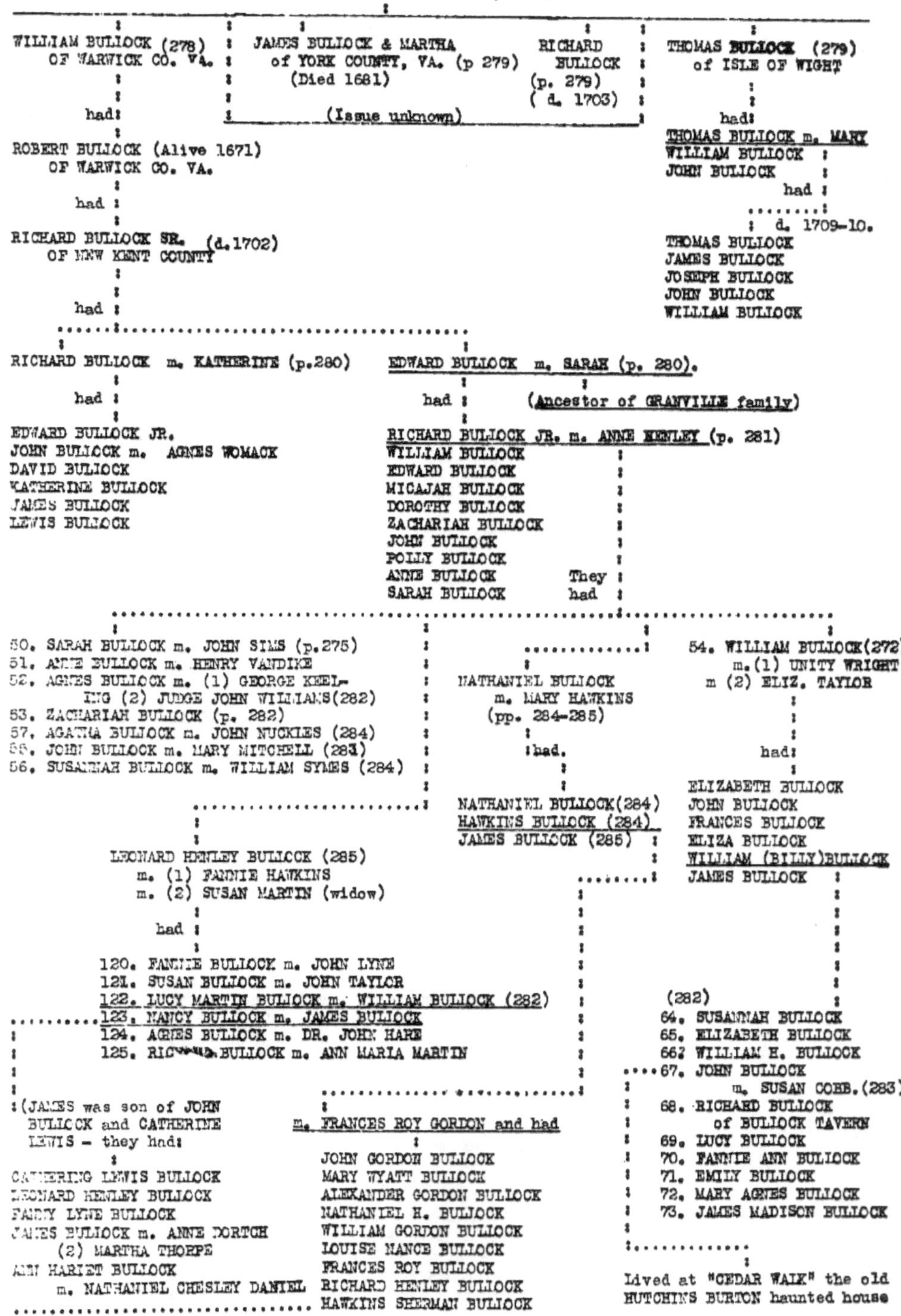

WILLIAM BULLOCK (278)
OF WARWICK CO. VA.
had:
ROBERT BULLOCK (Alive 1671)
OF WARWICK CO. VA.
had:
RICHARD BULLOCK SR. (d.1702)
OF NEW KENT COUNTY
had:
JAMES BULLOCK & MARTHA
of YORK COUNTY, VA. (p 279)
(Died 1681)
RICHARD
BULLOCK
(p. 279)
(d. 1703)
(Issue unknown)
THOMAS BULLOCK (279)
of ISLE OF WIGHT
had:
THOMAS BULLOCK m. MARY
WILLIAM BULLOCK
JOHN BULLOCK
had
d. 1709-10.
THOMAS BULLOCK
JAMES BULLOCK
JOSEPH BULLOCK
JOHN BULLOCK
WILLIAM BULLOCK
RICHARD BULLOCK m. KATHERINE (p.280)
had:
EDWARD BULLOCK JR.
JOHN BULLOCK m. AGNES WOMACK
DAVID BULLOCK
KATHERINE BULLOCK
JAMES BULLOCK
LEWIS BULLOCK
EDWARD BULLOCK m. SARAH (p. 280).
had
(Ancestor of GRANVILLE family)
RICHARD BULLOCK JR. m. ANNE HENLEY (p. 281)
WILLIAM BULLOCK
EDWARD BULLOCK
MICAJAH BULLOCK
DOROTHY BULLOCK
ZACHARIAH BULLOCK
JOHN BULLOCK
POLLY BULLOCK
ANNE BULLOCK
SARAH BULLOCK
They
had
50. SARAH BULLOCK m. JOHN SIMS (p.275)
51. ANNE BULLOCK m. HENRY VANDIKE
52. AGNES BULLOCK m. (1) GEORGE KEEL-
ING (2) JUDGE JOHN WILLIAMS(282)
53. ZACHARIAH BULLOCK (p. 282)
57. AGATHA BULLOCK m. JOHN NUCKLES (284)
55. JOHN BULLOCK m. MARY MITCHELL (283)
56. SUSANNAH BULLOCK m. WILLIAM SYMES (284)
NATHANIEL BULLOCK
m. MARY HAWKINS
(pp. 284-285)
had.
NATHANIEL BULLOCK(284)
HAWKINS BULLOCK (284)
JAMES BULLOCK (285)
54. WILLIAM BULLOCK(272)
m.(1) UNITY WRIGHT
m (2) ELIZ. TAYLOR
had:
ELIZABETH BULLOCK
JOHN BULLOCK
FRANCES BULLOCK
ELIZA BULLOCK
WILLIAM (BILLY)BULLOCK
JAMES BULLOCK
LEONARD HENLEY BULLOCK (285)
m. (1) FANNIE HAWKINS
m. (2) SUSAN MARTIN (widow)
had
120. FANNIE BULLOCK m. JOHN LYNE
121. SUSAN BULLOCK m. JOHN TAYLOR
122. LUCY MARTIN BULLOCK m. WILLIAM BULLOCK (282)
123. NANCY BULLOCK m. JAMES BULLOCK
124. AGNES BULLOCK m. DR. JOHN HARE
125. RICHARD BULLOCK m. ANN MARIA MARTIN
(282)
64. SUSANNAH BULLOCK
65. ELIZABETH BULLOCK
66. WILLIAM H. BULLOCK
67. JOHN BULLOCK
m. SUSAN COBB.(283)
68. RICHARD BULLOCK
of BULLOCK TAVERN
69. LUCY BULLOCK
70. FANNIE ANN BULLOCK
71. EMILY BULLOCK
72. MARY AGNES BULLOCK
73. JAMES MADISON BULLOCK
(JAMES was son of JOHN
BULLOCK and CATHERINE
LEWIS - they had:
CATHERINE LEWIS BULLOCK
LEONARD HENLEY BULLOCK
FANNY LYNE BULLOCK
JAMES BULLOCK m. ANNE DORTCH
(2) MARTHA THORPE
ANN HARIET BULLOCK
m. NATHANIEL CHESLEY DANIEL
m. FRANCES ROY GORDON and had
JOHN GORDON BULLOCK
MARY WYATT BULLOCK
ALEXANDER GORDON BULLOCK
NATHANIEL H. BULLOCK
WILLIAM GORDON BULLOCK
LOUISE NANCE BULLOCK
FRANCES ROY BULLOCK
RICHARD HENLEY BULLOCK
HAWKINS SHERMAN BULLOCK
Lived at "CEDAR WALK" the old
HUTCHINS BURTON haunted house

(88) JOHN DANIEL. This man and his descendants have been heretofore covered in these notes. Abstract of his will on page 212, with notes following later. Mrs. Hallie Lee (High) Royster says the Daniel farm in the Nutbush Sec. on of Granville County was afterwards known as the "TURNER PLACE".

(89) REUBEN SEARCY. The account of the SEARCY family, beginning with REUBEN, who was an early Sheriff of GRANVILLE COUNTY, begins on page 217, under the head of the "SEARCY FAMILY OF GRANVILLE".

THE HAWKINS FAMILY OF GRANVILLE COUNTY

(92) PHILEMON HAWKINS (See SEARCY MAP) must have been one of the earliest settlers who came down from VIRGINIA and located South of the ROANOKE RIVER as far West as the original Granville County territory. He was living in what afterwards became a part of old extinct BUTE County, in 1754, when his distinguished son, COL. BENJAMIN HAWKINS was born on August 15, 1754. The early records of YORK and GLOUCESTER Counties, Virginia, carry frequent reference to the name HAWKINS. It is a mere conjecture (but probably correct,at that) that he was the son of a COL. JOHN HAWKINS who lived in ESSEX COUNTY, Virginia, whither he had drifted northward with the WILLIAMS and other families, from GLOUCESTER and YORK COUNTIES. One writer has stated that he was born in GLOUCESTER COUNTY, Virginia, Sept. 28, 1717 and that he came to NORTH CAROLINA and settled when only twenty years of age, which would have been in 1737. One JOHN HAWKINS was in ALBEMARLE PRECINCT and a Lord Deputy of the Province in 1707, with GOV. WILLIAM GLOVER (See p. 62 of this completed Volume), but as there does not appear anywhere among these earlier members of the Hawkins family, one named PHILEMON, it is unlikely that the GRANVILLE PHILEMON descended from that branch of the family, though I have no doubt they were of the same family or tribe.

Col. PHILEMON HAWKINS married DELIA MARTIN. He died in 1801 at the age of 83 years, and left the following children:

1. COL. JOHN HAWKINS
2. COL. PHILEMON HAWKINS, JR.
3. COL. BENJAMIN HAWKINS (b. 1754)
4. COL. JOSEPH HAWKINS
5. FANNIE HAWKINS married LEONARD HENLEY BULLOCK
6. ANN HAWKINS married MICAJAH THOMAS, JR.
7. MARY HAWKINS married NATHANIEL BULLOCK (1760).

1. COL. JOHN HAWKINS, the name of whose wife is unknown to the compiler, was the father of an interesting family. He had:

10. PHILEMON HAWKINS (Of LOUISBURG).
11. GEN. JOHN H. HAWKINS
12. GEN. MICAJAH THOMAS HAWKINS (b. 1786 in WARREN COUNTY).
13. COL. JOSEPH HAWKINS.
(and several daughters)

2. COL. PHILEMON HAWKINS, JR., the name of whose wife the compiler has been unable to learn, was the father of the following children:

20. WILLIAM HAWKINS, who was Governor of NORTH CAROLINA (1811-1814).
21. JOHN D. HAWKINS
22. JOSEPH W. HAWKINS
23. BENJAMIN F. HAWKINS married SALLIE PEARSON.
24. PHILEMON HAWKINS
25. FRANK HAWKINS
26. GEORGE W. HAWKINS
27. ELIZANOR HAWKINS married SHERWOOD HAYWOOD.
28. ANN HAWKINS married WILLIAM P. LITTLE.
29. DELIA HAWKINS married STEPHEN HAYWOOD.
30. SARAH HAWKINS married COL. WILLIAM POLK.
31. LUCY DAVIS RUFFIN HAWKINS married LOUIS D. HENRY, of RALEIGH.

3. COL. BENJAMIN HAWKINS. He was born in August 15, 1754, according to WHEELER, who is in error for the reason that BUTE was not erected until 1764; therefore Col. Benjamin Hawkins was really a native of GRANVILLE COUNTY. He died in the CREEK NATION the 6th of June, 1816, in the exercise of his functions as Superintendent of Indian Affairs. A particular record to this effect was made at the time of his death by his elder brother, Col. Philemon Hawkins, in his family Bible, with the additional remark that he had been in public life thirty-six years. He served in the Congress of the United States, and on the 21st of March, 1785, being then a member, he was appointed by Congress, a Commissioner, together with DANIEL CARROLL and WILLIAM PERRY to treat with the Cherokee Indians; the same year he was appointed by Congress with GEN. ANDREW PICKENS, JOSEPH MARTIN and LAUCHLIN McINTOSH to negotiate with the CREEK INDIANS. These duties were performed, and in 1786 he was again elected to Congress. In 1789, with SAMUEL JOHNSTON he was elected UNITED STATES SENATOR from North Carolina. He served out his full term of six years in the United States Senate, after which Gen. Washington appointed him Superintendent and Agent for all the Indians South of the Ohio. He appointed his nephew 24. PHILEMON HAWKINS to serve as his assistant. COL. BENJAMIN HAWKINS left one son (WILLIAM HAWKINS) and five daughters.

(93) SAMUEL HENDERSON (Searcy Map). An account of his family, together with a list of his children, will be found on page 221. About two miles South of MIDDLEBURG in what is now Vance county there is dirt road turns to the right off the highway, which leads to ASHLAND, the old HENDERSON HOME. It is a two story house, three bays wide, has a doorway on the right hand bay and a story and a half addition on the right with end chimneys matching the twin chimneys on the left side of the main house. The beaded weatherboarding is painted white, and both eaves and window headings have well-designed cornices. A later porch extending the entire facade is supported by Roman Doric columns, supplemented by log posts. The place is said to have been built 200 years ago (1746) by SAMUEL HENDERSON, farmer and miller, who was one time High Sheriff of GRANVILLE COUNTY and the father of numerous children, including JUDGE RICHARD HENDERSON.

(104) RICHARD HENDERSON, the founder of TRANSYLVANIA, and an early JUDGE in NORTH CAROLINA. The account of the HENDERSON FAMILY (p. 221) includes the names of his children and of some of his descendants.

(120) JONATHAN KITTRELL. The town of KITTRELL named for his family is fourteen miles South of MIDDLEBURG. The KITTRELL family came to North Carolina from NANSEMOND and ISLE OF WIGHT County, Virginia, and first settled on BENNETT'S CREEK in BERTIE PRECINCT, perhaps, and moved to the GRANVILLE COUNTY territory probably in about 1745. Jonathan Kittrell sold lands on BENNETT'S CREEK in 1718, and his wife was ANN (See INDEX to Hathaway's p. 86). See also page 87 for an account of JONATHAN KITTRELL.

((122) "SPELLING" JOHN ALLEN. See account on page 269.

(123) GREEN HILL (SEARCY MAP). This GREEN HILL was the son of a GREEN HILL who married GRACE BENNETT, a daughter of WILLIAM BENNETT of Northampton County, North Carolina. The old GREEN HILL home is on the South side of the HAW RIVER in the outskirts of LOUISBURG, in what is now Franklin County. Here it was that Bishop Coke held the first North Carolina Metchodist Conference in 1785. The home is now a well-preserved white frame house with dormer windows, three big brick end chimneys and high porches. This particular GREEN HILL was prominent in State, as well as religious affairs, representing BUTE COUNTY (a part of the original GRANVILLE in the provisional Congress. He was also a Major of the BUTE MILITIA in the revolution. He became a minister and moved to the general vicinity of Nashville, Tenn.

(125) PHILLIP PIERCE was a resident of what is now FRANKLIN COUNTY (a part of the original GRANVILLE) and is distinguished in History mainly because of the fact that he was the father of one great Southern Preacher, and the grandfather of another who was a beloved BISHOP of the Methodist Church, REV. GEORGE F. PIERCE, of HANCOCK COUNTY, Georgia, known and loved by members of his denomination throughout the entire South. See items from the records of Franklin County on page 207 relating to transactions of PHILLIP PIERCE, and his family.

(133) EDWARD JONES (Searcy Map). See the records of GRANVILLE COUNTY and its earliest organization, beginning on page 209 for information in regard to EDWARD JONES. There is also an account of EDWARD JONES on page 43 (Of the INDEX SECTION) in connection with an account of COL. WILLIAM EATON and his genealogy. He was the father of PRISCILLA JONES who became of the wife of GIDEON MACON. Any purported account of the early history of GRANVILLE COUNTY could not be written without mention of EDWARD JONES and his descendants who exercised a wide influence on the destinies of the Province of North Carolina, and particularly GRANVILLE COUNTY.

(140) WILLIAM EATON. A genealogical account of his family, briefly outlined is to be found on page 43 (Index Section of the "Lost Tribes"). He was from YORK COUNTY, Virginia to North Carolina. The roster of his GRANVILLE COUNTY regiment will be given later.

(145) ISHAM HARRISON (Searcy Map) was a son of JOHN HARRISON and his wife SARAH DANIEL, daughter of JOHN DANIEL who died in Granville County in 1763 (See page 212). The ISHAM HARRISON who was on the tax list of GRANVILLE COUNTY in 1788 may have been a son, as he was only assessed with one poll, and at that time may not have been married. (145) ISHAM HARRISON moved to South Carolina, along the Pacolet, with some of the HENDERSONS and others, as did JOHN HARRISON, who may have been another son of ISHAM. For an account of the descendants of JOHN HARRISON and his wife SARAH, see beginning on page 255.

(153) NATHANIEL MACON was born in 1758 and died in 1837. He was three times Speaker of the House of Congress of the United States, from 1801 until 1807, and a member of the United States Senate from North Carolina from 1815 until 1828. He is said to have been one among North Carolina's foremost proponents of the political principles of Thomas Jefferson. His old home was at Buck Springs, four miles from the town of Vaughan, in what is now WARREN COUNTY. The place was restored in 1937 and stands in a great oak grove. NATHANIEL MACON was a grandson of EDWARD JONES (133 on the Searcy Map), his mother having been PRISCILLA JONES who married GIDEON MACON, whose sister MARTHA MACON married ORLANDO JONES, son of REV. ROWLAND JONES, Minister of BRUTON PARISH in YORK COUNTY, Virginia. This MARTHA MACON, the aunt of Nathaniel Macon, was the grandmother of MARTHA WASHINGTON, wife of the first President.

(155) CHRISTMAS RAY. He brought suit against DRURY GLOVER in GRANVILLE COUNTY, N. C. in 1765. He was a descendant of THOMAS RAY and MARY CHRISTMAS, of YORK COUNTY, Virginia, and a collateral kinsman of the writer.

(162) GIDEON MACON. He was a son in law of EDWARD JONES and is mentioned above.

(190) SUGAR JONES was a son of EDWARD JONES mentioned above. He married SARAH FRANKLIN, who after his death married NATHANIEL, the son of SAMUEL HENDERSON.

(136) WEST HARRIS (Of the SEARCY MAP), one of those who met at the home of EDWARD JONES, on December 2, 1746, to complete the organization of the original GRANVILLE COUNTY, was a member of an old VIRGINIA FAMILY (p. 209). This WEST HARRIS was related to EDWARD JONES, to GIDEON MACON, to the LANIERS, JENNINGS, HILLS and BENNETTS, but whether in an attempted review of the notes pertaining to this family of HARRIS, the writer can make this plain to the reader is questionable and I am sure will be questioned by others for the reason that the theories I will advance run counter to some of the writers who have attempted to set down the annals of the HARRIS FAMILY.

CAPT. THOMAS HARRIS, who on February 25, 1638, received a patent to 820 acres of land then known as LONGFIELD, but later known as "CURLES" on the JAMES RIVER, was the first AMERICAN ancestor of the GRANVILLE COUNTY HARRIS FAMILY. This land was afterwards claimed by NATHANIEL BACON "the Rebel" through WILLIAM HARRIS, a son, (pp. 1387 and 1959 of the Valentine Papers, quoting from the Records of HENRICO COUNTY), who sold the land to ROGER GREEN who promoted the first pilgrimage of Virginia settlers to the ALBEMARLE SOUND section of North Carolina. (Ibid & Dodd's Old South, p. 210). The name of the wife of CAPT. THOMAS HARRIS was DIANA. His widow, after his death, married (2nd) WILLIAM FOSTER, and finally, THOMAS WHITE. With her son JOHN she settled in North Carolina (p. 58 this work), perhaps at the instance of ROGER GREEN. She married WILLIAM FOSTER in 1675. The children of CAPT. THOMAS HARRIS and his wife DIANA were: (He died 1665) (3-274 NCHAG Reg.)

1. WILLIAM HARRIS
2. JOHN HARRIS (Dau. SARAH m. NATHANIEL NICHOLSON).
3. THOMAS HARRIS (d. 1672) married ALICE WEST
4. NICHOLAS HARRIS (York County, Va.)

EDWARD HARRIS, probably a brother of CAPT. THOMAS HARRIS, of Virginia. On November 23, 1638, in LONDON, ENGLAND, EDWARD HARRIS was the sole legatee, the executor and "kinsman" of JUDITH BENNETT, the widow of RICHARD BENNETT, who died in VIRGINIA, August 28, 1626. It is not improbable that JUDITH BENNETT, the widow, was born a HARRIS. (See Boddie's 17th Century Isle of Wight pp. 270-272.). The same authority shows that this RICHARD BENNETT, whose wife was possibly JUDITH HARRIS, was an uncle of GOV. RICHARD BENNETT, and brother of EDWARD BENNETT the father of SYLVESTRA HILL and MARY BLAND; thus the connection of the HARRIS FAMILY to the HILLS and BENNETTS shows up. This connection is supplemented by other connections that will follow. CHRISTOPHER HARRIS, who on January 30, 1659 in YORK COUNTY, with JOHN STANOP (?), ROBERT HARRISON and JOHN COTTEN, appraised the estate of FRANCIS WHEELER, the step-father of ROBERT HARRISON'S wife, was perhaps also connected with this HARRIS FAMILY of London and Virginia. The name of CHRISTOPHER HARRIS appears on the tax rolls of GRANVILLE COUNTY, N. C., and CHRISTOPHER HARRIS WILLIAMS was the father or Grandfather of HON. JOHN SHARP WILLIAMS, of Mississippi. (See WILLIAMS family herein.)

3. THOMAS HARRIS who married ALICE WEST, LATER SOJOURNER, and left a will in ISLE OF WIGHT COUNTY in March, 1672 (Vol. 7, W & M. (1) about p. 200-240), in which he mentioned only two sons JOHN HARRIS and THOMAS HARRIS, his daughter MARY "and other children". It is in the review of his family that we again run across the connection with the HILLS and BENNETTS, with evidence to add to what has been given. From other records we find he had children:

5. JOHN HARRIS
6. THOMAS HARRIS (Will Oct. 9, 1688)
7. MARY HARRIS m. ANTHONY SPILLTIMBER.
8. MARTHA HARRIS married JOHN JENNINGS.

MAJ. NICHOLAS HILL, whose wife was SILVESTRA, the daughter of EDWARD BENNETT (uncle of Gov. Richard Bennett) and JOHN JENNINGS, were named Executors of 3. THOMAS HARRIS' will. JOHN JENNINGS (it is presumed) after the death of MARTHA HARRIS, married one of the daughters of MAJ. NICHOLAS HILL, and a grand-daughter of EDWARD BENNETT.

---

6. THOMAS HARRIS, whose wife was apparently a MARTIN, left will in ISLE OF WIGHT COUNTY, VIRGINIA dated OCTOBER 9, 1688, which will shows that he had the following children:

10. EDWARD HARRIS
11. THOMAS HARRIS
12. ROBERT HARRIS
13. GEORGE HARRIS
14. MARTIN HARRIS
15. WILLIAM HARRIS
16. JANE HARRIS married a JONES.
17. ANNE HARRIS

The oldest son, EDWARD HARRIS, was made the executor of this will, according to the abstract which was found by the writer. In the account of the descendants of the children of the testator, the name of ROBERT HARRIS, who played so prominent a part in the political history of GRANVILLE COUNTY along during the last half of the eighteenth century, has not been found, but that is because only the descendants of 10. EDWARD HARRIS have been found (and not all of them). This ROBERT HARRIS of GRANVILLE certainly belonged in this family.

10. EDWARD HARRIS (son of THOMAS HARRIS, son of THOMAS HARRIS and ALICE WEST) married MARY, and died leaving a will in ISLE OF WIGHT COUNTY, Virginia, March 25, 1734, from which the names of his children appear to have been:

20. EDWARD HARRIS
21. JACOB HARRIS
22. NATHAN HARRIS (b. 1716). m. CATHERINE WALTON.
23. WEST HARRIS (said to have married MARY TURNER).
24. DANIEL HARRIS
25. ANNE HARRIS
26. MARTHA HARRIS married WILLIAMSON.

22. NATHAN HARRIS and CATHERINE WALTON were married in BRUNSWICK COUNTY, Virginia in 1737, and they were the parents of the following:

30. WALTON HARRIS born in Va. in 1739
31. NATHANIEL HARRIS
32. ISAAC HARRIS
33. DAVID HARRIS
34. ELIAS HARRIS
35. ROWLAND HARRIS
36. HERBERT HARRIS
36. GIDEON HARRIS
37. HOWELL HARRIS
38. JOHN HENRY HARRIS
39. CATHERINE HARRIS
40. MARTHA HARRIS
41. ELIZABETH HARRIS
42. ANN HARRIS

—he married REBECCA LANIER, the youngest daughter of SAMPSON LANIER and his wife ELIZABETH CHAMBERLAINE (See p. 99) and had children:

50. BUCKNER HARRIS
51. SAMPSON HARRIS
52. JOEL HARRIS
53. AUGUSTINE HARRIS
54. EDWIN HARRIS
55. NATHAN HARRIS
56. SIMEON HARRIS
57. WALTON HARRIS
58. ELIZABETH HARRIS
59. LITTLETON HARRIS
60. JEPTHA HARRIS.

57. WALTON HARRIS (moved to GEORGIA) and married VIRGINIA BILLUPS of MECKLENBURG COUNTY, VIRGINIA (Cumberland Parish p. 181), and they had children:

61. WALTON HARRIS, an attorney.
62. ELIZA HARRIS married a MR. BOOTHE.
63. CAROLINE HARRIS married DR. GIBBS.
64. AUGUSTINE HARRIS moved to ALABAMA.
65. MILTON HARRIS (d. infancy).
66. CATHERINE HARRIS (d. infancy).
67. ROBERT HARRIS (Lived in CLARKE CO. GEORGIA.)
68. MARY ANN HARRIS married DR. SWIFT.
69. YOUNG L. G. HARRIS, of ATHENS, GA.
70. JEPTHA HARRIS, of Columbus, Ga.
71. WILLIS HARRIS, also of GEORGIA.

---

23. WEST HARRIS (Same as (136) on the SEARCY MAP) married MARY TURNER, and had 11 children, as follows:

72. ISHAM HARRIS, who lived in GRANVILLE COUNTY
73. ELIZABETH HARRIS
74. TURNER HARRIS
75. ETHELRED HARRIS
76. PRISCILLA HARRIS
77. MARTHA HARRIS
78. ROWLAND HARRIS
79. WEST HARRIS
80. ARTHUR HARRIS
81. MARY HARRIS
82. PATIENCE HARRIS.

and who married and had EIGHT CHILDREN, as follows:

83. HARDY HARRIS
84. RANSOM HARRIS
85. NEWSOM HARRIS
86. BRITTON HARRIS
87. WILEY HARRIS
88. ISHAM HARRIS
89. JAMES HARRIS

---

88. ISHAM HARRIS married LUCY DAVIDSON, of FRANKLIN COUNTY, Tennessee, and they were the parents of NINE CHILDREN, as follows:

90. GEORGE W. D. HARRIS
91. RICHMOND P. HARRIS
92. WILLIAM R. HARRIS
93. JAMES T. HARRIS
94. PATSY G. HARRIS
95. MARY G. HARRIS
96. LUCY C. HARRIS
97. NANCY HARRIS
98. ISHAM G. HARRIS

98. ISHAM G. HARRIS, who was a GREAT GRANDSON of (136) WEST HARRIS, of early GRANVILLE COUNTY history was the beloved GOVERNOR ISHAM G. HARRIS, of the STATE OF TENNESSEE, during the dark days of reconstruction, an whose head "Parson" Brownlow place a price.

LIST OF EARLIEST INHABITANTS OF GRANVILLE COUNTY, NORTH CAROLINA

Authentic copy of the muster roll of a regiment of militia under the command of COLONEL WILLIAM EATON, as taken at a general muster of said regiment on OCTOBER 8, 754, as shown on pages 370 to 380 inclusive, of Volume 22, of the North Carolina STATE RECORDS, including the names of both officers and men.

WILLIAM EATON, ... COLONEL.
WILLIAM PERSON.......................... LIEUT. COLONEL.
JAMES PAINE.............................. MAJOR.

The Regiment consisted of EIGHT COMPANIES, in command of the following CAPTAINS:

1. CAPT. JOHN GLOVER .... 97 men.
2. CAPT. OSBORN JEFFREY....................... 83 men.
3. CAPT. RICHARD COLEMAN...................... 94 men.
4. CAPT. DANIEL HARRIS........................ 95 men.
5. CAPT. JOHN SALLIS.......................... 90 men.
6. CAPT. SUGAR JONES..........................140 men.
7. CAPT. BENJAMIN SIMMS....................... 75 men.
8. CAPT. ANDREW HAMPTON....................... 60 men.

The total number of men, exclusive of the commissioned officers of the Regiment and the companies was 734, and the entire personnel of the regiment probably represented every able bodied male person, subject to military duty at that time (1754) residing within the bounds of Colonial Granville County as shown on the SEARCY, and the accompanying sketched map, with possibly a very few exceptions.

Captain John Glover's Company.

George Glover, Lieut.
Evan Ragland, Ensign.
1. Henry Bishop, Sergeant.
2. William Glover, Sergeant.
3. Joseph Lindsay, Sergeant.
4. Joseph Bishop, Sergeant.
5. Thomas King, Corporal.
6. Richard Hargroves, Corpl.
7. Henry Fuller, Corpl.
8. Bartlet Searcey, Corpl.
9. Thomas Lowe.
10. John Gossard, Drummer.
11. John Blackman.
12. William Smith.
13. John Smith.
14. George Woodliffe.
15. Solomon Blackman.
16. William Lawrance.
17. Littleton Spivey.
18. Thomas Smith.
19. Stephen Smith.
20. Wm. Chavers, Negro.
21. Wm. Chavers, Jun., Mul.
22. Gilbert Chavers, Mulatto.
23. Thomas Woodliffe.
24. Thomas Smith, Merchant.
25. Littlebury Woodliffe.
26. William Woodliffe.
27. Ebenezer Wilson.
28. Edward Harris, Negro.
29. Daniel Potter.
30. Abraham Estice.
31. John Bishop.
32. George Bishop.
33. William Dickerson.
34. Emanuel Falkner.
35. Martin Dickerson.
36. Thomas Sing.
37. Thomas Wiggins.
38. James Welch.
39. John Waldrope.
40. Benjamin Ford.
41. William Holston.
42. Hugh Montgomery
43. John Kirkland.
44. John Hargrove
45. John Walker.
46. John Searcey, Junr.
47. Samuel Paschal.
48. John Paschal.
49. Thomas Adaman.
50. Leonard Lyndsey.
51. Elisha Jones.
52. Michael Bryant.
53. Edward Weaver.
54. James Morefield.
55. Alexander Burnet.
56. William Edwards.
57. Joseph Kimbal, Junr.
58. John Glover, Junr.
59. John Bird.
60. William Wagstaff.
61. Zachary Bullock.
62. Joseph Davenport.
63. Josiah Mitchel.
64. Joseph Grey.
65. John Strond.
66. Terence McMullin.
67. John Weaver.
68. Henry Vandyck.
69. James Trevillian.
70. John Trevillian.
71. Nathaniel Henderson.
72. John Smith Nut Bush.
73. William Woodward.
74. William Wood.
75. Penuel Wood.
76. William Byas.
77. Moses Harvel.
78. John Paterson.
79. William Cook.
80. Abraham Cook.
81. William Ford.
82. Charles King.
83. John Norwood.
84. Robert Mitchel.
85. John Williams.
86. Benjamin Wheatly.
87. John Williams, Junr.
88. Daniel Fluquinon.
89. Charles Williams.
90. Joseph Glover.
91. Henry Rearden.
92. Joseph Lindsay.
93. William Falkner.
94. Benjamin Edwards.
95. William Marlow.
96. William Strond.
97. William Williams.

Captain Osborn Jeffrey's Company.

Richard White, Lieutt.
John McKissick, Ensign.
1. Francis Bradley, Sergeant.
2. Howard Worley, Sergeant.
3. John Farrell, Sergeant.
4. William McBee, Corporal.
5. Thomas Cook, Corporal.
6. William Perry, Corporal.
7. John Martin, Corporal.
8. John Sandland, Senr.
9. Peter Vinson.
10. Philemon Bradford, Junr.
11. John Sutton.
12. Arthur Fuller.
13. Timothy Fuller.
14. Joseph Fuller.
15. James Sutton.
16. James Wade.
17. John Sandland, Junr.
18. Robert Allen.
19. Joseph Farrell.
20. William Moxley.
21. Robert Morgan.
22. Isaac Winston.
23. William White.
24. John Green.
25. Thomas Huland.
26. Thomas Mullins.
27. John Young.
28. William Porch.
29. Thomas Bridges.
30. Jeremiah Perry.
31. Ambrose Crane.
32. Francis Perry.
33. John Perry.
34. William Ridings.
35. William Smith.
36. Ezekiah Massey.
37. James Brogden.
38. John Golding.
39. Thomas Brogden.
40. John Davis.
41. Julius Alford.
42. Jacob Powel.
43. William Maynard.
44. Gibson Martin.
45. John Bradly.
46. Nathaniel Perry.
47. William Cade.
48. Andrew Harfield.
49. John Mooney.
50. Michael Perry.
51. William Brewer.
52. Francis Johnston.
53. John Booker.
54. Benjamin Arundel.
55. Thomas Arundel.
56. James Arundel.
57. Austin Honeycot
58. Joseph Bridges.

59. Roger Reese.
60. Thomas Jones.
61. William Taunt.
62. George Maynard.
63. Nathaniel Jones.
64. Andrew Martin.
65. Joseph Norris.
66. Richard Rayborn.
67. John Duncan.
68. William Adkinson.
69. Joseph Medlin.
70. James Bolton.
71. William Winston.
72. John Wright.
73. Samuel Carlisle.
75. John Wilder.
74. John Garret.
76. Anthony Lewis.
77. Nathan Grimes.

The next 5 are Mulattoes:

78. Thomas Gowen.
79. Michael Gowen.
80. Edward Gowen.
81. Robert Davis.
82. William Burnel.
83. William Mooney (white).

25. William Gilcrees.
26. William Read.
27. Samuel Bell.
28. William Acrey.
29. Thomas Worley.
30. Thomas Walker.
31. James Walker.
32. Charles Huckaby.
33. Charles Kimball.
34. Robert Ashley.
35. Moses Kennel.
36. Thomas Person.
37. Jennings Thompson.
55. John Campbel.
56. Isaac Johnson.
57. Daniel Colson.
58. William Hutchins.
59. Ephraim McLemore.
60. Giles Carter.
61. Robert Savage.
62. Robert Duke.
63. James Phillips.
64. Daniel Pegram.
65. Anthony Metcalfe.
66. William Downey.
67. Benjamin Carrol.

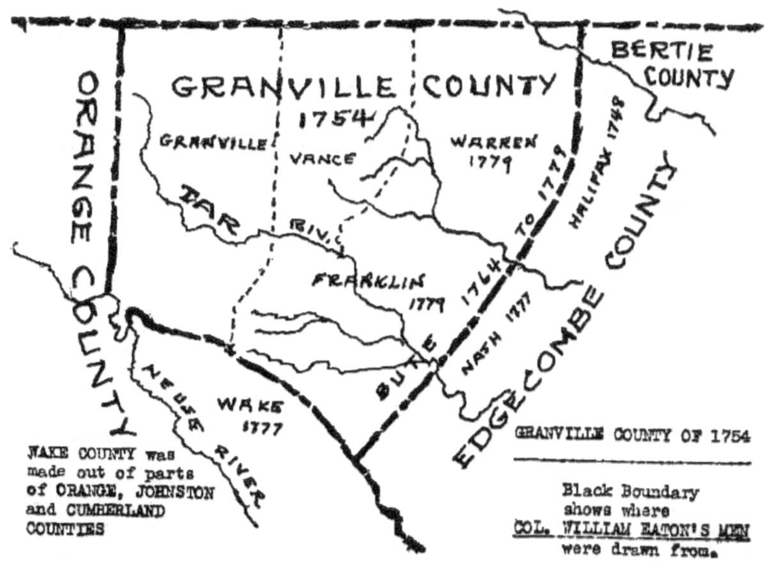

The 734 men and officers of COLONEL WILLIAM EATON'S Granville County Regiment here listed came from the territory represented by the black boundary lines of the above map. The list comprises, in our judgment, a practically complete roll of all of the able bodied men, subject to military duty in GRANVILLE COUNTY, North Carolina, at that time. So far as we have been able to ascertain no earlier list of the first citizenship of the county can be found.

CAPTAIN RICHARD COLEMAN'S COMPANY.

Robert Abernathy, Lieut.
Israel Robinson, Ensign.
1. William Sisson, Sergeant.
2. Thomas Harton, Sergeant.
3. Mathew Robinson, Sergeant.
4. William Stroud, Sergeant.
5. Moses Myrick.
6. George Rhodes.
7. John Shearing.
8. John Riggin.
9. Isaac Acrey.
10. John Dosier.
11 William Paschal.
12. William Paschal, Junr.
13. John Stroud.
14. Richard Jones.
15. Richard Coleman, Junr.
16. Richard Huckaby.
17. Jacob Dansby.
18. Israel Robinson, Junr.
19. William Young.
20. John Miller.
21. Jonathan Johnson.
22. William Moore.
23. William Dugger.
24. David King.
38. Thomas Campbel.
39. Thomas Howel.
40. James Young.
41. Daniel King.
42. John Morison.
43. Robert King.
44. Charles King.
45. John King.
46. Alexander Burnham.
47. Isaiah Paschal.
48. John Paschal.
49. William Marlow.
50. George King.
51. William Lewis.
52. Jesse Miller.
53. John Davis.
54. Robert Collier.
68. Nathaniel Nicholson.
69. William Smith.
70. John Ellis.
71. Edward Cary.
72. Samuel Thompson.
73. John Bradly.
74. Thomas Ballard.
75. John Woolbank.
76. William Collins.
77. Edmund Adcock.
78. Nicholas Robinson.
79. John Jones.
80. Richard Ballard.
81. Charles Edwards.
82. Leonard Griggs.
83. Benjamin Murphy.
84. John Robinson.

85. James Lester.
86. William Gamlin.
87. John Kendrick.
88. James Kendrick.
89. Alexander Berkley.
90. George Nichols.
91. Phillip Roberts.
92. James Nicholson
93. Thomas Johnson.
94. John Hawkins.

Captain Daniel Harris's Company.

Thomas Bell, Lieutt.
1. Smith Paterson, Sergeant.
2. Lawrance Lancaster, Sergt.
3. Robert Nutt, Sergeant.
4. Peter Green, Sergeant.
5. John McIlvail.
6. Henry Lauter.
7. James Maddrey.
8. John Leonard.
9. John Birch.
10. George Paterson.
11. William Burrows.
12. Isaac Mabry.
13. William Ellis.
14. John Wren.
15. Michael Harris.
16. Edward Holiman.
17. Benjamin Nicholson.
18. James Harris.
19. Benjamin Egerton.
20. Lewis Paterson.
21. Edward Narramore.
22. Robert Harris.
23. Ellis Marquis.
24. Joseph Hackney.
25. Joseph Trull.
26. Thomas Green.
27. Peter Kimball.
28. William Kimball.
29. Benjamin Kimball.
30. Jesse Edwards.
31. William House.
32. Edward Green.
33. Samuel Green.
34. John Cole.
35. William Duke.
36. William Duke, Junr.
37. Samuel Duke.
38. John Duke.
39. Joseph Duke.
40. Patric Harigall.
41. Richard Maddry.
42. Lewis Bobbet.
43. Miles Bobbet.
44. Charles Bartholomew.
45. Thomas Parish.
46. John Green.
47. William Cheek.
48. William Blake.
49. John Blake.
50. James Sensing.
51. Absalom Langston
52. John Smart.
53. Francis Capps.
54. James Langston.
55. Solomon Langston.
56. Joseph Green.
57. John Potts.
58. Peter Davis.
59. Richard Bennet.
60. John Mootlow.
61. John Person.
62. Joseph Person.
63. Solomon Atkinson.
64. William Mangham.
65. James Mangham.
66. William Mangham, Junr.
67. Eustace Daniel.
68. William Walker.
69. James Petty.
70. Edward Carlisle.
71. Richard Acock.
72. Francis Acock.
73. Daniel Prince.
74. Samuel Mangham.
75. Thomas Blancet.
76. William Cooper.
77. John Williams.
78. John Hudson.
79. Chamberlaine Hudson
80. Henry Hudson.
81. Isaac Hudson.
82. Edward Young, Junr.
83. Thomas Young.
84. William Davis.
85. Major Walker.
86. Peter Smart.
87. Charles Harris.
88. Joseph Harris.
89. Joseph Bell.
90. Arthur Robinson.
91. John Kicker.
92. William Meadows.
93. James Bettis.
94. Thomas Daniel.
95. Robert Moore.

Captain John Sallis's Company.

George Morris, Lieutenant.
James Mitchel, Ensign.
1. William Howlet, Sergeant.
2. Wm. Hollyman, Sergeant.
3. Richard Harris, Sergeant.
4. William Hicks, Corporal.
5. William Jordan, Corporal.
6. Henry Jordan, Corporal.
7. Thomas Morris, Corporal.
8. Thomas Newby, Corporal.
9. George King, Drummer.
10. John Craven, Drummer.
11. Thomas Bradford.
12. James Bandy.
13. Robert Bandy.
14. Jacob Perry.
15. Henry Day, Junr.
16. Simon Day.
17. Jeremiah Frazier.
18. Thomas Christian.
19. David Mitchel.
20. William Moore, Jr.
21. Henry Howard.
22. Nathaniel Holly.
23. William Holley.
24. Enoch Rentfrow.
25. Lewis Thomas.
26. Lewis Edwards.
27. John Smith.
28. Joseph Moore.
29. John Bains.
30. Richard Roberts.
31. Richard Roberts, Jun
32. John Thomason.
33. James Knott.
34. John Knott.
35. Martin Wheeler.
36. John Howard.
37. David Howard.
38. Solomon Howard.
39. Anthony Garnet.
40. Timothy Carter.
41. Samuel Carter.
42. John Stovall.
43. John Stovall, Junr.
44. Bartholomew Stovall.
45. Jeremiah Clayton.
46. William Clayton.
47. William Gowen.
48. John Gallimore.
49. Jesse Parker.
50. John Osborn.
51. William Cragg.
52. Jonathan Barret.
53. James Hembry.
54. Robert Glidewell.
55. William Manus.
56. Groves Howard.
57. John Johnston.
58. Francis King.
59. Thomas King, Junr.
60. Christopher Osborn.
61. Sherwood Harris.
62. Jonathan White, Junr.
63. George Jordan, Junr.
64. Henry Fegan.
65. John Parish.
66. William Ferguson.
67. James Reeves.
68. Harris Guillam.
69. Edward Loyd.
70. Robert Gilley.
71. William Gilley.
72. Mathew McKenny.
73. Claiborn Harris.
74. David Parish.
75. James Ferguson.
76. John Yancey.
77. Bartlet Yancey.
78. Joseph Gowen.
79. John Cragg.
80. James Roberts, Junr.
81. Osborn Hedgpeth.
82. John Simmons.
83. Christopher Harris.
84. Benjamin Simmons.
85. Joshua Nogins.
86. Bartlet Shepardson.
87. Lewis Anderson.
88. William Bass.
89. George Anderson.
90. George Pettiford.

Captain Sugan Jones's Company.

James Mosely, Lieut.
1. Francis Walker, Senr.
2. William Wood.
3. Miles Jones.
4. Denis Lindsey.
5. Aaron Fussell.
6. Benjamin Ward.
7. Shirley Watley.
8. John Burford.
9. John Thornton.
10. William Beckham.
11. William Wheeler.
12. Robert Whitaker.
13. Robert Day
14. Abraham Green.
15. John Green.
16. John Gibbs.
17. Theophilus Goodwin.
18. Theophilus Goodwin, Jr.
19. Thomas Goodwin.
20. John Goodwin.
21. Edward Thomas.
22. Benjamin Cowherd.
23. James White.
24. John Gant.
25. John Gant, Junr.
26. William Gant.
27. Isham Gant.
28. John Colley.
29. Richard Halcomb.
30. John Halcomb.
31. Joseph Halcomb.
32. Henry Thornton.
33. Benjamin Halcomb.
34. Roger Thornton.
35. George Bledsoe.
36. William Bledsoe.
37. Joshua Perry.
38. William Richardson.
39. John Boyd.
40. Thomas Zachry.
41. John Zachry.
42. William Dickerson.
43. Thomas Fussill.
44. Arthur Crocker.
45. John Wood.
46. Jacob Crocker.
47. Reuben Lawson.

48. Absalom Wells.
49. Thomas Beckham.
50. Henry Weaver.
51. William Waters.
52. Thomas Putman.
53. William Cheek.
54. Robert Cheek.
55. Williamson Liles.
56. Benjamin Thomson, Jr.
57. John Thomson.
58. William Thomas.
59. Emanuel Falkner.
60. William Falkner.
61. Simon Beckham.
62. John Rainwater.
63. James Rainwater.
64. Lewis Brantly.
65. Joseph Brantly.
66. John Brantly, Junr.
67. Hopkin Wilder.
68. John Watson.
69. Thomas Cooper.
70. Browning Williams.
71. Hezekiah Terrell.
72. Francis Strother.
73. James Ray.
74. William Underwood.
75. William Watley.
76. Shirley Watley, Junr.
77. Henry Jennings.
78. Moses Smithy.
79. Thomas Harris.
80. William Gibbons.
81. Allan Montjoy.
82. Lawrance Kerwin.
83. William Smith.
84. James Petty.
85. Thomas Petty.
86. Lawrance Strother.
87. Charles Liles.
88. Thomas Cook.
89. William Vinson.
90. James Barnet.
91. William Beckham, Junr
92. Ephraim Estrige.
93. Aaron Sherard.
94. Thomas Wooten.
95. George Wooten.
96. Daniel Wooten.
97. Robert Vasser.
98. Richard Pinnel.
99. John Pinnel.
100. Joshua Pinnel.
101. William Saul.
102. Thomas Sing.
103. William Willis.
104. Thomas Martin.
105. Atkins McLemore.
106. James Talbot.
107. Joshua Yarbro.
108. Thomas Sale.
109. Jeremiah Wooten.
110. John Wooten.
111. James Wooten.
112. Thomas Delany.
113. John Mosely.
114. Thomas Crab.
115. John Persons.
116. Richard Parsons.
117. Joseph Martin.
118. William Martin.
119. Arthur Watson.
120. John Serug Askew.
121. Henry Brewer.
122. William Takewell.
123. William Halley.
124. Simon Taylor.
125. Ambrose Bearding.
126. Samuel Freeman.
127. Jeptha Terrell.
128. John Terrell, Junr.
129. John Debord.
130. James Morris.
131. Thomas Harris.
132. Joseph Harris.
133. John Stanfield.
134. Benjamin Rice.
135. Robert Clark.
136. Thomas Carter.
137. John Burdock.
138. Thomas Turner.
139. John Deer.
140. George Underwood.

Captain Benjamin Simm's Company.

John Burt, Lieut.
William Mercer, Ensign
1. Giles Bowers, Sergeant.
2. John Bishop, Sergeant.
3. William Eves, Sergeant
4. James Ross, Corporal.
5. John Meldey, Corporal.
6. Mathew Mathews, Corporal.
7. William Jones, Drummer.
8. Henry Ivey, Drummer.
9. William Jackson.
10. Thomas Smith.
11. William Moxley.
12. William Thomas.
13. Charles Ivey.
14. Daniel Carrol.
15. John Duncan.
16. Thos. Hunt, Little Creek.
17. Robert Smith.
18. Richard Crutchfield.
19. John Meekie.
20. Henry Clark.
21. Thos. Hunt, up the River
22. Saul Rackley.
23. William Pace, Jun.
24. Joseph Acom Hutson.
25. Christopher Clark.
26. Joseph Brantly.
27. James Brantly.
28. George Bledsoe.
29. Thomas Woodly.
30. Robert Moody, Junr.
31. William Hunt.
32. William Jerkins.
33. Lodowick Alford.
34. Joseph Jeffries.
35. William Hobbs.
36. Thomas Jones.
37. William Simmons.
38. William Jones.
39. James Hunt.
40. John Claiborn.
41. Robert Clark.
42. Benjamin Rice.
43. John Deer.
44. Aaron Sherrud.
45. William Vinson.
46. William Richardson.
47. James White.
48. Arthur Crocker.
49. Miles Rackley.
50. Parsons Rackley.
51. John Rainwater.
52. Thomas Tharrington.
53. Robert Butler.
54. Edward Thomas.
55. John Reeves.
56. William Smith.
57. John Smith.
58. George Woodly.
59. Joseph Wright.
60. John Wright.
61. James Massey.
62. John Douglas.
63. George Hill.
64. Francis Strother.
65. Thomas West.
66. Joseph Wright, Junr.
67. James Pace.
68. James Smith.
69. Nathaniel Smith.
70. John Parnal.
71. John Massey.
72. William Edwards.
73. John Simmons.
74. Barnaby Goodwin.
75. Samuel Fowler, Senr.

Captain Andrew Hampton's Company.

John Adcock, Lieutt.
Ephraim Hampton, Ensign.
1. Thomas Robinson, Sergeant.
2. Wm. Williams, Sergeant.
3. John Landres, Sergeant.
4. John Williams, Corporal.
5. Fran. Davenport, Corporal.
6. Absalom Baker, Corporal.
7. Richard Ceverinton, Corpl.
8. Carter Hedgpeth, Corporal.
9. Anthony Cassart, Drummer.
10. Darwin Elwick.
11. William Rose.
12. Francis Rann.
13. Thomas Goss.
14. Robert Boyd.
15. Ephraim Merrit.
16. William Washington.
17. James Meadows.
18. Benjamin Hubbard.
19. John Clark.
20. Valentine White.
21. John Jones.
22. Moses Coppock.
23. John Ogowine.
24. Patrick Lashley.
25. Mathew Myers.
26. David Cassart.
27. John Landres, Junr.
28. James Bolling.
29. William Bolling.
30. Nicholas Horton.
31. Giles Hedgpeth.
32. Francis Falkner.
33. Leonard Adcock.
34. John Marrowin.
35. Emanuel Falkner.
36. Benjamin Bolling.
37. Daniel Blackman.
38. Malachi Reeves.
39. Minos Greggs.
40. Francis West.
41. Thomas May.
42. Samuel Flaick.
43. Thomas Flaick.
44. Samuel Fuller.
45. David Strahan.
46. Owen Read.
47. Samuel Smith.
48. John Bolling.
49. Joseph Langston.
50. John Mathews.
51. James Morris.
52. Samuel Johnson.
53. David Stroud.
54. Ebenezer Wilson.
55. John Gibbs.
56. William Smith.
57. Joseph Halley.
58. Lawrence Pettiford.
59. Richard Watts.
60. Peter Marrown.

Glover's	97
Jeffries'	83
Coleman's	94
Harris's	95
Sallis's	90
Jones's	140
Simms's	75
Hampton's	60
Total	734

WILLIAM EATON

6 December, 1754.
(Endorsement.)
Granville.

TAX PAYERS OF GRANVILLE COUNTY FOR THE YEAR 1788

Following herewith is a list of the tax payers in GRANVILLE COUNTY, NORTH CAROLINA for the year 1788. The territory covered by this list includes the present area of the county, plus the area embraced in the present VANCE COUNTY, which had not been established at the time the list was made. This list appears in Vol. 26 of the North Carolina Records & was used by the Federal Government as a substitute for the first census of 1790. As we have arranged these names in alphabetical order, they will not be included in the index. Where a note follows the name, of course, that is by this compiler. The initialed symbols after the name represent the DISTRICT where the assessment was made, but often the person assessed had property in more than one district, which explains why the same name is sometimes repeated. The Districts and symbols were as follows:

ABRAHAM PLAINS DISTRICT .... APD
BEAVER DAM DISTRICT................. BDD
DUTCH DISTRICT...................... DD
EPPING FORREST DISTRICT............. EFD
FISHING CREEK DISTRICT.............. FCD
FORT CREEK DISTRICT.................FTCD
GOSHEN DISTRICT..................... GD
HENDERSON DISTRICT.................. HED
ISLAND CREEK DISTRICT............... ICD
KNAP OF LEED'S DISTRICT............. KLD
OXFORD DISTRICT..................... OXD
RAGLAND DISTRICT.................... RD
TABB'S CREEK DISTRICT............... TCD
TAR RIVER DISTRICT.................. TRD

ADCOCK, BOLLING DD
ADCOCK, EDWARD KLD
ADCOCK, JOHN DD
ADCOCK, ROBERT TRD
ADCOCK, LEONARD KLD
ADDAMS, SAMUEL KLD
AKIN, ISOM ICD
AKIN, JAMES ICD
AKIN, JAMES, SR. ICD
AKIN, JOSEPH ICD
The AKIN FAMILY apparently LIVED in the Island Creek District.
ALLEN, CHAMPION BDD
ALLEN, FRANCIS GD
ALLEN, CAPT. GRANT APD
ALLEN, ROBERT BDD
ALLEN, SAMUEL RD
ALLEY, ROSSER EFD
ALLISON, ROBERT TCD
ALLISON, ROBERT FTCD
ALSTON, GEORGE RD
AMIS, WILLIAM APD
ANDERSON, FRANK BDD
ANDERSON, JACOB FCD
ANDERSON, LEWIS OXD
APLIN, THOMAS GD
This man may have been named APPLING, of the family settled in Ga.
ARNOLD, WILLIAM KLD
ASHMAN, LEWIS GD
ASKEW, JOHN EFD
AUSTIN, VALENTINE BDD
BADGET, JOHN TRD
BADGET, PETER TRD
BADGET, WILLIAM TRD
BAILEY, JEREMIAH BDD
BAILEY, JOHN DD
BAILEY, JOHN BDD
BAILEY, RICHARD BDD
BAILEY, STEPHEN DD
BALL, ELIJAH FCD
BARKER, AMBROSE GD
BARNES, MIRIM'C HED
BARNETT, JESSE ICD
BARNETT, JOHN ICD
BARBETT, SARAH C. ICD
BARR, JAMES FCD
BARTON, WILLIAM TCD
Some of these BARTONS settled in Tennessee, and ISAAC BARTON was a Baptist minister in JEFFERSON COUNTY; his descendants to MISSOURI.
BASS, BENJAMIN, SR. TRD
BASS, BENJAMIN, JR. TRD
BASS, EDWARD RD
BASS, NATHAN FCD
BASS, REUBEN FCD
BASS, RICHARD TRD
This family was numerous in Prince Edward County, Virginia and JONES COUNTY, NC. C.
BATES, JOHN RD
John was a stray member of the Virginia BATES family - kin to JORDANS and DANIELS. See articles herein on both.
BAXTER, JOSEPH DD
BEARDEN, BENJAMIN OXD
BECK, FREDERICK DD
BECK, MICHAEL DD
BECK, WILLIAM DD
BEDFORD, JAMES GD
BEEZLEY, STEPHEN GD
BELL, JOSA RD
BENNETT, LEWIS GD
BENNETT, CAPT. PETER GD
BIRD, ROBERT OXD
BIRAM, JOHN TCD
This name was properly spelled BYRUM as is shown by other items from records.
BISHOP, JAMES RD
BLACKLEY, CHARLES FTCD
BLACKLEY, JAMES FTCD
BLACKWELL, JAMES FTCD
BLALOCK, DAVID FTCD
BLALOCK, JEREMIAH FTCD
BLANKS, JOSEPH GD
This man a descendant of the second wife of CORNELIUS CARGILL, of Mecklenburg County, Virginia, mentioned in the "Journey to the Land of Eden" by Col. William Byrd.
BOBBITT, WILLIAM EFD
BOERS, PHILEMON FTCD
BOROLEN, WILLIAM KLD
BOTTOMS, THOMAS L. DD
BOWDEN, FRANCIS HED
BOWDEN, JOHN SR. KLD
BOYD, JOHN OXD
(See page 274 for sketch of JOHN BOYD).
BRACK, SAMUEL HED
BRACK, SAMUEL JR. HED
BRADFORD, BENJAMIN FTCD
BRADFORD, BOOKER BDD
BRADFORD, DAVID BDD
BRADFORD, DAVID JR. BDD
BRADFORD, EPHRAIM BDD
BRADFORD, JOHN FTCD
BRADFORD, PHILEMON BDD
BRADFORD, PHILEMON JR. BDD
BRADFORD, RICHARD BDD
BRADLEY, JAMES DD
BRAME, JAMES HED
BRAME, THOMAS HED
BRASFIELD, CALEB DD
BRASFIELD, ELIZABETH DD
BRASFIELD, GEORGE DD
BRAZLETON, JACOB KLD
BREWER, AMERY TRD
BRIDGERS, DRURY BDD
BRIDGERS, JOHN BDD
BRIDGES, JOSEPH ICD
BRIGGS, RICHARD TRD
BRINKLEY, JAMES, SR. TRD
BRINKLEY, JAMES JR. TRD
BRINKLEY, PETER TRD
BRINKLEY, RICHARD TRD
BRISTOW, JAMES TCD
BRISTOW, JOHN TCD
BRISTOW, PHILEMON TCD
BRODIE, JOHN RD
BRUMMIT, NIMROD FCD
BRYANT, ROWLAND TCD
BUCHANAN, WILLIAM BDD
BULLOCK, CHARLES KLD
BULLOCK, JAMES ICD
BULLOCK, JEREMIAH KLD
BULLOCK, MICAJAH DD
BULLOCK, WILLIAM ICD
BUSH, NICHOLAS APD & ICD.

BURRAGE, EDWARD APD
BURROUGHS, JAMES ICD
BURDIN, JOHN HED
BUSSURE, FRANCIS OXD
BUTLER, ANNE APD
BUTLER, ISAAC OXD
BUTLER, REUBEN ICD
BUTLER, THOMAS OXD
BYARS, WILLIAM ICD
BYART, MARY DD
BYNUM, HENRY FCD
BROWN, JOHN BDD
CAPE, WILLIAMSON BDD
CARDEN, JAMES FCD
CARDWELL, THOMAS ICD
CARNES, JOSEPH DD
CARRELL, JOHN BDD
CARTER, ALEX FTCD
CARTER, JESSE FTCD
CARTER, THOMAS FTCD
CARVER, EDMUND DD
CASH, JOSEPH DD
CASH, PETER DD
CAVENAUGH, GEORGE BDD
CHADWICK, JOHN HED
CHAMBLESS, JOEL KLD
CHAMPION, CHARLES BDD
CHAMPION, JOHN FTCD
CHAMPION, JOHN SR. FTCD
CHAMPION, JOSEPH BDD
CHANDLER, JAMES GD
CHANDLER, JOSEPH GD
CHAPMAN, GEORGE ICD
CHAVENS, WILLIAM FCD
CHAVIS, JAMES APD
CHRISTIAN, GIDEON HED
CLARK, LEONARD TCD
CLARK, NATHANIEL TRD
CLAXTON, JAMES DD
CLAY, SAMUEL OXD
CLEMENT, JOHN KLD
CLEMENT, OBEDIAH KLD
CLEMENT, SAMUEL KLD
CLEMENTS, THOMAS DD
COCK, WILLIAM TRD
COCKER, WILLIAM ICD
COLE, WILLIAM KLD
COLLINS, JOHN ICD
COLLINS, THOMAS ICD
COOK, BLANTON EFD
COOK, WILLIAM EFD
COOKE, CLAIBORN FTCD
COOKE, RICHARD S. DD
COOKE, SHEM, SR. FTCD
COOPER, CORNELIUS FCD
COOPER, JOHN FCD
COOPER, KANNON EFD
CORK, JAMES FCD
COTHRAN, WILLIAM OXD
COZZART, ANN KLD
COZZART, BENJAMIN KLD
COZZART, DAVID KLD
COZZART, JACOB KLD
COZZART, JESSE DD
COX, CHARNICH HED
CRAFT, JOHN HED
CRAFT, THOMAS HED
CRAGG, JOHN SR. TRD
CRAGG, JOHN JR. TRD
CRAWLEY, ROBERT ICD
CRENSHAW, ABRAM APD
CREWS, CALEB OXD
CREWS, GIDEON RD
CREWS, JAMES RD
CREWS, THOMAS RD
CRITCHER, JAMES OXD
CRITCHER, THOMAS HED
CRIETH, SAMUEL APD
CROWDER, EWELL EFD
CULBERHOUSE, JEREMIAH DD
CULBERHOUSE, THOMAS W. DD
CURRIN, HUGH RD
DANIEL, CHESLEY GD
DANIEL, JOSEPH HED
DANIEL, MARTIN GD
DAVIS, ABSOLOM ICD
DAVIS, AUGUSTIN ICD
DAVIS, BAXTER APD

Baxter Davis was related to the KING FAMILY; his name appears often in FAIRFAX CO. and PITTSYLVANIA County, Va.

DAVIS, JOSEPH RD
DAVIS, P. RD
DAVIS, SOLOMON ICD
DEBRULER, MICAJAH TCD
DENTON, BENJAMIN HED
DICKERSON, JOHN FCD
DICKERSON, JOHN FCD
DICKERSON, JOHN JR. FCD
DICKERSON, WILLIAM FCD
DODSON, WILLIAM ICD
DOTSON, WILLIAM JR. ICD

The proper spelling of the name was DODSON.

DOTSON, CHARLES ICD
DOUGLASS, JOSEPH GD
DOWNEY, JAMES APD
DOWNEY, JAMES, JR. APD
DRISKILL, DENNIS RD
DRISKILL, TIMOTHY ICD
DUNCAN, WILLIAM ICD
DUNKIN, GEORGE TRD
DUNKIN, HARRISON TRD
DUNKIN, JOHN TCD

Proper spelling of these names was DUNCAN, of course.

DUTY, RICHARD GD

Duty wills will be found in Caswell County notes. CAS - WELL was really the home of the DUTY FAMILY.

EARIS, JESSE FCD
EARLES, JOHN SR. RD
EARLE, JOHN RD
EASTES, SYLVANUS KLD
EASTES, LODOWICK KLD
EASTWOOD, ISRAEL KLD
EATON, CHARLES R. EFD
EDWARDS, JOHN EFD
EDWARDS, THOMAS GD
ELLIS, JOSEPH KLD
EMMERY, EPHRAIM DD
EVINS, BURIL FCD

Of course this was BURWELL.

EVINS, BURREL EFD

And this one, also.

EVANS, JOHN GD
EVANS, MORRAN FTCD
FABER, SEARCY TCD
FARMER, JOHN DD
FERRYBOUGH, JACOB KLD
FINCH, GEORGE EFD
FINCH, JOHN SR. EFD
FINCH, JOHN JR EFD
FINCH, WILLIAMSON EFD
FLEMEN, HENRY ICD
FLOYD, MOSES EFD
FLOYD, WILLIAM EFD
FORDWINE, LEMUEL RD
FORSYTHE, JAMES TRD
FOUPE, MATTHEW RD
FOWLER, HENRY TCD
FOWLER, JAMES FCD
FOWLER, RICHARD TRD
FOWLER, WILLIAM EFD
FRASYIER, ARTHUR APD
FRAZER, EPHRAIM TRD
FRAZIER, JEREMIAH OXD
FRAISYIER, WILLIAM APD
FREEMAN, GIDEON DD
FULLER, BRITTON EFD
FULLER, DAVID BDD
FULLER, HENRY SR. EFD
FULLER, HENRY JR. EFD
FULLER, CAPT. JONES BDD
FULLER, SAMUEL EFD
FUSSEL, MOSES DD
GAFFORD, REUBEN KLD
GARROTT, JESSE FCD
GILL, WILLIAM TRD
GILLIAM, HARRIS FTCD
GILLIAM, WILLIAM HED
GILPIN, HENRY HED
GLASGOW, RICHARD BDD
GLASS, WILLIAM GD
GLOVER, CAPT. DANIEL ICD
GLOVER, JOAB ICD
GOBER, MARTHA ICD
GOBER, WILLIAM ICD

The researchers will fin these GOBERS down in Geo gia in Madison or Clarke Counties.

GOLDSMITH, THOMAS ICD
GOOCH, AMOS TRD
GOOCH, DANIEL TRD
GOOCH, GIDEON ICD
GOOCH, JOSEPH ICD

A sister of REV. ROWLAND JONES, of Bruton Parish married a GOOCH, and these are descendants; Cousins removed of GIDEO MACON, who married PRIS - CILLA JONES in GRANVILLE

GOODLOE, ROBERT BDD

Also related to the JONE tribe AND THE HARPERS.

GORCH, ROLEN KLD

This was ROWLAND GOOCH, member of the GOOCH fami- ly above mentioned.

GOSS, SHEARMAN TRD
GOSS, THOMAS KLD
GOWIN, JENKIN FTCD
GRANT, THOMAS GD
GRAVES, HENRY APD
GRAVES, HENRY JR. GD
GRAVES, MARY APD

The widow who married JO WILLIAMS DANIEL of WARRE COUNTY.

GRAVES, RALPH APD

Namesake of RALPH GRAVES of YORK COUNTY, Va. who married a PINKETHMAN.

GRAY, MORTON OXD
GREEN, DANIEL KLD
GREEN, HENRY KLD
GREEN, JOAB KLD
GREEN, WILLIAM DD
GRESHAM, RICHARD HED
GRISHAM, HENRY HED
GRISHAM, JAMES RD

Families of both spelling exist today, but I am of the opinion that these were both the same—GRES AM, not GRISHAM.

GRIZEL, HARLEY ICD
GUNTER, JESSE TRD

The name of
CLEMENT, SIMON BDD
was omitted from the 1st column on this page. Thi family was from NEW KENT COUNTY, Virginia.

HALL, FUTRIL DD
HAMMOND, JOAB ICD
HANCOCK, BENJAMIN ICD
HANKS, ARGUYLE ICD
HANKS, WILLIAM HED

The ARGYLE HANKS above is said to have been the ancestor of the famous NANCY HANKS & the claim has been made that NANCY herself for a time had her abode with relatives in the upper part of GRANVILLE County near the Virginia line. Considering all that has been written and said of LINCOLN'S mother, these may have been her relatives.

HARDING, STERLING HED
HARGROVE, JOHN ICD
HARGROVE, RICHARD ICD
HARGROVE, STEPHEN ICD

The HARGROVES were from SURRY and BRUNSWICK CO. Virginia.

HARP, HENRY BDD
HARP, JOHN FCD
HARP, JOHN EFD
HARP, SAMPSON FCD
HARP, THOMAS FCD
HARP, THOMAS EFD
HARP, THOMAS SR. FCD
HARPER, JESSE (Estate) ICD

His wife was DIANA GOODLOE

HARRIS, ANTHONY (Son of RICHARD HARRIS TED
HARRIS, CHARLES GD
HARRIS, CHARLES OXD
HARRIS, CHRISTOPHER BDD
HARRIS, CHRISTOPHER ICD
HARRIS, CLAIBORN KLD
HARRIS, DARNIN RD
HARRIS, EDWARD BDD
HARRIS, GEORGE RD
HARRIS, HARRISON BDD

The last named was a revolutionary soldier and died in WOODFORD COUNTY, KY. leaving will and six children 1795. The children were DAVID, RANDOLPH, NATHANIEL m. Mary HOWARD, SUSANNA, MARY m. HICKS and MOURNING married ADAMS. - Bailey's Hist. of Woodford County, Ky.

HARRIS, JOHN GD
HARRIS, JOHN HED
HARRIS, JOHN BDD
HARRIS, RICHARD KLD
HARRIS, ROBERT OXD
HARRIS, ROBERT GD
HARRIS SAMUEL OXD

Sam lived in VIRGINIA.

HARRIS, SHERWOOD OXD
HARRISON, ISHAM HED

This was not the son in law of REV. HENRY PATTILLO. This ISHAM was not married in 1788.

HARRISON, SARAH DD

This was SARAH (DANIEL) HARRISON, daughter of JOHN DANIEL, in her old age living in GRANVILLE

[illegible] .... AFD
HAWKINS, JAMES DD
HAWKINS, JOHN KLD
HAWKINS, MATTHEW KLD
HAWLEY, JACOB BDD
HAWLEY, NATHANIEL AFD
HAYES, JOSEPH TCD
HAYS, HENRY JR. FCD
HAYS, JOSHUA RD
HAYS, JOSHUA TCD
HAYS, LEONARD BDD
HAYS, SARAH EFD
HAYS, THEOPHILUS TCD
HAYSLIP, LABORN FCD

Generally spelled on the records as HAIRSLIP.

HEDGEPETH, CARTER TCD
HEFLIN, CHARLES FTCD
HEFLIN, FIELDING BDD
HEFLIN, JOHN BDD
HEFLIN, WILLIAM BDD

This was the ancestrial family of U. S. Senator HEFLIN of ALABAMA.

HENDERSON, PLEASANT HED
HENDERSON, RICHARD HED

These were two famous brothers, both sons of SAMUEL HENDERSON (See page 221)

HENDLEY, WILLIAM BDD
HENDRICKSON, EZEKIEL AFD
HESTER, ABRAHAM ICD
HESTER, FRANCIS OXD
HESTER, JOSEPH EFD
HESTER, ROBERT GD
HESTER, WILLIAM AFD
HESTER, WILLIAM TED
HESTER, ZACHARIAH ICD
HESTER, ZACHARIAH OXD

This does not mean there were two of the same name; but that the one owned property in two different districts which was assessed to him separately. Of course, sometimes there WERE two of the same name.

HICKMAN, CORBIN EFD
HICKS, BISHOP RD
HICKS, DAVID TCD
HICKS, HARRIS ED
HICKS, ROBERT OXD
HICKS, SAMUEL TCD
HICKS, THOMAS RD
HICKS, THOMAS OXD
HICKS, WILLIAM TCD
HICKS, WILLIAM JR. RD
HIGGS, LEONARD EFD
HIGGS, ZACHARIAH TCD

The HIGGS FAMILY came to GRANVILLE from BERTIE.

HIGHFIELD, HEZEKIAH EFD
HILL, JOHN TED
HILLIARD, JAMES OXD
HOLT, JOHN BDD
HOMES, SAMUEL (HOLMES?) FTCD
HOOFMAN, JACOB DD

This was HOFFMAN.

HOOKER, JOHN BDD
HOOKER, JOHN JR. BDD
HOPGOOD, HEZEKIAH TED
HOPKINS, ANN TCD
HOPKINS, GEORGE OXD
HORN, HOWELL BDD
HORNSBY, WILLIAM EFD
HOWARD, ALLEN OXD
HOWARD, GROVES TED
HOWARD, JOHN AFD
HOWELL, JOHN ICD
HOWELL, THOMAS OXD
HUDDLESTON, JOHN FTCD
HUDSON, DRURY BDD

HUNT, DANIEL FCD
HUNT, GEORGE OXD
HUNT, GEORGE OXD
HUNT, JAMES KLD
HUNT, JOHN OXD
HUNT, JOHN EFD
HUNT, SAMUEL OXD
HUNT, WILLIAM FCD
HUNT, WILLIAM DD
HUSCATT, FARTHY BDD
HUTCHINSON, JOSHUA TCD
HYDE, ROBERT ICD
INSCOR, REUBEN SR. FCD
INSCOR, REUBEN JR. FCD
INSCHORE, STEPHEN FCD

INCORE, perhaps is the proper spelling.

JACKSON, SAMUEL KLD
JARRETT, JOHN DD
JEFFREYS, WILLIAM FTCD
JENKINS, JAMES FTCD
JENKINS, THOMAS DD
JETER, SAMUEL RD
JETT, STEPHEN TCD
JOHNSON, BENJAMIN EFD
JOHNSON, BENJAMIN ICD
JOHNSON, GIDEON TCD
JOHNSON, HENRY ICD
JOHNSON, ISHAM TED
JOHNSON, JOHN ICD
JOHNSON, JONATHAN TCD
JOHNSON, JOSEPH EFD
JOHNSON, NOEL TCD
JOHNSON, THOMAS TCD
JOHNSON, WILLIAM JR. TCD
JOHNSTON, JAMES AFD
JOHNSTON, SAMUEL OXD
JOHNSTON, WILLIAM SR. TCD

Little dependence to be put on spelling of these names for here is a Sr. & Jr. same District spelled differently.

JONES, ABRAHAM FTCD
JONES, AMBROSE SR. GD
JONES BRERETON KLD
JONES, CHARLES KLD
JONES, EDWARD KLD
JONES, FRANCIS BDD
JONES, JOHN TED
JONES, JONATHAN FTCD
JONES, MOSES KLD
JONES, REUBEN GD
JONES, SAMUEL BDD
JONES, THOMAS DD
JONES, VINKLER ICD
JONES WILLIAM (BIG) KLD
JONES, WILLIAM KLD
JONES, WILLIAM JR. DD
JORDAN, ARTHUR HED
JORDAN, ROBERT GD
KELLEY, THOMAS ICD
KIMBALL, BATHOL HED
KIMBALL, HENRY RD
KENDRICK, THOMAS ICD
KENNON, JOHN GD
KNOTT, DAVID GD
KNOTT, JAMES KLD
KNOTT, JOHN GD
KNOWLAND, CHARLES FTCD
KNOWLAND, DANIEL JR. FTCD
KITTLE, CHRISTOPHER FTCD
KITTRELL, JONATHAN SR EFD
KITTRELL, JONATHAN JR. EFD
KITTRELL, JOSHUA EFD
KITTRELL, SAMUEL EFD
KNIGHT, JOHN AFD
KNIGHT, JONATHAN AFD
KNIGHT, WILLIAM AFD

GRIFFIN, LAWRENCE BDD

LAMSDEN, JOHN GD
LANDISH, JOSEPH DD
LANKFORD, BARRISH FCD
LANKFORD, HENRY FCD
LANKFORD, JOHN FCD
LANFORD, JESSE TCD
LANIER, LEWIS ICD
LANIER, THOMAS ICD

Father in law of COL. JOSEPH and ROBERT WILLIAMS of NUTBUSH. Also of JOSEPH WILLIAMS of SHALLOW FORD.

LASSITER, WILLIAM GD
LAURENCE, DEBORAH EFD
LAURENCE, JOHN EFD
LAWRENCE, ABRAHAM DD
LAWRENCE, WILLIAM BDD
LEATHERS, JAMES BDD
LEAVEL, EDWARD APD
LEEMAN, WILLIAM EFD
LeMAY, SAMUEL GD
LeMAY, SUSANNAH (Est) GD
LEWIS, FRANCIS ICD
LEWIS, HOWELL APD
LEWIS, HOWELL, JR. APD
LEWIS, JAMES ICD
LEWIS, NATHANIEL GD
LEWISTON, JAMES FTCD
LIGON, THOMAS GD
LINDSAY, ELIJAH RD
LINDSAY, SARAH OXD

From ESSEX COUNTY, Va. or CAROLINE; the widow of JAMES LINDSAY & the daughter of WILLIAM DANIEL.

LOCK, JONA. OXD
LOCK, WILLIAM EFD
LOCUST, VALENTINE OXD
LONG, CHARLES TRD
LONG, GEORGE KLD
LONGMIN, WILLIAM OXD
LOYD, WILLIAM GD
LOYD, EDWARD RD
LLOYD, ISAIAH EFD
LOVE, ALLEN, EST. APD
LUMPKIN, ANTHONY TRD
LYLES, WILLIAM BDD
LYNE, HENRY ICD
LYNE, JAMES ICD

These LYNES married into the TAYLOR and BULLOCK FAMILIES in both Virginia and N. Carolina.

MACON, JOHN HED
MAGEHEE, BENJ. SR. FTCD
MAGEHEE, BENJ. FTCD
MAGEHEE, JESSE FTCD
MAGEHEE, JOSIAH FTCD
MAGEHEE, NATHAN FTCD
MAGEHEE, NATHAN FTCD
MAGEHEE, ROBERT FTCD

These Fort Creek MAGEHEES were doubtless the McGEHEES of Virginia and later of GEORGIA, Tennessee & TEXAS.

MALONEY, WILLIAM OXD
MANGUM, ABSOLOM BDD
MANGUM, HOWELL KLD
MANGUM, JOSEPH KLD

These were the ancestors of the famous N. Carolina WILEY MANGUM —Statesman.

MANN, ARNOLD BDD
MARON, DANIEL ICD
MARSHALL, JOHN OXD
MARSHALL, WILLIAM ICD
MASON, DAVID ICD

Daniel "Maron" above was perhaps DANIEL MASON.

MATTHEWS, JAMES ICD
MATTHEWS, JOHN TRD
MATTHEWS, LITTLEBURY OXD
MATHIS, WILLIAM TCD
MAUIER, JOHN WILLIAM KLD
MAYFIELD, ABRAHAM FTCD
MAYFIELD, VALENTINE FTCD
McDANIEL, JAMES EFD
McDANIEL, JOSEPH EFD
McLEMORE, JAMES DD
MEADOWS, JAMES TRD
MEADOWS, JESSE KLD
MEADOWS, MICHAEL TRD
MELONE, ROBERT APD
MELTON, HENRY ICD
MERRIMAN, MALACHIAH DD
MERRIMAN, WILLIAM DD
MERRITT, STEPHEN KLD
MILENER, JAMES TRD
MILINDER, WILLIAM GD
MINOR, JOHN OXD
MINOR, WILLIAM FCD
MILLS, ROBERT BDD
MILLS, WILLIAM TCD
MITCHELL, ARCHIBALD OXD
MITCHELL, CHARLES OXD
MITCHELL, DAVID HED
MITCHELL, ELY HED
MITCHELL, JACOB APD
MITCHELL, ISOM BDD
MITCHELL, JAMES GD
MITCHELL, JOSIAH GD
MITCHELL, MAJOR HED
MITCHELL, PHILLIPS HED

JOAB MITCHELL, of this family married the widow of the younger DANIEL WILLIAMS of Island Creek, and moved down on the PACOLET in South Carolina before this tax list was made in 1788. See HENDERSON family.

MONTAGUE, HENRY APD
MONTAGUE, LATTEMEY APD
MONTAGUE, YOUNG APD
MOORE, BENJAMIN DD
MOORE, CHARLES JR. EFD
MOORE, CHARLES SR. EFD
MOORE, CHARLES JR. FCD
MOORE, GEORGE L. DD
MOORE, JOEL FCD
MOORE, JOHN BDD
MOORE, JOHN APD
MOORE, MAJOR BDD
MOORE, WILLIAM ICD
MOORE, WILLIAM ICD
MORGAN, ELIZABETH APD
MORRIS, HENRY TCD
MORRIS, JOHN OXD
MORSE, JOHN HED
MORSE, PHILLIS HED
MORSE, REUBEN HED
MUTTER, THOMAS APD
MYARS, JACOB FTCD
MANGUM, JAMES BDD
NAILING, WILLIAM FTCD
NANCE, HARROD BDD
NANCE, RICHARD BDD
NEISTER, BENJAMIN RD
NEWBY, THOMAS SR. FCD
NICHOLSON, GEORGE BDD
NOLAND, EDWARD OXD
NORMAN, GEORGE APD
NORMAN, THOMAS RD
NORRIS, JAMES FTCD
NORWOOD, BENJAMIN ICD
NORWOOD, JORDAN ICD
OAKEY, JOSEPH KLD
OAKEY, JOSEPH JR. DD
OAKEY, MICAJAH KLD
OAKLEY, THOMAS TRD
OAKLEY, WILLIAM TRD
OGILVIE, HARRIS DD
OGILVIE, KIMBROUGH DD
OGILVIE, SMITH KLD
OGILVIE, WILLIAM KLD
OLIVER, JOHN GD
OLIVER, MARY APD
OLIVER, PETER GD
OLIVER, (WIDOW) APD
OBRIAN, PATRICK GD
OENNERY, RICHARD DD
OWEN, FREDERICK APD
OWEN, JACOB APD
OWEN, JOHN SR. GD
OWEN, JOHN APD
OWEN, JOHN JR. GD
OWEN, THOMAS GD
OWEN, WILLIAM APD

William Owen was the son of a JAMES OWEN. RICHARDSON OWEN, a descendant of the famous WELCH POET was in CASWELL CO. at this time and was an ancestor of THOMAS McADORY OWEN of Alabama, the Southern Historian. They were related to the DUTY FAMILY of Caswell.

PAGE, LEWIS TCD
PARK, WILLIAM ICD
PALMER, WILLIAM GD
PARRIS, CLAIBORN RD
PARRIS, THOMAS RD
PARHAM, CANNON TCD
PARHAM, EPHRAIM TCD
PARHAM, ISHAM TCD
PARHAM, ISHAM, JR TCD
PARHAM, JOHN TCD
PARHAM, JOHN JR. TCD
PARHAM, THOMAS SR. TCD
PARHAM, THOMAS JR. TCD
PARHAM, WILLIAM OXD
PARHAM, WILLIAM TCD

Without doubt the home of the PARHAM FAMILY was in TABB'S CREEK DISTRICT.

PARKER, AMOS KLD
PARKER, JEPTHA OXD
PARKER, SAMUEL DD
PARRISH, BRISSE EFD
PARRISH, CHARLES RD
PARRISH, DAVID TCD
PARRISH, DAVID RD
PARRISH, ELIJAH FCD
PARRISH, HUMPHREY ICD
PARRISH, JESSE FCD
PARRISH, JOHN GD
PARRISH, WILLIAM SR. RD
PARRISH, WILLIAM JR. RD
PARTEE, CHARLES KLD
PATERSON, ANDREW GD
PATILLO, REV. HENRY ICD

We dislike to impeach the generally accepted tradition that Rev. Patillo was born in Scotland. The will of his father, JAMES PATILLO, of Prince George Co. Va. shows he was born in Virginia in 1730. JAMES patented lands in Pr. Geo in 1728.

PASCALL, JAMES BDD
PARHAM, AVERY TCD
PEACE, JOHN SR. FCD
PEACE, JOHN JR. FTCD
PEACE, JOSEPH SR. FCD
PEACE, JOSEPH FCD
Same PEACE family that settled later in RA - LEIGH.
PEEK, JOHN C. DD
PEET, JOHN BDD
PENN, JOHN ICD
The son of MOSES and his wife MISS TAYLOR, and the "SIGNER". The will is on file at OXFORD in his own handwriting.
PERDUE, GEORGE HED
PERKINSON, JOEJ KLD
PERRY, PETER ICD
PERSON, THOMAS, ESQ. GD
The relationship of THOMAS PERSON to WILLIAM PERSON is conjectural. WILLIAM is listed as of FRANKLIN COUNTY in 1790 without a family. PERSON COUNTY was named for THOMAS PERSON.
PETTYFORD, DRURY ED
PETTIFORD, GEORGE TRD
PETTIFORD, JOHN GD
PETTIFORD, SETH GD
PETTIFORD, WILLIAM FCD
It may appear fantastic but I have an idea that the name PETTIFORD grew out of PETTIVER (p. 128) which in YORK COUNTY, VA was PETTIFER. The name SETH is the key to this idea.
PHILLIPS, BENNETT KLD
PHILPOT, WILLIAM TRD
PITCHFORD, DANIEL ICD
PITTARD, JOHN APD
PIZOR, MATHEW DD
PLUMMER, ZEPHANIAH ED
POINTER, SAMUEL GD
POLLIN, WILLIAM HED
POOL, THOMAS GD
POPE, JOHN BDD
POPE, JOHN JR. BDD
POPE, OSBORN BDD
POTTER, LEWIS DD
PRIDDY, GEORGE FTCD
PRIDDY, ROBERT FTCD
PRIDDY, WILLIAM FCD
PRIMROSE, WILLIAM KLD
PULLIAM, BARNETT TRD
PULLIAM, BARNETT KLD
PULLIAM, JOHN OXD
PUTNAM, BENJAMIN TRD
RAGLAND, AMIS ED
RAGLAND, REUBEN ED
RAGLAND, STEPHEN (EST) GD
RAGLAND, WILLIAM ED
RAGSBILL, BAXTER EFD
RAGSDALE, DAVID EFD
RAINWATER, JOHN HED
RAVEN, JOHN APD
RAVEN, JOHN JR. APD
REAVES, HARDY TCD
REAVES, SAMUEL HED
REAVES, WILLIAM TCD
REVES, SAMUEL HED
RICE, THOMAS ED
RIDLEY, BROMFIELD ED
RIGGS, ZACHARIAH TCD
RIVIS, LAN ED
ROBARDS, JOHN OXD
Some of the BURTONS married into this family. So did ANDREW JACKSON.
ROBERTS, ISAAC EFD
ROBERTS, JAMES TRD
ROBERTS, THOMAS BDD
ROBERTS, WILLIAM EFD
ROBERTS, WILLIS APD
ROBERSON, NICHOLAS EFD
ROBERSON, ROBERT EFD
ROBERTSON, BENJAMIN ICD
ROBERTSON, HENRY ICD
ROBERTSON, MARY ICD
ROGERS, JOHN FTCD
ROGERS, JOSEPH EFD
ROGERS, WILLIAM EFD
ROGERS, WILSON FTCD
ROLAND, THOMAS HED
ROSE, THOMAS OXD
ROSE, FREDERICK KLD
ROWLER, JAMES EFD
RUSSELL, JOHN TRD
RUST, GEORGE FTCD
RUST, JOHN SR. FTCD
RUST, SAMUEL FTCD
The RUST FAMILY came to GRANVILLE COUNTY from WESTMORELAND COUNTY, Virginia; related to the HARRISONS. There is a book called the "RUST FAMILY".
RUTH, DAVID ICD
REDD, FIELD ICD

SOME NAMES OMITTED ABOVE

O'BRYAN, DENNIS TRD
PARTIC, BENJ. KLD
PHILLIPS, DAVID BDD
PHILLIPS, GARLAND FTCD
REAVES, FREDERICK TCD

SAMPLE, JOHN OXD
SANDFORD, ROBERT GD
SATTERWHITE, JAMES ICD
SATTERWHITE, MICHAEL GD
SATTERWHITE, THOMAS HED
These are without doubt of the YORK COUNTY, VA. SATTERWHITES.
SCOTT, JOHN ICD
SCURRY, BENJAMIN ICD
SEARCY, WILLIAM HARGROVE OXD
SEARS, JOHN ED
SEARS, JOSEPH HED
SHEARMAN, MICHAEL TRD
SHEMWELL, JAMES TCD
SHULLHINES, JOHN HED
SIDDLER, JESSE APD
SIMMONS, JAMES FTCD
SIMMONS, JOHN SR. FTCD
SLAUGHTER, JACOB SR. TRD
SLAUGHTER, JACOB (TAYLOR) TRD
SLAUGHTER, JACOB JR. TRD
SMITH, ANDERSON APD
SMITH, EDMUND HED
Son in law of JAMES DANIEL named in will 1785.
SMITH, EDWARD TCD
SMITH, HENRY ICD
SMITH, JAMES FCD
SMITH, JAMES ICD
SMITH, JOHN SR. FCD
SMITH, JOHN JR. FCD
SMITH, JOHN APD
SMITH, JOSEPH ICD
SMITH, LEONARD ICD
SMITH, RANSOM HED
SMITH, SAMUEL ICD
SMITH, SAMUEL JR. APD
SMITH, SAMUEL APD
SMITH, THOMAS EFD
SNEED, DUDLEY ICD
SNEED, STEPHEN HED
SNELLINGS, ANN FCD
SNELLINGS, BARNET FCD
SNELLINGS, HUGH FCD
SNIPER, NATHANIEL OXD
SPEARS, JOHN EFD
SPEARS, PHILLIP EFD
STAMPER, JOHN APD
STEW, JACOB DD
STORY, GEORGE DD
STRINGFELLOW, RICHARD HED
STROME, BARTHOLOMEW ICD
STUBBS, WILLIAM ICD
SUITE, DENT. ICD
SUMMERHILL, CHARLES ICD
SUMMERVILLE, JOHN ICD
I am sure both of these were spelled the same way.
SUTE, JOHN (SUTE or SUITE) TCD
SWINNEY, THOMAS DD
SWINNEY, WILLIAM DD
This surely was SWEENEY, instead of SWINNEY.
TABURN, DRURY OXD
TACK, JOHN GD
TAGGIE, JOHN DD
TALLEY, REUBEN OXD
TANNER, FENNINGS BDD
TANNER, WILLIAM BDD
TATOM, BARNARD TCD
TATOM, JOHN DD
TATOM, WILLIAM KLD
TAYLOR, EDMUND FTCD
TAYLOR, ELIZABETH ICD
TAYLOR, EDWARD SR. OXD
TAYLOR, GEORGE BDD
TAYLOR, JOHN (EST. OF) ICD
TAYLOR, JOHN (BR. G.) ICD
TAYLOR, JOSEPH OXD
TAYLOR, LEWIS FTCD
TAYLOR, WILLIAM ED
These were all the TAYLORS from CAROLINE CO. VA., who were related to the LEWIS FAMILY, etc.
TEDDER, JAMES EFD
TEMERSON, WILLIAM HED
TERRY, JAMES TRD
TERRY, JAMES ICD
TERRY, ROLAND ICD
TERRY, STEPHEN ICD
TERRY, STEPHEN KLD
THOMASON, JOHN TRD
THOMASON, RICHARD EFD
These the ancestors of CAPT. JOHN W. THOMASON of "Fix Bayonets" fame - married into the KITTRELS and HUNTS.
THOMAS, CHRISTIAN FCD
THOMAS, JOHN BDD
THOMPSON, THOMAS ED
THORNTON, SOLOMON FCD
THORP, JOHN SR. TRD
THORP, JOHN JR. TRD
TIMS, AMOS KLD
TIMS, HOLLIS KLD
TINDALL, JOHN APD
TIPPETT, JOHN DD

TOMASON, THOMAS OXD
TOLLER, JOHN DD
TOWELL, JAMES OXD
TOWNS, HENRY APD
TUCKER, FREDERICK DD
TUCKER, THOMAS DD
TURNER, CHARLES DD
TYLER, BARTLETT FCD
UPCHURCH, WILLIAM OXD
VEASEY, ELIJAH DD
VEASEY, ZEBULON KLD
VINCENT, ALEXANDER FTCD
VINCENT, ISAAC FTCD
VINCENT, JACOB FTCD
VINCENT, PETER FTCD
WADE, ANNA DD
WADE, CHARLES GD
WADE, ROBERT GD
WALKER, JAMES DD
WALKER, JOHN OXD
WALKER, MARY KLD
WALKER, NATHANIEL DD
WALKER, SAMUEL SR. FCD
WALKER, SAMUEL OXD
WALKER, SOLOMON OXD
WALKER, WILLIAM FCD
WALLER, JOSEPH KLD
WALLER, ZEPHANIAH KLD
WASFF, GEORGE RD
WASHINGTON, JOHN, ESQ. TRD
WEATHERS, JAMES BDD
WEBB, JOHN GD
WEBB, WILLIAM KLD
WEAVER, EDWARD HED
WEAVER, JOHN HED
WEAVER, MINOR HED
WEAVER, WILLIAM BDD
WELCH, JOHN FTCD
WELLS, MILES TRD
WEST, JAMES APD
WESTON, JAMES GD
WHEELER, BENJAMIN DD
WHITE, COLEMAN FTCD
WHITE, GEORGE FTCD
WHITE, JOHN FTCD
WHITE, JONATHAN OXD
WHITE, MARK EFD
WHITE, PHILLIP SR. OXD
WHITE, PHILLIP JR. OXD
WHITE, SHARL FTCD
WHITE, THOMAS EFD
WHITE, VALENTINE EFD
WHITE, WILLIAM ROADS FTCD
WHITFIELD, JOHN BDD
WHITLAR, NICHOLAS FTCD
WHITLOW, JORDAN ICD
WHITLOW, NATHAN TCD
WICKER, THOMAS RD
WIGGINS, THOMAS HED
WILBURN, ZACHARIAH KLD
WILLARD, AUGUSTINE E. DD
WILKINS, THOMAS RD
WILKINS, RICHARD RD
WILKERSON, DAVID GD
WILKERSON, FRANCIS GD
WILKERSON, WILLIAM BDD
WILKERSON, WYATT DD
WILLIAMS, CHARLES RD
WILLIAMS, DANIEL ICD
WILLIAMS, GIDEON GD
WILLIAMS, JEREMIAH FTCD
WILLIAMS, CAPT. JOHN TRD
WILLIAMS, JOHN ESQ. HED
WILLIAMS, JOHN DD
WILLIAMS, NATHANIEL RD
WILLIAMS, SAMUEL HED
WILLIAMS, SOLOMON TRD
WILLIAMS, THOMAS OXD
WILLIAMS, THOMAS APD
WILLIAMS, WALTER FCD
WILLIAMS, WILLIAM FCD
WILLIAMSON, THOMAS APD
WILLSON, JOHN RD
WILSON, HENRY ICD
WINFREY, JAMES GD
WINNINGHAM, JOHN BDD
WITHUS, WILLIAM DD
WOOD, JOHN TRD
WOODALL, ABSOLOM TCD
WRIGHT, FRANCIS GD
WRIGHT, HANNAH BDD
WRIGHT, JOHN RD
WRIGHT, WILLIAM KLD
WRIGHT, WILLIAM TCD
YANCEY, STERLING HED
YORK, THOMAS FCD

THE LARGEST LAND OWNERS OF GRANVILLE COUNTY IN 1788, AS SHOWN BY THE ABOVE LIST.

According to the Assessment rolls for 1788, by far the largest land owner in GRANVILLE County at that period was THOMAS PERSON, ESQ. whose name appears in the GOSHEN DISTRICT in the Western part of the present GRANVILLE COUNTY. His Granville County holdings amounted to 34,760 acres; in addition he owned 5,546 acres in Warren and 1,000 acres in another tract in that county; 5,447 acres in Franklin, 6825½ acres in Caswell, 8,000 in Halifax and 16,417 acres in SUMNER and GREEN COUNTIES on the "Western Waters" - Tennessee.

Other large land owners in the GOSHEN DISTRICT were THOMAS GRANT, with 1690 acres, JOHN KENNON 1537 acres, CHESLEY DANIEL with his "Tranquility" tract, containing 1250 acres; CHARLES WADE had 1010 acres, JOHN KNOTT 1190 acres, JOHN OWEN JR. 1006, with AMBROSE BARKER, CHARLES HARRIS, THOMAS POOL, WILLIAM PALMER, SAMUEL POINTER and ROBERT HESTER, each having over 500, but less than 1000 acres.

JOHN DICKERSON, of FISHING CREEK owned 4579 acres, and JOHN PEACE, SR. and THOMAS NEWBY SR. each had 900 acres in this District, while SAMUEL WALKER had 978 acres. DANIEL HUNT and THOMAS YORK had around 700 acres.

CHARLES PORTER was the largest land owner in KNAP O' LEED'S DISTRICT, he having 5000 acres; ZEB VEASEY had 3587 acres, JOSEPH MANGUM 1206, ISRAEL EASTWOOD 1117 and ROWLAND GOOCH, whose assessment was in the name of "ROLAN GORCH" had 832½ acres of land.

ANDERSON and SAMUEL SMITH of the ABRAHAM PLAINS DISTRICT were well to do; SAMUEL SMITH owned 4324 acres and ANDERSON 2683 acres; HOWELL LEWIS came next with two tracts comprising a total of 3485 acres, while THOMAS MUTTER had 2580 acres, including some of the lands in the town of OXFORD. MARY GRAVES, the widow of JOHN W. GRAVES, who afterwards married JOHN WILLIAMS DANIEL, of WARREN COUNTY owned 1212 acres, HENRY GRAVES had 983 acres, JONATHAN KNIGHT 682 acres and BAXTER DAVIS 1057 acres. JAMES DOWNEY owned 1818 acres and JAKE MITCHELL 1022 acres.

In the BEAVER DAM DISTRICT, ROBERT GOODLOE (with 6600 acres) and DAVID and PHILEMON BRADFORD were the really big land owners.

JAMES LEWIS <u>next to</u> largest tax payer or land owner on ISLAND CREEK with 2181 acres & his kinsman, HENRY LYNE had 1945. GIDEON GOOCH had 1110 acres, JOHN TAYLOR 1411 acres, the estate of JESSE HARPER 1350 acres, JOHN SUMMERVILLE nearly as much as JAMES LEWIS but part of it was in HALIFAX COUNTY. The largest ISLAND CREEK land owner, however, was JOHN PENN, the SIGNER, who had 7712 acres assessed to him. REV. HENRY PATILLO owned only 300 acres, and DANIEL WILLIAMS 607 1-2 acres. SOLOMON and ABSOLOM DAVIS had nearly 1000 acres each.

BROMFIELD RIDLEY was the largest land owner in RAGLAND DISTRICT, with 1714 acres, and GEORGE HARRIS had 1437 and JOHN BRODIE 1115.

HON. ROBERT BURTON headed the list of big land owners in the HENDERSON DISTRICT (on NUTBUSH CREEK) with 3854 acres, while his father in law JUDGE JOHN WILLIAMS came next with lands aggregating 2405 acres; RICHARD HENDERSON had 1250 acres, and THOMAS SATTERWHITE and DAVID MITCHELL came next.

JOSEPH TAYLOR owned over 5000 acres in the OXFORD DISTRICT, SOLOMON WALKER 2000 and EDWARD TAYLOR Sr. about 2000 acres.

WILLIAM GILL had 1670 acres on TAR RIVER (DISTRICT) with 2200 in TENNESSEE; JOHN WASHINGTON owned 1247 acres. MICAJAH BULLOCK owned 4040 acres in DUTCH DISTRICT.

MARRIAGE BONDS
(See also pages 215-16)

Jeremiah Walker and Hannah Daniel, November 11, 1775; John Walker, security.
Solomon Walker and Martha Mitchell, August 9, 1799; Thomas Satterwhite, security.
William Walker and Phereby Miller (no date).
William Rose Walker (bride's name omitted), February 10, 1790; Solomon Williams sec.
Daniel Walker and Nancy Bailey, June 27, 1798; William Walker, security.
William Walker and Sally Jarrett, February 4, 1799.
William Walker and Rutha Baxter, July 31, 1824.
John Walker and Lucy McFarlin, March 12, 1823.
David Walker and Martha Gooch, January 17, 1792.
Henry Walker and Mary Sample, December 28, 1795.
David Walker and Rebecca Adams, December 6,1789; David Bridges, security.
Daniel Morrow and Fanny H. Smith, August 31, 1789; William Blackwell, security.
Robert Washington and Agnes Terrell, September 14, 1761; James Washington, security.
William Washington and Elizabeth Jones, August 1, 1807; Daniel Dean, security.
Woodson Washington and Sallie Blalock, September 12, 1817.
Mary Taylor and Robert Crawley, July 15, 1767.
Mary Taylor and James Anderson, August 23, 1770.
Mary Taylor and John Brodie, February 3, 1779.
Elizabeth Taylor and Josiah Rucks, August 14, 1780.
Jennie Taylor and Silas Parshall, September 18, 1787.
Polly Taylor and John Noland, 1788.
Mary Anne Taylor and Elias Jenkins, Dec. 19, 1789.
Keenhappoch Taylor and Benjamin Denny, December 19, 1798.
Jane Taylor and Benjamin Thorp, January 6,1800.
Frances A. Taylor and John Summerville, Jr., December 8, 1804.

LIST OF HUNT MARRIAGES IN GRANVILLE COUNTY:

David Alexander Hunt to Elizabeth Herndon, May 19, 1852.
Edward Hunt to Lucy Howard, November 4, 1806.
Frankey Hunt to Michael Hunt in 1812.
George Hunt to Lucy Woodfork, January 15, 1781.
George Washington Hunt to Susannah Crews, October 25, 1848.
James Hunt to Ann Satterwhite, July 21, 1785.
James Hunt to Ann Thompson, 1814.
John Hunt to Frances Penn, daughter of Joseph and Mary Taylor Penn, August 5, 1771.
John Hunt to Betsy Taylor, September 17, 1804.
John Penn Hunt to Sally Longmire, December 19, 1811.
Joseph Hunt to Nancy Hester, 1820.
Mary Hunt to Thomas Snipes, December 28, 1793.
Mourning Hunt, widow of John Hunt, married William Hicks, May 27, 1778.
Robert L. Hunt married Narcissa C. White, December 3, 1856.
Samuel Hunt to Sarah Howard, May 20, 1780.
Samuel Hunt to Sarah Hester, 1834.
Solomon Hunt to Elizabeth Sneed, 1817.
William Hunt to Mansey Kittrell, January 24, 1780.
William Hunt to Elizabeth Taylor, October 25, 1782.
William Hunt to Patsy Knott, December 22, 1807

SOME UNREGISTERED GRANVILLE COUNTY WILLS.

RICHARD WHITE, SR. Will dated in 1757, in which he names sons WILLIAM, NICHOLAS & RICHARD WHITE.

JONATHAN WHITE. Will in 1772 in which he mentions his wife SARAH and sons JONATHAN, BURGESS, WILLIAM and PHILEMON WHITE.

THOMAS WILLIAMS. Will in 1761, in which the name of his wife is not mentioned, but who names sons ROGER, SAMUEL, WILLIAM and THOMAS WILLIAMS.

PHILLIP TAYLOR. Will in 1765, in which he mentions his wife MARY and sons JOHN, PHILIP and JAMES TAYLOR.

WILLIAM MOORE. Will dated in 1761, in which he fails to give the name of his wife, but mentions his children, RICHARD, ANNE, WILLIAM, JAMES, JOHN, HOLLY, SARAH, EDNA and SUSANNAH MOORE.

SOME MORE DANIEL MARRIAGES IN GRANVILLE COUNTY.

Ashley Daniel to Louisa J. Robinson, Feb. 24, 1852.
Theophilus Daniel to Susan M. Robinson, Dec. 22, 1853.
George Daniel to Armon Brown, December 15, 1797.
Gilliam Daniel to Elizabeth Vaughan, July 23, 1838.
Hezekiah Daniel to Nancy L. Tarpley, December 23, 1806.
Hezekiah Daniel to Mary Hammonds, April 13, 1840.
Joseph Daniel to Sally Cords, January 15, 1798.
Joseph Daniel to Sarah J. Pritchett, September 25, 1844.
Matthew Daniel to Elizabeth D. Clarke, 1833.
Peter Daniel to Elizabeth Parker, 1816.
Robert Daniel to Martha Hawks, January 9,1791.
Mary Ann Daniel to Jeremiah Allen. September 21, 1815.
Stephen Barnes to Sarah Johnson, December 23, 1786.
Eliza A. Daniel to John J. Barnes, September 23, 1835.
Alex Andrews to Martha Moore, June 8, 1798.
Mary Walker to William Wallace, Apr. 19, 1769.

WILLIAMS FAMILY MARRIAGES IN GRANVILLE COUNTY

William Williams to Sarah Dean, March 29,1798.
Lucy Williams to Joseph King, August 11, 1762.
Sarah Williams to Thomas Lowe, Aug. 14, 1770.
Robert Williams to Sarah Williams, Oct. 10, 1774. (She was Sarah Lanier Williams).
Agatha Williams to Robert Burton, Oct. 12, 1785.
Mary Williams to Stephen Sneed Dec. 20, 1779.
Elleanor Williams to Laban Hairslip Feb. 1779.
Priscilla Williams to James Bowdin Oct. 1785.
Polly Williams to Samuel Craft Dec. 21, 1796.
Polly Williams to John Turner Nov. 6, 1798.
Martha Williams to Clarke Catlett, Feb. 1800.
Agnes Williams to Evan Ragland Jan. 19, 1802.
Nanny Williams to ISHAM Mouse, Nov. 18, 1802.
Polly Williams to Jordan Wright, Dec.24,1804.

NOTES FROM THE RECORDS OF WARREN COUNTY, NORTH CAROLINA

GENEALOGY OF WARREN COUNTY, N. C.

WARREN and FRANKLIN COUNTIES were both a part of old BUTE COUNTY, which came out of GRANVILLE'S original territory in 1764, and existed for FIFTEEN YEARS, but went out of existence when WARREN and FRANKLIN were created. GRANVILLE, of course, came from EDGECOMBE's vast territory in 1746, and EDGECOMBE came from CRAVEN. It was in 1786, seven years after the date that WARREN COUNTY was erected out of BUTE that JOHN MASON, PLEASANT HENDERSON and JOHN WILLIAMS DANIEL madetheir report as Commissioners to run the line between GRANVILLE and WARREN (See page 210 herein). Why this was so long delayed is not explained by any record we have found.

So, WARREN COUNTY, of course, was part of COLONIAL GRANVILLE COUNTY, as was FRANKLIN, its neighbor below.

JOHN WILLIAMS DANIEL, one of the Commissioners to run the line between GRANVILLE and WARREN COUNTIES, lived in WARREN COUNTY, though he was the son of JOHN DANIEL, who died in GRANVILLE in 1765 leaving a will (p. 212); He died in Warren County in the year 1808, leaving a will that was probated in May, 1809, of which the following is an abstract:

1. My beloved wife MARY DANIEL, the use of my estate, both real and personal during her natural life; and after her death
2. To my son ZADOCK DANIEL, my land and plantation whereon I now live, together with my two negroes Dan and Jerry.
3. To my daughter MARTHA VAUGHAN, my two negroes Luke and Lucy and fifty dollars cash.
4. To my daughter, MARY STAMPER, my negroes Peter, Jinney and Ceely and their increase.
5. To my step-son JONATHAN GRAVES one hundred dollars.
6. To my step-daughter FRANCES TRICE, a box of furniture and my cubbord, and old negroes Sam and Nancy.
7. My son ZADOCK DANIEL and son in law, WILLIAM STAMPER.

The witnesses to this will were JAMES BULLOCK, FRANCIS TUCKER and WILEY SMITH.

From a deed record in Deed Book 14, of Warren County we learn that the husband of the daughter MARTHA (DANIEL) VAUGHAN was one VINCENT VAUGHAN.

(The name of VINCENT VAUGHAN appears on the Quit Rent Rolls of NEW KENT COUNTY, Virginia in 1704).

ANN RAY. Her will appears on the records of Warren County dated in May, 1796 (Vol. 8, p. 336), in which she mentions the following legatees:

Nancy Rodwell.
Betty Gardner
Mary Pryor
Patty Myrick.

JOHN LYNCH. The will of JOHN LYNCH is in Vol 3 p. 8 of the Warren County records, in which he mentions only one legatee:

David Lynch.

JOSEPH LINDSAY. His will was offered for probate in Warren County in March. 1784. and in it he mentions only three children of legatees, as follows:

Caleb Lindsay
Rachel Lindsay
Laban Lindsay.

This JOSEPH LINDSAY lived in NUTBUSH DISTRICT in Granville County in 1756, and he is mentioned in the diary of the Rev. Hugh McAden who "went home with him" when on his tour through Granville County in that year. It was while on this visit to JOSEPH LINDSAY that the Rev. McAden wrote his impressions of the people of the Nutbush section of Granville County, mentioned in Wheeler's and other North Carolina books.

WILLIAM DANIEL left a nuncupative will which was probated in WARREN COUNTY, on November 24, 1794, in which he left all his property to be equally divided between Edmund Smith, Howell Moss, Joseph Daniel and John Daniel. This will was proven by the oath of Mary x Fleming and Daniel Key

The wife of Daniel Key was Sallie Daniel the daughter of Joseph Daniel, but they were not married until 1796, two years after this will was proven. (p. 215).

On August 28, 1795, a legatee of WILLIAMS DANIEL, deceased * * three surveys of land of 94 3/4 acres; also surveyed to Howell Moss, and the said John Daniel having bought said Howell Moss's part; 95 3/4 acres surveyed to Joseph Daniel and the same amount to Edmund Smith. Signed by

John W. Daniel
Isham Harris
Vincent Vaughan

Witnessed by W. Duke Johnson.

From Deed Book 14 (1796-1798):

Sterling Clack deeded lands to Peter Daniel of Warren County. p. 34.

John W. Daniel deeded lands to Zadock Daniel of Warren County. p. 260.

Richard Wadkins bought land from J. Williams Daniel p. 181.

1810-1815: James Bullock bought lands from Zadock Daniel p. 336.

Edmund Mayfield bought lands from Peter Daniel of Warren County.

Green Duke, in 1810-1816 record, bought land from William and Mary Cunningham in Warren County.

(Dr. Thomas Hunt of Granville County, married a daughter of Green Duke, who was from Virginia.)

Between 1821-1823, Anthony Davis of Warren County sold lands to A. and R. M. Cunningham. Record, p. 219.

William Davis bought lands from Eustice Daniel between 1764 and 1766, but at that time what is now Warren County was in BUTE. Other deeds to lands of that same period in BUTE County is one from Thomas Daniel to Jesse Rowland, and from Joseph Wright to Charles Daniel.

There was a Samuel Person who lived in Warren County in 1791-4 who sold a tract of land to a LEWIS DANIEL. This Lewis Daniel was perhaps from Halifax, son of a William.

(WARREN COUNTY, CONTINUED)

WILLS:

PETER MOORE, will in 1790. Mentions only MARTHA G. MOORE.

MARK MOORE. Will in 1794. Legatees were JOHN, MARY, OWEN and DAVID MOORE.

JOHN CHRISTMAS JR. Will in 1777. Legatees were ANN, HENRY, MARY and MARTHA CHRISTMAS.

DREWERY CHRISTMAS. Will in 1785. Legatees were JESSE and WILLIAM CHRISTMAS. (This is the WILLIAM who "laid off" the towns of WAR - RENTON and RALEIGH.)

HENRY CHRISTMAS. Will in 1789. Legatees were MARY and PATSY CHRISTMAS.

SAMUEL CRUTCHFIELD. Will in 1795. Mentions only SARAH CRUTCHFIELD.

MARY WILLIAMS. Left a will in 1797 in which she names only LEWIS and AMERICA JONES.

WILLIAM MOORE. Will in 1781. Names his wife as SARAH, and the following children:
- Lewis Moore
- William Moore
- John Moore
- Rebecca Moore
- Susannah Moore
- Edward Moore
- Mark Moore
- Nancy Moore
- Patsy Moore
- Elizabeth Moore.

JAMES JONES. Will in 1777. Names his wife CHARITY. She was Charity Alston, the daughter of SOLOMON ALSTON who married SARAH HINTON, and he was the son of EDWARD JONES and the brother of CAPT. SUGAR JONES. The children named were:
- Thomas Jones
- James Jones
- Willis Jones
- Mary Jones
- Priscilla Jones
- Rachel Jones.

THOMAS JONES. Will in 1779. Names wife FRANCES and THOMAS, WILLIS and FRED JONES.

WILLIS JONES. Will in 1779. Legatees were FRED and WILLIS JONES.

ALBRIDGETON JONES. Will in 1787. Names wife MARY, and children WILLIAM, WILLIS, and JEREMIAH JONES and son in law PENNY HARDY.

WILLIAM JONES, SR. Will in 1790. Names wife MARTHA, and children:
- James Jones
- Williams Jones
- Patsy Jones
- Sally Jones
- Polly Jones
- Betsy Jones married STURDIVANT.
- EDITH JONES married a KING.

DAVID HORTON, SR. Will in 1784. His wife was ANNE, and his children were DAVID, CONSTANT, SALLY, CHARLES, SAMUEL, NATHAN, WILLIAM, AMELIA and MATHIAS HORTON. He had daughter GRACE HORTON who married a man named ARENDALL.

WOODSON DANIEL. The will of a WOODSON DANIEL was probated in WARREN COUNTY, according to my notes in 1791. He names his wife NANCY, and children:
- JAMES DANIEL
- JOHN DANIEL
- DAVID DANIEL
- FRANKY DANIEL
- POLLY DANIEL
- WILLIAM DANIEL

I failed to get the book and page of this entry and am under the impression that he died in WAKE COUNTY, though I am unable to locate the record at this time.

THE ZADOCK DANIEL FAMILY - WARREN

ZADOCK DANIEL, the son of JOHN WILLIAMS DANIEL of WARREN COUNTY (p. 302) married ELIZABETH LEWIS in GRANVILLE COUNTY, N. C. July 26, 1792. One of his sons wrote the following account of the family June 26, in 1879:

"ZADOCK DANIEL, my father, married ELIZABETH LEWIS, of GRANVILLE COUNTY, N. C. on the 26th day of July, 1792. She was born on March 20, 1777, and died March 5, 1826. Her mother's name was ANDERSON and her father was JAMES LEWIS, and they had two sons, WILLIAM & JAMES LEWIS. My great grand-mother's name was FANNIE CLARK. She had two sons who left no issue, and had seven or eight daughters, who married into the best families of VIRGINIA and NORTH CAROLINA, namely, the TAYLORS, VENABLES and HUNTS. I am proud of my LEWIS and ANDERSON blood, for no grander man or nobler woman ever existed."

ZADOCK DANIEL and ELIZABETH LEWIS were the parents of the following children:

1. Susannah Daniel (b. 1793).
2. John Williams Lewis Daniel (b. 1794)
3. Mary (Polly) Daniel (b. 1798).
4. James Lewis Daniel (b. 1800).
5. William Daniel (b. 1802).
6. Dudley Daniel (b. 1804).
7. Sarah Lewis Daniel (b. 1806).
8. Lewis Daniel (b. 1808).
9. Zadock Daniel (b. 1810)
10. Elizabeth Ann Daniel (b. 1812).
11. Fannie Anderson Daniel (b. 1815)
12. Charles Daniel (b. 1817).

ZADOCK DANIEL and ELIZABETH LEWIS moved from WARREN to WAKE COUNTY, North Carolina in 1815.

4. JAMES LEWIS, their second son, was born in WARREN COUNTY, N. C. January 6, 1800, and moved to WAKE COUNTY with his parents in 1815. He married MATILDA GANNT in Merriwether County, Ga. October 12, 1830, and by her had eight children:

20. JOHN WILMOITE LEWIS DANIEL
21. Mary Ann Daniel
22. Elizabeth Lewis Daniel
23. Emma Josephine Daniel
24. Susan Artimina Daniel
25. Charles Parmly Sparks Daniel
26. Edwin Fletcher Daniel (b. 1853)
27. Dudley Daniel (b. 1855).

The parents of these children both died in EUFAULA, ALABAMA, where descendants live.

THE WILLIAM EATON FAMILY OF WARREN COUNTY.

COL. WILLIAM EATON patented lands in what was then GRANVILLE COUNTY in 1746 about the time the county was erected from territory taken from EDGECOMBE. He was Colonel of the GRANVILLE COUNTY Regiment of Militia (p. 291), and was the main leader in the organization of the County with EDWARD JONES (p. 209). He died in 1759 and his will was probated in GRANVILLE COUNTY on March 20th of that year (p. 42-43 of this work and Grimes' Abstracts p. 108.) His will names children:

1. William Eaton
2. Thomas Eaton
3. Charles Rust Eaton
4. Jane Eaton married Col. Nathaniel Edwards
5. Anne Eaton married Andrew Haynes
6. Mary Eaton married Robert Jones .
7. Sarah Eaton married Charles Johnson.
8. Elizabeth Eaton married Daniel Weldon.
9. Martha Eaton.

The family genealogy of COL. WILLIAM EATON will be found on page 43 of the Index & Digest to Hathaway's made a part of this work when finally completed. The descendants of Col. William Eaton (some of them, at least) still reside in WARREN COUNTY. The old Eaton home is located at 306 North Main Street in the town of WARRENTON. It was built in 1843 by a WILLIAM EATON SR. who was perhaps a grandson or great grandson of COL. EATON of the above will. He is accredited with being perhaps the wealthiest owner of lands and slaves on the Roanoke River & is said to have built this place as a summer home for his daughter ELLA.

ELLA EATON, in his old age, became the wife of HON. PETER HANSBOROUGH BELL, a retired Governor of Texas (1849-1854) who in his older days became impoverished, which fact, when made known to the people of Texas, resulted in a Legislative pension being granted to tide him over the remainder of his life, though he did not live long afterwards. PETER HANSBORO BELL was a native of Virginia and related to the family of the same name who settled in GRANVILLE COUNTY. (See page 214).

RARE LIST OF THE EARLIEST FAMILIES IN GRANVILLE COUNTY

The compiler is indebted to MR. FRANCIS B. HAYS, of OXFORD, NORTH CAROLINA, for the following very rare list of early GRANVILLE COUNTY FAMILIES:

Adcock, Allen, Allison, Alston, Amis, Anderson and Arnold.

Badgett, Bailey, Ballard, Banks, Booker, Barnes, Bass, Beardon, Beasley, Beckham, Bennett, Benton, Bishop, Blackwell, Blalock, Blacknall, Blanks, Bobbitt, Bonner, Boswell, Bowden, Boyd, Bradford, Bragg, Brassfield, Brissie, Bristow, Brown, Bruce, Brummitt, Buchanan, Bullock, Burden, Burton, Burwell, Butler, Byers.

Cannady, Carnall, Carroll, Cash, Cavendish, Cawthorn, Champion, Chandler, Chavis, Cheatham, Clark, Clay, Clement, Cobb, Cocke, Coghill, Colclough, Coley, Coleman, Collins, Compton, Cock(e), Cottrell, Cosart, Crabtree, Craft, Crawley, Crews, Critcher, Currin.

Dalby, Daniel, Davis, Dean, Dickerson, Dodson, Douglass, Downey, Drewry, Duncan, Dutch, Dutton, Duty.

Earl, Eastwood, Eaton, Edwards, Ellington, Elliott, Ellis, Ellixon, Epps, Evans.

Farrar, Finch, Floyd, Forsythe, Fowler, Frazier, Freeman, Fuller, Fullilove.

Gill, Gilliam, Glaze, Glover, Gober, Gooch, Goodloe, Goodwin, Gordon, Goss, Grant, Graves, Green, Gregory, Griffin, Grimsley, Grissom.

Hamilton, Hanks, Hare, Hargrove, Harper, Harris, Harrison, Hart, Hatcher, Hoskins, Hawkins, Hayes, Heflin, Heggie, Henderson, Hendrick, Hernden, Hester, Hicks, Hillyard, Hobgood, Hockaday, Hodge, Holstein, Holt, Hooker, Howard, Howell, Hubbell, Huckaby Hudspeth, Hunt, Husketh.

Ingles.

Jeffrey, Jenkins, Jeter, Johnson, Jones and Jordan.

Keeble, Keeling, Kennon, Kimball, King, Kittrell, Knight, Knott, Knowland.

Landis, Langston, Lanier, Lassiter, Lawrence, Laws, Leith, Lemay, Lewis, Lindsey, Littlejohn, Locke, Longmire, Lowe, Loyd, Lyle, Lyne, Lyon.

McClanahan, Mallory, Malone, Morrow, Mann, Marshall, Martin, Mayes, Mayfield, Meadows, Merritt, Marryman, Milton, Minor, Mitchell, Montague, Moody, Moore, Moss, Mutter and Murray.

Neal, Newby, Newport, Night, Norman, Norwood, Nuttall.

O'Brien, Oakley, Oliver, Overton, Owen.

Pannill, Parham, Parker, Parrish, Patillo, Peace, Peck, Penn, Perry, Person, Pettypool, Peyton, Philpot, Pierce, Pittard, Pool, Pope, Potter, Powell, Priddy, Pryor, Pulliam and Puryear.

Ragland, Raede, Reavis, Reeks, Richardson, Ridley, Robards, Roberts, Robertson, Rogers, Rowland, Royster, Rush, Russell, Rust, Ruth and Rux.

Sale, Sanford, Satterwhite, Saunders, Searcy, Sears, Seawell, Shemwell, Shepherd, Sherman (Shearman?), Sims, Slaughter, Smith, Sneed, Snelling, Spaulding, Spears, Speed, Springer, Stamper, Stork, Staunton, Stem, Stone, Stovall, Suit, Summerville, Sweaney and Simpson.

Taylor, Terry, Thomas, Thompson, Thorp, Traylor, Tucker and Tudor.

Umstead and Usry.

Valentine, Vandyke, Vass, Vaughan, Veasey and Vincent.

Wade, Walker, Waller, Ward, Washington, Weathers, Weaver, Webb, White, Whitfield, Whitlock, Wiggins, Wilborn, Wilkerson, Williams, Wilson, Wimbish, Winfree, Winningham, Winston, Wood, Woodworth, Wortham, Wright, Wyche.

Yancey, York and Young.

INDEX TO NAMES

PAGES 193 TO 304 INCLUSIVE

INDEX TO PLACES AND LOCALITIES

PAGES 193 TO 304 INCLUSIVE